Sentence Essentials:

A Grammar Guide

Instructor's Annotated Edition

Sentence Essentials:

A Grammar Guide

Instructor's Annotated Edition

Linda Wong
Lane Community College

Houghton Mifflin Company

Boston   New York

Editor-in-Chief: Patricia A. Coryell
Senior Sponsoring Editor: Mary Jo Southern
Senior Developmental Editor: Martha Bustin
Associate Editor: Kellie Cardone
Associate Project Editor: Cecilia Molinari
Editorial Assistant: Kristin Penta
Production Design Coordinator: Lisa Jelly Smith
Senior Manufacturing Coordinator: Marie Barnes
Marketing Manager: Annamarie Rice

Cover Image by David W. Fogle. © 1998 STOCKART.COM

Permission to reprint the following information is gratefully acknowledged:

Page 18: "Helping Athletes Go for the Gold" by Robert Epstein. Reprinted with permission from *Psychology Today Magazine,* Copyright © 1999 by Sussex Publishers, Inc.

Page 100: "Annual Wake-up Ritual Kept Alive." Reprinted with permission of The Associated Press.

Page 112: Colleen Smith, "The Nature of Bats," *The Denver Post,* October 31, 1999.

Page 115: Definition of "dig". Copyright © 1999 by Houghton Mifflin Company. Reproduced by permission from *Webster's II New College Dictionary.*

Page 180: "Kids Hear a Whale of a Tale" by Bill Bishop. Reprinted with permission. Copyright © 2000 by The Register-Guard.

Pages 207–208: "Cruise the Nile to View Wonders of Egypt" by Vijay Joshi. Reprinted with permission of The Associated Press.

Pages 225–226: "Century from Now, U.S. May Double Population" by Randolph Schmid. Reprinted with permission of The Associated Press.

Page 243: Jeannet/Hennessey, "Packaging for Global Markets," from *Global Marketing Strategies,* Fourth Edition, © 1998 by the Houghton Mifflin Company.

Page 248: "Miser Bequeaths Millions to Charity." Reprinted with permission of The Associated Press.

Pages 281–282: Robert Epstein, "Folk Wisdom," from *Psychology Today,* Nov. Dec. 1997, pp. 46–49, 76.

Pages 314–315: "Irene Inundates North Carolina." Reprinted with permission of The Associated Press.

Printed in the U.S.A.

Library of Congress Control Number: 00133913
ISBN: 0-618-154825
ISBN: 0-618-000364

3 4 5 6 7 8 9 – WEB – 05 04 03 02

BRIEF CONTENTS

CONTENTS

CHAPTER 7

MODIFIERS 185

CHAPTER 8

COMPOUND SENTENCES 215

CHAPTER 9

COMPLEX SENTENCES 249

PREFACE

Sentence Essentials: A Grammar Guide, with an annotated version for instructors, is a carefully structured, easy-to-use work text designed to teach fundamental sentence-writing skills to college students. It provides a strong and thorough foundation for the advanced writing skills students need in higher-level writing courses. As students master the sentence-level skills in this textbook, they gain confidence and become interested and involved in the process of writing, and they strengthen their understanding of sentence structure and enhance their ability to express ideas effectively in writing.

Instructional Approach

The instructional approach used in *Sentence Essentials: A Grammar Guide* has been carefully developed and class tested with students to focus on *what works.* The key features of this book include the following:

☼ A step-by-step approach to understanding the function of words in sentences (parts of speech) and subject-verb patterns in simple, compound, complex, and compound-complex sentences

☼ Sentence-writing and paragraph-writing exercises that encourage the application of the skills

☼ Instruction on grammar, punctuation, sentence patterns, and sentence combining integrated through identification and application exercises

☼ Grammar and punctuation rules presented in an easy-to-understand language without the confusion frequently caused by extensive use of complex terminology

☼ Easy-to-understand definitions and explanations with clearly labeled examples and model sentences

☼ Ample exercises with student answer keys to promote independent learning and a wealth of interesting, informative, and challenging exercises that can be used in class, independently as homework, or in small groups or with partners to promote collaborative learning

☼ An ongoing review and application of skills learned in previous chapters

☼ Special emphasis on strategies to correct common writing errors, such as fragments, run-on sentences, comma splice errors, subject-verb agreement problems, pronoun-antecedent agreement problems, and dangling modifiers

 ☼ A web site for each chapter including companion activities, indicated with this icon

Special Features

Chapter Introductions

Chapter introductions provide students with a quick overview of new and upcoming topics. A bulleted list explains the purpose for learning these skills and incorporates the skills into the larger goal of becoming a more effective writer.

Definitions

All new terms are systematically defined in easy-to-understand language. Clear examples follow each definition.

Charts

Comprehensive charts appear throughout the textbook. The charts serve as quick references for lists of words that belong to a specific category. The charts quickly become a valuable resource for students.

Just So You Know

The *Just So You Know* boxes provide additional explanations and alternative terminology for the concepts presented in the chapter. The boxes expose students to the higher-level concepts that they may encounter later in more advanced writing classes.

Practice Exercises

The practice exercises reinforce the new skills in each chapter. These practice exercises are self-correcting; the answer keys are in Appendix B. The answer keys provide students with immediate feedback on the accuracy of their work, promote independent study, and facilitate self-correcting for class, small group, partner, or individual work in the classroom.

Comma Sense

Rules that govern the use of commas are interwoven throughout all the chapters. Each of the comma rules relates to the concepts and skills presented in the chapter. This approach is more effective than attempting to teach all the rules that govern commas at once.

Exercises

Exercises at the end of each chapter do not have answer keys in Appendix B. These exercises can be used for classroom activities or instruction. They can be discussed as a class or completed in small groups, with partners, or independently in class or as assigned homework. Instructors may want to grade these exercises or use them as assessment tools.

Internet Icon

The icon that appears throughout the textbook indicates that supplementary activities or Internet links to related sites are available at the web site for this textbook. Web activities may be assigned, or they may be used by students as supplementary practice or drill work.

Chapter Summary

Each chapter summary highlights the terminology and the skills presented in the chapter. Because this summary provides a quick overview of the chapter, reading the summary before beginning work in the chapter is beneficial.

Writing Topics

Several optional writing topics that relate to the content of the chapter provide students with the opportunity to apply their newly acquired sentence-level skills to paragraph writing. These high-interest topics motivate students to write informative, entertaining paragraphs and provide students with new material to practice their proofreading, punctuation, and sentence-combining skills.

Chapter Review

The chapter review is an assessment tool for the skills presented in the chapter. Each chapter review is based on a 50-point system. Multiplying a student's score by 2 results in a percentage score. Instructors may use chapter reviews as a final review or as a graded test. Students do not have answer keys for the chapter reviews.

Content and Organization

Chapter 1: An Introduction to the Writing Process discusses the benefits of building a strong foundation in the areas of grammar and sentence-level skills. A writer's inventory gives students the opportunity to identify their personal writing and error patterns that they can reduce or eliminate through the mastery of the skills in this textbook. This chapter also introduces the steps in the writing process and emphasizes the recursive nature of writing. Key elements of paragraph structure provide students with a paragraph-writing model to use in their paragraph-writing assignments.

Chapter 2: Nouns begins the study of the parts of speech. New terminology includes *concrete, abstract, singular, plural, common,* and *proper nouns.* Thorough coverage of *noun markers* helps students identify nouns in sentences. Thirteen rules for capitalizing proper nouns, reinforced through practice exercises, end the instructional section of Chapter 2. Twelve practice exercises, including noun identification skills in the three-paragraph excerpt "Sports Psychology," can be used for class activities or homework assignments. Appendix B has answer keys for independent study and self-correcting work with these twelve exercises. *Comma Sense,* a feature that runs through all the chapters, begins the introduction of comma rules with two rules related to nouns in sentences. Four exercises, including the multiparagraph excerpt "Stellar Athletes," can be used as class activities or for individual assessment of Chapter 2 skills. Students do not have access to the answer keys for these four exercises. Chapter 2 concludes with a chapter summary of the essential skills in Chapter 2, writing topic options, and a 50-point chapter review test.

Chapter 3: Prepositions explains the value of identifying prepositions and prepositional phrases when analyzing subject-verb and sentence patterns. New terminology includes *prepositions, prepositional phrases, objects of the prepositions, object pronouns,* and *infinitives.* A discussion of objects of prepositions leads to a review of nouns and an introduction of objective pronouns. The chapter also explains the difference between a prepositional phrase that begins with *to* and an infinitive. Six practice exercises have self-correcting answer keys in Appendix B. *Comma Sense* covers two new comma rules that relate to prepositional phrases. The five exercises without student answer keys begin with the six-paragraph excerpt "The Peanuts Gang" and ends with original sentence-writing assignments. Chapter 3 concludes with a chapter summary, a list of writing topics, and a 50-point chapter review test.

Chapter 4: Subjects and Verbs in Simple Sentences launches the instruction for subject-verb and sentence patterns. New terminology includes *subjects, verbs, simple sentences, independent clauses,* and *subject pronouns,* which include *personal, indefinite,* and *relative pronouns.* Self-correcting practice exercises 1–4 provide practice identifying prepositional phrases, infinitives, subjects, and the correct subject or object pronoun. The sentence structure focus expands with the introduction of *action verbs, linking verbs, helping verbs, verb phrases, compound subjects,* and *compound verbs* in the simple sentence pattern. Self-correcting practice exercises 5–9 reinforce the skills of sentence combining and identification of subjects, verbs, prepositional phrases, and infinitives in simple sentences. Chapter 4 introduces strategies to correct *fragments,* a common writing error that is also addressed in several later chapters. Self-correcting practice exercises 10–13 reinforce the skills that cover identification of fragments and the location of subjects in various simple sentence patterns. *Comma Sense* summarizes three new comma rules. The multiparagraph excerpts "Chinese New Year" and "Annual Wake-Up Ritual" and five other exercises, which do not have self-correcting answer keys, provide students with practice using the simple sentence skills from the chapter. Chapter 4 concludes with a chapter summary, a list of writing topics, and a 50-point chapter review test.

Chapter 5: Verb Forms focuses on verbs, one of the most complicated yet interesting parts of speech. Essential functions and forms of verbs are included in this chapter, as reflected in the chapter's terminology: *verb form, tense, number,* and *person.* Chapter 5 discusses the *simple past, present,* and *future verb tenses, verb phrases, irregular verbs, past participles,* and *present participles.* Work with participles includes using participles as gerunds (nouns) and verbals (adjectives). The chapter also includes three ongoing skills that appear in many chapters: achieving subject-verb agreement in sentences, correcting fragment errors, and using commas correctly in sentences. Eighteen self-correcting practice exercises are also included in the chapter. Six exercises without self-correcting answer keys, beginning with the multiparagraph excerpt "Rabies," reinforce the skills in the chapter. Chapter 5 concludes with a chapter summary, a list of writing topics, and a 50-point chapter review test.

Chapter 6: Pronouns and Pronoun Agreement examines the role of pronouns in sentences. The chapter begins with an introduction to eight kinds of pronouns: *subjective, objective, possessive, reflexive, indefinite, demonstrative, interrogative,* and *relative.* Six self-correcting practice exercises focus on using the correct subject, object, possessive, and reflexive pronouns in sentences. In an easy-to-understand manner, Chapter 6 covers subject-verb agreement with singular and plural indefinite pronouns in present-tense sentences and pronoun-antecedent agreement. Four additional self-correcting practice exercises focus on pronoun agreement. *Comma Sense* adds two new comma rules to the ongoing instruction of the proper use of commas. Beginning with the six-paragraph proofreading article "Keiko," this chapter offers five exercises without answer keys to review and reinforce the chapter skills. Chapter 6 concludes with a chapter summary, a list of writing topics, and a 50-point chapter review test.

Chapter 7: Modifiers introduces adjectives and adverbs, words that add descriptive details and precise language to students' writing. Adjectives appear in two patterns: before nouns and after linking verbs (predicate adjectives). New terminology includes *adjectives, verbals* that work as adjectives, and *positive, comparative,* and *superlative adjectives* and *adverbs.* Eleven self-correcting practice exercises reinforce the skills in Chapter 7. *Comma Sense* covers two additional rules for using commas correctly. Five exercises without self-correcting answer keys provide additional identification and sentence-writing practice. Chapter 7 concludes with a chapter summary, a list of writing topics, and a 50-point chapter review test.

Chapter 8: Compound Sentences moves students from simple sentence structure to three compound sentence structures. New terminology includes *compound sentences, coordinating conjunctions, semicolons, conjunctive adverbs, run-on sentences,* and *comma splice errors.* The chapter includes comprehensive charts that explain the meaning of coordinating conjunctions and conjunctive adverbs. Emphasis in the chapter includes proper punctuation for compound sentences and methods for correcting run-on sentence and comma splice errors. *Comma Sense* adds three new rules for using commas correctly. Subject-verb agreement is reviewed and applied to compound sentences. Eleven self-correcting practice exercises provide ample opportunity to apply the skills of the chapter. Nine exercises without self-correcting answer keys, beginning with the multiparagraph excerpt "Sacagawea," emphasize proofreading, sentence-writing, and sentence-combining skills. Chapter 8 concludes with a chapter summary, a list of writing topics, and a 50-point chapter review test.

Chapter 9: Complex Sentences expands sentence-writing patterns to include complex sentences. New terminology in this chapter includes *complex sentences, dependent clauses, subordinate conjunctions, relative pronouns,* and *essential* and *nonessential dependent clauses.* Though the emphasis is not on labeling each of the three kinds of dependent clauses, the chapter discusses *adverb, adjective,* and *noun clauses.* Chapter 9 focuses on the proper punctuation for complex sentences, including essential and nonessential dependent clauses, correct usage of the relative pronouns *who, whom, that,* and *which,* and subject-verb agreement within relative pronoun clauses. *Comma Sense* adds two more rules for using commas correctly in sentences. Twelve self-correcting practice exercises focus on identifying, punctuating, and using correct conjunctions and relative pronouns in sentences. This chapter includes additional strategies for correcting fragments. Four exercises without self-correcting answer keys, beginning with the multiparagraph excerpt "Folk Wisdom," provide additional practice for proofreading, punctuation, sentence-writing, and sentence-combining skills. Chapter 9 concludes with a chapter summary, a list of writing topics, and a 50-point chapter review test.

Chapter 10: Sentence Builders continues to develop students' sentence-writing skills with more sophisticated sentence-combining techniques and a fourth sentence structure, the compound-complex sentence. New terminology in this chapter includes *appositives, participial phrases, words in a series, compound-complex sentences, dangling modifiers,* and *parallelism.* Emphasis continues throughout the chapter on the proper punctuation to use when combining phrases and clauses into one simple, compound, complex, or compound-complex sentence. *Comma Sense* closes the ongoing development of comma rules with the final four rules for using commas correctly. Chapter 10 also includes comprehensive summary charts that show common simple, compound, and complex sentence patterns, the conjunctions and punctuation to use to form compound and complex sentences, and methods to correct various types of fragments. Nine self-correcting practice exercises focus on compound-complex sentences and the new sentence-writing and sentence-combining skills. The last five exercises in Chapter 10, which are not self-correcting exercises, emphasize application of the sentence-combining skills presented in this final chapter of the textbook. Chapter 10 concludes with a chapter summary, a list of writing topics, and a 50-point chapter review test.

Appendix A: Punctuation Guide provides students with rules for the most commonly used punctuation marks. The various forms of punctuation are organized alphabetically; clear examples and explanations follow each rule.

Appendix B: Student Answer Keys provides students with answers to all the *practice* exercises that are interwoven throughout the instructional portions of the textbook in each chapter. These answer keys provide students with instant feedback on their work and promote independent study.

Instructional Notes

Instructor's Annotated Edition

The instructor's annotated edition includes answers for practices, exercises, and chapter reviews. With the annotations, classroom instruction and grading are easier and more convenient.

Lesson Plans: Classroom Approach

In a classroom approach, the following daily format works effectively:

1. Begin the class with a brief review of the skills studied in the previous class.

2. Introduce the new skills for the day. Sections of the textbook may be photocopied for use as overhead transparencies to introduce and explain new skills.

3. Use the self-correcting practices or the exercises without answer keys for class, small group, partner, or individual work. Consider using a collaborative approach at least once each week; providing students with opportunities to discuss the skills and complete assignments together promotes interaction, understanding, and peer tutoring. After students complete the assignment, ask them to check their accuracy with the answer key in Appendix B or with an annotated answer key that you copy from your teacher's edition.

In a classroom approach, planning topics, specific activities, and assignments one or two weeks in advance and providing students with a weekly assignment sheet are strongly recommended. The following example of a weekly assignment sheet for Chapter 2 includes class topics and homework assignments.

WEEK 2 ASSIGNMENT SHEET SENTENCE ESSENTIALS

Monday

In class: Introduction to Nouns, pages 11–13 and 17–20
Partner work: Practice 4: Sports Psychology
Check your answers with the answer key in the Appendix.

Homework: *Practice 1, 2, and 3. Check your work with the Answer Key.*
Practice 5 and 6. Check your work with the Answer Key.

Wednesday

In class: Review of definitions for Chapter 2
Exercise 2.2
Introduction: Rules of Capitalization, pages 22–28
Practice 10

Homework: *Practice 11 and 12. Check your answers with*
the Answer Key.
Exercises 2.3 and 2.4

Friday

In class: Partner work: Exercise 2.1
Chapter 2 Review, pages 39–40
Discuss this week's writing assignment.

Homework: *Select one activity on the web site to complete.*
Do one writing assignment by Monday.

Lesson Plans: Individualized Approach

In an individualized approach, the following strategies work effectively:

1. Create weekly goals and expectations with individual students. Provide the desired level of structure to reduce student procrastination and assist students who may have difficulty meeting the responsibilities required for independent study.

2. Create an assignment chart that shows specific assignments and scores. This record-keeping system also serves as a checklist for students to monitor their pace and understand the course requirements.

The following example shows the beginning portion of an assignment chart for an independent study approach to the textbook. At appropriate points on the assignment sheet, you may also assign web site activities.

	INDEPENDENT STUDY SENTENCE ESSENTIALS **Read each assignment carefully. Place the date next to the assignment to show when you completed it. Write your score in the column on the right.**	
Date	Assignment	Score
	1. Chapter 1. Read pages 1–8.	X
	2. Complete the Writer's Inventory on pages 4–5. On your own paper, summarize what you learned about yourself from this inventory.	X
	3. Chapter 2. Carefully read pages 9–11. Do Practice 1 on page 14. Check your answers with the answer key. In the score column, write your number of errors.	
	4. Read pages 14–15. Do Practice 2. Check and record your score.	
	5. Do Practice 3. Check and record your score.	
	6. By yourself or with a partner, do Practice 4. Check and record your score.	

Overhead Transparencies

Use these techniques to make overhead transparencies for any portion of the textbook you would like to use in class:

1. Photocopy the pages that you would like to have on overhead transparencies.

2. Cut and paste the sections you would like to have on overheads. Enlarge the information if you wish before you make a transparency.

3. Use the master with any copy machine that makes transparencies.

Annotated Student Answer Keys for Student Use

When you assign practices or exercises for small group or partner work, you can photocopy annotated answer keys on colored paper for students to correct their work together. Collect the answer keys upon completion of the work so they can be used for future classes.

Correcting Paragraph-Writing Assignments

The paragraph-writing assignments at the end of each chapter provide students with the opportunity to apply their sentence-writing skills to longer pieces of writing. Though the paragraph-writing topics are optional, consider including a paragraph-writing activity at least three times during the term. You can use your own method for grading the paragraph-writing assignments, or you can use the following:

1. In the margin of the student's paper and on the line where an error occurs, indicate the type of error. If the error involves a skill that you have already discussed in class, encourage the student to locate and correct the error without your assistance.

2. If the error involves a skill that you have not yet discussed in class, correct the error so the student can see how to correct that type of error. Offer a short explanation of the error in the margin.

3. For spelling errors, write *sp* above the error. Encourage students to use a spell checker or a dictionary to correct the spelling error.

4. Ask students to revise the paragraph and submit the draft and the revision to you for grading.

Ancillary Materials

Textbook Web Site

A comprehensive web site accompanies this textbook. Icons throughout the text indicate supplementary activities that are online. For Chapters 2–10, the web site features the following items:

1. Supplementary interactive exercises and quizzes that are corrected online

2. Supplementary sentence-writing exercises with text boxes that allow students to print their answers or email them to their instructor

3. Additional worksheets that students can download or print for additional practice

4. Links to other writing web sites with additional instruction, explanations, exercises, and resources

5. For teachers, a sentence bank with additional simple, compound, complex, and compound-complex sentences to use to make additional exercises or tests

Test Bank with Chapter Tests

The test bank for *Sentence Essentials* provides you with additional materials to use as tests or quizzes. The questions and the activities in the test bank use a flexible format. You may design or customize your own test by cutting and pasting sections from Form A, B, or C, rearranging them in your preferred order, and printing them for students. The test bank is a separate product; visit the Houghton Mifflin College Division web site at http://college.hmco.com to order your copy of the test bank that accompanies this text.

Author Contact

The author welcomes feedback, comments, and questions from teachers using *Sentence Essentials: A Grammar Guide.* The author's email address is posted on the textbook web site.

To the Student

You are about to begin the important study of sentence-level skills, which include grammar, punctuation, sentence structure, and sentence-combining skills. You may be excited about the opportunity to strengthen your ability to express your ideas clearly and powerfully on paper, or you may be apprehensive about tackling the skills in this course. A primary goal of this textbook is to provide you with easy-to-understand instructions and a set of practical skills that will help you develop an attitude of appreciation and enjoyment of the process of writing.

You will find the following key elements in this textbook:

- ☼ An easy-to-understand approach that explains rules for sentence-writing and grammar skills, without relying on complex language or excessive labeling or diagramming.

- ☼ Instruction that begins by analyzing key elements in prepared sentences and modeling effective, error-free sentences. In this way, you can more easily identify—or better yet, more easily avoid—many common writing errors. The learning sequence becomes *see, understand,* and then *apply* the skills to your own writing.

- ☼ Ample examples that help you understand new terminology and skills. You will be able to study the examples and see clearly how the new skills are applied to sentence-level work.

- ☼ Answer keys provided for some of the practice exercises. You will be able to use the answer keys in Appendix B to check the accuracy of your work and receive immediate feedback.

- ☼ An emphasis on using the terminology correctly and discussing exercises in small groups or with a partner.

- ☼ Interesting and informative content and intriguing, thought-provoking topics. Careful attention has been given to the selection of material to use for this book.

- ☼ An instructional approach that is sequential. Skills are continually reviewed and applied throughout the textbook. As you progress through the chapters, you will find yourself building a strong foundation for writing that will make higher-level writing classes easier to complete successfully.

- ☼ A comprehensive web site for additional exploration and practice. The web site for this textbook includes companion activities that reinforce the skills in the textbook and links to other web sites with related information. You will find that the activities and links on the web site for this textbook are valuable tools and resources for supplemental work.

As you work through the chapters in this textbook, you will become more aware of the fact that writing is a *recursive* rather than a linear process. In other words, you will often revisit earlier stages of the writing process in the course of revision and rethinking. Because of the recursive nature of writing, the writing process is never truly finished. There are always numerous ways to reword your ideas and restructure your sentences. Your goal as a writer should be to understand the options that are available to express your ideas clearly in language that is free of grammatical or sentence-level errors. Learning the sentence-level and grammar skills in this textbook will empower you with the strong skill foundation that is essential to the entire writing process.

Special Features Designed for You

To gain the greatest benefits from this textbook, use the following features in each chapter:

Chapter Introductions

The short chapter introductions provide you with a "big picture" of the chapter's contents. In addition, you will learn the importance of these skills to the overall writing process.

Definitions

Building a strong foundation of sentence-level skills involves learning basic definitions of terminology. Terminology provides you with a method for discussing your work and a communication system that you and your instructor can use. These strategies can help you learn the terminology:

1. Highlight the definitions in each chapter to make them stand out in your memory.

2. Create flash cards that you can use to practice reciting the definitions. Place the word on the front of the flash card. Write the definition and an example on the back of the flash card. Looking at the front of the flash card, practice explaining the definition *in your own words.* Turn the card over to check your accuracy. Review your flash cards each week to keep the information in your active memory.

Noun	A noun names a person, place, thing, or idea. *child, friend, bank, office, box, movie, beauty, fear*

Examples

Study the examples carefully. They show you how the specific skills work in sentences.

Instructional Information and Special Notes

Read the instructional information and the Special Notes carefully. Highlight key words, phrases, or sentences to make the information stand out on the page. *Ask questions* in class about information that you need to understand more thoroughly.

Just So You Know

The special sidebar boxes called *Just So You Know* provide you with additional explanations or terminology. Unless your instructor informs you otherwise, this information does not need to be memorized. If future classes use more complex terminology, you will have it available in this textbook for reference.

Practice Activities

The practice activities in each chapter provide you with the opportunity to demonstrate your understanding of the new skills. Complete each activity that your instructor assigns. Work carefully, giving thought to all of your answers. Check your accuracy by comparing your answers to the answer key in Appendix B in the back of your book. Consider the following suggestions:

1. Remove Appendix B from the back of your book. Punch holes in the pages so you can keep them in your notebook. Separating the pages from the book makes self-correcting easier.

2. After you correct your work, examine any errors that you made. Try to understand why you made the mistakes. Write any questions you have in the margins of your book next to the practice activities. Discuss your questions in class with your instructor.

3. Use a colored pen to write the correct answers. The learning process always involves correcting and refining, so look at errors as simply a part of the learning process.

Exercises

The exercises in the second half of each chapter provide you with additional opportunities to apply the new skills to new material. You do not have answer keys for these exercises. Complete each exercise that your instructor assigns. Work carefully and thoughtfully.

Charts

Quick reference charts appear throughout this textbook. The following suggestions will help you locate the charts quickly:

1. Attach an index tab to the page with the chart. Label the tab so you can quickly go to the chart when you need it for your work.

2. Photocopy the chart. You can block off the surrounding text or cut the chart from the page and photocopy it once again. In your notebook, create a section for quick reference charts.

Chapter Summary

Read each chapter summary carefully. After you read an item on the summary, pause to think about the information. Can you picture the concept clearly? Can you visualize examples? Can you explain the concept in your own words and with additional details? If you answer *no* to any of these questions, review the section of the chapter that discusses the specific skills or concept.

Writing Topics

If your instructor assigns a writing topic, allow yourself sufficient time to complete the writing assignment. Do not wait until the last minute to write a draft. Plan to spend time gathering information, formulating your ideas, and writing a draft. Proofread your draft carefully. Pay special attention to each sentence; check that it demonstrates correct usage of the writing skills that you have already learned in the textbook. Remember that writing is *recursive;* it involves proofreading and revision work.

Chapter Review

Each chapter review provides you with the opportunity to show how much you have learned. Read the directions carefully. Allow yourself sufficient time to complete the work. You do not have answer keys for the chapter reviews. Your work will be corrected by your instructor or in class.

Web Site Activities

Throughout each textbook chapter, this icon indicates skills that you can reinforce through activities on the Internet. Your instructor may assign some of the online activities, or you may wish to explore them on your own. If you own a computer, consider *bookmarking* the web site so you can quickly go to the site for supplementary work. If you do not own a computer, locate a place on campus where you can gain Internet access. Type in the web site address (the URL) in the address box that appears on the top of the screen after you are connected to the Internet.

http://college.hmco.com. Click on "Students." Type *Sentence Essentials* in the "Jump to Textbook Sites" box. Click "go" and then bookmark the site.

Acknowledgments

Developing and producing an effective textbook requires the expertise of many individuals. I would like to thank the following reviewers for their insightful and helpful feedback and recommendations:

Chandler Clifton, Edmonds Community College
Mark Connelly, Milwaukee Area Technical College
Judy D. Covington, Trident Technical College
Catherine Decker, Chaffey College
Jeanne Gilligan, Delaware Technical and Community College
Philip Herter, Fordham University
Mary Ann Merz, Oklahoma City Community College
Phyllis Moseley MacCameron, Erie Community College
Kevin Nebergall, Kirkwood Community College
Anne-Marie Schlender, California State University—Hayward
Michelle W. Zollars, Patrick Henry Community College

I would also like to extend my appreciation to the many individuals in the Houghton Mifflin College Division Developmental English Department who were instrumental in the development and production of this textbook. Without their work, dedication, and interest, *Sentence Essentials: A Grammar Guide* would not have been possible. Thank you, Mary Jo Southern, for your leadership and steadfast support of this textbook. Thank you, Martha Bustin, Kellie Cardone, Danielle Richardson, and Cecilia Molinari, for your expert editing skills, attention to detail, and commitment to working as a highly orchestrated team. I appreciate you all and feel honored to be a part of your team.

Linda Wong
Lane Community College

A Closing Comment

You are now ready to begin the process of building a strong foundation for sentence-level writing skills. The value of learning these new skills reaches far beyond the classroom and the completion of this course. You are building a strong writing foundation that will benefit you in higher-level classes, in your personal life, and in the work force. May you enjoy the process and feel an empowering sense of confidence and success as you become an effective, powerful writer!

CHAPTER 1

An Introduction to the Writing Process

In Chapter 1, you will learn about the benefits of a strong grammar foundation in college, the workplace, and other settings. A Writer's Inventory will help you identify some of your writing problems and error patterns; these errors can be reduced or eliminated as you learn the skills presented in this textbook. This chapter also includes the steps in the writing process and a discussion of the key elements of paragraph structure.

Understanding the writing process will help you do the following:

1. Form an overall picture of the writing process
2. Identify the key components you will learn to master
3. Prepare your paragraph writing assignments
4. Recognize the multiple reasons for building a strong grammar foundation

Benefits of a Strong Grammar Foundation

You may be asking yourself, "Why do I need to learn grammar to write?" This is a valid question and a timely one as you launch into a renewed study of grammar. Understanding why the mastery of grammar skills is important will lead to stronger motivation and a deeper sense of purpose.

Some of you do not have problems getting your ideas down on paper. You are able to write fluently and abundantly. The quality of your ideas and the clarity of your expression are excellent. Yet you may feel frustrated when your papers are returned with numerous red marks and corrections written throughout the margins. *Fragment, comma splice, dangling modifier,* and *incorrect verb tense* are examples of comments that may appear. Though the content of your paper is sound and appropriate, elements at the sentence level may be flawed, distracting your reader. Successful writing involves both expressing ideas clearly and using language free of grammatical or sentence-level errors. Writing is a process that leads to a powerful, effective, polished product, and knowing grammar is part of that process.

The benefits of knowing grammar go beyond being able to produce a finished, error-free paper. A good grasp of grammar allows you to express yourself to your readers more confidently and with more depth and impact. You may have noticed that your thoughts seem to lose energy and creativity when set down on paper or on a computer screen. Instead of communicating articulately and eloquently, you may find yourself expressing ideas in a stilted, shortened, or simplified version. Why do people sometimes have problems expressing themselves in writing? Often, the answer involves a lack of a strong foundation in grammar. By understanding the function of words in sentences, you can learn to express your ideas clearly and with more variety. You can use numerous options to combine ideas in powerful ways. You can move with confidence beyond choppy or wordy sentences and into the realm of more graceful, sophisticated sentence structures.

Benefits in the College Setting

Now that we have looked at two general reasons for studying grammar—error-free work and more flexibility in expressing your ideas—let us summarize the benefits of a strong grammar foundation in the college setting in particular. Most people like to see some kind of reward for their effort and their work. As a college student who is studying grammar, you will receive many rewards for your effort and your work. With stronger grammar skills, you will be able to do the following:

- Improve the quality of your written expression
- Produce higher-quality papers and reports for your classes

- Write more effective answers on tests
- Maneuver language to reach desired outcomes
- Become more comfortable with experimenting with options for expressing ideas
- Increase your enjoyment of writing
- Understand the grammatical comments written on your papers by teachers and tutors
- Communicate with others about grammar, proofreading, and correction methods
- Create a valuable foundation for learning foreign languages
- Experience less stress in writing
- Recognize effective sentence structure in other writers' work

Benefits in the Workplace and Other Settings

The benefits of becoming a strong writer are also apparent in areas of life outside of school. Numerous surveys indicate employers' desire and need to have employees with high levels of writing skills. Thus, advancement within a company or organization and better job opportunities often rest on a person's ability to communicate effectively in writing—that is, to produce documents such as these:

- Letters and memos
- Reports
- Training manuals
- Job assignments or directions for others to follow
- Budget requests and justification for funding
- Descriptions for new job postings
- Employee evaluations for personnel files
- Media releases
- Marketing brochures or flyers
- Letters of recommendation

In your personal life, strong writing skills are required for many daily tasks:

- Personal letters and email messages to family and friends
- Correspondence to request a specific service, get information, or file a complaint
- Personal diary or journal

- Cover letters, applications, and resumés for employment

In short, the effort you put into mastering *Sentence Essentials* will pay many direct, practical, and far-reaching dividends.

Writer's Inventory

The following inventory will help you identify writing problems and error patterns you may be making as you write. Recognizing these patterns will allow you to be more focused and effective in your grammar study.

Complete the following writing inventory by checking the box that is most appropriate for you.

	NEVER	SOMETIMES	OFTEN	NOT SURE
1. I have difficulty expressing my ideas on paper.				
2. I have difficulty organizing information on paper.				
3. My written expression is less sophisticated than my oral expression.				
4. I am not sure how to combine ideas, so I use short, simple sentences to express myself.				
5. Others do not understand what I am trying to say.				
6. I am not sure how to use commas correctly.				
7. I am not sure how to use semicolons correctly.				
8. I have problems using verb tenses correctly.				
9. I have difficulty proofreading my work.				
10. I use little variety in the kinds of sentences I write.				
11. I tend to be too wordy.				
12. I omit words when I write sentences.				
13. I make mistakes with pronouns, such as I/me, who/whom, he/him, she/her, or we/us.				
14. I write incomplete sentences (fragments).				

(Continue on page 5)

	NEVER	SOMETIMES	OFTEN	NOT SURE
15. I write run-on sentences without proper punctuation.				
16. I join two sentences by using commas (comma splice).				
17. I have difficulty with subject-verb agreement.				
18. I have problems knowing how to correct grammatical errors in my work without someone else's help.				

Checkmarks in the *Sometimes* and *Often* categories indicate a need to build a stronger grammar foundation. Checkmarks in the *Not Sure* column may indicate a lack of familiarity with the terminology or a lack of recent writing experience. In all cases, you can successfully build a stronger grammar foundation and become a stronger writer.

Steps in the Writing Process

As noted earlier, writing is a process, and grammar is part of that process. The series of steps in the writing process vary slightly with different kinds of writing projects, and the process is *recursive*—that is, you will often circle back and return to earlier steps as the need arises. Before you begin with the actual steps in the writing process, carefully read the directions for your writing assignment. Identify the type of writing and the length that is expected and appropriate. You will then be ready to begin the steps to produce an effective, powerful, well-developed writing assignment.

1. **Generate ideas.** Prewriting techniques, such as brainstorming, listing and categorizing, free-writing, clustering, outlining, and creating hierarchies can help you to generate ideas for your writing assignment.

2. **Get a focus.** Narrow the topic so that it is a manageable size for a paragraph; you do not want your topic to be too general or too narrow. Your topic should be well focused and interesting to both you and your reader.

3. **Gather and organize your information.** Sometimes writing is based primarily on personal experience or knowledge. Other writing is based on reference materials, textbook information, or other resources that you must locate, read, and evaluate. Library resources, the Internet, and interviews with experts in the field can be excellent sources of information. Keep track of the sources you consult and give credit in your paper. The techniques used to generate ideas can also be used to gather and organize your information. Once you have chosen a topic

and gathered information, develop a question you are going to answer or a distinctive point you are going to make. This will be your topic sentence. Write several possible topic sentences until you come up with one that tells your reader what you want to express in the paragraph.

4. **Write the first draft.** Double- or triple-space the draft so you will have room to mark it up later as you revise. The goal for a first draft is to get your ideas down in written form so you can then scrutinize, modify, and strengthen them as you revise.

5. **Revise, revise, and revise the draft.** Writers often select a specific aspect of the paragraph to examine and revise. For example, you may begin by looking for ways to strengthen the organization of your paragraph by revising the topic sentence, adding supporting details, deleting ineffective supporting details, and strengthening the concluding sentence. For a second revision, your goal may be to clarify wording and transitions and to consider ways to combine ideas or to present your main point or information more concisely. Get feedback from teachers, peers, or tutors; suggestions from a fresh perspective can be valuable and may lead to yet another revision.

Allow time so you can set your writing aside for a day or two. Examine your draft at a later date and make any additional revisions to improve the impact, clarity, and readability of your piece. Good writers often revise multiple times before a final version is produced. Reserve sufficient time for the revision process.

During the revision process, look at your writing style. The following questions can help you revise and strengthen your writing:

a. Do you use effective word choice and make good use of descriptive adjectives and adverbs to create a strong image in your reader's mind?

b. Do you use more action verbs than linking verbs?

c. Do you use a variety of sentence patterns?

d. Are sentences combined in meaningful, logical ways?

e. Do you avoid unnecessary wordiness? Is your writing crisp and concise?

f. Does your writing clearly express the thoughts, feelings, or purpose you intended to convey to the reader?

6. **Proofread and edit your paragraph.** Examine your writing for mechanical errors to make sure it is grammatically correct and polished. Ask yourself the following questions:

Grammar

a. Does each sentence have a subject and a verb? Have fragments, comma splices, and run-on sentence errors been corrected?

b. Do the subject and verb of each sentence agree?

c. Are the correct verbs and verb tenses used in each sentence?

d. In sentences with pronouns, do the pronouns agree with their antecedents?

e. Are modifiers placed appropriately in each sentence?

f. Are transition words used correctly to show the relationship between clauses?

Punctuation, Spelling, and Capitalization

g. Is correct punctuation used in compound, complex, and compound-complex sentences?

h. Is correct punctuation used with appositives and participial phrases?

i. Are all words spelled and hyphenated correctly? Use a spell checker or dictionary to verify questionable spellings.

j. Are capital letters used on all proper nouns?

7. **Prepare the final version of your writing.** Examine the format of your writing. If required by your instructor, is your work double-spaced, with a title and proper heading stating the date, course, and instructor's name? If hand-written, is your writing neat and legible?

These topics and more are covered in *Sentence Essentials*.

Writing Paragraphs

Although *Sentence Essentials* focuses primarily on grammar and sentence-writing skills, each chapter suggests some writing topics so you can apply the grammar skills to writing paragraphs. The following section provides you with basic guidelines for organizing your ideas and information into well-structured, effective paragraphs.

PARAGRAPH   A paragraph is a unit or series of sentences that are organized around one idea or topic. All the details in the paragraph are closely related to the main idea.

 ## Key Elements of Paragraph Structure

A paragraph that stands by itself and is not a part of a larger piece of writing, such as an essay, a report, or a chapter, consists of three main parts: the topic sentence, the body of the paragraph, and the concluding sentence. (Paragraphs that are a part of a larger piece of writing do not always have concluding sentences. Instead, the last sentence of the paragraph often serves as a transition sentence to connect it to the paragraph that follows.)

TOPIC SENTENCE   The topic sentence expresses the main idea of the entire paragraph. It controls the content of the paragraph.

The topic sentence

1. narrows the topic to a manageable size appropriate for a paragraph

2. names the specific subject of the paragraph

3. provides the reader with a sense of the direction, purpose, or point of view that is expressed in the paragraph

4. captures the reader's attention and interest

BODY OF THE PARAGRAPH   The body of the paragraph consists of sentences with details, examples, and explanations that support the main idea. The sentences in the body of the paragraph develop the subject that is expressed in the topic sentence.

The body of the paragraph

1. includes sufficient details and supporting points to explain, strengthen, and prove the main idea that is stated in the topic sentence (adequate development)

2. presents the supporting details and points in an orderly, logical sequence (coherence)

3. includes only sentences and ideas that are directly related to the topic sentence (unity)

4. flows smoothly with appropriate transition words between sentences

5. keeps the reader's interest and provides relevant information

CONCLUDING SENTENCE   The concluding sentence summarizes the topic sentence.

The concluding sentence

1. signals the end of the paragraph

2. summarizes the key ideas in the paragraph or echoes (restates) the topic sentence

Model of a Paragraph

The following model shows a standard format for any style of paragraph:

The topic sentence expresses the main idea.

The sentences in the body show unity, coherence, and adequate development. They provide the supporting details that are necessary to develop the topic sentence. While the number of sentences for a well-developed paragraph varies, five to ten sentences in the body is typical.

The concluding sentence echoes the topic sentence, summarizes the key points made in the paragraph, or signals the end of the paragraph in another way.

The topic sentence _____ _____
The body of the paragraph _____ _____ _____ _____ _____ _____ _____ _____
The concluding sentence _____ _____ _____ _____

Getting Started

Let us review the main ideas of this chapter:

- Writing is a process.
- Grammar is an important part of the writing process.
- Well-developed paragraphs are an effective way to put your sentence-level skills into action.

As you put these ideas into practice, you will find yourself becoming a stronger and more confident writer. Though writing in general and the study of grammar in particular may sometimes seem like an enormously complex process to master, keep in mind that the rewards and benefits of mastery are great and the satisfactions many.

Web Site Learning Experiences

See the web site for this book to locate companion exercises and links related to the writing topics in this chapter. At this point, go to the web site and spend a few minutes browsing and familiarizing yourself with its elements.

Directions to the Web Site

Go to: http://college.hmco.com. Click on "Students." Type *Sentence Essentials* in the "Jump to Textbook Sites" box. Click "go," and then bookmark this site if you have your own computer. Click on Chapter 1, and then click on the items that you wish to explore further.

How the Web Site is Organized

At this point, you are just browsing to familiarize yourself with the web site. In future chapters, you will proceed through the following steps.

1. After you locate the web site, click on the chapter you are currently studying.

2. You will see a list of different kinds of interactive exercises. After you finish some of the exercises, the directions ask you to click on SUBMIT. You can then get your score. For some of the other interactive exercises, the directions ask you to click on EMAIL to send your work to your instructor or to click on PRINT to make a hard copy for your instructor.

3. On the bottom of each chapter home page, you will also see "Links to Other Sites." When you click on this entry, you will see a list of topics and brief descriptions. Click on any one item to travel to another web site.

4. This web site provides you with hundreds of supplementary exercises and instructional sites. Enjoy the opportunity to explore the web and learn more about grammar and the writing process.

CHAPTER 2

Nouns

In Chapter 2, you will learn about **nouns,** which are words that name people, places, things, and ideas. You will learn that nouns can be singular or plural, and concrete or abstract. You will learn to use **noun markers** to help identify nouns in sentences. Some nouns, called proper nouns, name specific nouns and must be capitalized. Rules for capitalizing nouns are also included in this chapter.

> ### Understanding nouns will help you do the following:
> 1. Identify and write subjects of sentences
> 2. Analyze and correct subject-verb agreement errors
> 3. Locate the end of prepositional phrases
> 4. Recognize and use direct and indirect objects
> 5. Analyze and write sentences with a variety of sentence patterns and appropriate punctuation

NOUN   **A noun is a word that names a person, place, thing, or idea.**

Nouns can be found in many locations throughout a sentence. All of the words in the following chart can work as nouns.

NOUNS			
PERSON	PLACE	THING	IDEA
child	airport	box	beauty
clerk	bank	engine	belief
cousin	beach	foot	creativity
friend	kitchen	movie	envy
senator	library	traffic	fear
student	office	Ford Expedition	socialism
Russell	Hudson Bay	Macintosh	Catholicism

CONCRETE NOUN   A concrete noun names a thing you can see.

The nouns listed in the first three columns above are concrete nouns.

ABSTRACT NOUN   An abstract noun names a feeling, an emotion, an idea, or a concept. These nouns name things that exist but that cannot be seen.

The nouns listed in the right-hand column in the chart above are all abstract nouns.

Special Notes About Nouns

1. The grammatical term *parts of speech* refers to the function of words within sentences. (See the inside back cover for definitions of the eight parts of speech.) Some words may work as more than one part of speech. Sometimes the word may act as a noun; other times the word may act as a verb (an action) or as an adjective (a word that describes or modifies a noun). The following examples demonstrate how a word may shift from one part of speech to another.

   The *fish* feed near the bridge.
   [*Fish* is working as a noun (a thing). *Bridge* is also a noun.]

   Dad made *fish* chowder.
   [*Fish* is working as an adjective to describe the noun *chowder*. *Dad* is also a noun.]

   We *fish* from the banks of the river.
   [*Fish* shows the action of the sentence (the verb). *Banks* and *river* are nouns.]

   My *love* of music is well known.
   [*Love* is working as a noun (an idea). *Music* is also a noun.]

Leah received several *love* letters.
[*Love* is working as an adjective to describe the noun *letters*.
Leah is also a noun.]

Mary and Donald *love* to travel by train.
[*Love* shows the action of the sentence (the verb). *Mary,
Donald*, and *train* are nouns.]

2. Nouns work as *subjects* in many sentences. Subjects are one of the essential elements in sentences. The subjects are the *actors* or *doers* of the sentence. Subjects frequently appear in the front part of sentences, but they can be inverted and appear after the verb or the action of the sentence. (See Chapter 4.)

3. Nouns can be placed in many locations throughout a sentence, not just at the beginning. In the following examples, all the words in italics are nouns. Some of the words are inside prepositional phrases. (Prepositions are words that show a relationship between a noun and other words in the sentence. Prepositions appear at the beginning of a group of words called a prepositional phrase. See Chapter 3.)

noun / prepositional phrase noun / prepositional phrase noun
The *child* slipped off the *dock* and into the *river*.

noun / noun / prepositional phrase noun
My *mother* and *sister* stood on the *pier*

prepositional phrase noun
next to the fishing *boats*.

noun / prepositional phrase noun / noun
The *waitress* with the high *heels* spilled hot *coffee*

prepositional phrase noun
on the *customer*.

noun / noun / prepositional phrase noun
Carlton practiced his *speech* for his closest *friends*.

4. To decide whether a word is a noun, ask yourself if it is something you can see or if it is an idea or concept that is abstract. To test a word, try putting it in this sentence:

(The) _____ is/are good.

Notice how the following words can be placed in the test sentence to see whether they can work as nouns: *entertainment, dreams, pretended,* and *motivation*.

The __entertainment__ is good.   ___Dreams___ are good.
[*Entertainment* is a noun.]   [*Dreams* is a noun.]

The __pretended__ is good.   The __motivation__ is good.
[*Pretended* is not a noun.]   [*Motivation* is a noun.]

Practice 1   *Identifying Nouns in Sentence*

Write **N** above all the words that are **nouns.** Remember that nouns name a person, place, thing, or idea.

Example: The college placed colorful signs and banners throughout
the campus.

1. The clown gave balloons to the children.

2. Your attitude is my main concern.

3. My art teacher praised my creativity.

4. Many parents worry about the effects of television on their
children.

5. The main engine on the ship quit in the middle of the ocean.

6. Many speeches given by activists contain words of hope and
wisdom.

7. The stalled van snarled traffic on the freeway.

8. My wife and her friend filled the basket with fresh produce and
flowers.

9. The final report was a success.

10. The marathon runner sprained his ankle.

JUST SO YOU KNOW...

The noun markers *a, an,* and *the* are also called *articles. The* is a *definite article. A* and *an* are *indefinite articles.* Articles may also be referred to as *determiners.*

NOUN MARKER   The words a, an, and the are noun markers. They signal that a noun will follow.

However, there may be one or more words (adjectives) between the noun marker and the noun. (An adjective describes the noun. See Chapter 7.) Notice how the noun markers in the following examples signal that a noun will soon follow.

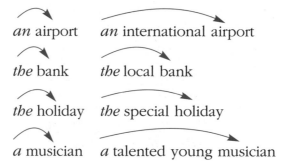

an airport   *an* international airport

the bank   *the* local bank

the holiday   *the* special holiday

a musician   *a* talented young musician

Use the noun marker *the* when you are referring to a specific or definite person, place, thing, or idea. Use the noun markers *a* and *an* when you are referring to a noun that is indefinite or not specific. Notice the differences in the following sentences between the definite and indefinite articles.

> **The girl won the race.** [*The* refers to a specific person.]
>
> **A girl won the race.** [*A* does not indicate a specific person.]
>
> **The umbrella was lost.** [*The* refers to a specific umbrella.]
>
> **An umbrella was lost.** [*An* does not refer to a specific umbrella.]

Special Notes About Noun Markers:

1. The noun markers *a* and *an* are used when the noun is not specific or definite. *A* and *an* are used only with singular nouns (nouns that represent a single item).

   Correct: a bicycle   *Incorrect:* a bicycles

   Correct: an ice cream cone   *Incorrect:* an ice cream cones

2. Use *a* before words that begin with a consonant. (Consonants are all the letters in the alphabet except *a, e, i, o, u,* and sometimes *y.* The letter *y* works as a consonant at the beginning of words. It works as a vowel at the end of words or in combination with another vowel, as in the words *hay, key,* and *toy.*)

   a box   a car   a hammer   a microwave   a yacht

3. Use *a* before words that begin with a long *u* sound. A long *u* sounds like the letter name "u."

   a university   a unique characteristic   a unicorn

4. Use *an* before words that begin with any vowel except a long *u.*

   an apple   an application

   an isolated cabin   an ugly duckling

5. Use *an* before words that begin with a silent *h.*

   an hour   an honor   an honest mistake   an herb garden

6. The noun marker *the* can be used for singular (one) and plural (more than one) nouns. The noun marker *the* is used with a specific or definite noun.

   the umpire   the umpires   the sign   the signs

7. Not all nouns have noun markers. Proper nouns (nouns that are capitalized), abstract nouns, and plural nouns frequently appear without noun markers.

Education improves a person's job *opportunities.*

New *positions* are posted at *school.*

Randy came out of *retirement.*

Candy rots *teeth* and causes *cavities.*

Fame and *fortune* are sought by young *actors.*

Dogs and *cats* are treated for *fleas.*

Practice 2   *A/An*

Write *a* or *an* to complete the following sentences. Write **N** above all the **nouns.**

Example: __An__ unusual situation occurred in the cafeteria.

1. Her husband ran __an__ errand.
2. The monkey ate __a__ banana.
3. Jamie asked for __an__ application.
4. Maria found __an__ unusual pattern.
5. __A__ magazine was on the table.
6. My mother is __an__ honorary member.
7. Sam has __an__ ulcer.
8. His team is __an__ unbeaten team.
9. Sue is __a__ union representative.
10. The seamstress needed __a__ hanger.
11. The book is about __an__ American hero.
12. My grandfather is __a__ hero to me.

Practice 3   *Identifying Words That Can Work as Nouns*

To determine whether a word can work as a noun, ask:

1. Is it a person, place, thing, or idea?

2. Does it make sense with a noun marker *(a, an, the)* in front of it?

3. Can it fit in the test sentence?

(The) _____ is/are good.

Use the questions above to help you identify and circle the words below that can work as nouns.

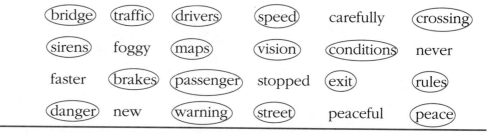

(bridge)   (traffic)   (drivers)   (speed)   carefully   (crossing)

(sirens)   foggy   (maps)   (vision)   (conditions)   never

faster   (brakes)   (passenger)   stopped   (exit)   (rules)

(danger)   new   (warning)   (street)   peaceful   (peace)

Additional Noun Markers

In addition to the noun markers *a, an,* and *the,* other words also work as noun markers. The following chart shows the articles and four additional kinds of noun markers. (Possessive pronouns are discussed in more detail in Chapters 4 and 6. Demonstrative pronouns are discussed in Chapter 7.) Note that possessive nouns always use an *apostrophe* to show ownership.

NOUN MARKERS					
NOUN	ARTICLES	POSSESSIVE PRONOUN	POSSESSIVE NOUN	NUMBER WORDS	DEMONSTRATIVE PRONOUNS
boat	**the** boat	**my** boat	**Sally's** boat	**one** boat	**this** boat
dream	**a** dream	**your** dream	**John's** dream	**two** dreams	**this** dream
identity	**an** identity	**her** identity	**Jill's** identity	**three** identities	**these** identities
unit	**a** unit	**his** unit	**Juan's** unit	**four** units	**these** units
friends	**the** friends	**our** friends	**family's** friends	**five** friends	**those** friends
toys	**the** toys	**their** toys	**children's** toys	**six** toys	**those** toys
idea	**an** idea	**their** idea	**parent's** idea	**seven** ideas	**that** idea
bone	**a** bone	**its** bone	**dog's** bone	**eight** bones	**that** bone

Practice 4   *Sports Psychology*

Work with a partner, in a small group, or on your own to complete this activity. Look at the words that are in bold print in the following passage. Write **N** above the word if it is working as a noun. Do not write anything above the words in bold print that are not working as nouns. Use noun markers as clues for identifying the nouns. Remember that some nouns can be used without noun markers.

SPORTS PSYCHOLOGY

Richard Suinn, Ph.D., is a sports **psychologist.** He was the first psychologist on a U.S. Olympic sports medicine **team.** He is currently the **head** of the American Psychological Association. In an **interview** with Robert Epstein, the two men **talked** about the body-mind connection for **athletes.** Important **ideas** from this interview are summarized below.

Modern sports psychology **started** in the early 1970s. The **focus** then and now has been on psychological **training** to **strengthen** the mental **skills** of athletes. With stronger mental skills, athletic **performance improves.** The mental skills include **stress management, self-regulation, visualization, goal-setting, concentration, focus,** and **relaxation.** For example, goal-setting affects **motivation.** Goal-setting **helps** to bring the **future** a little closer. Goal-setting breaks the future into little **steps** and helps the **athletes** see their **progress** week by **week.** Athletes can chart their progress, and the **small** steps of progress motivate them to stay with their **programs.** They focus on their ultimate **goals.**

Mental practice **is** also a **part** of sports psychology. Mental practice is also referred to as **visualization** or imagery rehearsal. Mental practice **begins** with twenty to thirty **minutes** of relaxation **training.** Relaxation is followed by the visualization of some **aspect** of the athlete's **game.** Mental practice is the **equivalent** of physical **practice.** For example, a **golfer** can visualize the **correct** swing. A golfer's **muscles** may actually **start** to learn the **swing** through this mental practice. **Performance** after relaxation and visualization often shows **improvement.**

[Adapted from Robert Epstein, Ph.D., "Helping Athletes Go for the Gold," *Psychology Today*, May/June 1999, p. 20.]

Practice 5   *Identifying Noun Markers and Nouns*

Write **N** above all the **nouns** in the following sentences. Use a highlighter to highlight the noun markers.

Example: Our closest friends live on your street near the high school.

1. Your wish is my command.

2. Three individuals reported the interference.

3. His beliefs are written in the introduction.

4. The fear in their eyes caught our attention.

5. My family's treasures are kept in this vault.

6. The beauty of the scenery was captured by the photographer.

7. The thought of his departure saddened me.

8. Ramon is a journalist for the tabloid.

9. His relatives bought five tickets for that track meet.

10. My group listed seven ideas for the class to consider.

SINGULAR NOUN   A singular noun names *one* person, place, thing, or idea.

The following words are singular nouns:

nurse	woman	river	religion
gentleman	inspiration	dog	barn

PLURAL NOUN   A plural noun names more *than one* person, place, thing, or idea.

Frequently the plural form of a noun is made by adding an -*s* or -*es* suffix to the singular form. Other times a spelling change is required. Guidelines for forming plural nouns are shown in the following charts.

GUIDELINES FOR REGULAR PLURAL FORMS	SINGULAR FORM → PLURAL FORM
Add -*s* to the singular form.	friend → friends movie → movies plan → plans
Add -*s* to words that end with *ay, ey, oy, uy*, and sometimes *o*.	tray → trays turkey → turkeys toy → toys guy → guys solo → solos piano → pianos

(Continue on page 20)

GUIDELINES FOR REGULAR PLURAL FORMS	SINGULAR FORM → PLURAL FORM	
Add -es to words that end in s, x, z, sh, ch, and sometimes o.	success → successes ax → axes brush → brushes tomato → tomatoes	pass → passes buzz → buzzes branch → branches hero → heroes
For most words that end with f or fe, when you say the plural, you hear a v sound. In such cases, change the f to v and add -es. (If you continue to hear the f sound, keep the letter f in the spelling.)	wolf → wolves knife → knives calf → calves chief → chiefs cuff → cuffs	
For words that end with a consonant + y, change the y to i and add -es.	mystery → mysteries baby → babies country → countries library → libraries	

GUIDELINES FOR IRREGULAR PLURAL FORMS	SINGULAR FORM → PLURAL FORM	
In some instances, a new word is used to form the plural.	analysis → analyses axis → axes crisis → crises foot → feet man → men mouse → mice ox → oxen radius → radii woman → women	antenna → antennae child → children die → dice goose → geese medium → media oasis → oases parenthesis → parentheses tooth → teeth phenomenon → phenomena
In some instances, no change is made in the singular form to make the plural.	deer → deer moose → moose	elk → elk sheep → sheep

Special Notes About Singular and Plural Nouns

1. A common error made with plural nouns is to use an apostrophe. Do not make plural nouns by using an apostrophe. An apostrophe is used to show possession, not plural form.

    Three ~~pilot's~~ spoke. _(pilots)_

    My ~~dog's~~ are registered. _(dogs)_

2. The noun markers *a* and *an* are used only with singular nouns. The noun marker *the* may be used with both singular and plural nouns.

<u>Singular:</u>	<u>Plural:</u>
An umpire made the call.	*Umpires* made the call.
	[Incorrect: *An umpires* made the call.]
A woman smiled at me.	*Women* smiled at me.
	[Incorrect: *A women* smiled at me.]
The rope was tangled.	*The ropes* were tangled.

COMMON NOUN   **A common noun is a general noun. It does not name a specific or unique person, place, thing, or idea. Common nouns are not capitalized.**

The following words are common nouns:

man   night   book   shoe   park   class   belief

PROPER NOUN   **A proper noun names a specific or unique person, place, thing, or idea. Proper nouns must be capitalized.**

The following words are proper nouns.

Mr. Wallace	Lynn Lee
Sometimes a Great Notion	China
Nike	Yellowstone National Park
English 210	Democracy

Practice 6   *Naming Proper Nouns*

A list of common nouns is given below. Next to each common noun, write a proper noun (the name of a *specific* person, place, thing, or idea). *Answers will vary. Possible answers are given.*

Examples: a family member ___Dion___   an ocean _Pacific Ocean_

1. a teacher ___Rob Smith___
2. an inventor ___Eli Whitney___
3. a mountain ___Mount Rainier___
4. a song _Star Spangled Banner_
5. a religion ___Buddhism___

6. a river ___Mississippi River___
7. your governor ___(for your state)___
8. a shampoo ___Herbal Essences___
9. a foreign language ___French___
10. a holiday ___Thanksgiving___

Rules of Capitalization: People

1. Capitalize names of specific people and words that indicate the following family relationships: parents, grandparents, aunts, and uncles.

Jordan	Mom	Grandma Dora	Papa
Auntie Rose	Uncle Lionell	Grandfather	Father

Do not capitalize *mother, father, grandmother, grandfather, uncle,* or *aunt* when the words appear with a noun marker.

the mother	my mom	his father	her aunt
their dad	our uncle	your grandmother	our grandpa

Usually *brother, sister, cousin, niece, nephew, grandparent,* or *grandchild* are not capitalized when they refer to family relationships. (Note in Rule 2 that *brother* and *sister* will be capitalized when they represent a religious title before a person's name.)

sister	brother	your nephew	cousin
niece	my grandson	their grandmother	grandchildren

2. Capitalize titles that come right before a person's name.

Mayor Goldstein	Officer Wallace
President Lincoln	Vice President Jackson
Coach Green	Captain Bellows
General Patton	Superintendent Walters
Senator Smith	Queen Elizabeth
Professor Ruiz	Ambassador Black
Governor Lacey	Dr. Cary
Rabbi Levins	Father Joseph
Sister Rosaria	Mother Teresa
Brother Malcolm	King Solomon
Mr. Chung	Mrs. O'Reilly
Miss Lancaster	Ms. Lopez

3. Capitalize nouns (and words made from nouns) that identify or refer to specific nationalities, races, ethnic groups, tribes, languages, and political parties.

Italians	Native Americans	African-American
Cherokee	Caucasian	Spanish
German	Mayans	Latino
Latina	Democrats	Republican

Do not capitalize common nouns that follow proper nouns.

Japanese tradition   *French* cuisine

Chinese imports   *Russian* alphabet

English teacher   *Greek* ruins

Latin music   *Native American* burial grounds

Spanish language   *Democratic* agenda

JUST SO YOU KNOW...

Proper nouns function as adjectives when they are followed by common nouns. They describe or modify the noun. As you will learn in Chapter 7, the italicized words in the examples on the right are adjectives.

Practice 7   *Capitalizing Proper Nouns Related to People*

Add capital letters to the proper nouns in the following sentences.

1. Chuck, mike, and jimmy plan to take father danielson fishing this weekend.
   (M, J, F, D)

2. Mary, aunt sue, and I wanted to give my mom and my dad a surprise party.
   (A, S)

3. The exchange rate for the canadian dollar and the american dollar was high.
   (C, A)

4. Many native american legends have been written about chief joseph.
   (N, A, C, J)

5. Most of the crew on the norwegian cruise ship spoke two or more languages.
   (N)

Rules of Capitalization: Places

4. Capitalize specific names of real or imaginary geographical locations, such as streets, cities, states, countries, mountains, rivers, oceans, planets, stars, and galaxies. Do not capitalize small words such as *of* that are inside the names.

Mississippi River	New Orleans	Pacific Ocean
People's Republic of China	Rocky Mountains	Panama Canal
River Road	Washington, D.C.	Atlantis
El Dorado	Jupiter	Milky Way

5. Capitalize specific names of places and institutions, such as parks, buildings, monuments, businesses, and schools. Do not capitalize small words such as *of* that are inside the names.

Empire State Building	WalMart	Central Park
Institute of Technology	Disneyland	Harvard
Wild Life Safari	House of Wax	Washington Memorial

6. Capitalize "direction words" only when they refer to a specific region of the country.

relocated out West	established in the South
occurs in the Mideast	shipped to the West Coast
known in the East	explored the Northwest

Do not capitalize "direction words" when they refer to a direction as shown on a compass.

climbed the western slopes	headed north
drove south of Paris	lived east of Memphis
moved south of the border	blew to the northeast

Practice 8   *Capitalizing Proper Nouns Related to Places*

Add capital letters to the proper nouns in the following sentences.

Example: The space needle in seattle and mount st. helens in
southern washington are two well-known landmarks.

1. The black hills of south dakota attract thousands of tourists each
   year.
   <small>B . H . . S . . D</small>

2. The mississippi river empties into the gulf of mexico.
   <small>M . R . . . G . M</small>

3. The famous ski resort of sun valley is situated east of boise, idaho.
   <small>S . V . . . . . B . I</small>

4. The hoover tower on the stanford university campus houses
   historical documents.
   <small>H . T . . S . U</small>

5. The dream of finding gold brought many settlers to the west.
   <small>W</small>

6. The ambulance raced down broadway avenue and headed south to
   the accident.
   <small>B . . A</small>

7. The only latin american country that does not have spanish as the
   national language is brazil.
   <small>L . A . . . . . S . . B</small>

8. A valid passport is required for americans to travel to singapore.
   <small>A . . S</small>

---

www Rules of Capitalization: Things

7. Capitalize specific names of companies, products, trademarks, and
   brand names.

   PepsiCola   Ameritrade   Tide   Sunny Delight   Maytag

8. Capitalize specific names of organizations and government
   agencies. Also capitalize abbreviations used to represent the name
   of an organization or agency.

   Internal Revenue Service (IRS)

   Rainbow Coalition

   Supreme Court

   United Parcel Service (UPS)

   League of Women Voters (LWV)

   United States Senate

9. Capitalize specific names of religions, followers of specific religious beliefs, religious books or documents, and references to a supreme being.

Catholics	Muslims	Protestants
the Qur'an	Allah	God
the Almighty	Holy Spirit	the Bible
the Old Testament	Buddhist temple	Jewish leaders
Methodist minister	Christian beliefs	Greek Orthodox custom

JUST SO YOU KNOW...

Proper nouns placed before common nouns function as adjectives. (See Chapter 7.)

10. Capitalize specific historical periods, events, and historical documents.

Renaissance	World War II
Great Depression	Declaration of Independence
Desert Storm	Stone Age
Boston Tea Party	Fifth Amendment

11. Capitalize specific holidays that are identified on calendars, days, and months of the year. Do not capitalize the seasons of the year (fall/autumn, winter, spring, or summer).

Veterans Day	Hanukkah	Easter	New Year's Eve
Yom Kippur	January	Thursday	Fourth of July

Practice 9   *Capitalizing Proper Nouns Related to Things*

Add capital letters to the proper nouns in the following sentences.

1. One jewish festival, passover, commemorates the exodus from egypt.
   <small>J   P   E   E</small>

2. The chapter focuses on the early period of human culture called the stone age.
   <small>S   A</small>

3. Both democratic and republican candidates spoke to the members of the local chamber of commerce.
   <small>D   R   C   C</small>

4. The federal reserve board announced a change in the national interest rate.
   <small>F   R   B</small>

5. Thirty students became members of the national honor society on wednesday.
   <small>N   H   S</small>
   <small>W</small>

Rules of Capitalization: Literary Works and Academic Courses

12. Capitalize specific titles of literary works. Do not capitalize the smaller words *the, a, an, of,* or *and* when they are in the middle of the title. The titles of long literary works (plays and musical compositions) and complete titles of books, movies, magazines, journals, newspapers, pieces of art, television series, radio programs, and software programs are underlined or placed in italics.

Beauty and the Beast	*The Client*
Who Wants to Be a Millionaire?	*The View*
New York Times	*The Star Tribune*
The Titanic	*The Best Man*

The titles of short stories, short plays, poems, articles, essays, chapters, songs, or other short literary works are placed inside quotation marks.

"Smooth" by Santana (song)

"The Empire of Liberty 1801–1824" (chapter)

"Stellar Athletes" (article)

"Spirits Sag as Aloha State Hits 40" (article)

"Self-Reliance" by Emerson (essay)

"The Raven" by Edgar Allan Poe (poem)

13. Capitalize specific names of courses when they are written as they would appear in a formal catalog.

English Literature 101	English Composition 123
European History 203	Graphic Design 2
Spanish III	History of Western Art

Do not capitalize nonspecific courses naming a general subject area.

an English course	a history course
my computer class	a French class
a course in biology	one of three math courses

Note that *English* and *French* are capitalized because they name specific languages.

Practice 10   *Working with Common and Proper Nouns*

Work with a partner, in a small group, or on your own. Use a highlighter to highlight all the nouns in the following sentences. Add capital letters to all the proper nouns.

1. The international students enrolled in conversational english II

   last winter term.

2. My entire family watches *touched by an angel* every week after

   dinner.

3. Colin powell's book my american journey was on the the

   best-seller list.

4. I subscribe to the *wall street journal* and *psychology today*.

5. I chose to read toni morrison's book *beloved* for my english

   literature assignment.

6. Professor long, the instructor of psychology 202, discussed the

   concepts presented in steven reiss's article "secrets of happiness."

Two or More Words That Function as One Noun

As you have likely already noticed, some proper nouns, such as a name, are expressed in two or more words. The words function together as one noun. Names or titles of people, geographic locations, businesses, organizations, holidays, product and brand names, religious and historical documents or events, literary works, and academic courses work together as one noun.

The following examples show how you would mark these proper noun combinations.

James Michener wrote *Tales of the South Pacific* in 1947.

Times Square in New York City attracts thousands of

people on New Year's Eve.

N
Medical Law and Ethics is my most challenging course
                                                    N

this semester.
          N

Aunt Betty lives near the French Quarter in New Orleans.
     N   N   N

Some word combinations made by two or more common nouns work together as a singular noun. These combinations work together as one concept and lose their intended meaning if they are separated. The following examples show two or more words that work together as one noun.

N
Ice cream is my favorite dessert.
                          N
[Ice is not your favorite dessert. Neither is cream your favorite dessert. In addition, *ice* is not an adjective that describes a type of cream. Therefore, *ice cream* works as one noun.]

N
We purchased a *money order* at the supermarket.
                                        N
[We did not purchase money, nor did we purchase an order. *Money* is not working as an adjective to describe a type of order. Therefore, *money order* works as one noun.]

The following word combinations also work as singular nouns:

purchase order	potato chip	notary public
room and board	runner-up	root beer
table tennis	home economics	daylight-saving time
movie star	mother-in-law	editor in chief
loan shark	macaroni and cheese	teddy bear
jump rope	chickenpox	comic strip
flea market	chow mein	television set
hocus-pocus	jumper cable	walkie-talkie
disc jockey	bread and butter	safe-deposit box
pen pal	vinegar and oil	cable car
field goal	pilot light	poison ivy

Practice 11   *Identifying Nouns*

Work with a partner, in a small group, or on your own to complete this activity. Highlight all the common and proper nouns in the following sentences.

1. Your [replacement] will arrive from [Cleveland] next [week].

2. A [lot] of the [commotion] started near the fire [station] on [Fifth Avenue].

3. The [flatness] of the [desert] surprised the Japanese [tourists].

4. The [elder] lost his [composure] in the [middle] of his [speech].

5. The [teller] at [Norwest Bank] completed the [transaction] quickly and efficiently.

6. The [conductor] on the [train] strolled through the [cars] and collected the [tickets].

7. [Laziness], [carelessness], and [irresponsibility] will not be tolerated in this [office].

8. [Lisa] received an [award] from the [Rotary Club] for her [excellence].

9. The [reputation] of our marketing [company] rests on the [performance] of our [employees].

10. The [shortage] of skilled [teachers] will soon be a national [problem].

Practice 12   *Identifying Nouns and Noun Markers*

Circle all the noun markers. Write **N** above all the **nouns.**

Example: You can purchase tickets to (the) football game at (the) main
entrance.

1. (The) quartet on (the) stage harmonizes well.

2. (The) blow to (my) funny bone caused (my) arm to tingle.

3. The period of European history between ancient and modern times is called the Middle Ages.

4. The cosmetologist plucked her eyebrows.

5. My uncle's negative criticism hurt my feelings.

6. The circular staircase in that church attracts curious tourists.

7. OPEC is the acronym for the Organization of Petroleum Exporting Countries.

8. The Richter scale is used to measure the intensity of earthquakes.

9. Five neighborhoods met to begin Neighborhood Watch programs.

10. The patient asked his doctor for a prognosis.

COMMA SENSE

Use a comma to separate nouns in a series of three or more nouns.

The bikes, wagons, toys, and skates were in the driveway.

The hurricane will hit Cuba, Haiti, or the Bahamas.

Use a comma between the name of a city and the state or country.

Use a comma after the state or country to separate it from the remainder of the sentence.

Seattle, Washington, is the home of the Seahawks.

We landed safely in Rio de Janeiro, Brazil, after a very long flight.

Fisherman's Wharf in San Francisco, California, is a world-renowned tourist attraction.

© AFP/Corbis Images

David J. Philip/© AP-Wide World Photos

© AP-Wide World Photos

Work with a partner, in a small group, or on your own to complete the following activity. Read the paragraphs carefully. Add capital letters above all the proper nouns. Add missing commas between nouns in a series or between cities and states.

STELLAR ATHLETES

Within a three-week period in 1999, sports fans around the world bade farewell to three of america's stellar athletes. Heads were bowed prior to the beginning of games, tributes were paid during tournaments, and television specials were broadcast frequently.

On october 12, Wilt Chamberlain died of an apparent heart attack at the age of 63. This basketball legend had a major impact on the game of basketball. Rules were changed to try to slow him down on the court. In high school in philadelphia, he scored 90 points in one 32-minute game. He began his professional basketball career with the harlem globetrotters. He was nicknamed "Wilt the Stilt" because he stood 7 feet 1¾ inches tall. Chamberlain then played in the NBA (national basketball association) for fourteen years. Chamberlain scored 31,419 points during his career. Many of his records still remain and may never be broken. No NBA player has yet threatened chamberlain's career rebound record of 23,924 rebounds. He holds the single-game rebound record with 55 rebounds in 1960. In 1962, he set an nba record for most points scored by an individual player in one game (100 points). His 1962 record for the highest season average (50 points per game) still stands.

Almost two weeks later, on october 25, the sports world mourned the death of a great golfer. Payne stewart won the USPGA tournament and two U.S. Opens, including the 1999 U.S. Open. He and other americans also played on two winning ryder cup teams. Stewart died at the age of 42. He and five other people were on his private jet. They left orlando, florida, and were headed to a golf tournament in dallas, texas. Shortly after takeoff, a loss of air pressure in the cabin of the jet occurred. All the passengers and the pilot passed out. The jet traveled on its own for more than 1,500 miles before its fuel finally ran out. The jet with the pilot, payne stewart, and four other passengers crashed in south dakota. Payne stewart will always be remembered for his playful spirit, his unique sense of golf fashion, and his talent with his golf clubs. In his memory at a tournament after his death, many of his golfing friends wore his outrageously colorful knickerbockers.

One week later, the nation observed the loss of football star walter payton. Payton was born in columbia, mississippi. Payton was nicknamed "Sweetness" for his "sweet" moves on the field and his "sweet" disposition off the field. His stamina and work ethic made him an all-time leading rusher and a football legend. His thirteen-year NFL (national football league) career was with the chicago bears. Payton still holds several league records. He carried the ball 3,838 times and rushed for 16,726 yards. He was a nine-time pro bowl player and was voted into the football hall of fame in 1993. Walter payton died of a rare liver disease at the age of 45. In february, he and his son told the nation about his disease. He was on a liver transplant waiting list at the mayo clinic, but the disease spread too quickly. Rev. jesse jackson, mike singletary, family, friends, and fans remembered payton in a special ceremony at soldier field in chicago, illinois.

At the end of 1999, many sports fans around the nation remembered these three athletes. The television stations, radio stations, newspapers, and magazines all covered in depth the deaths of these three sports legends. Who would have thought that three stellar athletes would die within three weeks of each other and at such young ages?

Part I: Circle the correct noun marker in each of the following sentences.

1. The speaker ended his speech with (**a**, an) hilarious anecdote.
2. He has (a, **an**) additional retirement fund.
3. That was truly (a, **an**) act of random kindness.
4. She has a secret about (a, **an**) upcoming event.
5. They wanted to present (**a**, an) united front.
6. Randy received (a, **an**) honorable mention.

Part II: Write **N** above all the words that are working as **nouns.** Use a highlighter to highlight all the noun markers. Note that not all of the nouns have noun markers.

1. Mom defrosted [the] freezer and threw out [the] old meat.
2. [The] plantations in [the] South produced [a] lot of [the] country's cotton and tobacco.
3. [A] look of disappointment crossed [his] face.
4. [The] play was [a] farce about American families.
5. [Our] tour took us through Greece, Spain, Portugal, and Italy.

Part III: Write a noun on the blanks to complete each sentence. *Answers will vary. Possible answers are given.*

1. We went to the ____store____ to purchase a ____heater____.
2. I despise ____okra____, ____yams____, and ____cauliflower____.
3. The ____bread____ and the ____jam____ cost $5.00 at the ____supermarket____.
4. I will never go to the ____movies____ again with my granddaughter.
5. The children sat on the ____bench____ and talked about ____baseball____.
6. My best ____friend____ gave me a ____present____.

EXERCISE 2.3   **Proofreading**   Name _____ Date _____

Proofread the following sentences for errors. Check carefully for missing capital letters and missing commas. Correct the errors by writing the capital letters above the proper nouns and by adding commas where they are needed. Write **C** in the margin if the sentence is **correct.**

Example: The multicultural club raised five hundred dollars for the
$\overset{M}{ }$ $\overset{C}{ }$
$\overset{C}{ }$ $\overset{S}{ }$
cancer society.

1. Our tour guide, $\overset{N}{n}$ancy $\overset{J}{j}$enkins, moved from $\overset{L}{l}$os $\overset{A}{a}$ngeles to $\overset{A}{a}$tlanta,
$\overset{G}{g}$eorgia.

2. The church group has done volunteer work in $\overset{C}{c}$osta $\overset{R}{r}$ica, $\overset{M}{m}$exico,
and $\overset{B}{b}$elize.

3. Key $\overset{W}{w}$est, $\overset{F}{f}$lorida, is on the southern tip of the state.

4. Jamaal has studied $\overset{F}{f}$rench, $\overset{S}{s}$panish, and $\overset{S}{s}$wahili at the university.

5. Every $\overset{F}{f}$riday night, we order $\overset{C}{c}$hinese food or pizza to be delivered
at home.

6. The $\overset{L}{l}$ions $\overset{C}{c}$lub served $\overset{P}{p}$olish sausages and corn on the cob at the
$\overset{O}{o}$regon $\overset{S}{s}$tate $\overset{F}{f}$air.

c 7. The weather to the east is warmer and drier.

8. The $\overset{A}{a}$pache, the $\overset{N}{n}$avaho, and the $\overset{H}{h}$opi are located in the $\overset{S}{s}$outhwest.

9. The $\overset{S}{s}$uper $\overset{B}{b}$owl is held the last $\overset{S}{s}$unday in $\overset{J}{j}$anuary.

10. Bill, $\overset{D}{d}$ad, and my sister went to $\overset{L}{l}$ookout $\overset{P}{p}$ass to cut our $\overset{C}{c}$hristmas
tree.

EXERCISE 2.4 **Sentence Writing** Name _____ Date _____

The sentences below begin with a noun marker and a noun, which is the subject of the sentence. The subject of a sentence is the *actor* or the *doer* of the sentence. The subject tells *who* or *what* the sentence is about. The subjects are underlined. Finish writing the sentences with your own thoughts. Highlight all the words in your sentences that work as nouns. *Answers will vary. Possible answers are given.*

1. A songwriter spends many hours at a keyboard _____

_____.

2. The students met to discuss the test _____

_____.

3. The retired plumber does freelance work for friends _____

_____.

4. Your imagination can get you in trouble _____

_____.

5. An athlete spends many hours in training _____

_____.

6. The psychologist completed her report _____

_____.

7. The bulldozer roared down the street _____

_____.

8. The shady oak tree is a landmark _____

_____.

9. Kim's favorite recording artist released a new album _____

_____.

10. My swollen ankle aches _____

_____.

Chapter 2 Summary

1. **Nouns** are words that name a person, place, thing, or idea.

2. Nouns can be divided into several categories:

   concrete nouns and **abstract nouns**

   singular nouns and **plural nouns**

   common nouns and **proper nouns**

3. **Noun markers** signal that a noun follows. These are common noun markers:

   a, an, the   my, your, his, her, our, their, its

   one, two, three   this, that, these, those

4. **Proper nouns** name specific people, places, things, or ideas. Proper nouns must always be capitalized.

5. Thirteen rules of capitalization govern proper nouns.

   Rule 1: Capitalize names of people and words that indicate family relationships (parents, grandparents, aunts, and uncles) when the words appear without noun markers.

   Rule 2: Capitalize titles that come before a person's name.

   Rule 3: Capitalize nouns (and words made from nouns) that identify or refer to nationalities, ethnic groups, tribes, languages, and political parties.

   Rule 4: Capitalize specific names of real or imaginary geographical locations (streets, cities, states, countries, mountains, rivers, oceans, planets, stars, and galaxies).

   Rule 5: Capitalize specific names of places and institutions (parks, buildings, monuments, businesses, and schools).

   Rule 6: Capitalize "direction words" only when they refer to a specific region of the country (the South, the Northwest).

   Rule 7: Capitalize specific names of companies, products, trademarks, and brand names.

   Rule 8: Capitalize specific names of organizations and government agencies. Also capitalize abbreviations used to represent the name of an organization or agency.

   Rule 9: Capitalize specific names of religions, followers of specific religious beliefs, religious books or documents, and references to a supreme being.

   Rule 10: Capitalize specific historical periods, events, and historical documents.

Rule 11: Capitalize specific holidays that are identified on calendars, days, and months of the year. Do not capitalize the seasons of the year.

Rule 12: Capitalize specific titles of literary works (books, movies, magazines, journals, newspapers, pieces of art, television series, radio programs, software programs, short stories, plays, poems, articles, essays, chapters, and songs).

Rule 13: Capitalize specific names of courses when they are written as they would appear in a formal catalog.

6. **Commas** are used to separate

- three or more nouns in a series.
- the name of a city from the name of the state or country.
- a city and state (or city and country) from the remainder of the sentence.

Writing Topics for Chapter 2

A *Writing Topics* section appears in each chapter and provides you with the opportunity to apply your sentence-writing skills to interesting topics that can be developed into paragraphs. Chapter 1 introduced you to the basic format of a paragraph. While you are learning to express your ideas on paper, strive to organize them into a paragraph format. These basic guidelines can be used for the *Writing Topics* in each chapter:

1. Select the main idea for the paragraph. Place the main idea first in your paragraph.

2. Avoid unnecessary paragraph introductions such as the following:

   Today I am going to tell you about . . .

   I am going to write about . . .

3. Make a brief outline or a plan for your paragraph. Organize the details in a logical sequence. The ideas should flow together smoothly.

4. Check the mechanics of your paragraph. As you progress through this textbook, you will learn many techniques for proofreading and strengthening your writing. For now, do your best with your current understanding of grammar and punctuation. Check for correct spelling. Read each sentence by itself to determine whether it sounds complete and makes sense. Check that you did not omit any words that you intended to write.

5. End your paragraph with a short conclusion.

Select one of the following writing options. Write one or two paragraphs about this topic. Proofread the draft of your work before you turn it in. Writing topics with the computer icon indicate that the Internet may be used to locate information for the assignment; however, access to the Internet is not essential to complete the assignment.

 1. Within your lifetime, you have encountered many sports legends. Write about a sports legend who is familiar to you. Use a sports magazine, the Internet, or the library to locate specific facts about the person you selected. Include a copy of any articles that you use for your information.

2. Every sport has record holders for various athletic feats accomplished by talented individuals. However, our world is also filled with individuals who have accomplished other kinds of great feats, overcome adversity, or performed worthwhile deeds or humanitarian acts. Select a person you know personally who has accomplished something extraordinary. Write about this person. Who is he or she? What is the person's special accomplishment?

Web Site Learning Experiences

See the web site for this book to locate companion exercises and links related to the grammar topics in this chapter.

Go to: http://college.hmco.com. Click on "Students." Type *Sentence Essentials* in the "Jump to Textbook Sites" box. Click "go," and then bookmark the site. Click on Chapter 2.

CHAPTER 2 • Review   Name _____ Date _____

Total Possible: 50   Your Score: _____

Part I: Identification of Nouns (25 points)

Highlight all the nouns in the following sentences. *Give 1 point for each correctly identified noun. Subtract ½ point for each incorrect answer.*

1. The young detective solved the mystery.

2. The tourists hauled blankets and sunscreen to the beach.

3. The clerk was not excited about the upcoming holiday.

4. Love, tenderness, and broken hearts are themes of many

   country western tunes.

5. Your rude comments hit a nerve.

6. A station in Kansas City picked up the signals.

7. The cheesecake was quite a temptation.

8. Freedom is not a universal reality.

9. Your level of confidence will affect your performance.

Part II: Capitalization and Commas (25 points—$\frac{1}{2}$ point each answer)
Proofread the following sentences. Add the missing capital letters and the missing commas.

1. Tiger woods, michael jordan, and the minnesota twins have
   appeared on wheaties boxes. 8 = 4 pts.

2. Josh studied latin, hebrew, and arabic. 5 = $2\frac{1}{2}$ pts.

3. I had two dreams about going to maui, oahu, and kauai. 5 = $2\frac{1}{2}$ pts.

4. El paso, texas, is located right on the mexican border. 5 = $2\frac{1}{2}$ pts.

5. The spokesperson for the pilots' association discussed the strike.
   2 = 1 pt.

6. The humidity in the midwest is extremely high in the summer.
   1 = $\frac{1}{2}$ pt.

7. The presbyterian, methodist, and lutheran churches conduct
   christmas eve services. 7 = $3\frac{1}{2}$ pts.

8. Mass production in most factories began during the industrial
   revolution. 2 = 1 pt.

9. The washington monument, arlington cemetery, and the vietnam
   veterans' memorial are located in our nation's capital. 9 = $4\frac{1}{2}$ pts.

10. The european tourists skated at rockefeller plaza in new york city.
    6 = 3 pts.

CHAPTER 3

Prepositions

In Chapter 3, you will learn about **prepositions,** which are connective words that join nouns or pronouns to other parts of the sentence. Prepositions indicate time, location, direction, and other kinds of relationships. Prepositions appear in prepositional phrases.

Understanding prepositions will help you do the following:

1. Identify prepositional phrases in sentences

2. Eliminate prepositional phrases from sentences when you are working with subject and verb patterns since subjects and verbs are never inside prepositional phrases

3. Strengthen your writing by adding more detail to your sentences through the use of prepositional phrases

PREPOSITION **A preposition is a connective word that joins a noun or a pronoun to the remainder of the sentence and indicates time, location, direction, or other kinds of relationships.**

Time:
> The computer technician arrived *before* you.
> The power shortage occurred *during* a heat wave.

Location:
> Spot hid *underneath* the front porch.
> I parked *in* the new parking structure.

Direction:
> The rafters floated *toward* the bridge.
> The cat climbed *up* the tree.

Other Relationships:
> The package arrived *via* a messenger.
> Everyone is going to the wedding *except* me.
> *Contrary to* public opinion, he is trustworthy.

PREPOSITIONS			
about*	beneath*	in regard to	round*
above*	beside*	inside*	since*
according to	between	in spite of	subsequent to
across*	beyond*	instead of	through*
after*	but*	into	throughout*
against	by*	like*	till*
ahead of	by means of	near*	to*
along*	concerning	next to	together with
along with	contrary to	of	toward
amid	despite	off*	under*
among	down*	on*	underneath*
around*	due to	on account of	unlike*
as*	during	onto	until*
aside from	except	opposite*	up*
as to	for*	out*	upon
as well as	from	out of	via
at	in*	outside*	with
away from	in addition to	over*	within*
because of	in front of	past*	without*
before*	in lieu of	per	
behind*	in order to	prior to	
below*	in place of	regarding*	

*These words can also work as other parts of speech.

PREPOSITIONAL PHRASE A prepositional phrase is a group of words that begins with a preposition and ends with a noun or a pronoun. The preposition shows a relationship, such as time, location, or direction, between the noun and the remainder of the sentence.

about the movie	*above* the counter	*according to* Jim
across the street	*after* the fireworks	*against* my wishes
ahead of the crowd	*along* the river	*along with* Cindy

The main function of prepositional phrases is to show relationships. The three most common relationships are time, location, and direction. However, you will encounter other prepositional phrases that show additional kinds of relationships. In the following examples, the prepositional phrases are related to the verbs, or action words, in the sentences. Prepositional phrases are shown in italics and placed inside parentheses. In this textbook, we will use parentheses ( ) to mark or to separate prepositional phrases from other parts of the sentence.

The "No Smoking" sign hung *(above the door)*.
[The preposition *above* shows **location** and the relationship between the door and the sign.]

The motorcade moved *(past the White House)*.
[*Past* shows **direction** and the relationship between the White House and the motorcade.]

The player kicked the ball *(between the goal posts)*.
[*Between* shows **direction** and the relationship between the ball and the goal posts.]

The fax arrived *(before noon)* *(on Friday)*.
[*Before* and *on* show **time;** the prepositions show the relationship of the fax to the time of day and the day of the week.]

Eager tourists arrived *(in cars and vans)* to see the Grand Canyon.
[*In* tells **how** the tourists arrived and shows the relationship between the cars and vans and the tourists.]

Prepositional phrases can add more details to sentences by describing nouns or pronouns. In the following examples, the prepositions show time, location, direction, and other relationships; they also describe nouns or pronouns. They describe *which* people, *which* woman, *which* migration, *which* man, *which* movie, and *which* agreement. Again, the prepositional phrases are marked with parentheses.

The people *(on the dock)* watched the migration *(of the whales)*.

The woman *(with the camera)* shot many pictures.

The migration *(from northern waters) (to warmer waters)* is annual.

A man *(in a heavy coat)* had watched the migration all day.

The movie *(about Hurricane Carter)* had a strong social message.

The agreement *(between Carlos and Miguel)* is binding.

Special Notes About Prepositions

1. Many prepositions consist of one word. However, two-word and sometimes three-word combinations are also considered prepositions.

One-word prepositions:	*about, above, at, behind, below, for, from, into, off*
Two-word prepositions:	*according to, along with, prior to, together with*
Three-word prepositions:	*as well as, by means of, in addition to, in lieu of*

2. The prepositions on page 42 that are marked with an asterisk (*) can also work as other parts of speech (nouns, adjectives, verbs, adverbs, or conjunctions). You will learn more about these other parts of speech in later chapters. For now, it is important to realize that all of the prepositions listed on page 42 will not always be prepositions when they are used in sentences. The following examples demonstrate ways in which some of the words that are marked with an asterisk can work as a noun, an adjective, a verb, an adverb, or a conjunction.

   The *till* was left unattended for five minutes.
   [*Till* is a noun.]

   Martinez and I have *opposite* interests.
   [*Opposite* is an adjective.]

   Most students *like* the new computer labs.
   [*Like* is a verb.]

   We moved the furniture *inside.*
   [*Inside* is an adverb.]

   I knew about the secret *before* you told me.
   [*Before* is a conjunction.]

3. Prepositional phrases are sentence "extras." They provide additional information to the sentence, but they are not a part of the main subject-verb pattern of the sentence. Though details and descriptions are lacking, complete sentences exist when the prepositional phrases are removed.

> The migration (from northern waters) (to warmer waters) is annual.

> A man (in a heavy coat) had watched the migration all day.

4. Knowing how to identify prepositional phrases will make finding the subjects and verbs of sentences much easier because **subjects and verbs are never found within prepositional phrases.** In the next chapter, you will be encouraged to remove all prepositional phrases before you identify subjects and verbs.

Practice 1   *Writing Prepositional Phrases*

Work with a partner, in a small group, or on your own. Using the list of prepositions on page 42, complete each of the following sentences by writing a preposition to show the relationship of the prepositional phrase to the rest of the sentence. In some sentences, more than one preposition can be used to complete the prepositional phrases. *Answers will vary. Possible answers are given.*

1. The doctor had to take an important call(____from____ the lab).

2. (____For____ many years), I was afraid to drive(____across____ the bridge).

3. The parade moved(____through____ the downtown area).

4. Children often put their baby teeth(____under____ their pillows) (____for____ the tooth fairy).

5. (____Before____ the test), I felt very confident.

6. The special coupon was inserted(____inside____ the magazine).

7. Chito lives(____next to____ the university).

8. Cynthia was pleased(____with____ her campaign)(____despite____ her loss).

9. I sat(____by____ the pond) and watched the children play (____in____ the water).

10. (____Throughout____ the entire ordeal), the flight attendants remained calm.

OBJECT OF THE PREPOSITION **The noun or pronoun that ends a prepositional phrase is called the *object of the preposition.***

You can easily find the object of the preposition and the end of the prepositional phrase by asking "Whom?" or "What?" after you identify the preposition.

preposition

Pam hid the box *beneath* the bed.

[Ask yourself, "Beneath what?" The answer is "beneath the
bed." The noun *bed* is the object of the preposition. The entire
prepositional phrase is *beneath the bed.*]

preposition

Lamar left his books *in* the living room.

[Ask yourself, "In what?" The answer is "in the living room."
The noun *living room* is the object of the preposition. The
entire prepositional phrase is *in the living room.*]

preposition

I went shopping *with* Larry's brother.

[Ask yourself, "With whom?" The answer is "Larry's brother."
The noun *brother* is the object of the preposition. The entire
prepositional phrase is *with Larry's brother.*]

Special Notes About Nouns and Noun Markers in Prepositional Phrases

1. As we saw in Chapter 2, **noun markers** signal that a noun will
   follow. Noun markers are frequently found before the noun within
   prepositional phrases.

   noun
   preposition marker noun

   We walked (through *the* crowd).

   Termites multiplied (underneath *the* logs).

   We moved (next to *Joe's* house) (in Phoenix).

   The forest ranger waved (to *my* brother).

2. One or more adjectives, or words that describe the noun, may
   appear between the noun marker and the noun within a
   prepositional phrase.

   noun
   preposition marker adjective noun

   We walked (through the *angry* crowd).

   Termites multiplied (underneath the *decayed* logs).

   We moved (from the *sickening* smog) (of Phoenix).

   The land (beyond the *first* ridge) was unfamiliar (to the
   amateur hikers).

3. The following combinations are frequently used in sentences with prepositional phrases:

preposition + noun
(for happiness)

noun
preposition + marker + noun
(to the library)

preposition + adj + noun
(with red roses)

noun
preposition + marker + adj + noun
(by an old cabin)

Practice 2   *Identifying Prepositional Phrases with Noun Objects*

Locate and mark all the prepositional phrases in the following sentences. Use parentheses to show the beginning and end of each prepositional phrase. Remember that a prepositional phrase must begin with a preposition and end with a noun or a pronoun. You may refer to the list of prepositions on page 42.

Example: The garbage bag (with the turkey bones) has a hole (in the bottom) (of it).

1. The librarian read a story (about the lost sailors).

2. (Above the fireplace) hung a picture (of four generations).

3. (According to leading authorities), visualization strengthens a person's immune system.

4. The investigators are searching (for relevant facts).

5. (As children), we were all very close (to our parents).

6. The train arrived (in San Diego)(around noon).

7. I will be (at the movie theater)(by seven o'clock).

8. The firewood was stacked (behind the garage).

9. His baggy pants hung (below his waist).

10. The girls raced (around the brick building).

Pronouns as Objects of the Preposition

PRONOUN   A pronoun is a word that replaces or renames a noun that was mentioned earlier.

Two categories of pronouns that you will frequently use in your writing are *subject pronouns* and *object pronouns*. (See page 67 in Chapter 4 for a list of subject pronouns.) For now, our attention is on *object pronouns,* which can be used as objects of the preposition.

JUST SO YOU KNOW...

Object pronouns can work as **direct objects:**

We tricked *her.*
I called *him.*
They notified *us.*

Object pronouns can also work as **indirect objects:**

We wrote *him* a letter.
I gave *her* a gift.

(See Chapter 4.)

OBJECT PRONOUN   An object pronoun, which is also called an objective pronoun, is a pronoun that is used instead of a noun at the end of a prepositional phrase.

The following pronouns are all object pronouns:

me   you   her   him   us   them   it   whom   whomever

In the following examples, object pronouns are used at the end of prepositional phrases. Each pronoun is the object of the preposition.

We wanted to buy flowers (for *her*).

The secret is (about *me*).

The actors sat (next to *us*).

The bonds are strong (between *us*).

The dog went (with *them*).

Practice 3   *Using Object Pronouns in Prepositional Phrases*

Use the pronoun choices at the beginning of the sentences. Write the correct object pronoun to complete the prepositional phrase. Mark the prepositional phrases with parentheses.

Example: he, him   The prescription is (for ____*him*____)

I, me   1. My dog heels (beside ____me____.)

her, she   2. I won the scholarship (because of ____her____.)

he, him   3. The divers swam (toward ____him____.)

them, they   4. Matt hid beneath the bridge (with ____them____.)

whoever, whomever   5. You can go (with ____whomever____) you want.

who, whom   6. (To ____whom____) should I address this card?

us, we   7. Communications will take place (through ____me____.)

he, him   8. You parked (behind ___him___) in the parking lot.

I, me   9. (Between you and ___me___), I want to vote (for Matt.)

them, they   10. I do not like to be (around ___them___.)

them, they   11. The rent will be shared (between ___them___.)

her, she   12. (With ___her___), he feels confident and happy.

who, whom   13. Sandra went out (to dinner) (with ___whom___?)

us, we   14. The president (of the youth group) rode (with ___us___.)

her, she   15. (Prior to ___her___), there was no leadership.

Practice 4   *Identifying Prepositional Phrases*

Mark with parentheses all the prepositional phrases in the sentences below.

1. The security guard hurried (to the phone) (with her report).

2. The newly adopted puppy went (with them) willingly.

3. I was fascinated (by the exotic fish) (in the new aquarium).

4. The birthday cards (on the table) (as well as the flowers) came (from her son).

5. (According to my grandfather), lessons can be learned (in all situations).

6. I often purchase coffee (on my way) (to work).

7. We planned the reunion (for the week) (after their wedding).

8. Martha stayed (with her sick grandfather) (throughout his illness).

9. A large crowd (of protesters) gathered (outside the courthouse).

10. The best man searched (in his pockets), (under the furniture), and (throughout his car) (for the ring).

Prepositions with Two or More Objects

Sometimes a prepositional phrase may have more than one noun or pronoun as the object of the preposition. A conjunction (connector) such as *and* or *or* will be used. After you identify the preposition, ask yourself, "Whom?" or "What?" If the answer is more than one noun or pronoun, include the additional nouns or pronouns in the prepositional phrase. Each of the following examples has two nouns or pronouns as objects of the preposition.

> **The players went (with the *coach* and the *manager*).**
> [The players did not go only with the coach or only with the manager.]
>
> **The drum was made (from *rawhide* and *sheepskin*).**
> [The drum was made from both rawhide and sheepskin.]
>
> **You need to choose (between *him* and *me*).**
> [The preposition *between* always requires two nouns, two pronouns, or a plural noun such as *them* or *both*.]

Practice 5 *Identifying Prepositional Phrases*

Mark with parentheses the complete prepositional phrases below.

1. The couple (with the rowdy children) quieted them (with hamburgers and milk shakes).

2. The differences (between you and her) are creating conflicts.

3. (Between you and me) I do not like the color (of her hair).

4. The salad was seasoned (with salt and pepper).

5. A child was crying (amid the chaos)(of the fire).

6. Everyone was surprised (but me).

7. The airport was closed (due to snow and ice)(on the runways).

8. The family requested a donation (to a charity)(in lieu of flowers or gifts).

9. The relationship (between parent and child) varies (from one culture) (to another).

10. A volunteer sunflower sprang up (among the tomatoes and green peppers).

To as a Preposition or as Part of an Infinitive

As we have seen, the word *to* often works as a preposition that shows a position, location, or direction. When *to* works as a preposition, it forms a prepositional phrase, as in the following examples:

preposition   noun

The company party was moved (*to* the Armory).

The hikers climbed (*to* the peak) of the mountain.

I sent the letter (*to* Arkansas).

This package is addressed (*to* you).

The word *to* can also work as part of a verb form called an **infinitive.** An infinitive is the beginning form, or base form, of a verb. An infinitive is not a prepositional phrase. Instead of seeing a noun or a pronoun after the word *to,* you will see a word that shows action. The following examples use *to* as a part of an infinitive:

to be	to call	to dance	to eat
to finance	to give	to have	to laugh
to manage	to prepare	to quit	to smell

Notice in the following sentences that *to* is followed by an action word and that the word group is not a prepositional phrase. In this textbook, brackets [ ] will be used to mark infinitives:

infinitive

The committee voted [*to move*] the party.

The hikers wanted [*to climb*] the mountain.

I need [*to send*] an email message.

The Cub Scouts hope [*to raise*] funds for the jamboree.

The players need [*to run*] ten laps.

Unlike prepositional phrases, infinitives are not sentence "extras." Infinitives cannot be deleted from a sentence without changing the meaning or the completeness of the sentence. The following sentences would not be complete or would not have the intended meaning if the infinitives were removed.

The family gathered [*to celebrate*] Grandma's eightieth birthday.

My partner and I planned [*to finance*] the remodeling with a second mortgage.

Most graduates are eager [*to find*] new employment opportunities.

Practice 6   *Identifying Prepositional Phrases and Infinitives*

Work with a partner, in a small group, or on your own to locate prepositional phrases and infinitives. Use parentheses ( ) to mark the prepositional phrases and brackets [ ] to mark the infinitives.

Example: The bridge (between Springdale and Four Rivers) has started [to deteriorate].

1. The team flew (to Memphis)(in two hours).

2. They wanted [to stay](in the downtown area).

3. They arrived (in town)[to play] a night game.

4. Time was allotted [to eat], [to stretch], and [to relax](in the hotel).

5. Some players went (to the lounge) [to play] video games.

6. Others chose [to go](to their rooms)[to read] or [to nap].

7. Many players wanted [to call] their families (from their rooms).

8. However, they had [to call](from pay phones)(in the lobby).

9. Curfew (for the players) was set (for eleven o'clock).

10. Few (of the players) were able [to sleep].

C O M M A   S E N S E

Use a comma after an introductory phrase at the beginning of a sentence. The introductory phrase may be a prepositional phrase or an infinitive.

These are examples of introductory prepositional phrases:

For them, the consequences were severe.
After the dance, the chaperons collapsed from exhaustion.
According to Lisa, the event was a huge success.
By the end of the day, all the papers were graded.
Between the audience and the performer, an immediate
   rapport was established.

These are examples of introductory infinitives and infinitive phrases:

To be honest, I did not enjoy the meal at that restaurant.
To know for sure, you will need to take the test.
To survive, they ate berries and snow.
To find her, we had to check several telephone directories.
To pass, you must complete all of the graded homework.

EXERCISE 3.1   **The Peanuts Gang**   Name _____ Date _____

© PEANUTS reprinted by permission of United Feature Syndicate, Inc.

© Douglas Kirkland/Corbis Images

Work with a partner, in a small group, or on your own to highlight all the prepositional phrases and mark the infinitives with brackets. Add capital letters wherever they are needed.

THE PEANUTS GANG

"Good grief!" Think about this expression. How can grief be good? For fifty years, Charlie Brown, snoopy, lucy, Linus, Sally, and other members of the "Peanuts Gang" delivered words of wisdom in a light-hearted manner. Readers could recognize themselves in the fears, foibles, insecurities, and failures of the comic strip characters. The messages were subtle and simplistic, yet profound. For example, in a February 1997 comic strip, sally declared, "I think I've discovered the secret to life. You just hang around until you're used to it."

Each of the "Peanuts" characters had a well-defined personality and significant role in the popularity of the comic strip. Charlie brown continued his determination in the face of constant defeat. He did not realize that he would never kick the football. Each of his mild, childhood misfortunes was faced with a mild "Good grief!" Snoopy, Charlie Brown's wise but eccentric beagle, would escape from his routine with an occasional flight of fancy back to world war I and a battle with the Red Baron. Other times he would perch on the top of his doghouse and use his typewriter [to reveal] his insights. Lucy never tried [to conceal] her crabbiness. She often yelled so loudly that her head tilted back and her entire face became her mouth. This self-righteous little girl always had inexpensive advice [to hand out]. Her advice cost a nickel. The sign on her famous lemonade stand said, "The doctor is IN." Linus, lucy's little brother, was filled with insecurities. He dragged his security blanket with him at all times. Yet, this insecure character never doubted his own convictions and belief in the Great Pumpkin. Other characters dealt with loneliness, poor grades, rejection, and plain looks.

Charles Schulz once wrote, "All the loves in the strip are unrequited. All the baseball games are lost. All the test scores are D-minuses. The Great Pumpkin never comes. The football is always pulled away." At first glance, one might think that "Peanuts" was all about failure. Schulz's biographer said that Schulz "spent a lifetime perfecting failure." However, failure was not the focus of the comic strip. Perseverance, determination, humor, and wisdom are the underlying themes developed over the course of fifty years.

In 1947, Schulz developed the comic strip "Li'l Folks" for his hometown newspaper, the *St. Paul pioneer press*. In 1950, his comic strip was sold to a syndicate and renamed "Peanuts." Within the following fifty years, Schulz penned more than 18,250 comic strips. "Peanuts" ran seven days a week for fifty years. Approximately 2,600 newspapers featured his comic strip. Over 355 million readers in 75 countries looked to his comic strip for humor and gentle advice. This comic strip with simple outlines, limited details, and well-defined personalities won Schulz international fame and enormous commercial success.

In January 2000, Charles M. Schulz announced his retirement. He wanted [to spend] more time with his family without worrying about daily deadlines. He also wanted [to focus] on his health. He had been diagnosed with cancer and had suffered a series of small strokes during an emergency operation. Schulz once explained why he had spent so many years drawing cartoons. He said he drew "for the same reason musicians compose. They do it because life wouldn't have any meaning for them if they didn't. That's why I draw cartoons. It's my life."

Charles Schulz died in his sleep on February 12, 2000, on the eve of the last publication of "Peanuts". Ellen Goodman, in her syndicated column, commented, "It was an eerie coincidence said some, a fine piece of symmetry said others. Charles M. Schulz died in his sleep just as the last 'Peanuts' loaded on to the last trucks for the last home delivery. His life and his work were completed on the same day, sharing the same national curtain call."

[Adapted from Ellen Goodman, "Schulz, Like His Subjects, Persevered," *Register Guard*, 2-13-00, page 16A, and Mary Ann Lickteig, "Peanuts' Creator Schulz Dies at Age 77," *Register Guard*, 2-13-00, 1A, 14A]

EXERCISE 3.2   **Identifying Prepositional Phrases and Infinitives**

Name _____ Date _____

In the following sentences, use parentheses to mark the prepositional phrases and brackets to mark the infinitives.

Example: He wanted [to re-establish] a friendship (with Mary).

1. The latest version (of the textbook) will be available (in July).

2. They plan [to air] the first (of several interviews)(on Tuesday night).

3. The reason (for his rudeness)(during the lecture) is unknown.

4. All (of us) wanted [to sign] the petition.

5. The chance (of a tribal dispute) continues [to exist].

6. The entire trip will be charged (to their credit card).

7. Sailing today is prohibited (due to the oncoming storm).

8. I love [to spend] hours browsing (through books)(in the new bookstore).

9. My in-laws spent several days (at the quaint fishing village)(in Spain).

10. The farmer caught the horse (by its reins) and tied it (to a tree).

List all the prepositions you identified in the above sentences. Do not list the same preposition more than once.

1. _____

2. _____

3. _____

4. _____

5. _____

6. _____

7. _____

8. _____

9. _____

10. _____

EXERCISE 3.3 Marking and Proofreading

Name _____ Date _____

In the following sentences, use parentheses to mark the prepositional phrases and brackets to mark the infinitives. Add any missing commas and capital letters.

Example: The amtrak train is scheduled [to pass] (through portland,
                 salem, eugene, and chiloquin).

1. (Throughout the game), the announcer continued [to

    mispronounce] several (of the players' names).

2. The red sea is located (between egypt and saudi arabia).

3. The pacific ocean is (off the west coast), and the atlantic ocean is

    (off the east coast).

4. An atrium (in ancient roman architecture) is an open-air courtyard.

5. (In the fifteenth and sixteenth centuries), the renaissance flourished

    (in italy).

6. notre dame (in paris) is a prime example (of gothic architecture).

7. (In 1988), dustin hoffman won an academy award (for the movie

    rain man).

8. the audubon society is named (after john james audubon).

9. The qur'an is the holy scripture (of the islamic religion).

10. Many amish and mennonites decided [to emigrate] (to the united

    states) and [to settle] (in pennsylvania).

EXERCISE 3.4   Adding Prepositional Phrases

Name _____ Date _____

Prepositional phrases can be added to sentences to enhance the meaning by providing more details. Enhance the following sentences by adding prepositional phrases. Remember that prepositional phrases may appear at the beginning, in the middle, or at the end of sentences. *Answers will vary. Possible answers are shown below.*
Example: The chair broke. The chair (with the straw seat) broke.

1. The new instructor is nervous. The new instructor (at our school) is nervous (about her first day) (of classes).

2. The sound was deafening. The sound (from the security alarm system) (in our home) was deafening.

3. The girls played football. Five (of the girls) (in our dorm) played football (with the boys) (on Saturday).

4. The contracts were finalized. (On Monday), the contracts (with the builder and the architect) were finalized (for our new deck) (in the backyard).

5. The dedication was taped. The dedication (for the new library) was taped (by the local news channel) (for the six o'clock news.)

6. The details were inaccurate. The details (in the newspaper) (about my uncle) were inaccurate.

7. Some resigned their positions. Some (of the top managers) (at the lumber mill) resigned their positions (on Friday).

8. The stereo system is compact. The stereo system (on the shelf) (in Karen's apartment) is compact.

9. John arrived. (Within minutes), John arrived (with his tools) to fix the pipe (under my sink).

10. Our basketball team won. (Despite the loss) (of our star player), our basketball team won the championship (in Portland) (on Saturday).

11. The circuits are busy. The telephone circuits (to Los Angeles) are often busy (during the prime time) (on national holidays).

12. All had melted. All (of the ice) (on the sidewalks) had melted (by noon).

13. We cried. (After the movie), we cried (about the ending) (for hours).

14. The people received recognition. (During my graduation ceremony), the people (with high grades) received recognition (from the dean) (of their school).

EXERCISE 3.5 **Sentence Writing** Name _____ Date _____

Follow the sentence-writing directions given below. Write your answers on separate paper. In each of your sentences, use parentheses to mark the prepositional phrases. *Answers will vary. Check that the students followed the directions for each sentence.*

1. Write two sentences that begin with introductory prepositional phrases.

   Example: (Despite the setback), I was determined to finish the term.

2. Write two sentences that have prepositional phrases that end with proper nouns.

   Example: The bus terminal (in Springfield) is always busy.

3. Write two sentences that have a common noun as the object of a preposition.

   Example: I arrived (at the airport) (with two huge suitcases).

4. Write two sentences that have prepositional phrases that end with object pronouns.

   Example: The computer lab will remain open (for us.)

5. Write two sentences that have two or more prepositional phrases.

   Example: The train will arrive (on time) (in Oakland).

6. Write sentences using each of the following prepositions.

   a. from   e. in spite of

   b. across   f. without

   c. underneath g. among

   d. instead of h. between

Chapter 3 Summary

1. A **preposition** is a word that shows a relationship between a noun or a pronoun and other words in the sentence.

2. A prepositional phrase begins with a preposition and ends with a noun or a pronoun. The noun or the pronoun at the end of a prepositional phrase is called the **object of the preposition.**

3. The pronoun that is used as the object of a preposition must be an **object pronoun** (*me, you, her, him, us, them, it, whom,* or *whomever*).

4. Prepositional phrases may have two or more objects.

5. Prepositional phrases are sentence "extras" that are used to add more details or descriptions to sentences. Prepositional phrases can be deleted from sentences without affecting the intended meaning of the sentence.

6. The word *to* may be a preposition, or it may be a part of an **infinitive** (the basic form of a verb). An infinitive is not a prepositional phrase.

7. A comma is used after an introductory phrase at the beginning of a sentence. A prepositional phrase or an infinitive may be an introductory phrase.

Writing Topics for Chapter 3

Select one of the writing options below. Write one or two paragraphs for the topic you selected. Proofread the draft of your paper before you turn it in.

1. Discuss ways in which the "Peanuts" gang has been a part of your life. Did you have Charlie Brown or Snoopy items when you were young? Did you read the comic strip on a regular basis?

2. Do you think "profound wisdom" was really presented by the "Peanuts" comic strip? Locate a few examples of sayings or comic strips related to Charlie Brown or Snoopy. Comment on the types of messages these comic strips sent out to readers.

 3. Use the Internet to locate an article about one of your favorite comic strips. What is the style of this comic strip? What general themes, messages, or philosophies are portrayed? Print the article that you use for your writing.

⬛www Web Site Learning Experiences

See the web site for this book to locate companion exercises and links related to the grammar topics in this chapter.

Go to: http://college.hmco.com. Click on "Students." Type *Sentence Essentials* in the "Jump to Textbook Sites" box. Click "go" and then bookmark the site. Click on Chapter 3.

CHAPTER 3 • Review Name _____ Date _____

Total Possible: 50 Your Score: _____

Part I: Identification of Prepositional Phrases and Use of Commas (20 points)

Use parentheses to mark all the prepositional phrases. Add any missing commas.

1. (From the beginning), Elizabeth had problems (with the other employees). 3 points

2. (In spite of her efforts), the strike was called (by the union members)(at midnight). 4 points

3. Arizona is a good place (for retired people). 1 point

4. (During spring break), many students go (to the coast)(for fun). 4 points

5. Snow (in the mountains) is expected (for the next two weeks). 2 points

6. The clown (with the red nose and yellow hair) made the children laugh. 1 point

7. The cat likes to lie (on the rug)(in front of the fireplace). 2 points

8. (During the lecture), many students were not able to concentrate (on the topic). 3 points

Part II: Identification of Prepositions and Infinitives (20 points)

Use parentheses to mark the prepositional phrases and brackets to mark the infinitives.

1. (Without a truck), we cannot move (out of the house)(on time). 3 points

2. I wanted [to invite] them (to our house)(for a quiet dinner). 3 points

3. (By the way), this telephone bill (for fifty dollars) is yours. 2 points

4. (Contrary to popular belief), many individuals (on public assistance) work (outside the home). 3 points

5. Mayumi correctly answered the quiz show question (without any hesitation). 1 point

6. Middle-aged women should consume (about 1200 milligrams) (of calcium) (per day). 3 points

7. (After the debate), the analysts argued (about the effectiveness) (of each candidate). 3 points

8. (Without written approval), surgeons are not allowed [to perform] many operations. 2 points

Part III: Object Pronouns   (6 points)
Circle the correct pronoun.

1. All of the letters were returned to (us, we).

2. Between Ben and (he, him), they had four dollars.

3. With (her, she) and Bob, life seems to be one continuous, happy adventure.

4. Sam sat near the door with (I, me).

5. I decided to go to the reception for (her, she).

6. My cousins went right past (them, they) without stopping.

Part IV: Sentence Writing   (4 points, 1 per sentence)
Write four sentences that use the following prepositions:

1. over

   _____

2. away from

   _____

3. between

   _____

4. about

   _____

CHAPTER 4

Subjects and Verbs in Simple Sentences

In Chapter 4, you will learn about **simple** and **compound subjects** and **simple** and **compound verbs** in **simple sentences.** You will also learn to combine sentences and avoid fragments.

Understanding subjects, verbs, and simple sentences will help you do the following:

1. Lay a strong foundation for more advanced writing skills

2. Write grammatically correct sentences void of fragments, pronoun errors, run-ons, comma splices, and other common writing errors that are discussed in later chapters

3. Combine two or more sentences into one simple sentence to avoid wordiness

4. Write grammatically correct compound and complex sentences in later chapters

5. Use correct subject and verb agreement, pronoun agreement, and punctuation in more advanced sentence patterns

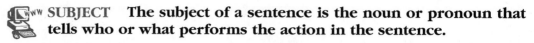 **SUBJECT** **The subject of a sentence is the noun or pronoun that tells who or what performs the action in the sentence.**

The subject is the *actor* or the *doer* of the action, which is also called the verb. The subject frequently appears in the first part of a sentence. The subject is never found inside a prepositional phrase.

subject
Many *athletes* train for the Olympics.

subject
They want to compete for their country.

subject
The *training* is difficult.

VERB **A verb is a word or group of words that expresses the action that is done by the subject or expresses the state of being of the subject.**

The verb portion of a sentence is also called the *predicate*. The verb usually follows the subject. The verb of a sentence is never an infinitive.

action verb
Many athletes *train* for the Olympics.

action verb
They *want* to compete for their country.

state of being verb
The training *is* difficult.

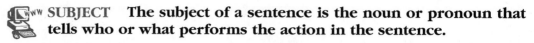 **SIMPLE SENTENCE** **A simple sentence has a subject and a verb and forms a complete thought.**

A simple sentence consists of one main or *independent clause*. A simple sentence can stand on its own without other clauses. This is a simple sentence:

My shoes were muddy.

This is also one independent clause:

My shoes were muddy.

Simple sentences do not need to be short sentences. They may include prepositional phrases, infinitives, and adjectives, as well as other parts of speech that will be covered later. As discussed in Chapter 2, adjectives may appear between noun markers and nouns. Other adjective positions will be discussed more thoroughly in Chapter 7. The following examples are simple sentences:

adjective   noun subject   adjective   verb
The pedigreed dog (with the rhinestone collar) ran

(down the street) (without a leash).

adjective noun subject   adjective   verb   infinitive

The irate owner (of the pedigreed dog) had [to chase]

adjective

the dog (for six blocks).

INDEPENDENT CLAUSE   An independent clause is a group of related words with a subject and a verb that can stand on its own as a simple sentence.

The following examples are all independent clauses; therefore, they are all simple sentences.

noun subject   verb

The thunderstorms produced rain.

noun subject   verb

The rain flooded the streets.

noun subject   verb

The situation was serious.

The following examples are not simple sentences, because the sentences contain more than one independent clause.

independent clause   independent clause

My shoes were muddy, and my socks were wet.

independent clause   independent clause

My shoes were muddy, but my pants did not get dirty.

independent clause   independent clause

My shoes were muddy, so I did not go into the house.

JUST SO YOU KNOW...

Sentences that consist of two or more independent clauses are called *compound sentences.* See Chapter 8.

JUST SO YOU KNOW...

Sentences with one independent clause and one or more dependent clauses are called *complex sentences.* Dependent clauses usually begin with a subordinate conjunction or a relative pronoun. See Chapter 9.

The following examples are also *not* simple sentences, because they consist of an independent clause and a *dependent clause.* A dependent clause is a group of words with a subject and verb that cannot stand on its own as a simple sentence.

independent clause   dependent clause

My shoes were muddy because I walked through the field.

independent clause   dependent clause

The field is behind the school that I attended as a child.

Subjects in Simple Sentences

You now know that the subject of a sentence is a noun or pronoun. The subject tells who or what performs the action of the sentence. The subject frequently appears in the first part of a sentence. The subject is never found inside a prepositional phrase. Learning to identify subjects in sentences is an essential skill for writing grammatically correct sentences. You will be able to use these skills later to form sentences with correct subject and verb agreement and to combine sentences to avoid wordiness. In this textbook, a single line under the word or words that work as the subject of a sentence will be used to differentiate the subject from other nouns and pronouns in the sentence.

Many <u>athletes</u> train for the Olympics.

<u>They</u> want to compete for their country.

The <u>training</u> is difficult.

The pedigreed <u>dog</u> with the rhinestone collar ran down the street without a leash.

The irate <u>owner</u> of the pedigreed dog had to chase the dog for six blocks.

Steps Used to Identify Subjects

Use the following steps to identify and mark the subjects of sentences.

Step 1: **Identify all the prepositional phrases and the infinitives.** The subject will not be inside prepositional phrases or infinitives, so prepositional phrases and infinitives can be crossed out and ignored.

The scientist (in the white lab coat) gave a slide presentation (to the reporters).

Step 2: **Ask yourself "who" or "what" is doing the action of the sentence.** If there is no action in the sentence, ask "who" or "what" exists or is shown in a "state of being." Look for a noun or pronoun toward the front of the sentence.

The *scientist* (in the white lab coat) gave a slide presentation (to the reporters).

Step 3: **Check that the word or word group that you identify as the subject is a noun or a pronoun.**

Is the word *scientist* a noun or a pronoun?
Yes, it is a noun.

Practice 1   *Finding the Subjects of Sentences*

Use the three steps shown above to identify the subjects of the following sentences. Underline each subject with one line.

1. The <u>detective</u> (from the third precinct) followed his intuition.

2. My <u>friends</u> (from Costa Rica) visited me (during their summer vacation.)

3. (During the storm), my <u>neighbors</u> covered their windows (with pieces) of lumber.

4. <u>Lenny</u> wanted [to move] (to New Mexico) (at the end) (of the year.)

5. (In cold weather), an unusual <u>noise</u> comes (from under the hood) (of my car.)

6. A <u>deer</u> (with full antlers) roams (into our backyard) and eats our vegetables.

7. <u>Members</u> (of the tribe) paid tribute (to the elder.)

8. <u>Players</u> (in uniforms) paraded (onto the field) (prior to the opening ceremonies.)

9. Two <u>men</u> (on the corner) ran [to assist] the elderly woman (with bags) (of groceries.)

10. The <u>psychic</u> (on television) makes predictions (about events) (in people's lives.)

 SUBJECT PRONOUN   A subject pronoun is a word that replaces a subject noun. The subject pronoun tells *who* or *what* performs the action of the sentence.

The following kinds of pronouns are often found working as subjects of sentences.

SUBJECT PRONOUNS				
PERSONAL PRONOUNS	INDEFINITE PRONOUNS			RELATIVE PRONOUNS
I	all	everybody	none	who*
you	another	everyone	no one	whoever*
he	any	everything	nothing	
she	anybody	few	one	
it	anyone	many	several	
we	anything	more	some	
they	both	most	somebody	
	each	neither	someone	
	either	nobody	something	

*These pronouns are discussed in Chapter 6.

The following examples contain subject pronouns. Refer to the three steps on page 66 to identify subject pronouns.

subject pronoun
↓
(After the tornado), <u>they</u> needed food, clothing, and shelter.

subject pronoun
↓
(Between you and me), <u>she</u> is the best candidate (for the job).

subject pronoun
↓
<u>Each</u> (of the members) has a right (to one vote).

subject pronoun
↓
<u>Some</u> (of the people) (in line) are willing [to wait] (for hours).

subject pronoun
↓
<u>They</u> hired a consultant [to deal] (with the problems).

subject pronoun
↓
<u>Neither</u> (of the children) wants [to go] (on the ride).

subject pronoun
↓
<u>More</u> (of the fabric) is needed [to finish] the curtains (for the nursery).

Practice 2   *Identifying Subject Pronouns*

Use parentheses to mark the prepositional phrases and brackets to mark the infinitives in the following sentences. Then ask *who* or *what* is doing the action of the sentence. Check that the word you identify as the subject is toward the beginning of the sentence and that it is a noun or a pronoun. Underline the subject of each sentence with one line.

1. <u>Everyone</u> (at the assembly) applauded the keynote speaker.

2. Shortly (after midnight), <u>all</u> (of the emergency sirens) stopped.

3. <u>You</u> will like the new counselor (in the Career Information Center).

4. <u>None</u> (of these books) discussed the early romantic or classical composers.

5. (During the early years) (of her life), <u>she</u> frequently traveled (to Japan) [to visit] her sisters.

6. <u>Several</u> (of the wealthy aristocrats) sponsored composers.

7. (According to the salesman), <u>neither</u> (of the stereo systems) comes (with a five-year warranty).

8. <u>All</u> (of my closest friends) have already seen the movie (about outer space aliens).

9. <u>Many</u> (of the applicants) (for the management position) graduated (from Stanford).

10. <u>Some</u> (of the sculptures) (in her garden) were done (by her nephew).

 COMPOUND SUBJECT   **A compound subject occurs when two or more subjects are joined together to tell who or what performs the action of the sentence.**

Each of the nouns or pronouns in the compound subject refers to the same verb. Compound subjects are usually joined by *and, or,* or *nor* and appear before the verb in the sentence. A comma is used between three or more subjects in a simple sentence.

<table>
<tr><td>subject</td><td>subject</td></tr>
</table>

The <u>soup</u> *and* the <u>bread</u> tasted good (to the hungry refugees).

Temporary <u>shelters</u> *and* medical <u>facilities</u> existed (in the camp).

<u>Boots</u> *or* <u>shoes</u> were distributed (to the children).

<u>Jackets</u> (with hoods) *or* heavy <u>sweaters</u> *and* <u>scarves</u> were given (to the refugees).

Neither <u>rain</u> *nor* <u>snow</u> stopped the volunteer efforts.

Either <u>milk</u> *or* <u>rice</u> should arrive (in the next shipment) (of supplies).

Military <u>personnel</u>, Red Cross <u>workers</u>, and United Nations <u>peacekeepers</u> provide services (in the camp).

Use caution when personal pronouns are used in a compound subject. *I, you, he, she, it, we,* and *they* are the subject pronouns that can be used in compound subjects. Personal pronouns, such as *me, him, her, us,* and *them* cannot be used in the subject position.

<u>You</u> and <s>me</s> ^I will be close friends forever.

^She <s><u>Her</u></s> and <u>Clay</u> will work to compile the data.

^He ^she <s><u>Him</u></s> and <s>her</s> make an attractive couple.

JUST SO YOU KNOW...

The words *and, or,* and *nor* are *conjunctions.* Conjunctions can be used to join two words, phrases, or clauses together. *Nor* and *or* can also be used in the following combinations to form compound subjects.

neither . . . nor
either . . . or

These combinations are called *correlative conjunctions.*

Practice 3   *Identifying Single and Compound Subjects*

Mark the prepositional phrases with parentheses and the infinitives with brackets. Use the three-step process to identify the subject or subjects of each sentence. Underline each subject with one line.

1. (According to Peter), the benefit dinner included salad, a main course, and dessert.

2. Mr. Lane and Mrs. Montague served spaghetti (with meat sauce) and hot French bread.

3. The tractor and the other farm equipment are stored (in the barn) (in the north field).

4. They and I want [to attend] the Monterey Jazz Festival together each year.

5. (In the morning), the kitten and the squirrel chased each other playfully (around the yard).

6. I left my glasses and my keys (on the table) (in the café).

7. My brother and the man (from next door) built a wheelchair ramp (into the house).

8. Several (of the workers) and two (of the managers) filed a discrimination complaint.

9. The newspaper and the Historical Society jointly published the document (about the first land deal).

10. The memory (in my computer, my modem, and my printer) is adequate.

11. Neither the plane tickets nor the hotel confirmation was (in the mail).

12. (In June), Mom and Dad plan [to travel] (to Hawaii).

13. The hula hoop and the pogo stick were fast-selling items (in the 1960s).

14. The public park and the fishing docks close (at ten o'clock) (in the evening).

15. Your sister and my brother have many common interests.

Practice 4   *Using Subject and Object Pronouns*

Mark the prepositional phrases with parentheses and the infinitives with brackets in the following sentences. Circle the correct subject or object pronoun. Remember to use a subject pronoun when the pronoun is the subject of the sentence and an object pronoun at the end of prepositional phrases. The chart below shows subject and object pronouns.

SUBJECT PRONOUNS	OBJECT PRONOUNS
I, you, she, he, we, they, it, who, whoever	me, you, her, him, us, them, it, whom, whomever

1. (She, Her) and Grandma are going [to shop] (at the new Kmart store).

2. (After the dance), Mark and (her, she) decided [to drive] (to the coast).

3. The unemployed workers came (to (we, us) (for retraining).

4. (Within minutes), the message was received (by (they, them)).

5. (He, Him) and I want [to request] a private meeting (with the manager).

6. I cannot choose (between you and (he, him)).

7. You and (I, me) make a perfect team (for this job).

8. (Them, They) and Mary seem [to disagree] (about everything).

9. (Without (he, him) and his dog), the house seems too quiet.

10. Exercising (with (they, them)) is rewarding and beneficial.

 SENTENCE COMBINING   Sentence combining involves properly joining two or more sentences to make one sentence. When two or more sentences have the same verb, the sentences can be combined into one simple sentence with compound subjects. A comma is used between three or more subjects in an independent clause.

Sentence combining can eliminate wordiness in your writing.

Sentence 1:   The *fans* gathered outside the stadium.

Sentence 2:   The sports *reporters* gathered outside the stadium.

Combined: The *fans* and the sports *reporters* gathered outside the stadium.

Sentence 1: Community *groups* [subject] use [verb] the new conference [verb] center.

Sentence 2: *Faculty* [subject] use [verb] the new conference center.

Sentence 3: Student *organizations* [subject] use [verb] the new conference center.

Combined: Community *groups* [subject], *faculty* [subject], and student *organizations* [subject] use [verb] the new conference center.

Practice 5 *Combining Sentences*

Combine the two sentences into one simple sentence that has compound subjects. Write your sentences on a separate piece of paper. *Answers will vary. Possible answers are given below.*

1. Mesh ^and plastic tarps^ can be used to make a tent. Plastic tarps can be used to make a tent.

2. Mangoes ^peaches, and plums^ have pits. Peaches and plums have pits.

3. Inflammation ^and itching^ may cause some discomfort. Itching may cause some discomfort.

4. Mason ^and Hector^ had the winning lottery ticket. Hector had the winning lottery ticket.

5. The dog ^and the policeman^ chased the car down the alley. The policeman chased the car down the alley.

6. ^Cory and^ I finished the summary last night. Cory finished the summary last night.

www Verbs in Simple Sentences

VERB   A verb is a word that expresses action or a state of being (nonaction).

action verb
↓
Pedro *bowled* a perfect game.

state of being verb
↓
Pedro *was* the winner.

To find the verbs in sentences, identify the subject. Then look for words that express the action done by the subject or the state of being of the subject. Just like subjects, verbs are never found inside a prepositional phrase.

ACTION VERB   An action verb expresses action done or being done by the subject.

After you have identified the subject, ask yourself these questions:

"What is the subject *doing?*"

"What has the subject *done?*"

"What is the subject *going to do?*"

These questions will lead you to the verb. To differentiate the verb from the subject in this textbook, two lines will be used to mark verbs.

<u>subject</u> <u>verb</u>
Pedro bowled a perfect game.

<u>subject</u> <u>verb</u>
He had a final score (of three hundred).

<u>subject</u>   <u>verb</u>
Pedro practices four times a week.

subject   verb
The owner (of the bowling alley) knows Pedro well.

subject   verb
Many (of the regular bowlers) like [to practice] with Pedro.

THREE KINDS OF ACTION VERBS		
VISIBLE ACTION VERBS	**INVISIBLE (MENTAL) ACTION VERBS**	**ACTION VERBS SHOWING POSSESSION**
write read	dream wish	have
sing dance	think consider	own
laugh cry	decide hope	possess
walk run	imagine pretend	
open close	create identify	

Special Notes About Forms of Verbs

The form of the verb can change depending on the following conditions (you will learn more about verb forms in Chapter 5).

1. Whether the subject is singular or plural:

Mohammed *likes* to study history. (singular subject)

The students *like* to study history. (plural subject)

2. The time the action occurs:

> The movie *opened* yesterday.   (past)
>
> The movie *opens* today.   (present)
>
> The movie *will open* this weekend.   (future)

3. Whether the subject is speaking (first person), is spoken to (second person), or is spoken about (third person):

> I *like* rap music.   (first person - I)
>
> You *like* rap music.   (second person - you)
>
> She *likes* rap music.   (third person singular - she)
>
> They *like* rap music.   (third person plural - they)

Practice 6   *Identifying Subjects and Action Verbs*

Mark the prepositional phrases with parentheses and the infinitives with brackets. Draw one line under the subjects. To find the verb in each sentence, ask yourself what the subject is doing, has done, or is going to do. Draw two lines under the verbs.

1. The children write thank-you letters (to their grandparents).

2. All (of the students) read several books each term.

3. They dream (of adventures)(in foreign countries).

4. She pretends [to be] a beautiful princess.

5. Every morning (by six o'clock), the newspaper lands (on my front porch).

6. The lake fills (with water)(during the spring).

7. Alice possesses an exceptional ability [to sing](without accompaniment).

8. (At midnight), the owner closed the store.

9. The anxious student opened her report card carefully.

10. We laughed (for several hours)(at her corny jokes).

LINKING VERB   A linking verb is a verb that expresses no action. Instead, it expresses a state of being or a condition of the subject.

A linking verb links the subject to the remainder of the words within the independent clause.

linking verb
Ingrid is forty-five years old.

linking verb
She appears younger.

linking verb
Ingrid feels healthy and happy.

The following chart shows three categories of linking, or nonaction, verbs that express a state of being or a condition.

LINKING VERBS THAT ARE FORMS OF THE VERB *TO BE*	LINKING VERBS THAT RELATE TO THE SENSES	OTHER LINKING VERBS
am is are was were	feel look taste smell sound	become seem appear remain grow

In each of the following examples, the linking verbs link or connect the subject to the remainder of the words within the independent clause.

FORMS OF THE VERB *TO BE*	LINKING VERBS RELATED TO THE SENSES	OTHER LINKING VERBS
I am a college graduate.	The idea feels right to me.	She becomes timid.
She is my best friend.	This report looks thorough.	The doctor seems competent.
His roommates are friendly.	The bread tastes fresh.	You appear to be annoyed.
Willie was too old for me.	I smell trouble.	Toddlers easily grow restless.
My advisers were excellent.	That sounds familiar to me.	The truth remains to be seen.

Special Notes About Linking Verbs

1. Notice which form of the verb *to be* is used in present tense and in past tense for the following singular or plural pronouns.

SINGULAR				PLURAL	
Present	Past	Present	Past	Present	Past
I am	I was	You are	You were	We are	We were
He is	He was	She is	She was	You are	You were
It is	It was			They are	They were

2. The following examples use forms of the verb *to be* in present tense and in past tense. Remember that the form of the verb will vary depending on whether the subject is singular or plural.

PRESENT TENSE	PAST TENSE
I <u>am</u> your lawyer.	Janice <u>was</u> a student last term.
Samuel <u>is</u> a student.	The telephone <u>operators</u> <u>were</u> busy.
The <u>results</u> <u>are</u> surprising.	The <u>prizes</u> <u>were</u> cute.

JUST SO YOU KNOW...

Nouns and adjectives that follow linking verbs are called *predicate nouns* and *predicate adjectives*. Because they describe or modify the subject, predicate nouns and predicate adjectives are *subject complements*.

3. The following examples show linking verbs in the present tense and the past tense. Remember that the form of the verb will vary depending on whether the subject is singular or plural. Notice how the verbs for singular subjects in the present tense end with *-s* or *-es*. Many, but not all, verbs in the past tense end with *-ed*. (See Chapter 5.)

PRESENT TENSE	PAST TENSE
<u>Cindy</u> <u>feels</u> silly in the chicken costume.	<u>You</u> <u>looked</u> frightened.
The <u>muffins</u> <u>smell</u> delicious.	The <u>milk</u> <u>tasted</u> sour.
The <u>parrot</u> <u>becomes</u> talkative in the morning.	The computer <u>technicians</u> <u>grew</u> weary.
The <u>painting</u> <u>looks</u> authentic.	<u>Raymond</u> <u>felt</u> conspicuous.

4. Some linking verbs can also work as action verbs. If the verb shows an action that is done by the subject, the verb is an action verb. If the verb is a state of being or a condition, the verb is a linking verb. Notice the subtle differences in these sentences.

ACTION	LINKING (STATE OF BEING)
A <u>cloud</u> <u>appears</u> (in the sky).	The <u>story</u> <u>appears</u> [to be] true.
<u>She</u> <u>feels</u> her keys (in the bottom) (of her purse).	<u>He</u> <u>feels</u> lousy.
<u>I</u> <u>smell</u> a strong perfume.	The <u>bread</u> <u>smells</u> good.

| Practice 7 | *Identifying Verbs in Simple Sentences* |

Work with a partner, in a small group, or on your own. Mark the prepositional phrases with parentheses and the infinitives with brackets. Underline the subject of each sentence with one line. Underline the verb with two lines.

Example: Fresh <u>bread</u> (from the bakery) <u>smells</u> wonderful.

1. The crescent <u>moon</u> <u>disappeared</u> (behind a bank)(of clouds).
2. (For an aerobic workout), <u>Nancy</u> <u>goes</u> (to the gym).
3. This new <u>cream</u> <u>does</u> wonders (for blemishes).
4. The <u>jury</u> <u>was</u> attentive (throughout the trial).
5. <u>Tortillas</u>, <u>rice</u>, and beans <u>are</u> staples (in many countries).
6. (After the movie), <u>I</u> <u>felt</u> uneasy and irritable.
7. My <u>father</u> and my <u>brother</u> <u>look</u> (to Mom)(for advice).
8. A <u>team</u> (of volunteers) <u>cleans</u> the beaches (during spring vacation).
9. The candy <u>machine</u> <u>is</u> empty today.
10. The <u>coins</u> (in my uncle's coin collection) <u>are</u> expensive [to insure].

 COMPOUND VERB   A compound verb consists of two or more verbs expressing the actions or state of being of the subject. For compound action verbs, the subject performs two or more separate actions.

Compound verbs are usually connected with the word *and* or the word *or*. A comma is used between three or more verbs or groups of words that express the action of the same subject.

The following examples show compound action verbs. Notice that each verb is underlined twice and each verb expresses the action of the subject.

The massive <u>bull</u> <u>snorted</u> *and* <u>pawed</u> the ground.

<u>George</u> <u>takes</u> many pictures *and* <u>develops</u> them himself.

The <u>chef</u> <u>mixed</u> the ingredients *and* <u>poured</u> the batter into molds.

<u>Teachers</u> <u>grade</u> papers *or* <u>plan</u> lessons every night of the week.

The fund-raising <u>event</u> <u>begins</u> at 7:00 P.M., <u>includes</u> a live auction, *and* <u>concludes</u> with dancing to a live band.

Special Notes About Compound Verbs

1. Both of the actions in a compound verb express the action done by the same subject. The verbs usually need to be in the same tense (past, present, or future).

> Correct: We removed the stakes and dismantled the tent.
> *past tense*   *past tense*

> Incorrect: We removed the stakes and dismantle the tent.
> *past tense*   *present tense*

> Correct: The mountaineer climbs mountains and scales cliffs.
> *present tense*   *present tense*

> Incorrect: The mountaineer climbs mountains and scaled cliffs.
> *present tense*   *past tense*

2. Two or more separate sentences can be combined into one simple sentence when each of the verbs in the independent clause expresses the action of the same subject.

> Sentence 1:   The boulder broke loose.

> Sentence 2:   The boulder tumbled down the hillside.

> Combined: The boulder broke loose and tumbled down the hillside.

Practice 8   *Identifying Subjects, Verbs, and Simple Sentence Patterns*

Work with a partner, in a small group, or on your own. Mark the prepositional phrases with parentheses and the infinitives with brackets. Then underline the subjects with one line and the verbs with two lines. Use the letters **S** (subject) and **V** (verb) to show the number of subjects and verbs in the following simple sentences.

> **S-V** = single subject and single verb
>
> **SS-V** = compound subject
>
> **S-VV** = compound verb

Example: _____S-VV_____   The Boys and Girls Club of America <u>provides</u> children and teenagers (with recreational opportunities) and <u>promotes</u> educational and personal growth.

_____S-VV_____   1. The <u>mechanic</u> <u>tuned</u> the engine and <u>rotated</u> the tires (on my car).

_____S-VV_____   2. <u>I</u> often <u>drink</u> coffee or <u>eat</u> lunch (at the restaurant) (on the corner).

_____SS-V_____   3. My <u>cat</u> and <u>dog</u> <u>wanted</u> [to get] (inside the house).

_____S-V_____   4. The <u>cost</u> (of the leather sofa) <u>was</u> excessive.

_____SS-V_____   5. The <u>Fire Department</u> and the <u>Police Department</u> <u>merged</u> (in January).

_____S-V_____   6. <u>Lenders</u> (of home mortgages) <u>advertise</u> (in the newspaper).

_____S-V_____   7. <u>I</u> <u>grew</u> [to enjoy] classical music (for relaxation).

_____S-V_____   8. <u>He</u> <u>has</u> many good qualities and unusual talents.

_____S-VV_____   9. <u>Anita</u> <u>hauled</u> the chairs (from the garage) and <u>washed</u> them thoroughly.

_____SS-V_____   10. <u>You</u> and <u>I</u> always <u>study</u> hard [to pass] all our courses.

 VERB PHRASE **A verb phrase consists of two or more verbs working together to show the action done by the subject.**

A verb phrase has a *helping verb* plus a main (or base form) verb, which may have suffixes attached. The following examples are verb phrases:

HELPING VERB	+	MAIN VERB WITHOUT SUFFIXES (BASE FORM)
can	+	agree
was	+	hit
did	+	call
will	+	plan
might	+	be

JUST SO YOU KNOW...

Helping verbs are also called *auxiliary verbs*. Helping verbs always appear in front of the main verb. Main verbs without suffixes are also called *base forms* or *infinitives*.

HELPING VERB	+	MAIN VERB WITH SUFFIXES
am	+	thinking
is	+	doing
would have	+	preferred
should have	+	bought
could have	+	charged

HELPING VERB   **A helping verb works in combination with another verb to indicate tense. Together they form a complete verb. A helping verb is usually some form of the verb *to do, to be, or to have.***

The following chart shows four different kinds of helping verbs. These helping verbs are joined to a main verb to form a verb phrase. Different kinds of verb phrases show different verb tenses. *Verb tense* means the time period in which the action occurs. (See Chapter 5.)

HELPING VERBS			
FORMS OF THE VERB *TO BE*	FORMS OF THE VERB *TO DO*	FORMS OF THE VERB *TO HAVE*	OTHER HELPING VERBS
am*	do[†]	has[†]	can
is*	does[†]	have[†]	will
are*	did[†]	had[†]	shall
was*			could
were*			should
be			would
being			may
been			might
			must

*When these verbs are not used in a verb phrase, they function as linking verbs.
[†]When these verbs are not used in a verb phrase, they function as action verbs.

Special Notes About Verbs

1. Infinitives are never the verbs in sentences. Infinitives always begin with the word *to.*

   to dream   to eat   to do   to go   to call

2. Verbs are never found inside prepositional phrases. Therefore, identifying verbs will be easier if you first identify the prepositional phrases and then ignore them.

> (After dinner), the players (on the team) were hoping [to have] time [to relax].

3. When marking verb phrases in sentences, both the helping verb and the main verb—in other words, the complete verb phrase—must be underlined with two lines.

> verb phrase
> The catering business is hiring new personnel.

> verb phrase
> I will apply (for a job) (on weekends).

> verb phrase   verb phrase
> I can use the extra money and can learn some new skills.

> verb phrase
> Ellie is hoping [to begin] a training program this weekend.

4. Sometimes other words called *adverbs* appear between the helping verb and the main verb. Words such as *not, never,* or *already* are examples of adverbs that appear in the middle of verb phrases. Do not mark the adverbs when you are marking the verbs. (See Chapter 7 for a list of adverbs).

> adverb
> She is not going (to the hairdresser) this week.

> adverb
> Grandma was always calling me late (at night.)

> adverb
> I will never move (beyond these borders.)

5. A verb phrase is not a compound verb. A compound verb expresses two or more separate actions done by the subject. A verb phrase expresses *one* action.

One verb:	Chris will find the perfect gift (for Gail).
One verb:	She is coming (to the shower) (with Lindy).
One verb:	Mathew had filed a complaint.
Compound verb:	Chris will find the perfect gift (for Gail) and will give it (to her) (on her birthday).

6. A sentence may have a *compound verb phrase,* which means that there are two separate actions. Frequently, the helping verb in the second verb phrase is omitted. The second helping verb is the same as the first helping verb; it is unstated but understood to be a part of the verb phrase. In the following pairs of sentences, each sentence is correct. However, the second sentence in each pair sounds better with the helping verb unstated.

> Correct: I <u>had called</u> Jim and <u>had left</u> a message several times.

> Better: I <u>had called</u> Jim and <u>left</u> a message several times.

> Correct: You <u>are doing</u> the work and <u>are receiving</u> a lot of credit.

> Better: You <u>are doing</u> the work and <u>receiving</u> a lot of credit.

Practice 9   *Reviewing Elements of a Sentence*

Work with a partner, in a small group, or on your own. Mark the prepositional phrases with parentheses and the infinitives with brackets. Then underline the subjects once and the verbs twice.

1. The <u>officials</u> <u>were watching</u> (for unsportsmanlike conduct).

2. <u>I</u> <u>will</u> never <u>understand</u> my teenage daughter.

3. The hungry <u>visitors</u> <u>had eaten</u> all (of the cheesecake).

4. <u>Rodents</u> <u>gnawed</u> (on the wood) and <u>damaged</u> the fence posts.

5. The <u>noise</u> (from the construction site) <u>is</u> <u>hindering</u> my ability [to concentrate].

6. (Aside from that one incident), <u>they</u> <u>have</u> always behaved politely and courteously.

7. The <u>report</u> <u>was read</u> and <u>approved</u> (by the board).

8. <u>You</u> <u>may apply</u> a second time (for the scholarship).

9. <u>You</u> <u>should go</u> (to the rally) (at noon).

10. The young <u>offender</u> <u>had</u> not <u>asked</u> (for a lawyer).

Avoiding Fragments

> **FRAGMENT** **A fragment is a part of a sentence that poses as a complete sentence. Fragments are incomplete sentences that lack a subject, a verb, or a complete thought.**

Following are three common types of fragment errors that you can correct with your understanding of subjects and verbs in simple sentences.

1. The fragment has a subject but no verb.

   The <u>kayakers</u> (with their new kayaks and white-water equipment).

   Method of correction: Add a verb.

   The <u>kayakers</u> (with their new kayaks and white-water equipment) <u>began</u> a two-week expedition.

2. The fragment has a verb but no subject.

   (Without electricity), <u>bundled up</u> [to keep] warm.

   Method of correction: Add a subject.

   (Without electricity), <u>we</u> <u>bundled up</u> [to keep] warm.

3. Part of the verb phrase is missing.

   The <u>women</u> <u>washing</u> their clothes (in the river).

   Method of correction: Add a helping verb.

   The <u>women</u> <u>were washing</u> their clothes (in the river).

Practice 10   *Identifying Fragments and Complete Sentences*

Analyze each of the following groups of words by marking the prepositional phrases with parentheses, the infinitives with brackets, the subjects with a single underline, and the verbs with a double underline. After you mark the sentence, examine whether the subjects and verbs are complete and whether the group of words is a complete thought. On the lines before each number, write **S** if it is a complete sentence. Write **F** if the group of words is a fragment.

Example: _____F_____ The caddies wanting [to be] a part (of the PGA tour).

_____S_____ 1. Delays (in Financial Aid) were (due to the national holiday).

_____S_____ 2. I had noticed an unfamiliar car (in the neighborhood).

_____F_____ 3. A sudden burst (of energy) (from the power bar).

_____F_____ 4. Andrew became the youngest student (at the state university).

_____F_____ 5. Flown (through the smoke) (from the fires) (in the northern part) (of the state).

_____F_____ 6. Wanted (for tampering) (with the fire alarms) (in the school).

_____S_____ 7. The team (of consultants) might consider the lucrative offer [to merge].

_____S_____ 8. Mario sometimes does attend the review sessions.

_____S_____ 9. Dune buggies and recreational vehicles destroyed the sand dunes.

_____F_____ 10. Both (of the candidates) (for the Senate seat) (in our state).

Placement of Nouns in Sentences

As we have seen, nouns can appear throughout a sentence. You should already understand the following rules for placement of nouns in sentences:

1. A noun that names the topic or is the actor of the sentence is the *subject* of the sentence.

2. A noun at the end of a prepositional phrase is the *object of the preposition*.

Nouns often appear in sentences in three additional locations and with three different functions:

1. A *direct object* is a noun or pronoun that receives the action of the verb. Do not confuse these nouns or pronouns with the subject of the sentence. Notice how the direct objects below follow an action verb and receive the action of the verb. The direct objects are italicized.

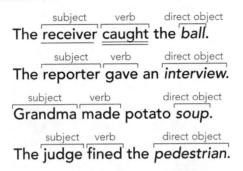

subject   verb   direct object
The receiver caught the *ball.*

subject   verb   direct object
The reporter gave an *interview.*

subject   verb   direct object
Grandma made potato *soup.*

subject   verb   direct object
The judge fined the *pedestrian.*

Verbs that require direct objects are called *transitive verbs.* The predicate, the verb part of a sentence, is not complete if a transitive verb is used without a direct object. Instead of having a complete sentence, the result is a *fragment.* Notice in the following examples how the thought of the sentence is incomplete without the direct object:

Incomplete thought: The receiver caught.

Incomplete thought: The reporter gave.

Incomplete thought: Grandma made.

Incomplete thought: The judge fined.

To find the direct object of a transitive verb, ask *Whom?* or *What?* after you identify the verb. The answer will be the direct object.

subject   verb
The librarian examined the books (on the shelf).

[Ask: *What* did the librarian examine?]

subject   verb
The superintendent notified the teachers (about the assembly).

[Ask: *Whom* did the superintendent notify?]

Just So You Know...

Direct objects and indirect objects are the complements of action verbs. They complete the thought of the verbs.

2. An *indirect object* is a noun or pronoun that names who benefits from the action of the verb or to whom or for whom the action is done. An indirect object can appear only in a sentence that has a transitive verb and a direct object. Asking the following kinds of questions can help you identify direct and indirect objects.

Marcus bought Karen a dozen red *roses.*
 [What did Marcus buy? *Roses* is the direct object.]
 [Who benefited or who received the roses? *Karen* is the indirect object.]

subject　verb　indirect object　direct object
Marcus bought Karen a dozen red *roses.*

Karen gave Marcus a hug.
 [What did Karen give? *Hug* is the direct object.]
 [Who benefited? Who got the hug? *Marcus* is the indirect object.]

subject　verb　indirect object　direct object
Karen gave Marcus a *hug.*

The pattern of both of the previous sentences is:

Subject - Transitive Verb - Indirect Object - Direct Object.

Indirect objects can be rewritten as prepositional phrases by using the preposition *to* or *for.* This is one way to test whether or not a noun is working as an indirect object.

Marcus bought a dozen red *roses* (for Karen).

Karen gave a *hug* (to Marcus).

Just So You Know...

Predicate nouns are also called *predicate nominatives.* Predicate nouns are subject complements.

3. A *predicate noun* can be placed after a linking verb and rename the subject. Predicate nouns are not found in sentences that have action verbs. Notice that predicate nouns look like direct objects; however, direct objects do not rename the subject.

subject　linking verb　predicate noun
Robert is a student.

subject　linking verb　predicate noun
My professor became a commercial photographer.

subject　linking verb　predicate noun
Rufus is my loyal dog

subject　linking verb　predicate noun
The leading man (in the play) is my uncle.

Other Subject-Verb Patterns in Simple Sentences

As you have noticed throughout this text, many simple sentence patterns begin with the subject(s) in the first part of the sentence and follow with the verb(s). The following sections show how this standard pattern is sometimes inverted or turned around. These are the three situations of inverted subject-verb patterns in simple sentences:

1. The sentence begins with the adverb *here* or *there.*

2. The sentence is written as a question.

3. The subject and verb pattern is intentionally inverted for personal style.

Sentences That Begin with *Here* or *There*

The subject of a sentence is always a noun or a pronoun. The words *here* or *there* are *adverbs.* An adverb cannot work as the subject of a sentence. When a sentence begins with *here* or *there,* the subject will be found after the verb. Notice the inverted subject and verb patterns in the following examples:

> Here <u>are</u> the latest <u>figures</u>.
> [This sentence can be turned around to read: The latest <u>figures</u> <u>are</u> here.]

> There <u>were</u> two <u>sailors</u> on the deck.
> [This sentence can be turned around to read: Two <u>sailors</u> <u>were</u> there on the deck.]

> **Just So You Know...**
>
> *Here is/are* and *There is/are* are called *expletives.* Expletives are not subjects of sentences but they point to the subject that appears after the linking verb.

Notice how the words *here* and *there* can often be omitted from the sentence when the sentence is no longer inverted.

Beginning sentences with the nonspecific words *here* or *there* often leads to weak, wordy, and less effective sentences. Keep this point in mind when you write, and reorder the subject(s) and verb(s) so they appear in a standard simple sentence form.

Weak:	There are four forms in the packet.
More direct:	Four forms are in the packet.
Weak:	Here is the taxi.
More direct:	The taxi is here.

Practice 11 *Rewriting Inverted Sentences*

Mark all the prepositional phrases in the following sentences. Underline the subjects once and the verbs twice. In inverted sentences, you will see the verb-subject pattern. Rewrite each sentence in the subject-verb pattern.

Example: There <u>were</u> four <u>suitcases</u> <u>sitting</u> (on the front porch).
Four suitcases were sitting on the front porch.

1. There <u>are</u> many <u>options</u> available.

   Many options are available.

2. Here <u>stands</u> a brave <u>woman</u>.

   A brave woman stands here.

3. There <u>are</u> <u>children</u> (in the park) every day.

   Children are in the park every day.

4. There <u>can be</u> four <u>candidates</u> (on the ballot.)

   Four candidates can be on the ballot.

5. Here <u>is</u> my <u>letter</u> (of resignation.)

   My letter of resignation is here.

6. Here <u>are</u> the <u>packages</u> (from today's delivery.)

   The packages from today's delivery are here.

Sentences Written as Questions

Declarative sentences tell, declare, or state information. Interrogative sentences ask questions. The subject-verb pattern is inverted in questions. The subject-verb patterns for interrogative sentences are more easily understood by converting the interrogative sentence into a declarative sentence and deleting the question words *how, why, when, who,* and *where* and some of the helping verbs that have no place in a declarative sentence. Study the subject-verb patterns in the following sentences.

INTERROGATIVE SENTENCES	DECLARATIVE SENTENCES
Are you nervous?	You are nervous.
Is she your niece?	She is your niece.
Were they accepted into the program?	They were accepted into the program.

(Continue on page 89)

INTERROGATIVE SENTENCES	DECLARATIVE SENTENCES
Do you like sushi?	You do like sushi. 　You like sushi.
Did the computer malfunction?	The computer did malfunction. 　The computer malfunctioned.
Has the college notified you about the loan?	The college has notified you about the loan.
Have you applied for the job?	You have applied for the job.
May officers in uniform enter the club?	Officers in uniform may enter the club.
Should I submit the report now?	You should submit the report now.
How humid is the weather?	The weather is humid.
Why are you laughing?	You are laughing.
When did he arrive?	He did arrive. 　He arrived.
Where does she perform this week?	She does perform this week. 　She performs this week.

Practice 12   *Finding Subjects and Verbs in Questions*

Mark the prepositional phrases with parentheses and the infinitives with brackets. Draw one line under the subjects and two lines under the verbs.

Example: When are you going [to graduate]?

1. Why did you honk (at me)?

2. Where did the Lewis and Clark expedition originate?

3. Were you prepared (for the test)?

4. Can you lend me some money?

5. Shall we schedule a meeting (with the president)?

6. Are all (of the verbs) action verbs?

7. How is the tax calculated?

8. Do all (of the students) need [to register] (for the workshop)?

9. Will they file a complaint?

10. Should we plan a study session (for Friday)?

Sentences Inverted for Personal Style

Writers have many options to use to express ideas. To add variety or alter the style of writing, sometimes writers intentionally choose to invert the subject and verb patterns in sentences. Often, however, the results confuse the reader. When you write, use the standard subject-verb pattern for simple sentences.

Inverted: (Behind the porch) <u>was</u> a huge <u>rat</u>.
                 verb *subject*

More direct: A huge <u>rat</u> <u>was</u> (behind the porch.)
              subject *verb*

Inverted: (Away from the crowd) and (out of sight)
                 (from the investigators) <u>stood</u> the <u>arsonist</u>.
                 verb *subject*

More direct: The <u>arsonist</u> <u>stood</u> away from the crowd
              subject *verb*
                 and (out of sight) (from the investigators.)

Inverted: (On the walls) (in the hotel lobby) <u>were</u>
                 verb
                 original <u>photographs</u> (from the Civil War
                 subject
                 years).

More direct: Original <u>photographs</u> (from the Civil War
              subject
                 years) <u>were</u> (on the walls) (in the hotel lobby.)
                 verb

Sentences with the Understood Subject *You*

Sentences that give an order, issue a command, or make a request are *imperative sentences.* When an order, a command, or a request is made, it is addressed directly to a specific person or group of people. The person (or people) is always *you,* so the subject of an imperative sentence is always *you.* Many times, however, the word *you* is omitted from sentences and simply understood to be there.

Stated subject: <u>You</u> please <u>take out</u> the garbage.

Understood subject: [You] Please <u>take out</u> the garbage.

Stated subject: <u>You</u> <u>study</u> this by Friday.

Understood subject: [You] <u>Study</u> this by Friday.

Practice 13   *Subjects and Verbs in Imperative and Declarative Sentences*

Work with a partner, in a small group, or on your own. Underline the subjects once and the verbs twice in the following sentences. If the subject is implied, write *You* in the subject position and underline it.

Example: <u>You</u>   <u>Plan</u> to arrive early.

<u>You</u>   1. Please <u>bake</u> a cake for the bake sale on Friday.

      2. There <u>are</u> four prizes this year.

<u>You</u>   3. <u>Close</u> the door, please.

<u>You</u>   4. <u>Attach</u> the sales receipt to the rebate form.

      5. Here <u>are</u> three ways to earn more money.

      6. At the end of the day, ^{you}∧<u>deliver</u> the posters to each

         department.

<u>You</u>   7. <u>Call</u> me later.

      8. Without hesitation, ^{you}∧<u>count</u> on me for help.

<u>You</u>   9. <u>Donate</u> blood this month to help those in need.

<u>You</u> 10. <u>File</u> the forms alphabetically.

<u>You</u> 11. <u>Drop</u> your applications into the basket by the door.

<u>You</u> 12. <u>Contact</u> every person on the list.

<u>You</u> 13. Do not <u>call</u> her by her first name.

     14. There <u>is</u> a <u>reason</u> for your signature.

<u>You</u> 15. <u>Create</u> a dynamic poster for this event.

COMMA SENSE

Use a comma between compound subjects with three or more subjects.

> Graduates, undergraduates, and faculty are invited to the ceremony.

> A spell checker, a dictionary, or a laptop computer may be used during the essay exam.

Use a comma between compound verbs with three or more verbs that express the action of the subject.

> The angry child yelled, kicked, and threw a temper tantrum.

> Carlos dug the hole, added fertilizer, and planted the bulbs.

Use a comma after a direct address (name of a person) in an imperative or an interrogative sentence.

> Janet, please call the director on Monday.

> Randy, did you receive the bonus yet?

EXERCISE 4.1   **Chinese New Year**   Name _____ Date _____

John G. Mabanglo/© Corbis Images

Work with a partner, in a small group, or on your own to complete this activity. Read the paragraphs carefully. Mark the prepositional phrases with parentheses and the infinitives with brackets. Underline the subjects once and the verbs twice. Add any missing commas.

CHINESE NEW YEAR

The Chinese astrological <u>calendar</u> <u>consists</u> (of twelve years). The <u>Dragon Year</u> <u>is</u> <u>considered</u> the luckiest year (of all). The Millennium <u>year</u> <u>is</u> <u>called</u> the "Qian Xi" ("the Year (of a Thousand Happinesses)"). <u>February 5, 2000,</u> <u>was</u> the beginning (of the Millennium Dragon Year). Chinese <u>communities</u> (in major cities)(throughout Asia) <u>celebrated</u> the new year (with fireworks, dragon dances, parades, and worship). The <u>celebrations</u> <u>were</u> especially significant (in Hong Kong). This former British <u>colony</u> <u>returned</u> (to Chinese rule)(in 1997). The <u>people</u> <u>survived</u> the economic recession and <u>wanted</u> [to renew] their wishes (for prosperity). The <u>parade</u> (in Hong Kong) <u>had</u> ten sets (of dragon dancers). One <u>dragon</u> <u>was</u> more than 300 yards long. (In New York City), <u>thousands</u> (of revelers) <u>crowded</u> Chinatown [to watch] the dragon dancers (in the streets). The <u>Empire State Building</u> <u>was bathed</u> (in red and gold lights)(for the holiday).

Many Chinese call themselves "the dragon's descendants." (In ancient times) emperors regarded themselves (as reincarnations)(of dragons). Dragon Year babies are considered blessed. Millennium Dragon Year babies are double joy and are expected [to excel] (beyond other babies).(As a result) millions (of Chinese mothers) are expected [to contribute] (to a big baby boom)(during the Year of the Dragon). Taiwanese officials expect a 20 percent increase (in the number)(of births)(during the Dragon Year). (In Singapore) officials expect a 10 to 15 percent rise (in the birthrate). Other factors also contribute (to the increase)(in birthrates) (during the Dragon Year). Many women waited (for the Dragon Year) and avoided pregnancy two years ago (in the Year of the Tiger). A Tiger Baby is considered rebellious. Many people also wanted a baby (in the Dragon Year) but not (in the following year). The following year is the Year (of the Snake). (In Hong Kong) junior high schools have just started [to expand] [to accommodate] the children (from the last dragon year). Even greater expansions will be required twelve years (from the Millennium Dragon Year) [to accommodate] this unusually large baby boom.

[Source: "Dragon Year Often Brings a Baby Boom," *Register Guard*, January 5, 2000.]

EXERCISE 4.2   Working with Simple Sentences

Name _____ Date _____

Mark the prepositional phrases with parentheses and the infinitives with brackets. Then underline the subjects once and the verbs twice. Add any missing commas. If the subject is implied, write *You* in the subject position and underline it.

1. (Without the truck), the project would have been difficult.

2. We collated, stapled, and punched holes (in the worksheets).

3. (Within one week), all (of the students) registered, bought books, and formed study groups.

4. Bob, Betty, Bruce, and Brian will represent the college (on the debate team).

5. (At the restaurant), the waitress took our orders, told a few jokes, and disappeared.

6. Each (of the dolphins) was swimming (in the huge tank).

7. A popular comedian stood (on the stage) and forgot his lines.

8. The weavers and the sculptors displayed their products (at the county fair).

9. Did you write letters, call your state representatives, or protest (in any way)?

You 10. Go (to the depot), buy a ticket, and get (on the next bus).

11. Anna Maria, please sort the mail and deliver it (to the managers).

12. Why are the men, women, and children separated (during the interviews)?

You 13. Report (to duty)(on the first day)(of the month).

You 14. Read, sign, and mail the forms back (by May 1).

15. You can create a flowchart [to show](to other students).

EXERCISE 4.3 **Compound Sentences** Name _____ Date _____

The following sentences share the same verb. Combine the sentences into one simple sentence with compound subjects. You may add or delete words as needed. An example is provided. Write your sentences on separate paper. *Answers may vary slightly.*

Two sentences with the same verb:

The American flag **flapped** in the wind above the Capitol.

The state flag **flapped** in the wind above the Capitol.

Combined sentence:

The American flag and the state flag flapped in the wind above the Capitol.

The snack bar and the cafeteria open at 8:00 A.M.
1. The snack bar opens at 8:00 A.M. The cafeteria opens at the same time as the snack bar.

My rent for a studio apartment and my electric bill each month are too high.
2. My rent for a studio apartment is too high. My electric bill each month is too high.

Getting better grades and learning computer skills are high priorities for me this year in school.
3. Getting better grades is a high priority for me. Learning computer skills is a high priority for me this year in school.

My roommate and I paid cash for our books this term.
4. My roommate paid cash for his books. I also paid cash for my books this term.

Cumulus clouds and stratus clouds often produce light showers.
5. Cumulus clouds often produce light showers. Stratus clouds can also produce light showers or drizzle.

Most doctors and many nutritionists recommend daily portions of fruits and vegetables.
6. Most doctors recommend daily portions of fruits and vegetables. Many nutritionists recommend daily consumption of fruits and vegetables.

The track coach and members of the track team jog five miles along the river every day.
7. The track coach jogs five miles along the river every day. The members of the track team also jog five miles every day with the track coach.

My lab notebook and my essay for my English class are due the last week of the term.
8. My lab notebook is due the last week of the term. My essay for my English class is due the last week of the term.

EXERCISE 4.4   **Sentence Elements**   Name _____ Date _____

In each of the following sentences, a word or a group of words appears in bold print. On the line, identify how the word or words in bold print are functioning. Use the following numbers to indicate your answers.

1 = noun subject	**5** = verb phrase
2 = pronoun subject	**6** = prepositional phrase
3 = action verb by itself	**7** = infinitive
4 = linking verb	**8** = none of the above

Example: ___5___   I **was sleeping** and **snoring** loudly.

___7___   1. Here is another idea for you **to consider.**

___3___   2. Linda **washed** the windows, **mopped** the floor, and **vacuumed** the rooms.

___4___   3. The salary and the benefits **were** excellent.

___5___   4. Adoption **will require** an extensive background check of each parent.

___6___   5. **In the process** of the divorce, Kathryn was firm but fair.

___5___   6. **Do** not **bother** me right now.

___2___   7. As a commuter, **I** often drove through horrendous traffic.

___6___   8. **Without the children** at home, life seemed dull and meaningless.

___1___   9. Did the **accountant** locate and correct the error?

___8___   10. Please take a **nap** for an hour or two.

___2___   11. Why are **you** tired?

___8___   12. **There** appears to be a disagreement between them.

___7___   13. Mary and Donald love **to solve** mysteries.

___5___   14. The smoke alarm **will sound** with this much smoke in the kitchen.

___1___   15. **Dr. Lin** and **Dr. Johnston** are in charge of the emergency room.

EXERCISE 4.5   Compound Verbs   Name _____ Date _____

Each of the pairs of sentences share the same subject. Combine the sentences into a simple sentence with compound verbs. An example is provided. Write your sentences on a separate piece of paper. *Answers may vary slightly.*

Two sentences with the same subject:

The <u>nurse</u> <u>held</u> the chart.

The <u>nurse</u> <u>told</u> me the results.

Combined sentence:

The <u>nurse</u> <u>held</u> the chart and <u>told</u> me the results.

The children stomped their feet and yelled his name.
1. ⌃The children stomped their feet. The children yelled his name.

The freshmen were grabbing doughnuts and hurrying off to class.
2. ⌃The freshmen were grabbing doughnuts. They were hurrying off to class.

The antique table stood in the corner and gathered dust.
3. ⌃The antique table stood in the corner. The antique table gathered dust.

The lone rider arrived in town and stopped to ask directions.
4. ⌃The lone rider arrived in town. He stopped to ask directions.

We arrived on campus Sunday, located our dorm room, unloaded our car, and started to settle in.
5. ⌃We arrived on campus Sunday. We located our dorm room. We unloaded our car and started to settle in.

The clothes hung on the clothesline and dried quickly in the hot sun.
6. The clothes hung on the clothesline. The clothes dried quickly in the hot sun.

Did you write down the address and get the phone number?
7. ⌃Did you write down the address? Did you get the phone number?

Write to me often and call me once a month.
8. ⌃Write to me often. Call me once a month.

The hospital volunteer delivers flowers and reads to some of the patients.
9. ⌃The hospital volunteer delivers flowers. She reads to some of the patients.

The kennels near the airport will be opening soon and offering special discounts.
10. ⌃The kennels near the airport will be opening soon. They will be offering special discounts.

The summary was written and copied for the lawyers.
11. ⌃The summary was written. It was copied for the lawyers.

The final exam will cover all the chapters and include an essay.
12. ⌃The final exam will cover all the chapters. The final exam will include an essay.

EXERCISE 4.6   **Subject and Object Pronouns**

Name _____ Date _____

Part I: Circle the correct subject or object pronoun in the following sentences.

1. (Her, She) and (I, me) are considering becoming roommates.

2. The utility bills and the food expenses will be divided equally between (she, her) and (I, me).

3. Apartments, townhouses, and duplexes are available for (we, us) to rent.

4. Without a doubt, (she, her) will be a good roommate.

5. Her parrot will stay with (she, her) in her room.

6. Did Sonya and (him, he) decide to get married?

7. The class president worked well with the administrator and (her, she).

8. Just between you and (I, me), Sr. Garcia seems depressed and frustrated.

9. My parents and (I, me) spend too little time together.

10. The stress and pressure of taking six classes have taken a toll on (I, me).

Part II: On a separate piece of paper, use each of the following pronouns in a simple sentence. The pronouns may appear anywhere in the sentence. Underline the subjects once and the verbs twice in your sentences. *Answers will vary*

1. her   6. he

2. them   7. us

3. they   8. him

4. she   9. I

5. me   10. we

EXERCISE 4.7   Annual Wake-Up Ritual

Name _____ Date _____

Identify the part of speech for each of the words in boldface print. Write **N** for noun, **V** for verb, **P** for pronoun, and **Prep** for preposition. The first sentence is done as an example.

ANNUAL WAKE-UP RITUAL KEPT ALIVE

Garla Mohammed Bayoumi **bundles** up against the winter **chill. She** treads a familiar path **through** the darkened streets of old **Cairo.** She thumps out a regular **rhythm** on a small drum and **pauses** to call sleeping **residents** by name. It is 2:30 A.M. Bayoumi **is performing** an annual **ritual** that dates back seven **generations** in her family. She is a *mesaharati,* a public waker. She rouses faithful Muslims for **prayers** and breakfast in the wee **hours** of the holy month of **Ramadan.**

During Ramadan, Muslims **abstain** from food, drink, smoking, and sex from sunrise to **sunset.** This is an **act** of **sacrifice** and purification. **They** break the fast **with** a sunset meal and then wake early to eat a predawn meal. Ramadan **ends with** the first sighting of the crescent moon. A three-day feast **begins** the following day.

Mesaharatis were once a common **sight** and sound in Cairo. Now many **neighborhoods** are **without** a traditional waker. Sometimes young **entrepreneurs** fill the **void.** They **clang** loud noisemakers through the streets. They **hope** to be paid **for** their services. But Bayoumi, 52, is from the old school. She was **trained** by her father. She had **accompanied** her father as a child and learned the names of every head **of** household **in** the neighborhood. She **became** the mesaharati of her **section** of town thirty-five years ago. She is a respected figure.

It is unusual **for** a woman to be a mesaharati, but Bayoumi's father had no **sons.** She **wanted** to keep the family **tradition** alive. The people of the neighborhood **supported** her. They turned away another mesaharati who tried to take over her **area** in 1992.

Her loud **voice** rises in **pitch** in the traditional call. Most people **respond** to her calls. The persistent **drumming** wakes all the others. Some nights, **Bayoumi** also carries a wooden walking stick and **raps** on the doors of those sound **sleepers** who have requested special **attention.** Most residents tip her. **They** pay a little **extra** for special services, such as an extra rap **on** the door or adding the name of their young son to her **repertoire during** the first fast.

[Adapted from "Annual Wake-Up Ritual Kept Alive," Associated Press, *Register Guard,* January 6, 2000, p. 10A.]

Chapter 4 Summary

1. The **subject** of a sentence is the noun or the pronoun that tells who or what performs the action in the sentence. The subject frequently appears in the front part of the sentence. The subject is never found inside a prepositional phrase.

2. The **verb** of a sentence is the word or group of words that expresses the action or the state of being of the subject. The verb usually follows the subject. The verb is never an infinitive.

3. A **simple sentence** consists of one independent or main clause that has a subject and a verb and forms a complete thought.

4. An **independent clause** is a group of related words with a subject and a verb that can stand on its own as a separate sentence.

5. A three-step approach can be used to identify subjects in sentences. First, identify and mark all the prepositional phrases and the infinitives. Second, look in the front part of the sentence for a word that tells *who* or *what* is doing the action of the sentence. Finally, confirm that the word or word group you select as the subject is a noun or a pronoun.

6. **Personal pronouns** and **indefinite pronouns** may work as **subject pronouns.**

7. Sentences may have **compound subjects** and/or **compound verbs.** Compound subjects occur when two or more subjects within one independent clause share the same verb. Compound verbs occur when two or more verbs within one independent clause express the action of the same subject.

8. **Action verbs** show the action done by the subject. **Linking verbs,** also known as **state of being verbs,** link the subject to the remainder of the information in the independent clause.

9. **Verb phrases** consist of one or more helping verbs joined to a main verb. **Helping verbs** may come from the verb *to be, to do,* or *to have,* or they may be verbs such as *can, will, could,* and so on.

10. **Fragments** are parts of a sentence that pose as complete sentences. Fragments by themselves are incomplete sentences that lack a subject, a verb, and/or a complete thought.

11. **Nouns** may appear throughout a sentence. Nouns may be subjects, objects of prepositions, direct objects, or indirect objects.

12. The basic **subject-verb pattern** in simple sentences may be **inverted** in three ways: (1) in sentences that begin with *here* or

there, (2) in **interrogative sentences** that ask questions, and (3) in sentences when an author inverts the pattern for style or emphasis.

13. An **imperative sentence** gives an order, a command, or a request. The understood subject is always *you.*

14. **Commas** are used

   a. between compound subjects with three or more subjects

   b. between compound verbs with three or more verbs that express the action of the subject

   c. after a direct address (the name of a person) in an imperative or interrogative sentence

Writing Topics for Chapter 4

Select one of the following writing options. Write one or two paragraphs about this topic. Proofread your work carefully. Make any necessary revisions.

1. Select a holiday tradition that you celebrate with your family or your friends. What is the tradition? Where did it originate? How many years have you practiced this tradition? Why is the tradition meaningful to you?

2. If you were asked to compile a list of three important "principles of life," what principles would you include in your list? Briefly name and discuss the three principles and why these principles are the ones that you value.

 3. Use the Internet or other resources to locate the Chinese astrological calendar with the twelve years in the Chinese zodiac. (You may also find this information on place mats in Chinese restaurants.) Briefly discuss each of the twelve years. What do they represent? What are the characteristics of people born in each year? Print any web pages you use as a source for your information. Attach them to your writing.

Web Site Learning Experiences

See the web site for this book to locate companion exercises and links related to the grammar and writing topics in this chapter.

Go to: http://college.hmco.com. Click on "Students." Type *Sentence Essentials* in the "Jump to Textbook Sites" box. Click "go" and then bookmark the site. Click on Chapter 4.

CHAPTER 4 • Review   Name _____   Date _____

Total Possible: 50   Your Score: _____

Part I: Identification of Subjects, Verbs, and Parts of Speech (27 pts.)

Underline the subjects with one line and the verbs with two lines. On the blank, identify the part of speech of the words printed in bold. Use these symbols: *Give one point for identification, one for each subject, and one for each complete verb.*

N = noun   **P = pronoun**

V = verb   **Prep = preposition**

INF = infinitive

_____P_____ 1. **Anyone** can learn to use a computer.   3 points

_____N_____ 2. Some of the rocks in Johnny's collection are natural **gems.**   3 points

_____Prep_____ 3. **Before** the final exam, Eduardo and Sue studied together in the library.   4 points

_____V_____ 4. She and I **have become** close friends.   4 points

_____V_____ 5. **Should** we **design** an evacuation plan?   3 points

_____Inf_____ 6. Does every student need **to have** a photo ID card?   3 points

_____V_____ 7. You
Value your friendships and personal goals.
3 points

_____Prep_____ 8. Taxpayers prepare and mail millions of tax forms **on** April 15.   4 points

Part II: Proofreading   (14 points)

Each of the following sentences has one or more errors. Add or delete words or punctuation to correct each error.

1. She
   ~~Her~~ and Chang study in the library every day after class.   1 point

2. Economics,X and graphic design are my favorite courses this term.
   1 point

3. The cold front moved ~~moves~~ through the Northwest and created record

   low temperatures.   1 point

C   F   D   F   A

4. The college finance department distributes financial aid checks,

collects special fees, and charges interest on late payments.
7 points

                                                     X

5. The teacher will either cancel the class, or arrange to have a

substitute.   1 point

                                          is a busy time. (Answers will vary.)

Frag 6. The end of the term on our campus,   1 point

7. Flowers, candy, and a small box arrived at the actor's new home.
1 point

                                                         him

8. The time for the presentation will be divided equally between ~~he~~

and Carlos.   1 point

Part III: Sentence Writing   (9 points)

Follow the directions for writing three different sentences. Underline the subject(s) once and the complete verb(s) twice. *Give one point for following the direction and one for each subject and verb identification.*

1. Write a simple sentence that is an *imperative sentence.* (Give an order or make a request.)

   _____

   _____

2. Write an *interrogative sentence.* (Ask a question.)

   _____

   _____

3. Combine the following sentences into one simple *declarative sentence:*

   I fell on the cement.   I banged my knee.   I bruised my arm.

   _____

   _____

CHAPTER 5

Verb Forms

In Chapter 5, you will learn about **verbs,** which are words that express the action or state of being expressed by the subject of the sentence. You will also learn about verb forms, tenses, number, and person. Past and present participles are also discussed in this chapter.

Understanding different verb forms will help you do the following:

1. Express the action of the verb in the correct verb tense or time period

2. Avoid common errors with subject and verb agreement, verb tenses, and verb forms

3. Avoid fragments that are caused by incomplete verbs

4. Write grammatically correct simple, compound, and complex sentences

---

Verbs are the most complicated part of speech, but they are also the most interesting and important. Within each sentence, verbs convey the subject's action or state of being. In Chapter 4, you learned about three kinds of verbs, summarized in the following chart.

KINDS OF VERBS		
ACTION VERBS (p. 73)	LINKING VERBS (p. 75)	HELPING VERBS (p. 80)
• Show visible action Examples: write, jump, hug • Show invisible, mental action Examples: think, consider, know, pretend • Show possession Examples: have, own, possess	• From the verb *to be:* am, is are, was, were • From verbs related to senses: feel, look, taste, smell, sound • From other verbs that show state of being or condition: become, seem, appear, grow, remain	• From the verb *to be:* am, is, are, was, were, be, being, been • From the verb *to do:* do, does, did • From the verb *to have:* has, have, had • Other helping verbs: can, will, shall, could, should, would, may, might, must

Before we begin to discuss verbs in greater detail, the following chart shows the five verb forms that exist for all verbs. The examples provide a brief look at each of the five verb forms. You will learn more about each of these verb forms in this chapter.

FIVE FORMS OF VERBS				
INFINITIVE: THE BASE FORM	PRESENT TENSE: -S OR -ES SUFFIX FOR THIRD PERSON	PAST TENSE: -ED SUFFIX FOR REGULAR VERBS AND OTHER FORMS FOR IRREGULAR VERBS	PRESENT PARTICIPLE: -ING SUFFIX	PAST PARTICIPLE: -ED SUFFIX FOR REGULAR VERBS AND OTHER FORMS FOR IRREGULAR VERBS
to plan	plan, plans	planned	planning	planned
to study	study, studies	studied	studying	studied
to show	show, shows	showed	showing	shown
to think	think, thinks	thought	thinking	thought
to sing	sing, sings	sang	singing	sung

In order to explain and discuss different verb forms, you will need to learn some basic grammar terminology and definitions. The following three terms are briefly introduced here but will be discussed throughout the chapter: *verb tense, number,* and *person.*

VERB TENSE **Tense tells when the action occurs or the state of being exists. It also indicates whether the action or the state of being is continued or completed.**

These are the six verb tenses:

1. Simple present tense: I *walk* to school every day.

2. Simple past tense: I *walked* to school last year.

3. Simple future tense: I *will walk* to school tomorrow.

4. Present perfect tense: I *have walked* to school for a long time.

5. Past perfect tense: I *had walked* to school in the past.

6. Future perfect tense: I *will have walked* to school for the entire term.

NUMBER   Number tells whether the subject is singular (one) or plural (more than one).

Singular: The *bus* arrives at 9:00 A.M.

Plural: The *buses* arrive at 9:00 A.M.

Singular: The *child* lives with his grandmother.

Plural: The *children* live with their grandmother.

PERSON   First, second, and third person are terms used to indicate whether the subject is speaking, spoken to, or spoken about.

PERSON			
PERSON	SHOWS . . .	SUBJECT NOUN OR PRONOUN	EXAMPLES
First-person singular	the subject is speaking	I	*I* study hard in college.
First-person plural	the subject is speaking	We	*We* study hard in college.
Second-person singular	who is being spoken to or addressed	You	*You* study hard in college. *You* passed your classes.
Second-person plural	who is being spoken to or addressed	You	*You* will receive your grades today. *You* are wonderful students.
Third-person singular	who is spoken about	He, she, it, or any singular noun or singular indefinite pronoun*	*He* plays the piano. *She* plays the guitar. *It* lasts three hours. *Stephanie* is tall. Our *roof* leaked. *Everyone* likes Raymond.
Third-person plural	who is spoken about	They or any plural nouns or plural indefinite pronouns*	*They* invited six people. *Picnics* are fun. *Many* expect bonuses.

*See Chapter 6, page 164 for a list of indefinite pronouns.

▦www Simple Verb Tenses

The three simple verb tenses are **simple present, simple past,** and **simple future.** These three time periods are shown in the following sentence patterns, which can be used with any action verbs. These sentence patterns show first person, but second or third person may also be used.

Present tense: Today I _____.
                Examples: Today I *go* to school.
                           Today I *need* to write to Dad.

Past tense: Yesterday I _____.
                Examples: Yesterday I *went* to school.
                           Yesterday I *needed* to write to Dad.

Future tense: Tomorrow I _____.
                Examples: Tomorrow I *will go* to school.
                           Tomorrow I *will need* to write to Dad.

SIMPLE PRESENT TENSE **Simple present tense tells about an action that occurs now or is a habitual or repeated action.**

The simple present tense verb is formed by one word. The only word ending, or suffix, that may be used on a simple present tense verb is an *-s* or an *-es* when the subject is in the third person.

I *like* my new software program.

She *swims* at noon every day.

Bubba *plays* chess at least three times a week.

SIMPLE PAST TENSE **Simple past tense tells about an action that has already taken place and is completed.**

The simple past tense verb is formed by one word. The simple past tense verb may have an *-ed* suffix or may take a form that is different from the base form of the verb.

I *liked* my new software program at first.

She *swam* at noon last Thursday.

Bubba *played* chess for the first time last week.

SIMPLE FUTURE TENSE **Simple future tense tells about an action that has not yet occurred; it will occur in the future.**

A verb phrase with the helping verb *will* is used to form the future tense.

The record industry *will protest* the court decision.

I *will drive* to the mountains at the end of the month.

Practice 1   *Simple Verb Tenses*

Mark prepositional phrases with parentheses and infinitives with brackets. Then underline the subjects once and the simple verbs twice. On the line, use one of these abbreviations to indicate the simple sentence verb tense that is used in the sentence:

PR = present   P = past   F = future

Example: __P__   The man (in the cannon) shot (through the air) and landed (in the net).

__P__   1. The fog settled (into the valley).

__PR__   2. I frequently search (for inexpensive train tickets) [to see] my parents.

__F__   3. The waitress will bring your order (to your table).

__PR__   4. You always get the best seat (in the movie theater).

__PR__   5. Ali arrives every day (by 7:00 A.M.)

__PR__   6. Little Latisha pretends [to be] a famous ballerina.

__P__   7. Daydreaming caused me too many problems (in school).

__P__   8. The lab assistant copied a set (of notes) (for me).

__F__   9. The taxi driver will get you (to the meeting) (on time).

__PR__   10. Your resume looks thorough and intriguing.

Simple Present Tense

To use the simple present tense correctly, you need to identify the subject and know whether it is first, second, or third person, and whether it is singular or plural. The form of a present tense verb remains the same for first, second, and third person except for third-person singular. For third-person singular, the verb must have an *-s* or an *-es* suffix. Notice how the verbs work in these examples:

First-person singular: I *sing* in the shower.

First-person plural: We *sing* in the shower.

Second-person singular and plural:	You *sing* in the shower.
Third-person singular:	He *sings* in the shower.
Third-person singular:	She *sings* in the shower.
Third-person singular:	The boxer *sings* in the shower.
Third-person plural:	The boxers *sing* in the shower.
Third-person plural:	They *sing* in the shower.

Practice 2   *Identifying Person*

Mark prepositional phrases with parentheses and infinitives with brackets. Then underline the subject once and the simple verbs twice. On the line, indicate whether the subject is in first, second, or third person by writing **1**, **2**, or **3.**

Example: __3__   Tofu and soy beans provide important nutrients (for vegetarian diets).

__3__   1. Wildflowers cover the valley floor.

__3__   2. Many people choose early retirement.

__1__   3. I plan [to attend] graduate school (in three years).

__2__   4. You spend too much time (on the phone).

__3__   5. My niece will compete (in a gymnastics tournament) this weekend.

__1__   6. We decided [to present] a skit (for our class project).

__3__   7. The electricians belong (to a union).

__3__   8. Court papers outline the grievances.

__3__   9. They care very much (about their possessions).

__3__   10. This exhibit is incredible.

 ## Special Notes About Subject-Verb Agreement

The subjects and the verbs in sentences must agree in number and person. Subject-verb agreement needs special attention when a sentence has a third-person subject. Use the following rules to make third-person subjects and verbs agree.

The spelling guidelines for using -s and -es to form plural nouns can also be used to form third-person singular verbs. See pages 19–20 in Chapter 2 to review the spelling rules for -s and -es suffixes.

1. Singular subjects in third person must use the singular form of the verb. The singular verb form has an -s or an -es suffix.

   singular subject   verb has -es
   A student writes many papers.

   singular subject   verb has -es
   My brother watches all the sports channels.

2. Plural subjects in third person must use the plural form of the verb. The plural form of the verb has no -s or -es suffix.

   plural subject   verb has no -s or -es
   Students write many papers.

   plural subject   verb has no -s or -es
   My brothers watch all the sports channels.

   plural subject   verb has no -s or -es
   My feet often ache after a long hike.

3. Put an -s or an -es either on the noun subject to make it plural or on the verb to make it singular. Either the subject or the verb will have the -s or the -es suffix, but not both. One exception to this rule occurs when the plural subject noun is an irregular plural form, such as *feet, women, men,* and *geese.* The irregular noun plural forms were discussed on page 20 in Chapter 2.

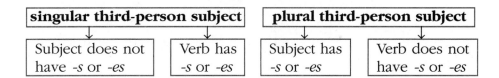

singular third-person subject		plural third-person subject	
Subject does not have -s or -es	Verb has -s or -es	Subject has -s or -es	Verb does not have -s or -es

Whenever you are using a third-person subject (singular or plural), carefully check the verb. To avoid errors with subject-verb agreement, train yourself to mark the prepositional phrases and the infinitives first and then identify the subject. Once you have identified the subject, you can check that you are using the correct verb form for third person in the present tense. Notice the importance of identifying the prepositional phrase first and looking outside the prepositional phrase for the subject.

Singular subject and verb: The ice (in the glasses) melts within minutes.

Singular subject and verb: The boy (with the red gloves) loves the snow.

Plural subject and verb: The boxes (under the bed) gather dust.

Plural subject and verb: The people (in the elevator) hear the alarm.

| Practice 3 | *Using Simple Present Tense* |

In the following sentences, begin by marking all the prepositional phrases with parentheses and the infinitives with brackets. Underline the subjects once. Then use a double underline to select the correct form of the simple present tense verb.

1. The tropical <u>desserts</u> (on the menu) (tempts, <u><u>tempt</u></u>) me [to try] something new.

2. <u>I</u> (enjoys, <u><u>enjoy</u></u>) your company.

3. <u>She</u> never (<u><u>wants</u></u>, want) [to go] (to the movies).

4. My <u>report</u> (about the floods) (<u><u>needs</u></u>, need) some graphics.

5. Your <u>friend</u> (with the two German shepherds) (<u><u>enters</u></u>, enter) many dog shows.

6. <u>They</u> (buys, <u><u>buy</u></u>) lottery tickets every week.

7. <u>We</u> often (consults, <u><u>consult</u></u>) (with our grandfather) (for advice).

8. <u>You</u> (needs, <u><u>need</u></u>) some medical attention.

9. The <u>storms</u> (in the Caribbean) often (develops, <u><u>develop</u></u>) (into hurricanes).

10. The <u>planes</u> (in Houston) usually (departs, <u><u>depart</u></u>) (on time).

| Practice 4 | *Proofreading for Subject-Verb Agreement* |

Carefully check the following paragraph for subject-verb agreement. Above any subject-verb agreement errors, write the correct subject or the correct verb form to eliminate the error.

Many species of bats ~~is~~ *are* considered endangered. The bat population worldwide ~~are~~ *is* declining. Bats in Colorado ~~is~~ *are* roosting in caves, hollow trees, beneath bridges, and in attics, cellars, and mine tunnels. In the past, inactive ~~mine~~ *mines* were closed to prevent danger to people. Mines were blasted to backfill the tunnels and to seal the openings with concrete. Thousands of bats were entombed alive. They were shut off from their food source and eventually starved to death. Now the Colorado Division of Wildlife ~~operate~~ *operates* a program to provide bat habitats in the inactive mines. "Bat gates" are installed to allow bats to fly in and out. The man-made habitats in Colorado ~~is~~ *are* important for the conservation and preservation of the bat species.

Simple Past Tense

You already know that simple past tense tells about an action that has already taken place and is completed. The simple past tense verb is formed by one word, not a verb phrase. To understand past tenses, you must first understand the terms **regular verb** and **irregular verb.**

REGULAR VERB **A regular verb is an action verb that uses the *-ed* suffix to form the simple past tense. Sometimes spelling changes occur when you add the *-ed* suffix.**

This pattern is also used to form the past participle, one of the verb forms that will be discussed later in this chapter. The majority of verbs in English are regular verbs. In the following chart, note the changes in the verb forms as the verbs move from the infinitive, which is the base form, to simple present tense, and then to simple past tense. Also note that some of the subjects are singular and some are plural. Both singular and plural subjects use the same form of the verb in simple past tense.

REGULAR VERBS		
INFINITIVE = BASE FORM	SIMPLE PRESENT TENSE	SIMPLE PAST TENSE
to bark	The brown <u>dog</u> <u>barks</u>.	The brown <u>dog</u> <u>barked</u>.
to match	The <u>jacket</u> <u>matches</u> his trousers.	The <u>jacket</u> <u>matched</u> his trousers.
to drip	The <u>faucet</u> <u>drips</u>.	The <u>faucet</u> <u>dripped</u> all weekend.
to slam	Bob <u>slams</u> the books down.	Bob <u>slammed</u> the books down.
to carry	Three <u>girls</u> <u>carry</u> purses.	Three <u>girls</u> <u>carried</u> purses

Practice 5 *Using Regular Action Verbs in Past Tense*

For each sentence below, write a regular action verb in simple past tense. All the simple past tense verbs must be made by adding an *-ed* suffix. Write only one word on each line. *Answers will vary. All verbs must have an -ed suffix.*

Example: The holiday sales __attracted__ thousands of shoppers to the mall.

1. The umpire __yelled__ at the batter.

2. The food coloring __stained__ the kitchen counter.

3. We __ordered__ salads and pizza.

4. The semi-truck __turned__ on the exit ramp.

5. The artist ____created____ a masterpiece.

6. All of the airline pilots ____signed____ a new contract.

7. Most students ____attended____ classes all term.

8. The baby ____cried____ all night.

9. The gale winds ____subsided____ overnight.

10. The engineer ____halted____ the train abruptly.

IRREGULAR VERB   An irregular verb is an action verb that does not use the -ed suffix to form the past tense. A set pattern is not used to make the simple past tense.

As you will see later in this chapter, past participles of irregular verbs also do not use a set pattern. In the following chart, note the changes in the verb forms as the verbs move from the infinitive to the simple present tense and then to the simple past tense. Also note that some of the subjects are singular and some are plural. Both singular and plural subjects use the same verb form in the simple past tense.

IRREGULAR VERBS		
INFINITIVE = BASE FORM	SIMPLE PRESENT TENSE	SIMPLE PAST TENSE
to catch	Mike catches the ball.	Mike caught the ball yesterday.
to read	I read two books every week.	I read two books last week.
to think	We often think about you.	We often thought about you.
to sink	The star player often sinks free throws.	The star player often sank free throws.
to write	She writes in her journal every day.	She wrote in her journal every day.
to cut	The florist cuts fresh flowers daily.	The florist cut fresh flowers daily.
to shut	They shut the garage door at night.	They shut the door and left.

Though the majority of verbs in English are regular verbs, attention must be given to the more than two hundred irregular verbs in English. Refer to the second column of the list on pages 128–130 for the simple past tense of the most common irregular verbs. Refer to dictionaries and spell checkers with dictionaries whenever you need to verify the past tense form of an irregular verb. Locate the word and the abbreviation *v.* (verb). Immediately following the abbreviation, and prior to the definitions, you will see the spelling for the past tense of the verb. For example, *Webster's II New College Dictionary* shows the following entry for the verb *to dig*.

word	pronunciation	verb	past tense	present participle	word history
dig	**(dĭg)**	**vt.**	**dug**	**dig•ging**	**[ME diggen]**

definitions
1. to break up, turn over, or remove (e.g., earth or sand)
2. to make (an excavation) 3. to obtain by digging . . .

Practice 6 *Using Irregular Action Verbs in Past Tense*

On each blank, write the past tense of the irregular verbs shown at the beginning of the line. If you are not sure of the correct simple past tense, refer to the list of past participles of irregular verbs on pages 128–130.

freeze, burst   1. The water pipes ____froze____ and ____burst____ last winter.

break   2. Miguel ____broke____ his leg in the last quarter.

deal, bid   3. She ____dealt____ all the cards and ____bid____ on her hand.

lead   4. The guide ____led____ the hikers to safety.

shrink   5. The sweatshirt ____shrank/shrunk____ in the hot water.

make, pay   6. She ____made____ the decision and ____paid____ the price.

strike, awake   7. The lightning ____struck____ the house and ____awoke____ the occupants.

flee   8. The villagers ____fled____ in the middle of the night.

swim, dive   9. We ____swam____ in the river and ____dove/dived____ off the rocks.

choose, fall   10. I ____chose____ a movie but ____fell____ asleep.

creep, hide   11. The frightened girl ____crept____ around the house and ____hid____ under the stairs.

lay, go   12. I _____laid_____ my books on the table and
_____went_____ into the kitchen.

quit, leave   13. The contractors _____quit_____ work early and
_____left_____ the construction site.

spin, weave   14. The weaver _____spun_____ her own yarn and
_____wove_____ a beautiful wall hanging.

swing, hit   15. The third batter _____swung_____ and _____hit_____ a
home run.

Practice 7   *Knowing Past Tense*

You will notice that some of the verbs in this practice are regular verbs and some are irregular verbs. Without referring to a dictionary or the list of past tenses of regular verbs, write the simple past tense for each of the following verbs.

Tip: For each numbered verb, first think to yourself:
Today I _____.
Yesterday I _____. [This second verb form will be your answer.]

Example: Today I _____run_____ laps at the school.
Yesterday I _____ran_____ laps at the school.

1. think _____thought_____   8. study _____studied_____   15. catch _____caught_____

2. plan _____planned_____   9. steal _____stole_____   16. hear _____heard_____

3. count _____counted_____   10. bottle _____bottled_____   17. cut _____cut_____

4. wake _____woke_____   11. stick _____stuck_____   18. deal _____dealt_____

5. speed _____sped_____   12. prove _____proved_____   19. feed _____fed_____

6. spring _____sprang/sprung_____ 13. strap _____strapped_____ 20. cry _____cried_____

7. choose _____chose_____   14. buy _____bought_____   21. spray _____sprayed_____

Simple Past and Present Tenses for the Verbs
To Be, To Have, and To Do

The verbs *to be, to have,* and *to do* are irregular verbs. You were first introduced to these verbs in Chapter 4. Review the present and past tense verb forms for these verbs. Pay close attention to the third-person singular verbs in present tense.

PRESENT TENSE			
	TO BE	TO HAVE	TO DO
First-person singular	I *am* a student.	I *have* new textbooks.	I *do* my homework.
First-person plural	We *are* students.	We *have* new textbooks.	We *do* our homework.
Second-person singular	You *are* a student.	You *have* new textbooks.	You *do* your homework.
Second-person plural	You *are* students.	You *have* new textbooks.	You *do* your homework.
Third-person singular	He/She *is* a student.	He/She *has* new textbooks.	He/she *does* his homework.
Third-person plural	They *are* students.	They *have* new textbooks.	They *do* their homework.

PAST TENSE			
	TO BE	TO HAVE	TO DO
First-person singular	I *was* happy.	I *had* new textbooks.	I *did* my homework.
First-person plural	We *were* happy.	We *had* new textbooks.	We *did* our homework.
Second-person singular	You *were* happy.	You *had* new textbooks.	You *did* your homework.
Second-person plural	You *were* happy.	You *had* new textbooks.	You *did* your homework.
Third-person singular	He/She *was* happy.	He/She *had* new textbooks.	He/she *does* his homework.
Third-person plural	They *were* happy.	They *had* new textbooks.	They *did* their homework.

Practice 8   *Using the Correct Verbs in Present Tense*

First, mark all the prepositional phrases with parentheses and the infinitives with brackets. Then underline the subjects once. Use a double underline to select the correct form of the simple present tense verb. Remember that the subjects and verbs must agree in number and person. Some of the sentences have inverted subject-verb patterns.

1. The cash <u>prizes</u> (in the contest) (is, <u>are</u>) huge.

2. Where (is, <u>are</u>) your <u>boots</u>?

3. (Is, <u>Are</u>) the <u>statues</u> (on the shelf) new?

4. The <u>waitresses</u> (at the diner) (has, <u>have</u>) long hours.

5. There (is, <u>are</u>) two <u>checks</u> (in the mail) (for you).

6. Where (<u>is</u>, are) the hot-air <u>balloon</u> now?

7. The pet <u>hogs</u> (on the farm) (has, <u>have</u>) a good life.

8. The tobacco <u>industry</u> (<u>has</u>, have) a statement [to make] (to the public).

9. (Is, <u>Are</u>) the <u>concerts</u> (in the park) free this summer?

10. How many <u>boxes</u> (in the storage room) (has, <u>have</u>) lids?

11. The <u>child</u> (in those commercials) (<u>has</u>, have) curly hair.

12. Here (is, <u>are</u>) the <u>results</u> (of the latest poll).

13. The <u>students</u> (in the media arts program) (has, <u>have</u>) a legitimate complaint.

14. The rescue <u>workers</u> (at the scene) (of the earthquake) (is, <u>are</u>) mostly volunteers.

15. (Is, <u>Are</u>) recent <u>photos</u> (of your child) available?

SIMPLE FUTURE TENSE **The future tense refers to actions that will take place in the future, after the time of writing.**

The future tense is always made by using a verb phrase. The helping verb *will* is combined with the basic form of the verb to make the future tense. The helping verb *shall,* which is more formal, is becoming outdated as a form of future tense.

In the following examples, notice how the entire verb phrase is marked as one verb because the phrase represents one action. You do not need to be concerned with singular or plural subjects, regular or irregular verbs, or first, second, or third person, since all the verbs use the same form.

<u>I</u> <u>will call</u> you tomorrow.   <u>We</u> <u>will attend</u> the ceremony.

<u>You</u> <u>will receive</u> a bonus.   <u>She</u> <u>will accept</u> the nomination.

<u>It</u> <u>will bring</u> good results.   The <u>checks</u> <u>will arrive</u> tomorrow.

Special Notes About Future Tense Verb Forms

Chapter 4 briefly discussed the following points about verb phrases. Reviewing these points will prepare you for a more in-depth understanding of different kinds of verb phrases.

1. When a compound verb is used, the helping verb is often understood to be a part of the second verb phrase even though it is not written.

   The <u>author</u> <u>will sign</u> autographs and <u>pose</u> for pictures.

   <u>Teachers</u> <u>will grade</u> the final exams and <u>calculate</u> the grades.

2. Also notice that some words, called *adverbs,* may appear between the helping verb and the base form of the verb. Common adverbs that appear between the helping verb and the base form of the verb are *not* and *never.* Other adverbs will be discussed in Chapter 7.

The <u>attorneys</u> <u>will</u> not <u>represent</u> her.

<u>She</u> <u>will</u> never <u>sign</u> those forms.

3. Interrogative sentences have inverted subject and verb patterns. The subject appears between the helping verb and the base form of the verb. Remember that the subject and verb patterns may be easier to identify when you convert the interrogative sentences to declarative sentences.

Interrogative: <u>Will</u> <u>Janice</u> <u>perform</u> on the main stage?

Declarative: <u>Janice</u> <u>will</u> <u>perform</u> on the main stage.

Interrogative: When <u>will</u> the <u>doctor</u> <u>talk</u> to you?

Declarative: The <u>doctor</u> <u>will</u> <u>talk</u> to you.

Practice 9   *Using Future Tense*

Mark all the prepositional phrases with parentheses and the infinitives with brackets. Underline the subjects once and the verbs twice.

1. <u>Alfredo</u> <u>will take</u> his placement test (on Tuesday).

2. <u>Will</u> <u>you</u> <u>submit</u> your resignation this week?

3. The <u>union</u> <u>will ask</u> its members [to vote].

4. The <u>rally</u> <u>will create</u> a challenge (for security).

5. The <u>photographs</u> <u>will appear</u> (in the Sunday paper).

6. <u>Investments</u> (on the Internet) <u>will</u> not <u>guarantee</u> profits.

7. The software <u>program</u> <u>will</u> not <u>include</u> backup disks.

8. When <u>will</u> <u>we</u> <u>plan</u> a reunion (for this summer)?

9. The travel <u>agent</u> <u>will book</u> the flight and <u>make</u> hotel reservations (for you).

10. Our <u>neighbors</u> <u>will watch</u> the house and <u>water</u> the yard.

Present and Past Participles

On page 106, you were introduced to the five forms of verbs shown below. Now that you understand simple verb tenses, you are familiar with the first three columns of this chart. Shift your attention to the last two columns on the right: present participles and past participles.

FIVE FORMS OF VERBS				
INFINITIVE	PRESENT TENSE	PAST TENSE	PRESENT PARTICIPLE	PAST PARTICIPLE
Use the word *to* to show the base form of the verb.	Use an *-s* or *-es* suffix for third person singular.	Use an *-ed* suffix for regular verbs and other forms for irregular verbs.	In a verb phrase, use an *-ing* suffix on the base form.	In a verb phrase, use an *-ed* suffix for regular verbs and other verb forms for irregular verbs.

Present participles and past participles are verb forms that are used in verb phrases. Verb phrases were first introduced on pages 79–82 in Chapter 4. Now that the term *base form* has been introduced, it will replace the term *main verb* that was used in Chapter 4.

VERB PHRASE   In a verb phrase, two or more verbs work to show the action done by the subject.

A verb phrase consists of a helping verb plus the base form of a verb, which may have suffixes attached.

HELPING VERB + BASE FORM	HELPING VERB + BASE FORM
is thinking	was hitting
had planned	have bought
will lead	will buy

HELPING VERB   A helping verb works in combination with another verb to form a verb phrase or a complete verb.

Four kinds of helping verbs are used to form verb phrases:

1. *To be* verbs: am, is, are, was, were, be, being, been
2. *To have* verbs: has, have, had
3. *To do* verbs: do, does, did
4. Other verbs, called *modals*. Modals always work as helping verbs in verb phrases: can, will, shall, could, should, would, may, might, and must.

Present Participles

Writers of English can use many different kinds of verb phrases to convey different tenses or actions performed by the subject. One common verb phrase uses an *-ing* suffix attached to the base form of the verb. This *-ing* form used in a verb phrase is called a *present participle*.

PRESENT PARTICIPLE   A present participle is a verb form in which the base verb has an *-ing* suffix.

Present participles are used to form verb phrases that begin with a helping verb from the verb *to be:* am, is, are, was, were, or will be. These verb phrases are called *progressive verbs* because they express an action that occurred continuously through a given time period.

PROGRESSIVE VERBS	
HELPING VERB *TO BE* +	PRESENT PARTICIPLE
am, is, are, was, were, will be +	base form with *-ing*
am	fixing
is	calling
are	preparing
were	running
will be	competing

Present participles are not the part of a verb phrase that shows the verb tense. The helping verbs in progressive verbs express the present, past, or future verb tense of the verb phrase.

Present Progressive The action continues at the present time.	I <u>am thinking</u> about the offer. You <u>are hoping</u> for a miracle. We <u>are resigning</u> our positions. She <u>is submitting</u> her application. The sun <u>is shining</u>. They <u>are driving</u> to the coast.
Past Progressive The action continued over a period of time in the past.	I <u>was thinking</u> about the offer. You <u>were hoping</u> for a miracle. We <u>were resigning</u> our positions. She <u>was submitting</u> her application. The sun <u>was shining</u>. They <u>were driving</u> to the coast.
Future Progressive The action will begin in the future and continue through a period of time in the future.	I <u>will be thinking</u> about the offer. You <u>will be hoping</u> for a miracle. We <u>will be resigning</u> our positions. She <u>will be submitting</u> her application. The sun <u>will be shining</u>. They <u>will be driving</u> to the coast.

At this point, you may be questioning the differences among simple past, present, and future verb tenses and past, present, and future progressive verbs. The main difference involves the period of time that is expressed by the verb. The simple tenses express that an action starts, finishes, or will occur in the future. Progressive verbs express a continued action of the verb through a specific period of time.

Simple present tense:	The auditor <u>reviews</u> the taxpayer's receipts. [The action occurs now.]
Present progressive tense:	The auditor <u>is reviewing</u> the taxpayer's receipts. [The action has started and continues in the present.]
Simple past tense:	The mayor <u>introduced</u> the city manager. [The action is completed.]
Past progressive tense:	The mayor <u>was introducing</u> the city manager. [The action started in the past and continued over time in the past.]
Simple future tense:	The managers <u>will work</u> longer hours. [The action will occur in the future.]
Future progressive tense:	The managers <u>will be working</u> longer hours. [Once the action begins, it will continue through a future period of time.]

Practice 10   *Forming Progressive Verb Phrases*

Complete each of the following sentences by adding a progressive verb phrase to the sentence. Create a present participle from the base verb given. You may choose any helping verb from the verb *to be* to indicate a verb tense that is appropriate for the sentence.

Example: select   Ramon and Lisa <u>are selecting</u> the same topic for their research papers.

consider   1. The administration <u>is/was considering</u> the students' request.

borrow   2. Samuel <u>is/was borrowing</u> his neighbor's pickup.

take   3. The manager <u>is/was taking</u> applications for five new jobs.

explore   4. The Cub Scouts <u>are/were exploring</u> the old coal mines.

inspect 5. The health officials <u>are/were inspecting</u> my apartment building.

fish 6. No one <u>was fishing</u> at the time of the accident.

talk 7. Several workers <u>are/were talking</u> about new safety procedures.

hope 8. Everyone <u>is/was hoping</u> to pass the test.

apply 9. I <u>am applying</u> the first formula to this math problem.

cook 10. The teenagers <u>are/were cooking</u> dinner for their parents.

Special Notes About Words That End with -ing

1. Words that end with *-ing* work as verb forms, known as present participles, only when they are a part of a verb phrase with a helping verb from the verb *to be*. An adverb, such as *not* or *never*, may be inserted in the verb phrase.

> She is not mailing the packages today.
> We are not sending out announcements.
> He was never running as a professional.
> They were never planning to elope.

2. To avoid *fragments*, do not try to use a present participle as a verb without using a helping verb. The result will be an incomplete verb and a sentence fragment.

> Incorrect: Eric trying to get a record deal.

> Correct: Eric was trying to get a record deal.

3. Words that end with *-ing* do not always work as verbs. Instead, they may function in sentences as nouns, which are known as **gerunds.** Gerunds name a specific activity, process, or action. Gerunds may be the subjects of sentences. Gerunds are not a part of a verb phrase and do not have helping verbs.

> Swimming is good exercise.
> [*Swimming* is a gerund.]

> We watched wrestling on television.
> [*Wrestling* is a gerund.]

> Shipping the boxes will be expensive.
> [*Shipping* is a gerund.]

4. Participles that end with *-ing* may also be adjectives. Adjectives are words in sentences that describe nouns. Be careful not to confuse these verbal adjectives with the verbs of the sentence. Verbals do not show the action that is being done by the subject and do not have helping verbs.

The boxing matches attract many young fans.
<small>adjective   noun</small>

This shipping tape is durable.
<small>adjective   noun</small>

The alarming statistics changed my mind.
<small>adjective   noun</small>

JUST SO YOU KNOW...

A verbal is a verb form that functions as a noun or an adjective, not a verb. There are three kinds of verbals:

1. Infinitives
2. Present participles
3. Past participles

Practice 11   *Identifying Subjects and Verbs*

Mark all the prepositional phrases with parentheses and the infinitives with brackets. Underline the subjects once and the verbs twice.

1. Four babies were crying (in the movie theater) (on Sunday).

2. Two (of the crying babies) were sick.

3. One elderly man was snoring loudly and whistling (through his teeth).

4. Three teenage boys were imitating the snoring man.

5. The girls (in the row) (behind me) were watching the boys.

6. Young children were running (in the aisles).

7. Parents were yelling (at the children) and telling them [to sit] down.

8. Ignoring all the activity was difficult.

9. Following the plot (of the movie) was impossible.

10. I will not be going (to Saturday matinees) (at this theater) again.

Practice 12   *Identifying Complete Sentences and Fragments*

Each of the following statements has a present participle. Write **F** for *fragment* if the statement is not a complete sentence. Write **S** for a complete *sentence* if the statement has a subject and a correct form of a verb and forms a complete thought.

_____S_____ 1. The night security was walking through the campus.

_____F_____ 2. One officer talking to the central dispatch.

_____F_____ 3. A suspicious man lurking in the bushes.

_____S_____ 4. The man was actually looking for his lost keys.

_____F_____ 5. Shining the flashlight in his face.

_____F_____ 6. The man trying to explain his situation.

_____S_____ 7. The officer was questioning the man carefully.

_____F_____ 8. The officer spotting the keys on the ground.

_____S_____ 9. The man was grinning at the security officer.

_____S_____ 10. Both men were shaking their heads.

Past Participles

Like present participles, past participles are verb forms that are used in verb phrases. The past participle is the last of the five forms of verbs shown in the chart on page 106.

PAST PARTICIPLE **A past participle is a verb form used in a verb phrase that uses a helping verb from the verb to have: have, has, or had.**

Past participles differ for regular and irregular verbs. Past participles for regular verbs use an *-ed* suffix. Past participles for irregular verbs use a different word form. Past participles create *perfect verb tenses,* which express an action that is perfected or completed within a specific time period.

PERFECT VERB TENSES	
HELPING VERB *TO HAVE* +	PAST PARTICIPLE
have, has, had, will have	+ base form with *-ed* for regular verbs or a different word form for irregular verbs

REGULAR VERBS	IRREGULAR VERBS
has rented	has spoken
have rejected	have begun
had negotiated	had shut
will have achieved	will have driven

Past participles are not the part of the verb phrase that shows the verb tense. The helping verbs in the perfect verb tenses express the present, past, or future perfect verb tense. In all perfect verb tenses, the verb phrase expresses an action that is perfected or completed within the specific time period of the present, the past, or the future. The following chart illustrates the present perfect, past perfect, and future perfect verb tenses that are constructed by using a helping verb from the verb *to have* and a past participle for a regular or an irregular verb.

Present Perfect Tense The action started in the past and continues in the present, or the action occurred at an unknown time in the past.	The Youth Council <u>has achieved</u> its goal. Everyone in my family <u>has flown</u> in a helicopter. We <u>have slept</u> under the stars. The lakes <u>have frozen</u> by now.
Past Perfect Tense The action started and ended in the past before a second action began.	The Youth Council <u>had achieved</u> its goal. Everyone in my family <u>had flown</u> in a helicopter. We <u>had slept</u> under the stars. The lake <u>had frozen</u> by then.
Future Perfect Tense The action will start and end in the future before a second action in the future begins.	The Youth Council <u>will have achieved</u> its goal. Everyone in my family <u>will have flown</u> in a helicopter. We <u>will have slept</u> under the stars. The lakes <u>will have frozen</u> by then.

Notice the difference in meaning in the following sentences. Simple present tense shows that the action occurs at the present time. Present perfect shows that an action started in the past and continues in the present. The same slight differences in meaning also occur for past and future tenses.

Simple present tense: She <u>completes</u> her homework by eight o'clock.

Present perfect tense: She <u>has completed</u> her homework by eight o'clock.

Simple past tense: I <u>called</u> my mother yesterday.

Past perfect tense: I <u>had called</u> my mother yesterday.

Simple future tense: The men <u>will lift</u> weights in the gym.

Present perfect tense: The men <u>will have lifted</u> weights in the gym.

The past participles for regular verbs are made by adding *-ed* to the base form of the verb. Notice that the past participles for regular verbs are the same verb form used for simple past tense.

REGULAR VERBS		
BASE FORM	SIMPLE PAST	PAST PARTICIPLE
The base form is the infinitive form.	The simple past tense for regular verbs has an *-ed* suffix.	The past participle for a regular verb has an *-ed* suffix and is used in a verb phrase with a helping verb from the verb *to have.* The helping verb expresses the verb tense.
to create	created	has created, have created, had created, will have created
to jog	jogged	has jogged, have jogged, had jogged, will have jogged

Irregular verbs do not use *-ed* to make a simple past tense. They also do not use *-ed* to make the past participle. For some irregular verbs, the past participle is the same word that is used for the simple past tense. However, for many other irregular verbs, a different word is used for the past participle. Refer to the list of past participles of irregular verbs on pages 128–130.

The following examples show three forms of irregular verbs: base form, simple past tense, and past participle. The fourth column uses the past participle in a verb phrase with a helping verb from the verb *to have.*

IRREGULAR VERBS			
BASE FORM	SIMPLE PAST TENSE	PAST PARTICIPLE	PERFECT TENSE VERB
to speak	spoke	spoken	has spoken, have spoken, had spoken, will have spoken
to go	went	gone	has gone, have gone, had gone, will have gone
to begin	began	begun	has begun, have begun, had begun, will have begun
to steal	stole	stolen	has stolen, have stolen, had stolen, will have stolen

Practice 13   *Reciting the Verb Forms*

Work with a partner for this reciting practice. Take turns reciting from the list of past participles of irregular verbs beginning below. Randomly select twenty infinitives to give to your partner. Ask your partner to recite the base form, the past tense, and the past participle without looking at the page. Then reverse roles so both partners have the opportunity to recite. Reciting should follow this pattern:

Base Form	Past Tense	Past Participle
begin	began	begun
choose	chose	chosen
give	gave	given

Tip: Practice this form of reciting frequently until you are familiar with the verb forms for these irregular verbs. To practice by yourself, cover up the past tense and the past participle when you recite. Then remove the paper to check your accuracy. Place a check mark next to the verb forms you need to continue to practice.

PAST PARTICIPLES OF IRREGULAR VERBS

Infinitive (base form)	Past (simple past)	Past Participle (Use with *has, have, had, will have*)	Infinitive (base form)	Past (simple past)	Past Participle (Use with *has, have, had, will have*)
abide	abode/abided	abode	cast	cast	cast
arise	arose	arisen	catch	caught	caught
awake	awoke	awaked	choose	chose	chosen
bear	bore	born, borne	cling	clung	clung
beat	beat	beat, beaten	come	came	come
become	became	become	cost	cost	cost
begin	began	begun	creep	crept	crept
bend	bent	bent	cut	cut	cut
bid	bid (offer), bade (command)	bid (offer), bidden (command)	deal	dealt	dealt
			dig	dug	dug
bind	bound	bound	dive	dove, dived	dived
bite	bit	bit, bitten	do	did	done
bleed	bled	bled	draw	drew	drawn
blow	blew	blown	dream	dreamed, dreamt	dreamed, dreamt
break	broke	broken			
bring	brought	brought	drink	drank	drunk
broadcast	broadcast	broadcast	drive	drove	driven
build	built	built	eat	ate	eaten
burst	burst	burst	fall	fell	fallen
buy	bought	bought	feed	fed	fed

(Continue on page 129)

PAST PARTICIPLES OF IRREGULAR VERBS

Infinitive (base form)	Past (simple past)	Past Participle (Use with *has, have, had, will have*)	Infinitive (base form)	Past (simple past)	Past Participle (Use with *has, have, had, will have*)
feel	felt	felt	mean	meant	meant
fight	fought	fought	meet	met	met
find	found	found	pay	paid	paid
flee	fled	fled	prove	proved	proved, proven
fling	flung	flung	put	put	put
fly	flew	flown	quit	quit	quit
forbid	forbade,	forbidden	read	read	read
	forbad	forbid	rid	rid, ridded	rid, ridded
forget	forgot	forgotten,	ride	rode	ridden
		forgot	ring	rang	rung
forsake	forsook	forsaken	rise	rose	risen
freeze	froze	frozen	run	ran	run
get	got	got, gotten	say	said	said
give	gave	given	see	saw	seen
go	went	gone	seek	sought	sought
grind	ground	ground	sell	sold	sold
grow	grew	grown	send	sent	sent
hang (an object)	hung	hung	set	set	set
have	had	had	sew	sewed	sewed, sewn
hear	heard	heard	shake	shook	shaken
hide	hid	hidden, hid	shine	shone	shone
hit	hit	hit	shoot	shot	shot
hold	held	held	show	showed	shown, showed
hurt	hurt	hurt	shrink	shrank,	shrunk,
keep	kept	kept		shrunk	shrunken
knit	knit, knitted	knit, knitted	shut	shut	shut
know	knew	known	sing	sang	sung
lay	laid	laid	sink	sank	sunk
lead	led	led	sit	sat	sat
leave	left	left	slay	slew	slain
lend	lent	lent	sleep	slept	slept
lie (recline)	lay	lain	slide	slid	slid
light	lit	lit, lighted	sling	slung	slung
lose	lost	lost	slink	slunk	slunk
make	made	made	slit	slit	slit

(Continue on page 130)

PAST PARTICIPLES OF IRREGULAR VERBS

Infinitive (base form)	Past (simple past)	Past Participle (Use with *has, have, had, will have*)	Infinitive (base form)	Past (simple past)	Past Participle (Use with *has, have, had, will have*)
sneak	sneaked, snuck	sneaked, snuck	swim	swam	swum
			swing	swung	swung
speak	spoke	spoken	take	took	taken
speed	sped	sped	teach	taught	taught
spend	spent	spent	tear	tore	torn
spin	spun	spun	tell	told	told
spread	spread	spread	think	thought	thought
spring	sprang, sprung	sprung	thrive	thrived, throve	thrived, thriven
stand	stood	stood			
steal	stole	stolen	throw	threw	thrown
stick	stuck	stuck	thrust	thrust	thrust
sting	stung	stung	understand	understood	understood
stink	stank, stunk	stunk	wake	woke	waked
stride	strode	stridden	wear	wore	worn
strike	struck	struck, stricken	weave	wove	woven
string	strung	strung	weep	wept	wept
strive	strove	striven, strived	win	won	won
swear	swore	sworn	wring	wrung	wrung
sweep	swept	swept	write	wrote	written

Practice 14   *Identifying Subjects and Perfect Tense Verbs*

Mark the prepositional phrases with parentheses and the infinitives with brackets. Underline the subjects once and the verbs twice. Be sure to watch for compound subjects and compound verbs.

1. The <u>drivers</u> <u><u>will have raced</u></u> (for five hours).

2. Our maternal <u>grandmother</u> <u><u>had reached</u></u> her one-hundredth birthday.

3. The solar <u>eclipse</u> <u><u>has appeared</u></u> (for the first time) this century.

4. The overhead <u>transparencies</u> and the colored <u>pens</u> <u><u>have improved</u></u> her lectures.

5. <u>Marcus</u> <u><u>had mastered</u></u> the game (of cribbage) (at an early age).

6. The grieving <u>widow</u> <u>had wanted</u> [to sell] her home.

7. The <u>roses</u> and the <u>daisies</u> (in the vase) <u>had wilted</u> (after one week).

8. The rushing <u>waters</u> <u>have overflowed</u> their banks and <u>flooded</u> the small town.

9. The taxi <u>driver</u> and the <u>passenger</u> <u>had exchanged</u> angry words.

10. <u>Rosie</u> and <u>Patrick</u> <u>will have dated</u> (for four years).

Practice 15   *Using Past Participles Correctly*

In each sentence below, draw two lines under the correct form of the verb to complete the verb phrase. Each verb phrase has a helping verb from the verb *to have*. You may refer to the past participle chart of irregular verbs on pages 128–130 to check the accuracy of your answers.

1. The rebels had (broke, <u>broken</u>) through the lines and entered the village.

2. They had (shooted, <u>shot</u>) and killed many people.

3. They had (<u>stolen</u>, stole) the livestock and personal belongings.

4. Many villagers had (fleed, <u>fled</u>) without taking many belongings.

5. They have (<u>gone</u>, went) to the other side of the mountain.

6. The village will have (<u>shrunk</u>, shrank) to a few dozen people.

7. Has the time (came, <u>come</u>) for help from the United Nations?

8. The wandering villagers have (became, <u>become</u>) hungry and weary.

9. The loss of their village has (took, <u>taken</u>) a heavy toll on them.

10. The children have not (<u>eaten</u>, ate) or (<u>drunk</u>, drank) for two days.

11. They have (sleeped, <u>slept</u>) on the hard ground without blankets.

12. The villagers have (chose, <u>chosen</u>) a leader to meet with the rebels.

13. The two sides have not (spoke, <u>spoken</u>) to each other before.

14. Perhaps the dispute has (hurted, <u>hurt</u>) both sides too much.

15. Both sides have (saw, <u>seen</u>) the need to end the fighting.

Practice 16   *Using Simple Past Tense and Participles*

Work with a partner, in a small group, or on your own for this practice with verb forms. Use the verb shown in the margin. First, write the simple past tense; then, in the second sentence, write the past participle to complete a verb phrase.

Example: see   The pilots _____saw_____ the cloud formations in the distance.
The pilots had _____seen_____ the cloud formations in the distance.

become   1. The hikers _____became_____ weary after hiking all day.
The hikers will have _____become_____ weary after hiking all day.

freeze   2. The water on the pond _____froze_____ overnight.
The water on the pond had _____frozen_____ overnight.

grow   3. The tomatoes in my garden _____grew_____ four inches.
The tomatoes in my garden will have _____grown_____ four inches.

hold   4. We _____held_____ on tightly to the side of the boat.
We had _____held_____ on tightly to the side of the boat.

feed   5. The mother _____fed_____ the children earlier in the day.
The mother had _____fed_____ the children earlier in the day.

cast   6. The fly fishermen _____cast_____ their lines into the river.
The fly fishermen have _____cast_____ their lines into the river.

forget   7. I _____forgot_____ your name.
I have _____forgotten_____ your name.

eat   8. No one _____ate_____ the contaminated salad.
No one had _____eaten_____ the contaminated salad.

Additional Verb Phrases

Chapter 4 introduced the four kinds of helping verbs: *to be, to have, to do,* and then a group of words that are always helping verbs. Only two forms of helping verbs remain to be discussed: verbs from the verb *to do* and the helping verbs, called *modals,* that work only as helping verbs to form verb phrases.

Verb Phrases with Helping Verbs From the Verb *To Do*

The pattern for a verb phrase that includes a helping verb from the verb *to do* is shown below. The helping verb forms *do, does,* or *did* express the verb tense. *Do* is used for sentences in the present tense with subjects that are first-person, second-person, or third-person plural. *Does* is used for sentences in the present tense with subjects that are third-person singular. *Did* is used for past tense.

HELPING VERB	+	BASE FORM [INFINITIVE]
do		wash
do		owe
does		care
does		earn
did		enjoy
did		exchange

Verb phrases with a helping verb from the verb *to do* work in three ways:

1. They are often used to construct interrogative sentences.

   Do you <u>intend</u> to make a reservation?

   Does she <u>organize</u> her lectures well?

   Did you <u>cancel</u> the magazine subscription?

2. They are used in declarative sentences with a negative adverb, such as *not*.

   I <u>do</u> not <u>spend</u> my money foolishly.

   The train <u>does</u> not <u>stop</u> on 43rd Street.

   We <u>did</u> not <u>like</u> the service at that restaurant.

3. They are used for emphasis. This is called an *emphatic* form.

   I <u>do want</u> to get an interview.

   She <u>does inspire</u> others.

   They <u>did recover</u> the bodies from the river.

Practice 17   *Identifying Verb Phrases*

In the following sentences, mark the prepositional phrases with parentheses and the infinitives with brackets. Underline the subjects once and the verbs twice. Remember, if the sentence has a verb phrase, you must underline the helping verb and the main verb.

1. I do not intend [to enroll] (in school) (during the summer).

2. Do you plan [to attend] summer school?

3. We had never seen a solar eclipse.

4. The defense attorney had proven her innocence (in front of a jury).

5. The professor does give difficult exams.

6. All (of the speakers) will have spoken (to the council members) (at the public forum).

7. I have not swept the kitchen floor this week.

8. The neighbors will be having a huge garage sale (on Saturday).

9. My parents had known all along.

10. Someone (in the cafeteria) had stolen my favorite compact disk.

11. The ducks and the geese had swum (near the docks).

12. The mourners had wept (for a long time) (at the grave).

13. Three (of the freshmen) did elect [to live] (off campus).

14. Have the nuns organized this event (in the past)?

15. The dean had posted the message and made the announcement.

Modals: Words That Are Always Helping Verbs

The final group of helping verbs, sometimes referred to as **modals,** are always helping verbs. The verb phrase expresses the verb in the following pattern:

HELPING VERB	+	BASE FORM
would		create
should		consider
might		play
must		clean
could		pretend
will		respond
can		attend
may		invite
shall		order

Modals provide writers with helping verbs that can be used to show different degrees of certainty, obligation, suggestion, or necessity. Selecting the best modal, or helping verb, depends on the conditions or situations expressed in your sentences. Review the list of modals and their meanings in the following chart. Notice that the verb phrase is made by joining the helping verb and the base form without any suffixes.

MODALS (HELPING VERBS)		
MODAL (HELPING VERB)	SHOWS . . .	EXAMPLES
can	ability	I can ride a bike.
could	condition	I could learn to ride a bike if I had more time.
would		I would ride my bike if it did not have a flat tire.
may	permission	May I please ride my bike to school today?
may	uncertainty	If it does not rain, I may ride my bike.
might		If I get up early enough, I might ride my bike.
must	necessity	I missed the bus, so I must ride my bike to school.
should	obligation	I should ride my bike in order to get some exercise.
will shall	intention	I will ride my bike tomorrow. Shall I ride my bike?

Special Notes About Modals

1. Modals often appear at the beginning of questions that ask permission, ask a favor, question an ability, or seek advice. The modal *will* is used to form the future tense.

INTERROGATIVE PATTERN

helping verb + subject + base form

May I call you tomorrow?
Can you run a five-minute mile?
Could you mail this package for me?
Should I tell the truth?
Must you smoke inside?
Would you drive the children to school today?
Will she marry Richard?

2. Modals that include a form of the helping verb *to have* require the use of the past participle.

Incorrect: I could have went to the fair on Friday.
Correct: I could have *gone* to the fair on Friday.

Incorrect: He should have drove the truck.
Correct: He should have *driven* the truck.

Incorrect: They may have drank the contaminated juice.
Correct: They may have *drunk* the contaminated juice.

3. **Contractions,** or shortened word forms, are created by joining two words together. An apostrophe indicates the place where letters have been omitted, usually in the second word. Avoid using contractions in formal writing; use the two separate words instead. In the following examples, notice that the adverb *not* (or its contracted form, *-n't*) is not included in the complete verb when you identify and underline verb phrases. For more information about contractions, see Appendix A.

Mandy should have taken the test yesterday.

Mandy should've taken the test yesterday.

Sammy could have thrown the ball farther.

Sammy could've thrown the ball farther.

You should not teach her bad habits.

You shouldn't teach her bad habits.

The receptionist did not recognize me.

The receptionist didn't recognize me.

4. Because of careless pronunciation, people often mistakenly write *of* instead of the helping verb *have* in verb phrases. The confusion probably stems from the similarity of sounds when the contraction -*'ve* is used for *have.*

Incorrect: You should *of* given him the answer.
Correct: You should *have* given him the answer.
Correct: You should*'ve* given him the answer.

Incorrect: She could *of* hidden the diary.
Correct: She could *have* hidden the diary.
Correct: She could*'ve* hidden the diary.

Practice 18   *Forming Verb Phrases*

In each of the following sentences, draw two lines under the correct verb form. Pay close attention to the helping verb when you make your selection. You may refer to the following chart of helping verbs to review the formation of verb phrases.

HAS, HAVE, HAD	DO, DOES, DID	MODALS (COULD, SHOULD, WOULD, ETC.)	MODAL + HAVE OR HAD
Use with the past participle.	Use with the base form (infinitive) without a suffix.	Use with the base form (infinitive) without a suffix.	Use with the past participle.

1. The explorer (had chose, <u>had chosen</u>) to move westward.

2. Mrs. Levins (could of, <u>could have</u>) already collected the money.

3. Malcolm (has edit, <u>has edited</u>) the manuscript.

4. The swimmer (must of set, <u>must have set</u>) a new school record.

5. The captain (had chose, <u>had chosen</u>) his crew.

6. The drivers (should have saw, <u>should have seen</u>) the road signs.

7. They (<u>had gone</u>, had went) to the park for a family picnic.

8. The poker player (had dealed, <u>had dealt</u>) the cards too quickly.

9. Robert's car (<u>must have cost</u>, must of cost) a lot of money.

10. The sponsors of the contest (must have gave, <u>must have given</u>) a million dollars.

11. The young child (<u>had stolen,</u> had stole) candy from the store.

12. You should not (have drank, <u>have drunk</u>) so much in the restaurant.

13. We (<u>had dived,</u> had dove) into the icy water.

14. By this time last year, we (had swam, <u>had swum</u>) across the lake already.

15. The tree branch (had broke, <u>had broken</u>) during the storm.

C O M M A   S E N S E

Use a comma between three or more verb phrases that tell the action of the subject. Note that the helping verb may be understood but not directly stated. When the same helping verb is used in each verb phrase, the helping verb does not need to be repeated.

> The rescue <u>workers</u> <u>had arrived</u> at noon, [had] <u>set up</u> a communication post, and [had] <u>organized</u> crews immediately.

> The rodeo clowns <u>were yelling</u> loudly, [were] <u>waving</u> their hands, and [were] <u>distracting</u> the raging bull.

> The drivers <u>are starting</u> their engines, [are] <u>moving</u> toward the line, and [are] <u>preparing</u> themselves mentally for a long race.

EXERCISE 5.1 Rabies Name _____ Date _____

Work with a partner, in a small group, or on your own for this activity. In the following article, mark the prepositional phrases with parentheses and the infinitives with brackets. Underline the subjects once and the complete verbs twice.

RABIES

Rabid animals are carriers (of the deadly rabies virus). (In most parts) (of the world), dogs are the main carriers (of rabies). More than 40,000 people worldwide die annually (from rabid dog bites). Leash laws, quarantines (of sick dogs), and the use (of rabies shots) (for dogs) (in the United States) have made deaths (from dog bites) almost nonexistent. Consequently, this deadly disease is seldom carried (in the United States) (by dogs or other domestic pets). Instead, rabies (in the United States) is more prevalent (in the skunk, raccoon, and bat populations). However, bites (from rabid skunks or raccoons) seldom result (in death). Usually people are very aware (of bites) (from skunks or raccoons). They tend [to seek] the series (of rabies shots) (from doctors or hospitals).

Bats are now the chief spreader (of the rabies virus) (in the United States). (For that reason), doctors advise people never [to handle] bats. The small, sharp teeth (of this flying mammal) can pierce the flesh (of a person) and leave no visible wounds. (Without the series of rabies shots), a bite (from any rabid animal) will likely result (in death). This virus attacks the nerve endings (in the skin) and spreads (throughout the brain). Common symptoms include fever, involuntary muscle movements, inability [to swallow], shallow breathing, and low blood pressure. (After any bite) (from any animal), a person should consult a doctor (for further testing and possible treatment).

[Adapted from Daniel Haney, AP, "Tests Trace Rabies Sources, Including Bats," *Register Guard*, October 17, 1999.]

Complete the following sentences with simple past, present, or future verb tenses. Use the correct form of the verb that is shown at the beginning of the sentence. The simple past tense and the simple present tense verbs must be expressed as a one-word verb. The simple future tense requires a verb phrase. Use the context of the sentence to determine the most appropriate verb tense.

Example: write   My father ____wrote____ to all the family members last week.

switch   1. I accidentally ____switched____ the two cables.

think   2. Mark ____thought____ seriously about the promotion for an entire week.

weave   3. The Navajo women ____wove____ these beautiful rugs last year.

steal   4. Two young girls ____stole____ the purses last Saturday.

cut   5. Marsha ____will cut____ her long hair next week.

cram   6. Only three students ____crammed____ over the weekend for today's test.

propel   7. The remote ____propels/propelled____ the model airplane.

stink   8. The garbage ____stank____ and needed to be removed immediately.

shoot   9. Two hunters ____shot____ an elk on Friday near Iron Mountain.

spin   10. The car ____spun____ out of control and caused a pileup.

refuse   11. The car dealers ____refused____ to discuss the current accusations at today's press conference.

present   12. The college ____will present____ the award at the end of this month.

bleed   13. The dog ____bled____ on the carpet and licked his wounded paw.

deal   14. Uncle Joe ____dealt____ himself a great poker hand and won.

begin   15. My cousin ____began____ his apprenticeship program last September.

EXERCISE 5.3   **Subject-Verb Agreement**   Name _____ Date _____

Write the correct verb forms of the simple present tense for the following sentences. Use the verb shown at the beginning of each sentence.

Examples: observe   The test proctor at my university _____observes_____ every student carefully.

hurry   Morning commuters _____hurry_____ to work along the freeway systems.

hate   1. The members of the orchestra _____hate_____ the eight o'clock rehearsals.

waste   2. Many people _____waste_____ a lot of food every day.

flatten   3. The heavy machinery _____flattens_____ the scrap metal.

stretch   4. Joseph _____stretches_____ the wet rawhide to make authentic drums.

plug   5. The kitchen sink _____plugs_____ up at least once a week.

recede   6. The floodwaters of the Siuslaw River always _____recede_____ in due time.

reduce   7. Eating less fat _____reduces_____ the risk of high cholesterol.

copy   8. My secretary _____copies_____ her work onto backup files.

piece   9. Grandma _____pieces_____ together her quilts with great care.

shield   10. Many parents _____shield_____ their children from violent movies.

believe   11. The members of the school board _____believe_____ your story.

envy   12. Lisa _____envies_____ her roommate's athletic abilities.

progress   13. The research work for a cure for cancer _____progresses_____ a little each year.

yield   14. Your latest investment _____yields_____ a monthly profit.

grieve   15. The family members _____grieve_____ the loss of the young child.

EXERCISE 5.4 **Selecting Verbs** Name _____ Date _____

Read each sentence carefully. Mark the prepositional phrases with parentheses and the infinitives with brackets. Underline the subjects with one line. Draw two lines under the correct verb for each sentence and also under any helping verbs that complete the verb phrase.

Examples: The bank (lended, lent) me the money [to buy] a new truck.
The people (in my neighborhood) (conducts, conduct) annual garage sales.

1. The architects (on the project) have (draw, drawn) hundreds (of blueprints).

2. The snow (on the roads) (melts, melt) (in the early spring).

3. The actress had (lay, laid) her gown carefully (on the bed).

4. Lydia (become, became) the first All-American (at my high school).

5. Sam and I had (flinged, flung) our hats (into the air).

6. We had (went, gone) (to the coast)(for the weekend).

7. We had (bade, bidden) farewell (for the last time).

8. (Do, Does) the drummers compete (in many powwows)?

9. Sponsors (of the scholarship)(wants, want) [to meet] the recipients.

10. The bell had (rang, rung) three times.

11. The newspapers and the magazines (cover, covers) the same current events.

12. My father had (casted, cast) his line (into the water).

13. I have (became, become) very skeptical (of special offers)(for new credit cards).

14. Adversity had (fell, fallen) (on the family)(for a second time) (in the same year).

15. The bats (in the old barn)(fly, flies)(at night).

EXERCISE 5.5 Sentence Writing   Name _____ Date _____

On a separate piece of paper, follow the directions below to write sentences that use different verb tenses. Use the following chart as a reference.

simple present:	The birds <u>fly</u> south for the winter.
present progressive:	The birds <u>are flying</u> south for the winter.
present perfect:	The birds <u>have flown</u> south for the winter.
simple past:	The birds <u>flew</u> south for the winter.
past progressive:	The birds <u>were flying</u> south for the winter.
past perfect:	The birds <u>had flown</u> south for the winter.
simple future:	The birds <u>will fly</u> south for the winter.
future progressive:	The birds <u>will be flying</u> south for the winter.
future perfect:	The birds <u>will have flown</u> south for the winter.

1. Use the verb *sweep* in simple present tense. sweep, sweeps

2. Use the verb *shake* in past perfect tense. had shaken

3. Use the verb *split* in present progressive tense. is/are splitting

4. Use the verb *drink* in past perfect tense. had drunk

5. Use the verb *break* in present perfect tense. has/have broken

6. Use the verb *build* in simple past tense. built

7. Use the verb *ring* in future progressive tense. will be ringing

8. Use the verb *mean* in simple future tense. will mean

9. Use the verb *sneak* in past progressive tense. was/were sneaking

10. Use the verb *think* in future perfect tense. will have thought

Each sentence has one word in bold print. On the line, write the part of speech for that word. Use these abbreviations for your answers:

N = noun   V = verb   Prep = preposition   Pro = pronoun

Examples: _N_   **Gerunds** are a special kind of noun.
             _V_   He **should** complete his electives as soon as possible.
             Pro Majoring in history is a wise choice for **you.**

_____V_____   1. The doctor **showed** them my x-ray.

____Pro____   2. The doctor had shown **them** my x-ray.

_____V_____   3. The boys **sneaked** out of their dorm rooms.

_____V_____   4. The boys **had** snuck out of their dorm rooms.

____Pro____   5. **Everyone** at the party had drunk nonalcoholic beverages.

_____V_____   6. Everyone at the party **drank** nonalcoholic beverages.

_____V_____   7. The masked man had **sprung** out of the bushes.

_____N_____   8. The masked man sprang out of the **bushes.**

_____V_____   9. All of the contestants **strove** for top scores.

_____N_____   10. All of the **contestants** had striven for top scores.

____Prep___   11. The young boys had shaken the apples **from** the tree.

_____N_____   12. The girls shook their heads in **disbelief.**

_____V_____   13. The clocks were **ticking** throughout the store.

_____V_____   14. The sound of running water **relaxes** me.

_____N_____   15. **Shopping** can be tedious.

Chapter 5 Summary

1. **Action verbs, linking verbs,** and **helping verbs** are the three kinds of verbs.

2. The term **number** indicates whether the subject is singular or plural. The term **person** indicates whether the subject is speaking, spoken to, or spoken about. **First, second,** and **third person** can be singular or plural. Understanding the number and the person in sentences helps you select the correct verb form, so sentences have subject-verb agreement.

3. **Third-person singular** in simple present tense requires special attention. To have subject-verb agreement, a singular subject requires a verb with an *-s* or an *-es* suffix. A plural subject requires a verb that does not have an *-s* or an *-es* suffix.

4. The five forms of verbs are: **infinitive, present tense, past tense, present participle,** and **past participle.** One-word verbs express the *simple present tense* and the *simple past tense. Simple future tense* is expressed as a verb phrase with the helping verb *will.*

5. **Regular verbs** are verbs that use an *-ed* suffix to make the simple past tense and past participle. **Irregular verbs** are verbs that do not use an *-ed* suffix to make the simple past tense or past participle; a different form of the verb makes the simple past tense.

6. You can review irregular verb forms by reciting the main verb forms in this order: base form - past tense - past participle.

   Example: sing – sang – sung

7. Verb phrases consist of helping verbs plus present participles and past participles. The helping verbs determine the verb tense. Present participles consist of the base verb + an *-ing* suffix. Past participles consist of the base verb + an *-ed* suffix or a special form of the verb that does not use an *-ed* suffix. Chapter 5 discusses four kinds of verb phrases:

Progressive verbs:	helping verbs from the verb *to be* + the present participle
	Example: are writing
Perfect verbs:	helping verbs from the verb *to have* + the past participle
	Example: has written
Phrases with *to do:*	helping verbs from *to do* + a base form of a verb
	Example: do write
Phrases with modals:	helping *modal* verbs + a base form of a verb.
	Example: could write

8. Words that end with an *-ing* suffix are not always verbs. Sometimes the words may function as nouns (called **gerunds**) or as adjectives

9. Commas should be used between three or more verb phrases that tell the action of the subject.

Writing Topics for Chapter 5

Select one of the writing options below. Write one or two paragraphs about this topic. Proofread the draft of your paper before you turn it in.

1. Discuss a frightening experience you had that involved an encounter with a wild or a domestic animal. Have you ever been threatened by a bat, a bear, a wild boar, a moose, or a skunk? Have you ever encountered a vicious dog that was possibly rabid? Use ample details to describe your experience and the ultimate outcome.

 2. Use the library or the Internet to locate information about the rabies virus or bats. Print a copy of the article you locate and attach it to your paper. Summarize the interesting information that you learned by reading the article.

 3. People can have many kinds of fears or phobias. Use the Internet, the library, or one of your textbooks to learn more about different kinds of phobias. Select one phobia to discuss in one or two paragraphs. How does such a phobia begin? What are some of the characteristic reactions? Are there ways the phobia can be overcome?

4. Select an interesting newspaper or magazine article about a current event. Assume the role of a teacher. Use the word *what, why,* or *how* to write one question about the main idea or content of the article. Then write a paragraph with details to answer your own question. Attach the article to your written work.

Web Site Learning Experiences

See the web site for this book to locate companion exercises and links related to the grammar and writing topics in this chapter.

Go to: http://college.hmco.com. Click on "Students." Type *Sentence Essentials* in the "Jump to Textbook Sites" box. Click "go" and then bookmark the site. Click on Chapter 5.

CHAPTER 5 • Review   Name _____ Date _____

Total Possible: 50   Your Score: _____

Part I: Identification of Subjects and Verbs   (20 points)

Underline the subjects with one line and the complete verbs with two lines. Give 1 point for the subject(s) and 1 for the verb(s) (2 points per sentence).

1. Her <u>mood</u> <u>was getting</u> serious.

2. The career <u>counselors</u> from all the high schools <u>had</u> not <u>met</u> for many months.

3. <u>We</u> <u>were yelling</u> and <u>waving</u> our hands to get the police officer's attention.

4. The <u>technician</u> <u>is installing</u> new software and <u>upgrading</u> the hard drive.

5. <u>Have</u> <u>any</u> of you <u>swum</u> in the Mississippi River?

6. My <u>brother</u> and my <u>sister</u> <u>have bused</u> tables at the local diner.

7. The <u>refugees</u> <u>fled</u> from the village on foot.

8. <u>You</u> <u>should have notified</u> your sister about the delay.

9. The math <u>group</u> <u>did</u> not <u>meet</u> on Saturday at Jim's house.

10. The track and field <u>judges</u> <u>had strung</u> the blue ribbon across the finish line.

Part II: Identification of Past Tense and Past Participles   (20 points)

The base form of a verb is shown in the first column. Write the simple past tense in the second column and the past participle in the third column. Give $\frac{1}{2}$ point per blank line.

Infinitive	Past Tense	Past Participle	Infinitive	Past Tense	Past Participle
1. break	broke	broken	4. fight	fought	fought
2. teach	taught	taught	5. freeze	froze	frozen
3. cost	cost	cost	6. tear	tore	torn

7. run   __ran__   __run__   14. smile   __smiled__   __smiled__

8. draw   __drew__   __drawn__   15. forget   __forgot__   __forgotten__

9. cut   __cut__   __cut__   16. enjoy   __enjoyed__   __enjoyed__

10. fall   __fell__   __fallen__   17. plan   __planned__   __planned__

11. take   __took__   __taken__   18. attend   __attended__   __attended__

12. shake   __shook__   __shaken__   19. choose   __chose__   __chosen__

13. begin   __began__   __begun__   20. slide   __slid__   __slid__

Part III: Proofreading   (10 points)

Proofread the following paragraph for ten verb errors. Correct the errors by writing the correct verb form above the errors. Give 1 point per correction.

For honeybees, swarming is a natural reproductive process. A mature bee colony typically ~~divide~~ [divides] into two units. One unit is called the reproductive unit. The other unit of bees ~~are~~ [is] called the parental colony. The reproductive unit is known as a swarm. The swarm ~~have~~ [has] one queen bee, a few drones, thousands of worker bees, and scout bees. The swarm ~~depart~~ [departs] the parental cavity, such as a hollow tree, to find a new temporary home. The experienced scout workers comb the countryside for a temporary home and then ~~searches~~ [search] for a permanent home near rich food sources. The mass of thousands of bees then ~~take~~ [takes] flight for the new home. The scouts ~~leads~~ [lead] the way and the swarm ~~follow~~ [follows]. The queen bee mates with the male bees, the drones. She may mate with up to seventeen drones over a two-day period. After the two days, she never mates again. The worker bees in the colony forage for nectar and pollen. They also ~~fed~~ [feed] and groom the queen bee. The second unit, the parental colony, ~~rear~~ [rears] a replacement queen. The reproductive process of the honeybees once again begins in the parental colony.

[Adapted from Gears: Internet Classroom http://gears.tucson.ars.ag.gov]

CHAPTER 6

Pronouns and Pronoun Agreement

In Chapter 6, you will learn about **pronouns,** which are words that rename or replace nouns. You will learn to use four kinds of personal pronouns as well as indefinite pronouns. Subject-verb agreement and pronoun-antecedent agreement are included in this chapter.

Understanding pronouns will help you do the following:

1. Avoid common writing errors with subject-verb and pronoun-antecedent agreement

2. Understand why pronouns can work as different parts of speech in sentences

3. Identify and write compound and complex sentences with more than one subject-verb combination

PRONOUN   **A pronoun replaces or renames a noun that has been previously mentioned.**

Pronouns serve many different functions in sentences. You have already completed some work with pronouns in previous chapters. This chapter will expand your understanding of pronouns and their functions in sentences. The following chart summarizes the various categories of pronouns. (See the Index in the back of this book to locate more information about each pronoun category.)

KINDS OF PRONOUNS							
SUBJECTIVE	OBJECTIVE	POSSESSIVE	REFLEXIVE	INDEFINITE	DEMONSTRATIVE	INTERROGATIVE	RELATIVE
singular:	*singular:*	*Before a noun:*	*singular:*	*singular:**	*singular:*	who	who
I	me	*singular:*	myself	anybody	this	whom	whom
you	you	my	yourself	each	that	whose	whose
yours	him	your	himself	either	*plural:*	which	which
he	her	his	herself	everyone	these	what	that
she	it	her	itself	neither	those		
it		its	oneself	no one			
plural:	*plural:*						
we	us	*plural:*	*plural:*	*plural:*			
you	you	our	ourselves	both			
yours	them	your	yourselves	few			
they		their	themselves	many			
				others			
		After a linking verb:		several			
		singular:		*singular or plural:*			
		mine		all			
		yours		any			
		his		more			
		hers		most			
		plural:		none			
		ours		some			
		yours					
		theirs					

*See page 164 for a complete list of singular indefinite pronouns.

Pronouns eliminate redundancy and boredom for the reader by replacing already mentioned nouns. In the following examples, notice the awkwardness of the sentences that include the same noun repeatedly. Then notice how pronouns make the sentences shorter, smoother, more interesting, and easier to read. Pronouns appear in italics.

Redundant use of nouns:	Payne Stewart was a popular golfer. Payne Stewart died in a plane crash in 1999. Payne Stewart, along with the pilot and the passengers in Payne Stewart's plane, lost consciousness.
Pronouns replace some nouns:	Payne Stewart was a popular golfer. *He* died in a plane crash in 1999. *He,* along with the pilot and the passengers in *his* plane, lost consciousness.
Redundant use of nouns:	Mary grew many tomatoes in Mary's garden. The tomatoes were ripe and juicy. Mary made tomato juice, and Mary canned the tomato juice. However, after several months, the tomato juice lost the tomato juice's flavor. Mary then used the tomato juice for cooking instead of drinking.
Pronouns replace some nouns:	Mary grew many tomatoes in *her* garden. The tomatoes were ripe and juicy. *She* made tomato juice and canned *it.* However, after several months, *it* lost *its* flavor. Mary then used *it* for cooking instead of drinking.
Redundant use of nouns:	Marcus, Troy, Brent, and Rory planned a trip together. Marcus, Troy, Brent, and Rory wanted to spend some time together without Marcus's, Troy's, Brent's, and Rory's other friends. Marcus, Troy, Brent, and Rory wanted to spend a weekend together at a lodge in the mountains. Marcus, Troy, Brent, and Rory made arrangements to go the first weekend in November.
Pronouns replace some nouns:	Marcus, Troy, Brent, and Rory planned planned a trip together. *They* wanted to spend some time together without *their* other friends. *They* wanted to spend a weekend together at a lodge in the mountains. *They* made arrangements to go the first weekend in November.

CASE   The term *case* refers to the relationship of a word to the other parts of a sentence. The relationship shows how the word functions in the sentence.

The three case forms for pronouns are nominative, objective, and possessive.

1. In the **nominative case,** also referred to as **subjective case,** the pronoun functions as the subject of the sentence. In Chapter 4 (page 67), you learned about pronouns as subjects of sentences.

2. In the **objective case,** the pronoun functions as a direct or indirect object of the verb or the object of the preposition. In Chapter 3 (page 48), you learned that some pronouns can be used to end a prepositional phrase as objects of the preposition. In this chapter, you will learn that pronouns may also work as direct and indirect objects in sentences with transitive verbs (pages 156–157).

3. In the **possessive case,** the pronoun signals ownership. In Chapter 2 (page 17), you learned that possessive pronouns can function as noun markers.

Four Kinds of Personal Pronouns

PERSONAL PRONOUN   A personal pronoun identifies the person speaking or the person who is spoken to or spoken about. Personal pronouns may also refer to places, things, or ideas.

There are four kinds of personal pronouns:

1. Subjective pronouns—the subjects of sentences:

    I often send birthday gifts to family members.

    He acknowledges my gifts.

    We exchange gifts at Christmas.

    They always receive the gifts early.

2. Objective pronouns—the objects of prepositions, direct objects, or indirect objects:

    I sent the gift (to *him*).

    She wrapped the boxes (for *us*).

    Cindy loved *it*.

    She thanked *me* for the gift.

    Marla baked *him* cookies.

3. Possessive pronouns—show ownership:

The trading card lost *its* value.

The player signed *his* card.

The avid fans traded *their* cards.

4. Reflexive pronouns—reflect back to the subject:

The members of the Alumni Club raised the money *themselves*.

The manager paid *himself* well.

Using Subject Pronouns

Subjective pronouns, or subject pronouns, show number and person; that is, they show singular or plural in first, second, or third person. (See Chapter 5, page 107.) The following chart reviews subject pronouns.

SUBJECT PRONOUNS		
PERSON	SINGULAR	PLURAL
First person	I	we
Second person	you	you
Third person	he, she, it	they

Subject pronouns must be used in the subject position of sentences. Errors with subject pronouns are infrequent when there is only one subject. However, errors often occur when a sentence has compound subjects.

          She
Her and I went to a hockey game.

          He
Him and my parents are planning a trip together.

Subject-verb agreement was introduced in Chapter 5 (pages 110–111) for noun subjects. The same rules used for subject-verb agreement for noun subjects are used for pronoun subjects. Remember to check the subject-verb agreement carefully when the subject pronoun is third person singular and the verb is in present tense.

PRESENT TENSE	
SINGULAR THIRD-PERSON SUBJECT	PLURAL THIRD-PERSON SUBJECT
Subject does not have *-s* or *-es*. Verb has *-s* or *-es*.	Subject has *-s* or *-es*. Verb does not have *-s* or *-es*.

Subjects and verbs must agree in number. Subject pronouns that are singular must use singular verb forms. In verb phrases, the helping verb must agree with the subject.

He <u>appears</u> in many movies.

He <u>has announced</u> his resignation.

She <u>participates</u> in community events.

She <u>is returning</u> to school in January.

It <u>happens</u> to me on a regular basis.

It <u>was falling</u> off the shelf.

Subject pronouns that are plural must use plural verb forms.

We <u>drive</u> to school every day.

We <u>are planning</u> to go to Maine.

Students, <u>you</u> <u>use</u> effective strategies.

Soldiers, <u>you</u> <u>are leaving</u> in May.

They <u>perform</u> on stage every week.

They <u>have announced</u> their engagement.

Pronoun-antecedent agreement is another form of agreement that occurs in sentences with pronouns. Remember that pronouns replace nouns. The noun that is replaced by a pronoun is called the **antecedent.**

antecedent
The <u>contest</u> will be televised.

pronoun
<u>It</u> will attract new advertisers.

antecedent
The <u>singers</u> performed in an outdoor amphitheater.

pronoun
<u>They</u> received a standing ovation.

If the antecedent is singular, you must use the singular form of the pronoun. Sometimes other words in the sentence also provide clues that the singular form is needed.

singular antecedent   singular verb
The <u>picture</u> on several magazine covers <u>was</u> unique.

It   was
~~They~~ ~~were~~ taken by an amateur.

If the antecedent is plural, you must use the plural form of the pronoun. Sometimes other words in the sentence also provide clues that the plural form is needed.

plural antecedent   plural verb
The <u>notes</u> for her novel <u>have been saved</u>.

They were
~~It was~~ on scraps of paper.

Practice 1   *Using Subject Pronouns*

Complete each sentence with a subject pronoun.

1. Raoul has worked at McDougals for fifteen years. _____He_____ manages five retail outlets.

2. The company employs three hundred people. _____It_____ is the largest firm in town.

3. Tina, Jim, and _____she, he, they_____ work at McDougals. _____They_____ like their jobs.

4. Two local firms decided to merge. _____They_____ completed the merger last week.

   Any two: He, she, we, they, I, you
5. _____↓_____ and _____↓_____ were promoted and given more responsibilities.

6. Two unprofitable outlets were closed as a way to cut costs. _____They_____ lost money for the company.

7. Mergers and acquisitions occur frequently in the business world. _____They_____ are done to cut costs, decrease competition, or expand production.

8. Spinoff is a business term. _____It_____ means to sell a portion of the company to cut costs.

9. Restructuring is another method used to cut costs. _____It_____ often leads to a reduction in the number of workers.

10. _____She, He, They_____ and Rachel lost their jobs at the firm during restructuring.

Special Notes About Subject Pronouns with Direct Quotations

Subject pronouns are used frequently with direct quotations. The subject pronoun followed by a verb may appear before or after a direct quotation. **Direct quotations** are statements that indicate the exact words spoken by an individual. Quotation marks are placed before and after the exact words.

> He told the graduates, "Your destiny is in your hands."

> "Your destiny is in your hands," he told the graduates.

A comma is used before a direct quotation when the sentence begins by identifying the speaker. A comma is used after the direct quotation when the sentence begins with the quotation.

Notice the use of the comma and the question mark when the direct quotation is a question.

> She boldly asked, "How much money do you make?"

> "How much money do you make?" she boldly asked.

Using Object Pronouns

Objective pronouns, or object pronouns, may be singular or plural in the first-, second-, or third-person form. Object pronouns may not be used as subjects of sentences.

OBJECT PRONOUNS		
PERSON	SINGULAR	PLURAL
First person	me	us
Second person	you	you
Third person	him, her, it	them

Object pronouns can have three different functions in sentences:

1. An object pronoun can be the object of a preposition.

> Mark went (with me) to see a counselor.

> My mother often talked (about us).

> The ball was thrown (at him).

> The keys are (under it).

> The officers walked (in front of us).

> The burden of proof is (on them).

2. An object pronoun can be a direct object. Direct objects are nouns or pronouns that receive the action of the verb. Direct objects complete the verb's meaning. After you identify the verb, you can find the direct object, if there is one, by asking "What?" or "Whom?" receives the action of the verb.

JUST SO YOU KNOW...

Direct objects follow transitive verbs. All transitive verbs need direct objects.

After running down the field for the ball, the <u>receiver</u> <u>caught</u> it in the end zone.

[Ask yourself, "Caught *what?*" The receiver caught *it*. *It* is the direct object. *Ball* is the antecedent of *it*.]

John was a campus activist. Three student <u>groups</u> <u>nominated</u> him for president.

[Ask yourself, "Nominated *whom?*" They nominated *him*. *Him* is the direct object. *John* is the antecedent of *him*.]

When a direct object is a pronoun, the full meaning of the sentence is linked to a noun, the *antecedent,* which was stated earlier. When you write, make sure that your readers can clearly identify the antecedent for the pronoun.

Before Lisa could find Sofia, the director called her into her office.

[The antecedent is not clear in this sentence. Does *her* refer to Lisa or Sofia?]

<u>Paolo</u> <u>received</u> it yesterday.

The <u>superintendent</u> <u>called</u> her about the situation.

The book <u>described</u> it perfectly.

The <u>stranger</u> <u>carried</u> them across the river.

In the first sentence above, the reader does not know what Paolo received because no antecedent is given to name what *it* represents. Did Paolo receive a box, a subpoena, a check, an award, a citation, a surprise, or a chair? The same is true for the other sentences. Though the sentences are complete, the meaning is not unless there is an antecedent in the previous sentence. As a writer, this writing convention must be rigorously attended to and checked during proofreading. If an antecedent is not used in the previous sentence, then a noun should be used instead of a pronoun.

3. An object pronoun can be an indirect object. An indirect object is a noun or pronoun that benefits from the action of the verb. It indicates *to whom* or *for whom* the action of the verb is performed. Indirect objects are found only in sentences that also have direct objects. An indirect object in a sentence can be rewritten as a prepositional phrase by using the preposition *to* or *for*.

Marcus <u>bought</u> her a dozen red roses.

[Direct object: "Marcus bought *what?*" The direct object is *roses*. Indirect object: "*Who* benefited from this?" "*For whom* did Marcus buy roses?" The indirect object is the pronoun *her*. The indirect object can be rewritten as a prepositional phrase using *to* or *for*: Marcus <u>bought</u> a dozen red roses (for her).]

Practice 2   *Using Object Pronouns*

Underline the subjects once and the verbs twice. Circle the correct pronouns.

1. <u>Karen</u> <u><u>watched</u></u> the stock car races with (I, (me)) last summer.

2. The <u>announcer</u> on the public address system <u><u>called</u></u> (he, (him)) to the lobby.

3. The flight <u>attendant</u> <u><u>gives</u></u> (they, (them)) pretzels and a choice of drinks.

4. Between (he, (him)) and (I, (me)), <u>we</u> <u><u>are</u></u> able to find solutions to most problems.

5. My <u>professor</u> <u><u>told</u></u> (we, (us)) the story about the fiasco.

6. With (he, (him)) by my side, <u>I</u> <u><u>am</u></u> not afraid to face my angry neighbor.

7. The <u>inspectors</u> <u><u>told</u></u> (she, (her)) to call an exterminator.

8. Most <u>magazines</u> <u><u>show</u></u> (they, (them)) as a happy couple.

9. For (we, (us)), the tax <u>refund</u> <u><u>will pay</u></u> some old bills.

10. The <u>sailors</u> on the deck of the ship <u><u>waved</u></u> at (we, (us)).

Using Possessive Pronouns

Possessive pronouns indicate possession or ownership. Possessive pronouns may be singular or plural for first, second, and third person, as shown in the following chart.

POSSESSIVE PRONOUNS		
PERSON	SINGULAR	PLURAL
First person	my, mine	our, ours
Second person	your, yours	your, yours
Third person	his, her, hers, its	their, theirs

Unlike possessive nouns, possessive pronouns do not use apostrophes.

The house is her's, but the land is her brother's. *(hers)*

The prizes are your's to keep. *(yours)*

The manager's goals were not compatible with our's. *(ours)*

The antique car lost it's lustrous shine. *(its)*

Possessive pronouns can appear at various places in sentences, as summarized in the following chart.

SENTENCE POSITION	EXAMPLES
As a noun marker (adjective)	**My** address will change in two months. Is this **your** final decision? The tree lost **its** leaves early this year.
After a linking verb to show ownership of the item in the subject position	This class schedule is **mine.** These concert tickets are **yours.** That convertible is **his.**
As the object of a preposition	I signed my name below **yours.** Her interview went better than **his.** You can put your laundry with **ours.**
As a direct object	They listed **theirs** in the newspaper. We filed **ours** before the deadline. She exhibited **hers** at the state fair last year.
As a subject	**Ours** is the house on the corner. **Yours** requires more extensive research. **Mine** should receive a perfect score.

Special Notes About Possessive Pronouns

1. Confusion often occurs with the pronoun *its.* Use the contraction *it's* (with the apostrophe) when you mean *it is* or *it has.* When *it's* is used, you will be able to substitute the words *it is* or *it has* into the sentence. Use *its* (without the apostrophe) when you want to use a possessive pronoun.

   its
   The maple tree shed it's leaves early this year.

   Its
   It's surface needs to be sanded and painted.

2. A possessive pronoun must agree with its antecedent in number and gender (masculine or feminine). If the antecedent is singular, you must use the singular form of the possessive pronoun. If the antecedent is masculine or feminine, you must use the corresponding masculine or feminine possessive pronoun. Use *his* when the antecedent is masculine (male), and use *her* or *hers* when the antecedent is feminine (female).

   singular   singular
   The *circus* had *its* last matinee on Sunday.

   singular   singular
   A young *girl* swung from *her* trapeze

   singular   singular
   The burly trapeze *artist* caught *his* partner.

If the antecedent is plural, use the plural form of the possessive pronoun.

plural   plural

The *performers* gave *their* last performance for the year.

plural   plural

We kept *our* commemorative programs and souvenirs.

Practice 3   *Working with Possessive Pronouns*

Circle all the possessive pronouns in the following sentences.

1. (Your) name was mentioned at (their) weekly meeting.

2. The leftovers are (yours) to take home with you.

3. The fruit punch lost (its) flavor after several hours.

4. I believe (his) story, not (yours).

5. I picked up (my) clothes from the cleaners, but not (yours).

6. That beach chair looks like one of (ours).

7. (Ours) is that old, beat-up motor home on the end.

8. You were asked to call (your) mother after work.

9. (Their) most noted achievements were recognized.

10. I bought (mine) at the Emporium.

Practice 4   *Working with* its *and* it's

Circle the correct word in parentheses to complete each sentence.

1. (It's, Its) going to rain this weekend.

2. The book cover is attractive. I like (it's, its) shiny finish.

3. The table is new. How did (it's, its) surface get scratched?

4. The puppy wanted (it's, its) mother.

5. In such a difficult race, (it's, its) hard to predict a winner.

6. (It's, Its) expensive to run for office.

7. The dog is loose. (It's, Its) leash snapped.

8. (It's, Its) been a very difficult experience.

9. My grandfather's death was a mystery. For several years, (it's, its) been on my mind.

10. We are concerned about the old mansion. (It's, Its) roof is going to cave in soon.

Practice 5   *Working with Pronoun Agreement*

Work with a partner, in a small group, or on your own. Select the appropriate pronoun in parentheses in the second sentence. Circle the *antecedent* (the noun that the pronoun replaces) in the first sentence.

Example: The ornaments are made from fabric. (It, They) sell for five dollars.

1. Robert writes movie reviews. He sells (it, them) to the local newspaper.

2. My aunt left her notes on my counter. She needed (it, them) later in the day.

3. The lawyer filed the papers with the judge. (It, They) were read by other lawyers.

4. The winds from the hurricane damaged the beaches. (It, They) destroyed many homes.

5. The power was knocked out during the storms. Then (it, they) was restored.

6. The students circulated the petition. Many students signed (it, them).

7. The door to the main gym was locked. The players could not open (them, it).

8. Sirens sounded throughout the city. (It, They) warned the citizens of a tornado.

9. The rocks from the archaeological dig were on display. (It, They) attracted many visitors.

10. Another archaeological dig was planned. Film crews wanted to document (them, it).

11. The remote controls are broken. (Its, Their) power switches do not work.

12. Norma and Raeleen need new track shoes. (Her, Their) mother helped them choose sturdy shoes.

13. The (children) always run for the swings. (He, (They)) want me to push them.

14. The (deer) pranced through the field with their fawns. (It, (They)) were graceful.

15. The golfers had problems putting on the ninth (green). (They, (It)) was fast and sloped.

Using Reflexive Pronouns

REFLEXIVE PRONOUN   A reflexive pronoun reflects on or refers to the subject of the sentence.

Reflexive pronouns are made by combining a personal pronoun with -self or -selves, depending on whether the pronoun is singular or plural. Reflexive pronouns appear after the verb.

REFLEXIVE PRONOUNS	
Singular	myself yourself himself oneself herself itself
Plural	ourselves yourselves themselves

The following examples show how reflexive pronouns refer to the subject.

I painted the entire house *myself.*

Professor Watson wrote the novel *himself.*

The marathon *runners* paced *themselves* well.

Reflexive pronouns should not be used as subjects or objects in sentences. Instead, use subject or object pronouns.

Sammy and ~~myself~~ prepared a special dinner together. *(I)*

The agreement on the rent was (between Carla and ~~myself~~). *(me)*

Special Notes About Reflexive Pronouns

1. The words *hisself* and *theirselves* should not be used. The correct forms to use are *himself* and *themselves.*

The night watchman locked the gates ~~hisself~~. *(himself.)*

The houseguests helped ~~theirselves~~ to a late-night snack. *(themselves)*

2. The same pronouns that are reflexive pronouns may also work as **intensive pronouns.** Intensive pronouns intensify or emphasize nouns or pronouns, but they are not necessary for the meaning of the sentence. An intensive pronoun, unlike a reflexive pronoun, appears immediately after the noun or the pronoun that it emphasizes. Notice how the intensive pronouns add intensity to the nouns or pronouns in these sentences.

Lucinda *herself* locked the safe at the end of the day.

I *myself* witnessed a robbery in progress.

He *himself* admitted his mistake.

They *themselves* decided to accept the challenge.

Practice 6   *Using Reflexive and Intensive Pronouns*

Write an appropriate reflexive or intensive pronoun to complete each of the following sentences.

1. The local detectives captured the alligator __themselves__.

2. The raccoon fed ____itself____ from the garbage can.

3. My aunt congratulates ___herself___ for her own accomplishments.

4. He ___himself___ is the sole heir.

5. I ___myself___ won five different scholarships.

6. The photographer captured __himself/herself__ on tape.

7. The referees blamed __themselves__ for the bad call.

8. We paid ___ourselves___ before we passed on the profits.

9. The science instructor graded all the tests __himself/herself__.

10. Maria complimented ___herself___ on her appearance.

Indefinite Pronouns

INDEFINITE PRONOUN   An indefinite pronoun replaces a noun that stands for a person, place, or thing that is indefinite or not clearly defined.

Some indefinite pronouns are always singular, some are always plural, and some can be singular or plural depending on their antecedents.

INDEFINITE PRONOUNS		
SINGULAR	PLURAL	SINGULAR OR PLURAL
another everything	both	all
anybody neither	few	any
anyone nobody	many	more
anything no one	others	most
each nothing	several	none
either one		some
everybody somebody		
everyone someone		
Helpful Hint 1: Ignore the nouns that may appear in prepositional phrases after the indefinite pronoun.	**Helpful Hint 2:** Ignore the nouns that may appear in prepositional phrases after the indefinite pronoun.	**Helpful Hint 3:** Look inside the prepositional phrase or other parts of the sentence for clues to determine whether the pronoun is singular or plural.

Some indefinite pronouns are always treated as singular when they are subjects of clauses.

> singular   singular
> **Everyone has** the right to vote in this election.

> singular   singular
> **Each** (of the fire alarms) **meets** the federal safety regulations.

Some indefinite pronouns are always treated as plural when they are subjects of clauses.

> plural   plural
> **Both want** to reconsider the contract.

> plural   plural
> **Others prefer** to retire early.

A third group of indefinite pronouns in the subject position of a clause can be singular or plural depending on their antecedent:

> singular   singular
> **All** (of the ice cream) **is** homemade.

> plural   plural
> **All** (of the desserts) **are** homemade.

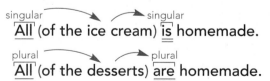

JUST SO YOU KNOW...

Indefinite pronouns can function as subjects, adjectives, noun markers, direct and indirect objects, subject complements, and objects of prepositions.

Indefinite pronouns are not always the subjects of sentences. Some indefinite pronouns may work as noun markers, or adjectives, to describe the subject noun. Adjectives will be discussed in the next chapter.

adjective   subject
Neither candidate is my choice.

Each child is precious.

One tree provides shade from the sun.

Both members want a new charter.

Few problems have no solutions.

Many students enjoy her class.

Several courses require lab work.

Most accidents occur in the home.

 ## Subject-Verb Agreement

Indefinite pronouns often create problems with subject-verb agreement. The *Helpful Hint* sections at the bottom of the indefinite pronouns chart on page 164 provides suggestions to help you determine whether an indefinite pronoun is singular or plural. The verb form then used with each indefinite pronoun must agree in number.

Following are the three *Helpful Hints* explained with examples. Study the examples carefully so you will know how to form subject-verb agreements when the subjects of sentences are indefinite pronouns.

Helpful Hint 1:
When the subject is a singular indefinite pronoun, use a singular verb. If a prepositional phrase follows the subect, *ignore the information inside the prepositional phrase.*

singular
Nobody (in my classes) *is* friendly.

singular
Everyone (on the team) *wants* to win this week's game.

singular
Anything (in these boxes) *is* free.

singular
Nothing (in these reports) *appears* to be suspicious.

singular
Neither (of the candidates) *is* my choice.

Helpful Hint 2:

When the subject is a plural indefinite pronoun, use a plural verb. If a prepositional phrase follows the subject, *ignore the information inside the prepositional phrase.*

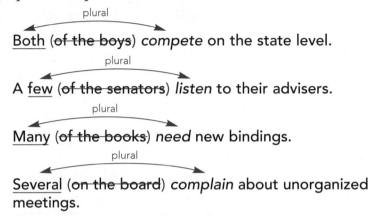

plural

<u>Both</u> (~~of the boys~~) *compete* on the state level.

plural

A <u>few</u> (~~of the senators~~) *listen* to their advisers.

plural

<u>Many</u> (~~of the books~~) *need* new bindings.

plural

<u>Several</u> (~~on the board~~) *complain* about unorganized meetings.

Helpful Hint 3:

When the subject is one of the indefinite pronouns *all, any, more, most, none,* or *some,* the verb may be singular or plural depending on the context of the sentence. If a prepositional phrase follows the subject, *look at the noun at the end of the prepositional phrase.* Use a singular verb when the noun (the direct object) is singular. Use a plural verb when the noun (the direct object) is plural.

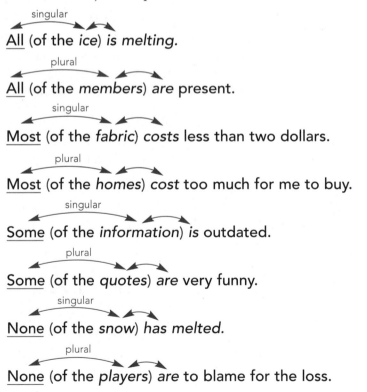

singular

<u>All</u> (of the *ice*) *is* melting.

plural

<u>All</u> (of the *members*) *are* present.

singular

<u>Most</u> (of the *fabric*) *costs* less than two dollars.

plural

<u>Most</u> (of the *homes*) *cost* too much for me to buy.

singular

<u>Some</u> (of the *information*) *is* outdated.

plural

<u>Some</u> (of the *quotes*) *are* very funny.

singular

<u>None</u> (of the *snow*) *has* melted.

plural

<u>None</u> (of the *players*) *are* to blame for the loss.

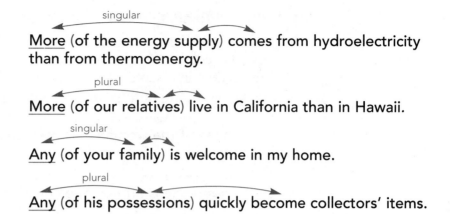

singular
More (of the energy supply) comes from hydroelectricity than from thermoenergy.

plural
More (of our relatives) live in California than in Hawaii.

singular
Any (of your family) is welcome in my home.

plural
Any (of his possessions) quickly become collectors' items.

Practice 7   *Working with Subject-Verb Agreement*

Mark the prepositional phrases with parentheses. Underline the subjects once. Use two lines to select the verb that agrees with each subject.

1. Everybody (make, makes) fun (of my colorful hair).

2. Both (of the movies) (is, are) (about historical events).

3. Most (of the garbage) (stink, stinks).

4. Neither (appeal, appeals) (to me).

5. Several (of my uncles) (work, works) (for Sony Disk Manufacturing).

6. None (of the current options) (match, matches) my goals.

7. Some (of the factories) (close, closes) (for the holidays).

8. Few writers (make, makes) a decent living.

9. Nobody (on the bus) (want, wants) to stand (for the duration) (of the trip).

10. Someone (was, were) knocking (at the door) (in the middle) (of the night).

11. Something (was, were) rattling (inside the mysterious box).

12. All (of the recycling) (save, saves) the company thousands (of dollars).

13. Few petitions (has, have) enough signatures.

14. All (of the loose change) (go, goes) (into a jar) (for a vacation).

15. Nothing (work, works) (on my new computer).

Pronoun-Antecedent Agreement

As we have discussed, a pronoun must agree in number and gender with its antecedent. When a singular indefinite pronoun appears first as the antecedent in a sentence, pronouns later in the sentence that refer to the indefinite pronoun must also be singular.

singular

<u>One</u> of the women <u>is</u> chosen each year to represent *her* county.

singular

<u>Everyone</u> <u>is</u> afraid to tell *his or her* mother.

When a plural indefinite pronoun appears as the antecedent in a sentence, pronouns placed later in the sentence that refer to the indefinite pronoun must also be plural.

plural

A <u>few</u> of the chefs <u>are</u> not willing to share *their* recipes.

plural

<u>Some</u> <u>choose</u> not to identify *their* ethnic backgrounds.

A singular pronoun must also agree with the gender (masculine or feminine) of the antecedent. If the gender is known, it is not difficult to determine the correct pronoun to use to match the gender of the antecedent. Problems in awkwardness, however, occur when the gender is not known. To use only *his* or only *her* would not be accurate. The correct wording is *his or her.* Frequently, writers try to avoid this situation by using plural subjects.

Singular, Gender Known

singular

<u>Each</u> (of the female basketball players) <u>receives</u> her uniform in October.

Singular, Gender Unknown

singular

<u>Each</u> (of the basketball players) <u>receives</u> his or her uniform in October.

Plural, Gender Reference Problems Do Not Occur

plural

The women basketball <u>players</u> <u>receive</u> their uniforms in October.

plural

The basketball <u>players</u> <u>receive</u> their uniforms in October.

Practice 8   *Working with Subject-Verb Agreement with Indefinite Pronouns*

Underline the subject once. Use two lines to select the verb that agrees with the subject.

1. <u>Each</u> of my dogs (<u>has</u>, have) a dog tag.

2. All <u>children</u> (<u>deserve</u>, deserves) love and nurturing.

3. <u>Some</u> (<u>believe</u>, believes) in excessive punishment for small mistakes.

4. One's <u>patience</u> sometimes (run, <u>runs</u>) thin with children.

5. <u>Anything</u> from the street market (need, <u>needs</u>) to be washed thoroughly.

6. <u>Someone</u> (need, <u>needs</u>) to read his or her essay in front of the class tomorrow.

7. <u>Both</u> of the children (<u>cry</u>, cries) for their mother.

8. <u>Most</u> of the invitations (has, <u>have</u>) been sent.

9. <u>She</u> and <u>one</u> of the other contestants (is, <u>are</u>) going to win a trip to New York.

10. All <u>employees</u> (<u>complete</u>, completes) a tax form each year.

11. <u>No one</u> (wait, <u>waits</u>) in a doctor's office for half a day.

12. <u>Many</u> (<u>arrive</u>, arrives) early at the airport to take a flight.

13. <u>Many</u> of the questions (is, <u>are</u>) difficult to answer.

14. <u>None</u> of the media coverage (tell, <u>tells</u>) the true story.

15. <u>All</u> of the desserts (<u>taste</u>, tastes) too sweet for me.

Practice 9   *Working with Pronoun and Verb Agreement*

Draw two lines under the correct verb and circle the correct pronoun inside the parentheses.

Example: Some of the players (<u>prefer</u>, prefers) to talk to (his, (their)) fans after a game.

1. One of my friends (love, <u>loves</u>) ((his), their) job at the new car dealership.

2. Everybody (<u>is</u>, are) entitled to ((his or her), their) opinion.

3. Both of my parents (has, _have_) worked (his or her, (their)) way through college.

4. Some of the students (forgets, _forget_) (his or her, (their)) books every day after class.

5. Everything in my office (_has_, have) (their, (its)) place.

6. Many businesses (_give_, gives) (its, (their)) business cards to every customer.

7. Everyone (lose, _loses_) ((his or her), their) confidence at some time.

8. Nobody (enter, _enters_) the reserved area without ((his or her), their) ticket.

9. Each (want, _wants_) to submit ((his or her), their) story for the competition.

10. Someone (leave, _leaves_) ((her), their) dishes every month at the women's potluck.

11. Everyone in the tournament (agree, _agrees_) to pay ((his or her), their) entrance fee on time.

12. No one (take, _takes_) ((his or her), their) health for granted.

13. All students (_pay_, pays) for (his or her, (their)) lab fees at the beginning of the term.

14. Everybody (leave, _leaves_) ((his or her), their) fingerprints on the doorknob.

15. Most of the men (_wear_, wears) (his, (their)) favorite T-shirts on the weekends.

Compound Subjects with _Either . . . Or_ or _Neither . . . Nor_

The indefinite pronouns _either_ and _neither_ are singular. However, combinations of _either . . . or_ and _neither . . . nor_ create different situations. Sometimes a singular verb is required for agreement; other times a plural verb is required. Examine the following situations to see how subject-verb agreement is achieved.

> Both subjects are singular. The conjunction *or* indicates that only one person creates the problem. The verb is singular.

Either <u>Ethel</u> or <u>Lucy</u> <u>creates</u> a problem on every show.

> Both subjects are plural. The verb is plural.

Either <u>eggs</u> or <u>egg substitutes</u> <u>are</u> needed in the recipe.

> The first subject is singular. The second subject is plural. Match the verb to the *closer* subject. The verb, therefore, must be plural.

Neither <u>Sammy</u> nor his <u>brothers</u> <u>live</u> in Arizona.

> The first subject is plural. The second subject is singular. Match the verb to the *closer* subject. The verb, therefore, must be singular.

Neither Sammy's <u>brothers</u> nor <u>Sammy</u> <u>lives</u> in Arizona.

Special Notes About Compound Subjects

1. *Neither . . . nor* is used to show negative elements in the sentence. The word *not* is reflected in the *neither . . . nor* pattern.

   Neither Bill nor Mary wants to drive to Seattle.
   [The *neither . . . nor* pattern means *not Bill and not Mary*.]

2. Problems with subject-verb agreement usually occur in third-person present tense, when one of the subjects is singular and the other is plural. The rule is to make the verb agree with the closer of the subjects.

   Either the Christmas <u>tree</u> or the <u>presents</u> <u>have</u> to wait for another week.

   Either the <u>presents</u> or the Christmas tree <u>has</u> to wait for another week.

3. Subject-verb agreement problems sometimes occur in present tense when one of the subjects is the first-person pronoun *(I)* or the second-person pronoun *(you)* and the other subject is third person singular. In this situation, match the verb to the closer of the subjects.

   third person   *first person*

   Either <u>Quincy</u> or <u>I</u> <u>need</u> to do the laundry this week.

   first person   *third person*

   Either <u>I</u> or <u>Quincy</u> <u>needs</u> to do the laundry this week.

   third person   *second person*

   Neither your <u>boyfriend</u> nor <u>you</u> <u>want</u> to see the relationship end.

   second person   *third person*

   Neither <u>you</u> nor your <u>boyfriend</u> <u>wants</u> to see the relationship end.

4. *Not only . . . but also* is another compound subject combination you may encounter or want to use in your writing. If both subjects are singular, use a singular verb. If both subjects are plural, use a plural verb. If one subject is singular and one subject is plural, match the verb form to the closer subject.

   Singular subjects:

   Not only the student body <u>president</u> but also the college's <u>president</u> <u>talks</u> about the need for a student lounge.

   Plural subjects:

   Not only <u>students</u> but also <u>teachers</u> <u>talk</u> about the need for a student lounge.

   Singular and plural subjects:

   singular   *plural*

   Not only the <u>horse</u> but also the <u>goats</u> <u>run</u> through the field.

   Plural and singular subjects:

   plural   *singular*

   Not only the <u>goats</u> but also the <u>horse</u> <u>runs</u> through the field.

5. If one of the subjects in a *not only . . . but also* combination is a pronoun, match the verb form to the closer subject.

   agree

   Not only my <u>brothers</u> but also <u>you</u> refuse to windsurf with me.

agree

Not only <u>you</u> but also my <u>sister</u> refuses to windsurf with me.

agree

Not only the <u>manager</u> but also <u>you</u> want the weekend off.

agree

Not only <u>you</u> but also the <u>manager</u> wants the weekend off.

Practice 10   *Working with* either . . . or *and* neither . . . nor

Underline the subjects once and the correct verb twice.

1. Neither <u>Purdue</u> nor <u>Notre Dame</u> (<u><u>was</u></u>, were) his first choice.

2. Either <u>psychology</u> or <u>sociology</u> (<u><u>is</u></u>, are) Mark's major.

3. Either a certified <u>check</u> or a credit <u>card</u> (<u><u>is</u></u>, are) required for the purchase.

4. Either a <u>salad</u> with dressing or a <u>platter</u> of vegetables (<u><u>is</u></u>, are) good for the potluck.

5. Neither <u>Paul</u> nor his <u>cousins</u> (wants, <u><u>want</u></u>) to go to the family reunion.

6. Neither <u>Francis</u> nor <u>Samuel</u> (<u><u>plays</u></u>, play) pool very well.

7. Neither the <u>instructor</u> nor the <u>students</u> (expects, <u><u>expect</u></u>) perfection.

8. Either a term <u>paper</u> or a class <u>presentation</u> (<u><u>is</u></u>, are) required to pass the class.

9. Neither the <u>salesmen</u> nor the <u>manager</u> (<u><u>works</u></u>, work) overtime.

10. Neither the <u>photographs</u> nor the <u>painting</u> above the fireplace (<u><u>was</u></u>, were) damaged.

11. Neither the <u>dogs</u> nor the <u>cat</u> (<u><u>is</u></u>, are) allowed in the living room.

12. Either the <u>chicken</u> or the <u>scallops</u> (was, <u><u>were</u></u>) contaminated.

13. Either <u>you</u> or <u>she</u> (<u><u>is</u></u>, are) to blame.

14. Either <u>you</u> or the <u>accountants</u> (is, <u><u>are</u></u>) responsible for this error.

15. Neither the <u>aunts</u> nor the <u>uncles</u> (is, <u><u>are</u></u>) in Grandfather's will.

COMMA SENSE

Use a comma after introductory information that is followed by a direct quotation. A direct quotation indicates the exact words that a person spoke. Quotation marks are used at the beginning and the end of the quotation.

> The president of the college said, "Either tuition increases or reduction in classes is required."

> The student body president replied, "Neither is acceptable."

> A faculty representative commented, "Administrators need to find ways to trim their budgets."

Use a comma after a direct quotation that is followed by identification of the speaker.

> "We need more money for computer upgrades," Professor Wilcox proclaimed.

> "Increased recruitment to attract students will increase revenues," said one manager.

| EXERCISE 6.1 | Keiko | Name _____ | Date _____ |

Jack Smith/© AP-Wide World Photos

Work with a partner, in a small group, or on your own to proofread the following paragraphs. Look for errors in capitalization, punctuation, pronouns, pronoun-antecedent agreement, verb forms, and subject-verb agreement. Write the corrections above the errors.

KEIKO

Who is Keiko? Keiko is a celebrity killer whale and the first captive killer whale to be released back into the wild. Keiko was captured at the age of two in the waters off iceland. He was trained to star in the movie *Free Willie*. After the movie, he was placed in an amusement park in Mexico city. He become ill. He was brought to the oregon coast aquarium in 1996 for rehabilitation. A large tank with glass walls for viewers were built for him. Thousands of people have went to Newport, Oregon, to see Keiko. In 1998, the Free willie foundation started plans to return Keiko to Iceland. The ocean future society were formed to supervise the move and coordinate the training of Keiko to prepare him to return to his natural environment.

In 1998, a huge air force cargo jet picked keiko up from newport, oregon, and flyed him to klettsvik bay in Iceland. They were put in a large floating pen in the bay. The pen was 100 feet by 250 feet. That pen are 60 percent larger than the pen in Oregon.

Keiko started getting acclimated to the cold waters of Iceland. He thrived and frolicked in the cold water and the icelandic storms. Researchers were pleased with their increased strength and stamina. Chances of survival for Keiko in the open ocean increased.

The next step was to extend ^Kkeiko's roaming space beyond his pen to the entire bay. The Ocean Future ^Ssociety built a large synthetic net across ^Kklettsvik ^Bbay to separate Keiko from the open seas. The net was 950 feet long and was attached to the floor of the bay and to the rocky cliffs. A smaller net was installed in front of the big net. They wanted to discourage ^Kkeiko from trying to ~~escaped~~ ^{escape} prematurely. Keiko was released from his pen and allowed to roam in the bay and dive deeper. Trainers also ~~wants~~ ^{wanted} Keiko to learn to find natural food sources, communicate with other orcas (whales), and be comfortable around other underwater creatures.

Eventually, Keiko will need to be accepted by the other whales and included in ~~his~~ ^{their} pod. A pod is the family unit of whales. The pod is important for survival. Scientists studied the language and the dialects of the resident orcas. Keiko's language is similar enough to that of the other orcas. He will be able to communicate with them and learn new social skills.

In ^Mmay 2000, Keiko started taking escorted tours into the ocean. ^Ssome harbor improvement projects were planned at that time. Trainers worried that ^Kkeiko's hearing would be damaged by the underwater drilling and blasting in the bay. The "ocean walks" reacquainted ^Kkeiko with ~~their~~ ^{his} native waters. Keiko was given time to explore the ocean freely and dive much deeper. Keiko encountered some traveling female whales with their calves. No interaction ~~taked~~ ^{took} place. Interaction and socializing usually ~~occurs~~ ^{occur} during whales' feeding times and not their traveling times. At the end of each excursion, ^Kkeiko always returned to the boat to be escorted back to the bay. He never wandered more than a few miles from his trainers' boat.

The final event will be the release of Keiko into ~~their~~ ^{his} natural environment. The plan is to lead ^Kkeiko to the middle of several groups of feeding whales. Trainers hope a pod of killer whales will accept ^Kkeiko as one of its own. Keiko's survival ~~depend~~ ^{depends} on breaking bonds with humans and creating bonds with other wild orcas. Before the final release, Keiko will be fitted with a transmitter. Scientists ~~wants~~ ^{want} to learn more about killer whales, ~~its~~ ^{their} habits, their socialization process, and the activities of the pod. The transmitter will help the trainers find Keiko if the natural environment is too difficult for him. Hundreds of thousands of dollars and thousands of people have backed this effort to "Free Willie."

EXERCISE 6.2   **Sentence Work**   Name _____ Date _____

Underline the subjects with one line and the verbs with two lines. Circle the correct pronoun in each sentence.

1. Sue and Ann visited the museum. Their classmates asked (her, them) about the exhibits.

2. The members of the local church had a bazaar. (It, They) attracted three hundred people.

3. We wanted to make new friends. Neighbors planned a party for (we, us).

4. Fireworks on the Fourth of July are a tradition. Many people watch (it, them) each year.

5. Stacks and stacks of mail clutter my desk. (It, They) need to be sorted and filed.

6. The chains for my truck broke. The dealer refused to give me a refund for (it, them).

7. My grandmother made her own jams. She gave (it, them) to family members.

8. Boxes of old books and clothing clutter my garage. I want to remove (it, them) by Thanksgiving.

9. Thin extension cords are dangerous. People should replace (it, them) with thicker cords.

10. The gutters are full of debris. I need to get on the roof to clean (them, it).

11. The debris comes from the large trees in my backyard. (They, It) clogs the gutters.

12. The store on Elm Lane sells video cameras. (It, They) cost under seven hundred dollars.

13. The geese landed gracefully on the lake. I heard (it, them) honking.

14. Three duck hunters sat behind a duck blind. (They, He) watched the decoys.

15. The decoys bobbed in the water near the duck blind. The hunters placed (it, them) in the water before dawn.

Follow the sentence writing directions below. Write each sentence in *present tense.* Check carefully that each sentence shows subject-verb agreement.

Part I: Use each of the following indefinite pronouns as the subject of a sentence.

Example: *Many* of the instructors expect students to actively participate in class.

1. Many _____ .

2. Either _____ .

3. Each _____ .

4. Everything _____ .

5. Both _____ .

6. Nothing _____ .

7. Neither . . . nor _____ .

Part II: Use each of the subject or object pronouns in a sentence. Use any verb tense.

Example: The box of chocolates is for *us* to share.

1. us _____ .

2. you _____ .

3. it _____ .

4. she _____ .

5. him _____ .

Part III: Use the following possessive pronouns in sentences.

Example: The videotape on the table is *his.*

1. mine _____ .

2. their _____ .

3. ours _____ .

4. its _____ .

5. theirs _____ .

EXERCISE 6.4   Subject-Verb Agreement   Name _____ Date _____

Use two lines to select the correct verbs for the following sentences so the subjects agree with the verbs. Underline the subjects once.

1. Neither <u>Emily</u> nor <u>Hannah</u> (receive, <u>receives</u>) tips at work.

2. Neither the <u>chef</u> nor the <u>hostesses</u> (<u>earn</u>, earns) tips for their work.

3. <u>All</u> of my former employers (<u>respect</u>, respects) my work ethic.

4. <u>None</u> of the fabric for my bridesmaids' dresses (<u>looks</u>, look) tacky.

5. Either the <u>referees</u> or the <u>clock keeper</u> (<u>is</u>, are) wrong.

6. <u>Somebody</u> really (care, <u>cares</u>) about you.

7. <u>Most</u> of the tickets (<u>sell</u>, sells) for more than fifty dollars.

8. <u>All</u> of my friends (<u>celebrate</u>, celebrates) their birthdays.

9. Neither <u>Dilbert</u> nor <u>Houston</u> (know, <u>knows</u>) about our plans for the evening.

10. <u>One</u> of you three girls (<u>has</u>, have) your picture in the paper.

11. Either my <u>dog</u> or <u>one</u> of my cats (eat, <u>eats</u>) leftovers from the garbage.

12. Little <u>Timmy</u> and his <u>friends</u> (<u>ask</u>, asks) for odd jobs every weekend.

13. The <u>desserts</u> for the day (is, <u>are</u>) on display behind the counter.

14. Neither the consulting <u>job</u> nor the sales <u>jobs</u> (was, <u>were</u>) fulfilling.

15. Neither the sales <u>jobs</u> nor the consulting <u>job</u> (<u>was</u>, were) profitable.

EXERCISE 6.5   Proofreading   Name _____ Date _____

Proofread the following paragraph. Add any missing punctuation and direct quotation marks. Correct verb errors by writing the correct form of the verb directly above the error.

Duncan Murrell is known as "The Whale Guy." He spends several months each year
on solo kayak excursions among the humpback whales. The humpbacks ~~migrates~~ [migrate] to
the channels between the islands of the Alaska peninsula. Murrell says‚ "I feel like I'm
an ambassador for the whales." He goes into elementary classrooms to teach children
about the whales. The whales and ~~him~~ [he] get close to each other. Sometimes he gets
close enough to see the crusty barnacles on ~~its~~ [their] necks and the golf ball–size bumps on
~~its~~ [their] heads. The bumps contain tiny hairs. These hairs ~~senses~~ [sense] movement of prey in dark
waters. Murrell explains the way humpbacks feed. The whales dive deep around a
school of fish and ~~swims~~ [swim] around them. They emit bubbles and ~~creates~~ [create] a dense bubble
curtain. It encloses the small fish. All at once the whales surge up through the middle
of the bubble net. Their huge mouths ~~scoops~~ [scoop] in a meal. They feed and ~~works~~ [work] together
as a team.

Chapter 6 Summary

1. **Pronouns** are words that replace and rename nouns that have been previously identified. This chapter focuses on **personal pronouns** and **indefinite pronouns.**

2. There are three kinds (cases) of **personal pronouns: subjective, objective,** and **possessive.** In the **subjective case** (also called nominative case), pronouns work as subjects of sentences. In the **objective case,** pronouns can be objects of prepositions, direct objects, or indirect objects. In the **possessive case,** pronouns show ownership.

3. **Reflexive pronouns,** which may also be used as **intensive pronouns,** are forms of the personal pronouns that include the suffix *-self* or *-selves.* Reflexive pronouns appear after the verb and refer to the subject. Intensive pronouns are reflexive pronouns that appear right after the noun; they intensify the noun in the sentence.

4. **Possessive pronouns** appear before nouns as noun markers, after linking verbs, or after prepositions. They also can appear as subjects or direct objects. An apostrophe is not used to make any of the possessive pronouns.

5. **Indefinite pronouns** refer to nouns that are not clearly stated. Some indefinite pronouns are always singular; other indefinite pronouns are always plural; with some, their number depends on context. The indefinite pronouns *all, any, more, most, none,* and *some* can be singular or plural; look inside the prepositional phrase or elsewhere in the sentence for clues.

6. Observe the rules of subject-verb agreement with all subject pronouns; pay special attention to the agreement when indefinite pronouns are the subjects. Singular indefinite pronouns require a singular verb form; plural indefinite pronouns require a plural verb form.

7. The noun that the pronoun renames and replaces is called the **antecedent.** The antecedent appears before the pronoun. The antecedent and the pronoun must agree in number (singular or plural) and gender (masculine or feminine). **Pronoun-antecedent agreement** occurs when singular pronouns replace singular nouns and when plural pronouns replace plural nouns.

8. Give compound subjects connected by **either . . . or** or **neither . . . nor** special attention to make sure subjects and verbs agree. If both subjects are singular, use a singular verb form. If both subjects are plural, use a plural verb form. If one subject is singular

and the other subject is plural, make the verb agree with the subject that is closer to the verb.

9. Use a comma with a direct quotation when the speaker is identified in the same sentence. Separate the speaker from the quotation with a comma.

Writing Topics for Chapter 6

Select one of the writing options below. Write a paragraph or two on this topic. Proofread the draft of your work before you turn it in.

 1. Use the Internet to learn more about whales or the whaling industry. Summarize your findings. With your summary, include a copy of the information you find on the Internet.

2. Use the Internet or library resources to find updated information on Keiko. Write one or two paragraphs to summarize the information. With your summary, include a copy of the information used for your writing.

3. Keiko the killer whale has spent twenty-one years of his life living in captivity in marine parks. He bonds with humans and has no experience bonding with wild whales. Millions of dollars have poured into rehabilitation efforts to prepare Keiko to survive in the wild waters off Iceland. Write a paragraph or two to express your opinion about the treatment, handling, and rehabilitation of Keiko. In your writing, provide sufficient details to support your opinion.

4. Write a story about a personal encounter you have had with a wild marine or land animal. Include specific facts that identify where you were, what happened, and how you felt about the experience. Your story, which is a narrative, should be written in chronological order to show a time sequence of events.

Web Site Learning Experiences

See the web site for this book to locate companion exercises and links related to the grammar topics in this chapter.

Go to: http://college.hmco.com. Click on "Students." Type *Sentence Essentials* in the "Jump to Textbook Sites" box. Click "go" and then bookmark the site. Click on Chapter 6.

CHAPTER 6 • Review   Name _____   Date _____

Total Possible: 50   Your Score: _____

Part I: Identifying the Correct Pronoun   (15 points)

Read each sentence carefully. Circle the pronoun that correctly completes each sentence. *Give one point per answer.*

1. His father and (**he**, him) talk openly about (his, **their**) feelings and opinions.

2. Either the home video or the photo album shows (**us**, we) with Perkins.

3. None of the boys wanted to walk to the lake by (himself, **themselves**).

4. (**Its**, It's) shine diminished over the years.

5. Benton hoped to buy (she, **her**) a basket of chocolates for Valentine's Day.

6. A strong bond has developed between you and (**me**, I).

7. Neither the river guide nor the rafters have seen (his or her, **their**) pictures yet.

8. My math tutor and (**I**, myself) went to the teacher for clarification.

9. The football trophy fell off (**its**, it's) stand and broke.

10. Either my roommate or (**I**, me) will pick (**him**, he) up for the meeting.

11. Both (**like**, likes) to debate about public policy issues.

12. Several (**volunteer**, volunteers) every year to help with community events.

Part II: Proofreading   (20 points)

Proofread the following sentences. Write the corrections above each error. Write **C** next to any sentences that have no errors. *Give one point per correction.*

1. The broadcaster said, "Neither the player's nor the coach have anything more to say."   (3 points)
   <small>[corrections above line: *players* (for "player's"), *has* (for "have")]</small>

2. One of the most important event's of the winter Olympics occur at the opening ceremony.   (2 points)
   <small>[corrections above line: *events* (for "event's"), *occurs* (for "occur")]</small>

3. Every year the raging water's get it's power from the rapid ice melt
~~waters~~ ~~their~~
from the mountains.   (2 points)

4. Kent hisself wanted to invite him and I to the party.   (2 points)
~~himself~~ ~~me~~

5. One of the volunteers always have their cellular phone available
~~has his or her~~

for I to use.   (3 points)
~~me~~

c 6. The board game lost its popularity after a few months.
(1 point for "C")

7. "Don't forget to buy today's paper," shouted Jake Manning from his
front porch.   (1 point)

8. None of the players wants ~~his or her~~ equipment to get dirty.
~~want~~ ~~their~~
(2 points)

9. Some of the players prefers to talk to his fans after every game.
~~prefer~~ ~~their~~
(2 points)

10. All of the magazines has the president on it's covers.   (2 points)
~~have~~ ~~their~~

Part III: Sentence Writing   (15 points)

Write a simple sentence for each of these pronouns. Underline the subjects once and the verbs twice. *Give one point for using the pronoun
correctly. Give one point for the subject and one point for the verb.*

1. its

_____ .

2. we

_____ .

3. himself

_____ .

4. none

_____ .

5. theirs

_____ .

CHAPTER 7

Modifiers

In Chapter 7, you will learn about **adjectives,** which are words that modify nouns or pronouns. You will learn how to incorporate these descriptive words into your writing. You will also learn about **adverbs,** which are words that modify verbs, adjectives, and other adverbs.

> **Understanding modifiers will help you do the following:**
>
> 1. Add detail and specificity to your writing
> 2. Create clear, vivid images in your reader's mind
> 3. Use adjectives effectively to modify nouns and use adverbs effectively to modify verbs, adjectives, and other adverbs
> 4. Add a level of sophistication to your writing by using more descriptive and precise language

MODIFIER   **A modifier is any word, phrase, or clause that describes another word or phrase.**

The two most common modifiers are adjectives and adverbs.

Adjectives

 ADJECTIVE   An adjective modifies (describes) a noun or a pronoun. Adjectives tell *which one, what kind, how many, what color,* or *whose.*

Use adjectives to add detail and specificity to your writing and to create clear pictures in the minds of your readers. Adjectives are especially important in descriptive writing, but they are important in other types of college writing as well. The following sentence can be used to test whether a word is an adjective. Words that can fit on the blanks are adjectives.

The ___[adjective]___ person seems ___[adjective]___.

           adjective   adjective
The *young* person seems *competent.*

The following chart summarizes the types of information expressed by adjectives. The adjectives are printed in **bold.**

ADJECTIVES				
WHICH ONE?	**WHAT KIND?**	**HOW MANY?**	**WHAT COLOR?**	**WHOSE?**
singular:	**responsible** citizen	*number words:*	**red** hat	*possessive nouns:*
this car	**creative** musician	**one** animal	**black** convertible	**Sam's** wallet
that report	**gigantic** glacier	**two** characters	**orange** hair	**Latisha's** ring
plural:	**bossy** cousin	**twenty-six** eggs	**beige** gloves	**students'** rights
these boxes	**beautiful** dream	**three hundred** homes	**lavender** umbrella	*possessive pronouns:*
those programs	**restful** vacation	*indefinite pronouns:*	**white** blanket	**my** consent
	unusual odor	**several** students	**turquoise** earrings	**our** agreement
	progressive ideas	**few** courses	**brown** water	**their** permission
		many letters		*indefinite pronouns + 's:*
		some writers		**somebody's** pen
				nobody's fault

Adjectives That Tell *Which One*

1. In Chapter 6, you learned that *this, that, these,* and *those* are demonstrative pronouns. Demonstrative pronouns can function as subject pronouns or, when they modify a noun, as adjectives.

   <u>This</u> <u>is</u> an interesting book.
   [*This* is the subject of the sentence.]

adjective   noun
This book is interesting.

[*This* modifies the noun *book. This* tells *which book.*]

2. *This* and *that* are singular and modify singular nouns. *These* and *those* are plural and modify plural nouns.

singular
This movie won an Oscar.

plural
These movies won Oscars.

Adjectives That Tell *What Kind*

1. Using precise and vivid adjectives that tell *what kind* requires a well-developed vocabulary. Overused words such as *big, cute, little,* or *nice* are not descriptive; that is, they do not create sharp, clear pictures in your reader's mind.

   mammoth
   A ~~big~~ redwood tree stands (in the center) (of the national forest).

   delightful
   The speaker has a ~~nice~~ personality.

2. Use a thesaurus or a dictionary of synonyms to identify more descriptive words when you write.

Adjectives That Tell *How Many*

1. In Chapter 2 (page 17), you learned that number words are noun markers; they signal that a noun follows. When a number word appears before a noun, it functions as an adjective.

   adjective   noun
   Five theories express the different approaches (to psychology).

   adjective   noun
   Thirty-two students enrolled (in his course).

   adjective   noun
   Five hundred people showed up for the grand opening of the museum.

2. Use the following guidelines when you are referring to number words or numerals in your writing.

NUMBERS	
Use a hyphen for numbers below one hundred that are expressed as two words.	twenty-two men ninety-nine cats
Do not use hyphens for numbers expressed in multiples of one hundred or one thousand.	one hundred homes three thousand bags
Use numerals rather than words to write numbers expressed in three words or more.	153 days 1,299 cars

3. In Chapter 4 (page 67), you learned that indefinite pronouns, such as *all, both, few, many, most, more, several,* and *some* can function as subjects of sentences. However, if these indefinite pronouns modify nouns and tell *how many*, the pronouns function as adjectives.

> *Few* <u>can admit</u> their own mistakes.
> [*Few* is the subject of the sentence.]

> adjective noun
> *Few* <u>people</u> <u>can admit</u> their own mistakes.
> [*Few* now modifies people, so it is functioning as an adjective.]

Adjectives That Tell *What Color*

Words that name a specific color and are used to modify a noun function as adjectives

>   adjective   noun
> <u>Members</u> (of the community) <u>tied</u> *yellow* ribbons (on the trees).

Adjectives That Tell *Whose*

1. You learned in Chapter 2 (page 17) that possessive nouns and possessive pronouns are two kinds of noun markers that signal that a noun follows. When possessive nouns and possessive pronouns modify or describe a noun, they function as adjectives.

2. *Possessive nouns can function as adjectives:*

>   adjective   noun
> *Joaquim's* <u>guitar</u> <u>sold</u> (for three hundred dollars).

>   adjective   noun
> The *driver's* <u>uniform</u> <u>was</u> immaculate.

Use an apostrophe with possessive nouns. The following chart shows the rules for adding an apostrophe to singular and plural nouns.

> **JUST SO YOU KNOW...**
>
> Words, phrases, and clauses that modify nouns are called *adjectivals*. Possessive nouns and possessive pronouns are adjectivals when they function as adjectives to modify nouns.

POSSESSIVE NOUNS	
Add *'s* to form the possessive noun for singular nouns, including singular nouns that end in *s*.	child's toy Kathryn's aunt boss's request Russ's truck bus's route James's wife
Add only an apostrophe to form the possessive noun for plural nouns that end in *s*. Notice that the word first appears in its plural form before the apostrophe is added.	voters' opinions waitresses' hours
Add *'s* to form the possessive noun for plural nouns that do not end in *s*.	men's attitudes teeth's enamel

3. *Possessive pronouns can function as adjectives:*

   adjective   noun
My <u>rollerblades</u> <u>can remain</u> (at your house).

   adjective noun
Your <u>computer</u> <u>has</u> many excellent features.

4. *Possessive indefinite pronouns can function as adjectives:*

Indefinite pronouns, such as *anyone, anybody, everyone, everybody, no one, nobody, someone,* and *somebody,* often function as subjects in sentences. However, in their possessive form, these indefinite pronouns can also modify nouns and function as adjectives.

<u>Everyone</u> <u>wants</u> [to complete] his or her paper (on time).

  adjective noun
Everyone's <u>paper</u> <u>must be</u> ready (by this Friday).

Practice 1   *Using Adjectives with Nouns*

In the first column, write a noun that can be modified by the adjective. In the second column, write an adjective that can modify the noun. *Answers will vary. Consider asking students to share their answers in class.*

Adjective	Noun		Adjective	Noun
1. enormous	dilemma	11.	violent	storm
2. rich		12.		shelter
3. three		13.		warnings
4. wild		14.		vehicles
5. simple		15.		people
6. tidy		16.		supplies
7. flat		17.		property
8. brave		18.		trees
9. exotic		19.		crew
10. ambitious		20.		weather

Adjective Patterns

Adjective Pattern 1: Adjectives Before Nouns

In this textbook, we will use the term *adjective pattern 1* to refer to an adjective or series of adjectives that comes directly before the noun that it describes. Adjective pattern 1 looks like this:

The (new) movie opens today.

All the adjectives discussed up to this point appear before the nouns that they modify and thus belong to adjective pattern 1. In the sentences below, the adjectives are circled. The arrows indicate the noun modified by the adjectives.

1. Adjectives may appear anywhere in the sentence where there is a noun. Adjectives may be found between the noun markers *a, an,* and *the* and the noun.

    The (dim) lights gave the room a (romantic) atmosphere.

2. Sentences may begin with adjectives. Two or more adjectives may modify the same noun.

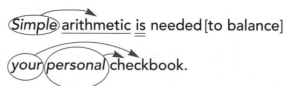

3. Adjectives may appear inside prepositional phrases.

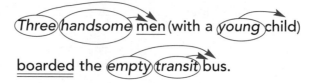

Practice 2   *Identifying Adjectives in Sentences*

Mark the prepositional phrases with parentheses, the infinitives with brackets, the subjects with one line, and the verbs with two lines. Circle the adjectives, including pronouns that are working as adjectives.

Example: The (marketing) expert met (with (her) staff) [to discuss]

the (new) (promotional) campaign.

1. (Our) firm landed a (sizable) contract [to market] an (innovative)

(electronic) toy.

2. The (managerial) meeting lasted (four) hours.

3. The vice president distributed (detailed) assignments (to every department) manager)

4. (Six) departments (within the (main) branch) agreed [to make] (this) (new) project a priority.

5. An (urgent) memo (to (each) employee) stated (several) deadlines.

6. (Many) (crucial) questions needed (immediate) answers.

7. A (detailed) list (of (mandatory) meetings) appeared (in the (company) newsletter)

8. (Fifty-two) employees signed up (for (additional) training and orientation)

9. Employees received (huge) bonuses and (overtime) pay.

10. Everyone (in this (marketing) firm) wanted [to be] a part (of (this) (unique) and (creative) project)

COMMA SENSE

Use a comma between two or more adjectives that describe the same noun whenever you can place the word *and* between the adjectives. The use of the comma between adjectives occurs when the adjectives tell *which kind*. Do not use the comma when one of the adjectives is a possessive pronoun, possessive noun, demonstrative pronoun, or number word that is working as an adjective.

> Comma needed:　　Melissa is a *talented, graceful* dancer.
> [Check by inserting the word *and*: Melissa is a talented *and* graceful dancer. This sentence makes sense with the word *and* between the adjectives; therefore, the comma is needed.]

> No comma needed:　*Jeff's old* guitar was sold at an auction.
> [Check by inserting the word *and*: Jeff's *and* old guitar was sold at an auction. This sentence does not make sense with the word *and* between the adjectives; therefore, no comma is needed.]

Practice 3   *Using Commas Between Adjectives*

Mark the prepositional phrases, the infinitives, the subjects, and the verbs. Circle all the adjectives. Add commas as needed between two or more adjectives that modify the same noun.

1. His father operates heavy machinery (at the old steel plant) (on Mill Street).

2. (In the quarterly reports), you will find unemployment figures.

3. Heather's older brother works long hours (at the family's equestrian center).

4. His inappropriate abusive language created many problems.

5. Marty's pleasant personality landed him many lucrative jobs.

6. An attractive detailed resumé often strengthens your application file.

7. Clarissa used an appropriate format (for her cover letter)(to the potential employer).

8. The confident, ambitious college graduate looked forward (to her first interview).

9. Pedro's closest friends envied his strong, articulate interviewing abilities.

10. Today's classified ads list eight jobs (in the popular field)(of data entry).

Verbals Working as Adjectives

By now you are aware that words can function in different ways in sentences. Some words can be nouns, verbs, or adjectives, depending on their function in a sentence. Many pronouns can function as subjects, objects, or adjectives. Different forms of verbs can also work in ways other than verb functions in sentences.

 VERBAL   A verbal is a word that comes from a verb but does not function as a verb in a sentence. It can function as a noun, adjective, or adverb.

Verbals take three forms: a **present participle,** which ends with an *-ing* suffix, a **past participle,** which ends with an *-ed* suffix for regular verbs or a different verb form for irregular verbs, and an **infinitive.** In this section, we will focus on verbals that function as adjectives to describe nouns.

1. *Present participles working as adjectives:*

             adjective   noun

   The (swimming) coach encouraged each swimmer to work hard.

         adjective   noun

   My (demanding) schedule will last three more weeks.

         adjective   noun

   A (participating) dealership honored the sale price.

2. *Past participles working as adjectives:*

         adjective   noun

   The (rented) office is (on the third floor).

                               adjective   noun   noun

   The post office has photos (of (wanted) men and women).

         adjective   noun

   The (broken) window will be expensive [to repair].

         adjective   noun

   This (frozen) dessert will serve six people.

Practice 4   *Identifying Adjectives*

Circle all the adjectives in the following sentences. The adjectives will appear before the nouns that they modify. Add commas if they are needed.

1. (My) (aging) (purebred) horse begs for (my) attention.

2. (Gradual) (weight) loss is recommended by (America's) (leading) physicians.

3. (Many) (concerned) citizens donated money to expand the (library's) services.

4. (Upscale) (furnished) homes rent for (two thousand) dollars a month.

5. A (brief) (peaceful) demonstration was held near the (old) courthouse.

6. The (diligent) detectives recovered (many) (stolen) artifacts.

7. A (perfect) grade on the (math) test would result in (special) recognition.

8. The (inactive) (nuclear) (power) plant emitted (toxic) fumes.

9. Working at the (airline's) (reservation) desk is a (stressful) job.

10. (One) (prominent) (local) family established a (scholarship) endowment at the college.

11. A (mysterious) (shiny) object appeared in the (dark) (autumn) sky.

12. (Every) (department) store offered (incredible) discounts for the (holiday) shoppers.

13. (Their) (dishonest) (business) dealings will be disclosed to the public.

14. (Betty's) enthusiasm and intelligence make her an (outstanding) candidate for the (administrative) position.

15. The (side) panel of the (medicine) box lists the (active) ingredients.

Adjective Pattern 2: Predicate Adjectives

We will use the term *adjective pattern 2* when an adjective follows a linking verb. The adjective describes the subject of the sentence and is called a **predicate adjective.** Adjective pattern 2 looks like this:

Subject verb *adjective*.

The <u>fee</u> <u>is</u> (*excessive*).

The following chart reviews the linking verbs. (See Chapter 4, page 75.)

LINKING VERBS				
am	is	are	was	were
feel	taste	sound	look	smell
become	appear	grow	seem	remain

Each of the following examples follows adjective pattern 2. Use this pattern only when the sentence has a linking verb, not an action verb. The arrows point to the noun, which is the subject, that is modified.

<u>Robert</u> <u>is</u> *successful* and *intelligent*.

<u>Students</u> often <u>grow</u> *impatient* and *confused* during her lectures.

The symphony's <u>music</u> <u>sounds</u> *beautiful*.

Grandma's <u>kitchen</u> always <u>smells</u> *spicy*.

<u>All</u> (of my grandchildren) <u>are</u> *young*.

Practice 5 *Identifying Subjects, Verbs, and Adjectives*

Underline the subjects once and the verbs twice in the following sentences. Circle all the adjectives in each sentence. Sentences may use adjective pattern 1, adjective pattern 2, or both.

Example: The (test) results were (predictable) and (exciting).

1. Each of the librarians is (knowledgeable) and (resourceful).

2. Many of (my) (closest) friends are (honest) and (ambitious).

3. (Many) drivers on the freeways are (careless), (dangerous), and (inconsiderate).

4. (Warm) (homemade) bread tastes (delicious).

5. The (new) product looks (exciting), (challenging), and (unique).

6. The voice on (my) (answering) machine sounded (distraught) and (confused).

7. Sharon feels (bad) about the incident.

8. All of the (porcelain) vases and plates on the mantel are (valuable).

9. Mark seemed (bothered) by (your) comments.

10. Several ballots were (invalid).

Positive, Comparative, and Superlative Adjectives

Adjectives change their form in relationships that express comparisons. The base form of an adjective, called the **positive** form, can be changed by adding an *-er* suffix to make a **comparative** form or an *-est* suffix to make a **superlative** form.

Positive	Comparative	Superlative
short	shorter	shortest
simple	simpler	simplest
rich	richer	richest
sweet	sweeter	sweetest
loud	louder	loudest

COMPARATIVE FORM The suffix *-er* is added to an adjective to compare two things. The suffix means *more*.

I am *taller* than my brother.

This term is *longer* than last term.

The word *more* is usually used instead of the *-er* suffix when the adjective has two or more syllables.

Positive	**Comparative**
enjoyable	more enjoyable
active	more active
timid	more timid
independent	more independent
beautiful	more beautiful

However, there is one exception. If the adjective ends in *y,* regardless of the number of syllables in the word, change the *y* to an *i* and add the *-er* suffix.

Positive	**Comparative**
lazy	lazier
friendly	friendlier
choppy	choppier
happy	happier

SUPERLATIVE FORM   **The suffix -est is added to an adjective to compare more than two things. The suffix means *the most.***

I am the *tallest* person in my family.

This term is the *longest* term of the school year.

The word *most* is usually used instead of the *-est* suffix when the adjective has two or more syllables.

Positive	**Comparative**	**Superlative**
enjoyable	more enjoyable	most enjoyable
active	more active	most active
timid	more timid	most timid
independent	more independent	most independent
beautiful	more beautiful	most beautiful

As with the comparative form, words that end in *y,* regardless of the number of syllables in the word, use the *-est* suffix, not the word *most* to make the superlative.

Positive	**Comparative**	**Superlative**
lazy	lazier	laziest
friendly	friendlier	friendliest
choppy	choppier	choppiest
happy	happier	happiest

Practice 6 *Identifying Adjectives*

Circle all the adjectives in the following sentences. Draw an arrow from the adjective to the noun it modifies.

Example: Thick fog and slippery roads created treacherous driving conditions.

1. The bronco rider had the wildest ride of his life last night.

2. The party was noisier after midnight.

3. This bread is fresher than that one.

4. Jazz dancing is livelier than the traditional waltz.

5. The heaviest box in the van is the last one.

6. *Dallas* was a successful television series for many years.

7. J. R. Ewing was a loathsome, egocentric, cunning man.

8. The famous restaurant on the pier serves the freshest fish in town.

9. Grapefruit is sweeter during the summer months.

10. The current weather predictions for the coastal areas are awful.

Special Notes About Irregular Comparatives and Superlatives

The common words in the following chart have irregular comparative and superlative forms. The pattern of using the suffix *-er* or the word *more* for comparisons and the suffix *-est* or the word *most* for superlatives is not followed for these irregular forms.

Positive	**Comparative**	**Superlative**
good	better	best
well (healthy)	better	best
little (quantity)	less	least
some, much, many (quantity)	more	most
far	farther, further	farthest, furthest
bad	worse	worst

Notice how these adjectives work in the following sentences:

Positive:	This storm was *bad.*
Comparative:	This storm was *worse* than yesterday's storm.
Superlative:	This was the *worst* storm of the year.
Positive:	This pie is *good.*
Comparative:	This pie is *better* than the mincemeat pie.
Superlative:	This pie is the *best* pie on the menu.
Positive:	I have *little* money.
Comparative:	I have *less* money than you.
Superlative:	I have the *least* money of anyone in the dorm.
Positive:	Penny has *many* brothers.
Comparative:	Jennie has *more* brothers than Penny.
Superlative:	Jason has the *most* brothers of any of us.

 Adverbs

ADVERB   An adverb modifies (describes) a verb, an adjective, or another adverb. Adverbs tell *how, when, where, how often,* and *to what extent.*

The men walked *carefully* on the thin ice. [*How?*]

The accident occurred *yesterday.* [*When?*]

The boxes are *here.* [*Where?*]

We *seldom* share expenses. [*How often?*]

Computer games are *quite* popular. [*To what extent?*]

Adverbs are sometimes a difficult part of speech to understand because they can modify three parts of speech (verbs, adjectives, and adverbs) and have several functions. The focus in this chapter is on individual words that function as adverbs. However, phrases and clauses can also function as adverbs.

prepositional phrase
I enjoy eating *in the cafeteria.* [*Where?*]

prepositional phrase
In the meantime, the relatives waited patiently. [*When?*]

dependent clause
When I lived in Brazil, I learned to speak Portuguese. [*When?*]

To identify adverbs, begin by labeling prepositions, verbs, nouns, and adjectives. Then examine the words that remain to determine whether they modify the verbs, adjectives, or other adverbs. If they do, they are adverbs. Also, ask yourself whether the individual words tell *how, when, where, how often,* or *to what extent.*

adverb
He *secretly* took the two hard drives (from the

N   adverb
hidden vaults) *yesterday.*

adverb
The governor was *too* tired [to return] my call.

adverbs
She is *not currently* planning [to sign] the agreement.

ADVERBS		
FUNCTION	COMMON CHARACTERISTIC	EXAMPLES
Modify action verbs, tell *how*	These adverbs often end with an *-ly* suffix. They usually appear just before or just after the verb.	My uncle *quickly* signed the papers. Each of the children answered *honestly.* The fans cheered *loudly.* The bus *frequently* stops along that route. The students listened *intently* to the lecturer.
Modify adjectives, tell *to what extent*	These adverbs are placed right before the adjective.	The tourists were *extremely* tired. The children were *very* polite. My jacket was *quite* snug. Your sister is *too* talkative. Roberto is the *most* motivated tennis player. The plot for that movie is *so* complex.
Modify other adverbs, tell *to what extent*	These adverbs are placed right before the adverb.	Many drivers act *quite* foolishly. Their actions were *not* racially motivated. The nurse spoke *very* softly to the patient. Your report is the *most* professionally written.

In addition to the numerous adverbs with *-ly* suffixes, the following words can also work as adverbs. Many of these adverbs describe *where, when, how often,* or *to what extent.*

ADVERBS			
above	everywhere	near	somewhere
again	far	never	soon
almost	here	not	still
already	home	now	then
also	how	nowhere	there
always	in(side)	often	today
anywhere	instead	out(side)	tomorrow
back	late	quite	too
behind	later	rather	up
down	least	really	upward
early	less	seldom	very
enough	more	so	well
even	most	sometimes	yesterday
ever	much	somewhat	yet

Special Notes About Adverbs

1. Adverbs may be found in various locations throughout a sentence, as shown below.

   At the beginning of the sentence:

   > *Never* did I expect to win the nomination.

   > *Fortunately,* all the children were safe.

   Before the adjectives they modify:

   > The voters were *very* angry and disappointed.

   > The fumes from the plant were *rather* noxious.

   Before the adverbs they modify:

   > The fire moved *extremely* quickly through the house.

   > The crowd cheered *more* loudly for you.

   Before or after the verbs they modify:

   > Marina dances *gracefully*.

   > The best man *joyfully* toasted the groom.

   Between the helping verb and main verb in a verb phrase:

   > Students should *not* attempt to cheat on tests.

I will *never* call him again in my life.

At the end of the sentence:

My parents plan to travel this year, *too.*

The business opened *yesterday.*

I am going to retire *early.*

2. Most adverbs that modify action verbs end in *-ly*. However, words that end in *-ly* may also be adjectives. How a word functions in a sentence determines whether a word is an adverb or some other part of speech. If a word that ends in *-ly* describes a noun, it is an adjective. If the word describes a verb, adjective, or other adverb, it is an adverb.

A *lovely* bouquet was delivered.
[*Lovely* describes a noun; it is an adjective.]

Your dog is *friendly.*
[*Friendly* describes a noun; it is an adjective.]

Maurice ran *quickly.*
[*Quickly* describes a verb; it is an adverb.]

Andy thought *quietly* before responding.
[*Quietly* describes a verb; it is an adverb.]

The market was *extremely* active.
[*Extremely* describes an adjective; it is an adverb.]

The mayor was *completely* honest with the press.
[*Completely* describes an adjective; it is an adverb.]

She speaks *surprisingly* well for a toddler.
[*Surprisingly* describes an adverb; it is an adverb.]

I *nearly* always drink herbal tea at bedtime.
[*Nearly* describes an adverb; it is an adverb.]

Practice 7   *Identifying Adjectives and Adverbs*

Decide whether the word in **bold print** is an adjective or an adverb. Circle **ADJ** for *adjective* if the word is describing a noun or a pronoun. Circle **ADV** for *adverb* if the word is describing a verb, an adjective, or another adverb.

(ADJ)   ADV   1. The **northerly** winds are brisk.

ADJ   (ADV)   2. The ducks and the geese fly **north** each year.

ADJ   (ADV)   3. The whales **seldom** migrate during the winter months.

ADJ   (ADV)   4. My uncle **frequently** fishes for coho salmon.

ADJ   (ADV)   5. Elk season will open **later** than usual this year.

ADJ   (ADV)   6. Hunting tags cost **too** much for our family to buy.

(ADJ)   ADV   7. There are **fewer** hunters in the woods each year.

(ADJ)   ADV   8. The **wooden** cabin was very isolated.

ADJ   (ADV)   9. We were **rather** tired after the long hike.

ADJ   (ADV)   10. The mountain peaks were **completely** covered with snow.

(ADJ)   ADV   11. **Several** glaciers attract tourists from all continents.

ADJ   (ADV)   12. The ice melts **slightly** during the summer months.

ADJ   (ADV)   13. My parents will **soon** take a cruise to Alaska.

ADJ   (ADV)   14. They do not **often** take vacations out of state.

(ADJ)   ADV   15. The airline industry often offers **promotional** fares.

Practice 8   *Identifying Adverbs*

Work with a partner, in a small group, or on your own. Draw a box around all the individual words that work as adverbs in the following sentences. You may refer to the chart on page 200 for a list of common adverbs.

Example: I am ⃞not⃞ ⃞quite⃞ ready to turn in my lab project ⃞today⃞.

1. ⃞Tomorrow⃞ is ⃞too⃞ ⃞soon⃞ to know the results of the contest.

2. The lecture at the museum was ⃞surprisingly⃞ ⃞quite⃞ interesting.

3. The plumber ⃞seldom⃞ arrives ⃞promptly⃞.

4. My science project is ⃞almost⃞ finished.

5. The fans ⃞never⃞ seem to understand the penalties.

6. Your parrot is ⃞really⃞ friendly.

7. Many voters are ⃞poorly⃞ informed.

8. The sun was ⃞too⃞ hot ⃞here⃞ ⃞yesterday⃞.

9. The professor is an extremely brilliant physicist.

10. You can be so stubborn.

11. We seldom buy a daily paper.

12. The plane arrived late from New York.

13. The furniture was much too expensive for us to buy.

14. The players were definitely ready for the game.

15. We did not go to bed early enough.

Practice 9   *Using Adjectives and Adverbs*

Read each sentence carefully to determine which modifier inside the parentheses will complete each sentence correctly. Notice that one word is an adjective and the other is an adverb.

1. The cat purred (happy, happily) in the sunshine.

2. My grandmother quilts (beautiful, beautifully).

3. The (nervous, nervously) freshmen attended the orientation session.

4. The electrician (quick, quickly) repaired the thermostat.

5. The dance instructor and her partner waltz (graceful, gracefully).

6. Someone in the audience coughed (loud, loudly) throughout the concert.

7. Mom seems (content, contently) to work part-time.

8. Warm bread from the oven smells (wonderful, wonderfully).

9. I was taught to eat dinner (slow, slowly).

10. The secretary opened the door very (quiet, quietly).

11. He always makes decisions too (quick, quickly).

12. The soloist (soft, softly) sang the hymn.

13. The color of your hair looks (different, differently) today.

14. I held on to the rail (tight, tightly).

15. The nanny had a (firm, firmly) grip on the child.

Positive, Comparative, and Superlative Adverbs

Like adjectives, many adverbs have positive, comparative, and superlative forms. As a general rule, adverbs that end in *-ly* and tell *how* form the comparative by adding the word *more* and the superlative by adding the word *most.*

Positive	Comparative	Superlative
cheerfully	more cheerfully	most cheerfully
angrily	more angrily	most angrily
politely	more politely	most politely
confidently	more confidently	most confidently

Adverbs that do not end in *-ly* usually use the suffix *-er* to form the comparative and the suffix *-est* to form the superlative.

Positive	Comparative	Superlative
soon	sooner	soonest
near	nearer	nearest
fast	faster	fastest

Some adverbs have irregular comparative and superlative forms.

Positive	Comparative	Superlative
badly	worse	worst
well	better	best

Good and Well

The words *good* and *well* are frequently used incorrectly. The following chart provides guidelines for using these two words correctly.

GOOD AND WELL		
WORD	FUNCTION	EXAMPLES
good	Use as an *adjective* before the noun it modifies or after a linking verb to describe the subject.	Studying brings *good* results. I had a *good* meal last night. As a pianist, she is very *good.* The actor looks *good* in that photograph. The fresh bread tastes *good.*
well	Use as an *adjective* only when it refers to health or well-being.	My grandmother is *well* again. I do not feel *well* today.
well	Use as an *adverb* to modify an action verb.	My aunt snowboards *well.* Sally dives and swims *well.* I do not speak French *well.*

Practice 10   *Using* **Good** *and* Well

Circle the word inside the parentheses that correctly completes each sentence.

1. The prime rib tastes very (**good**, well). linking verb → adjective

2. Samantha plays the piano extremely (good, **well**). action verb → adverb

3. I feel (**good**, well) about this new exercise program. linking verb → adjective

4. I always work (good, **well**) under pressure. action verb → adverb

5. Brush your teeth (good, **well**) after eating sweets. action verb → adverb

6. My boyfriend looks (**good**, well) in that new suit. linking verb → adjective

7. Candice did (good, **well**) in the audition. action verb → adverb

8. Your reasons for leaving are (**good**, well). linking verb → adjective

9. Many employees do their work (good, **well**). action verb → adverb

10. Jane speaks (good, **well**) in front of an audience. action verb → adverb

11. The toddlers play (good, **well**) together. action verb → adverb

12. The new dishwasher cleans dirty dishes (good, **well**). action verb → adverb

13. All the relatives had a (**good**, well) time at the reunion. adjective
    good time

14. I did not do (good, **well**) on the final exam. action verb → adverb

15. The lamp does not light the room (good, **well**) enough. action verb → adverb

Practice 11   *Using Adjectives and Adverbs*

Write ten descriptive sentences about an interesting place you have visited. Circle all the adjectives. Place a box around all the adverbs. Share your sentences with a partner. Ask your partner to check the accuracy of your work while you check the accuracy of your partner's work.

1. _____

2. _____

3. _____

4. _____

5. _____

6. _____

7. _____

8. _____

9. _____

10. _____

C O M M A   S E N S E

Use a comma between three or more adverbs whenever the word *and* can be placed between them. Adverbs that modify action verbs use this comma rule.

Commas are needed: The paramedics acted *quickly, professionally, and cautiously.*

Commas are not needed: My mother spoke *too loudly and carelessly.*

Usually use a comma after an introductory word at the beginning of a sentence. The comma indicates a pause in your voice. Many introductory words are adverbs.

Fortunately, the insurance premium is not due for another two months.

Consequently, the notices will be arriving late.

Other common introductory adverbs include these:

Accordingly,	Additionally,	Afterward,	Also,
Finally,	Furthermore,	Hence,	However,
Indeed,	Later,	Likewise,	Moreover,
Nevertheless,	Next,	Nonetheless,	Otherwise,
Similarly,	Still,	Subsequently,	Then,
Therefore,	Thus,	Unfortunately,	

EXERCISE 7.1   **The Nile**   Name _____   Date _____

© AP-Wide World Photos

Work with a partner, in a small group, or on your own. Read the paragraphs carefully. Circle all the words that are adjectives. Above as many adjectives as possible, substitute another adjective with a similar meaning. You may refer to your dictionary or thesaurus. *Synonym substitutions will vary. Possible answers are given.*

THE NILE

The pharaohs of (ancient) [old] Egypt had no use for roads. The Nile was (their) highway. The (thirty) dynasties of pharaohs ruled from 3050 B.C. to 340 B.C. The gently (flowing) (river's) (blue-green) [azure] waters have sustained life in Egypt for the (past) (12,000) years. Before (modern) travel, (caravan) journeys down the Nile were (arduous) [difficult]. (All) (commercial) activity passed up and down the Nile in barges and (sailing) vessels. (Common) [Ordinary] people were served by canoes of (papyrus) reeds.

Today, tourists can take (luxury) [expensive] cruises down the Nile. (Magnificent) [Marvelous] (stone) [rock] temples, intricately (decorated) [adorned] tombs, and (colossal) [immense] statues can be seen from the (luxury) (cruise) ships. Tourists view a portion of the (six-hundred-mile-long), (narrow) [thin] strip of (fertile) [rich] shores along the Nile. Approximately (250) (different) (cruise) ships make (their) way through the (purling) [swirling] waters and down the (mystical) [spiritual] river. The (cruise) ships offer (pampered) [catered] relaxation, (sumptuous) [delicious] food, (great) [breathtaking] sunsets, (romantic) [sentimental] interludes, and (guided) tours.

There are hundreds of (ancient) ruins to visit in Egypt. A cruise acquaints tourists with

the best of the (old) ruins. (Many) tourists long to return to Egypt for a more (leisurely)

ancient

slow-paced

visit. They want (more) time to explore the avenues of sphinxes, tombs of (famous)

well-known

pharaohs, (ancient) artifacts and hieroglyphs, and multitude of (rich) (carved) reliefs on

elaborate

the (limestone) walls of (pharaohs') tombs. (Many) tourists wish to experience more of the

numerous

(many) wonders of Egypt and the (legendary) Nile.

mythical

[Adapted from Vijay Joshi, AP, "Cruise the Nile to View Wonders of Egypt," *Register Guard*, January 16, 2000.]

EXERCISE 7.2 **New Adjectives** Name _____ Date _____

The following words can all be used as adjectives in adjective pattern 1 or adjective pattern 2. Use a dictionary to learn the meaning of any unfamiliar adjectives. Select any eight adjectives to use in original sentences. Write your sentences on separate paper. *Answers will vary.*

abrasive	adverse	amicable	arid	automatic
abstract	agile	anemic	artistic	auxiliary
absurd	allergic	antique	ashamed	average
abysmal	allusive	apologetic	astute	avid
accessible	amateur	appetizing	athletic	aware
acrylic	ambitious	applicable	attractive	awful
active	ambulatory	apprehensive	audible	awkward
addictive	amenable	aquatic	authentic	azure

1. _____

2. _____

3. _____

4. _____

5. _____

6. _____

7. _____

8. _____

EXERCISE 7.3   Verbals   Name _____ Date _____

Present and past participles, also called verbals, are listed in the box below. Select any ten verbals to use in sentences as adjectives. The verbals in your sentences must describe nouns or pronouns. *Write your sentences on separate paper.* Draw arrows to the nouns that are modified by the verbals. *Answers will vary.*

Example: *broken*   The *broken* glass cut my feet.

Present Participles		**Past Participles**	
dancing	missing	determined	frozen
jogging	wishing	embarrassed	hidden
pounding	planning	discarded	stolen
sleeping	caring	planned	torn

EXERCISE 7.4   Sentence Expansion   Name _____ Date _____

Add prepositional phrases, adjectives, and adverbs to expand the following sentences and provide the reader with more details and a more vivid image. *Rewrite each sentence on separate paper. Answers will vary.*

Example: The stadium was crowded.
The football stadium was extremely crowded with enthusiastic fans.

1. Wrap the box.

2. The news reporter responded.

3. The twins were screaming.

4. A power outage occurred.

5. Her hair flapped in the wind.

6. Bo's interests are unusual.

7. The philanthropist pledges money.

8. The accident snarled traffic.

9. The cabin became my haven.

10. The singer belted out a tune.

11. The notice cautioned online investors.

12. The exhibit attracted crowds.

Circle the correct word inside the parentheses to complete each sentence. On the line, write **ADJ** if the word is an *adjective*. Write **ADV** if the word is an *adverb*.

Examples: <u>ADJ</u>   Your reflexes seem to be ((good), well).
<u>ADV</u>   Your petition was read (thorough, (thoroughly)) by the review board.

<u>ADJ</u>   1. The pianist was ((exceptional), exceptionally) at an early age.

<u>ADV</u>   2. He played (beautiful, (beautifully)) during the rehearsals.

<u>ADV</u>   3. He played especially (good, (well)) at the opening recital.

<u>ADV</u>   4. I was (inexcusable, (inexcusably)) late for my dentist appointment.

<u>ADV</u>   5. Jeremy always does (poor, (poorly)) on essay exams.

<u>ADV</u>   6. The counselor listened (quiet, (quietly)) to my story.

<u>ADV</u>   7. All of the traffic moved (slow, (slowly)) on the bridge.

<u>ADV</u>   8. The fog appeared (unexpected, (unexpectedly)) in the valley.

<u>ADJ</u>   9. I try to send ((good), well) wishes to my close friends.

<u>ADV</u>   10. You handled that situation (nice, (nicely)).

<u>ADV</u>   11. An (extreme, (extremely)) popular newscaster underwent surgery today.

<u>ADV</u>   12. Walk across the frozen lake (careful, (carefully)).

<u>ADJ</u>   13. Jane's attire for the award ceremony looked ((beautiful), beautifully).

<u>ADV</u>   14. You always manage your financial affairs (wise, (wisely)).

<u>ADV</u>   15. The visiting professor ended his lecture (abrupt, (abruptly)).

Chapter 7 Summary

1. **Modifiers** are words, phrases, or clauses that describe other words or phrases. The two most common kinds of modifiers are adjectives and adverbs.

2. **Adjectives** modify or describe nouns or pronouns. Adjectives tell *which one, what kind, how many, what color,* or *whose.*

3. Sometimes possessive nouns, possessive pronouns, indefinite pronouns, and participles (also known as **verbals**) can work as adjectives in sentences.

4. Two adjective patterns are defined by the position of the adjective in the sentence. In **adjective pattern 1,** the adjective comes directly before the noun or pronoun it describes. In **adjective pattern 2,** the adjective follows a linking verb, not an action verb. The adjectives describe the subject of the sentence. Adjectives in adjective pattern 2 are also called **predicate adjectives.**

5. Adjectives and adverbs change their form in relationships that express comparisons. The **positive** is the base form of the adjective or the adverb. The **comparative** is the form used to compare two items; an *-er* suffix or the word *more* before the base form is used to form a comparative. The **superlative** form is used to compare three or more items; an *-est* suffix or the word *most* before the base form is used to form the superlative.

6. **Adverbs** are words that modify or describe verbs, adjectives, and other adverbs. Adverbs tell *how, when, where, how often,* and *to what extent.* Many adverbs end with the *-ly* suffix.

7. The words *good* and *well* are frequently confused. *Good* works as an adjective. *Well* works as an adjective only when it refers to health or well-being; *well* works as an adverb to modify action verbs.

8. Three new comma rules cover the following:

   - A comma is used between two or more adjectives that describe the same noun whenever the word *and* can be inserted between the adjectives.

   - A comma is used between three or more adverbs whenever the word *and* can be placed between them.

   - A comma is usually used after an introductory adverb at the beginning of a sentence.

Writing Topics for Chapter 7

Select one of the writing options below. Write a paragraph or two for this topic. Proofread the draft of your work before you turn it in.

 1. Use the Internet to find information about a place you would like to visit. Read the information. Then, without copying the information from your source, write a description of the place you would like to visit. With your description, turn in a copy of the information obtained from the Internet.

 2. Use the Internet or the library to find information about Egypt, the Nile, pharaohs, or pyramids. Choose one or two articles to read about your selected topic. Summarize the information you learned. With your summary, include a copy of the source of your information.

3. Select a person whom you know well. Write a paragraph that describes the person. You may wish to include his or her physical features, style of clothing, special interests, unique mannerisms, or unusual characteristics. Incorporate adjectives and adverbs in your paragraph to create vivid, descriptive details so that a strong image of the person will be created in the reader's mind.

4. Watch a travelogue on television. Travelogues are often televised on educational channels. Write the name of the show and the date you watched it. Take notes about information that is presented in the show and details you notice as you watch the show. Write a summary of the travelogue. With your summary, include a copy of your original notes.

Web Site Learning Experiences

See the web site for this book to locate companion exercises and links related to the grammar topics in this chapter.

Go to: http://college.hmco.com. Click on "Students." Type *Sentence Essentials* in the "Jump to Textbook Sites" box. Click "go" and then book-mark the site. Click on Chapter 7.

CHAPTER 7 • Review   Name _____   Date _____

Total Possible: 50   Your Score: _____

Part I: Identifying Adjectives and Adverbs (10 points)

Identify the word that appears in **bold print.** Write **ADJ** if the word is an *adjective* and **ADV** if the word is an *adverb*. Draw an arrow from the word in bold print to the word it modifies. *Give ½ point for the answer on the line and ½ point for a correct arrow.*

_____ADJ_____   1. The **unexpected** news surprised and delighted me.

_____ADV_____   2. The snowplows moved **slowly** through the city streets.

_____ADV_____   3. Dr. Simonton is **extremely** active in our community.

_____ADJ_____   4. The cosmetic surgery was too **expensive** for me to consider.

_____ADJ_____   5. There is a often a **dear** price to pay for vanity.

_____ADV_____   6. The elders **frequently** adorned themselves in traditional costumes.

_____ADJ_____   7. Is this your **best** paper this term?

_____ADV_____   8. The dog went into the river **willingly.**

_____ADV_____   9. The fire alarm **promptly** alerted the family to the smoke.

_____ADV_____   10. The punch at the reception was **too** sweet.

Part II: Sentence Expansion (10 points)

Expand each of the following sentences by adding at least one adjective and one adverb. Circle the adjective. Draw a box around the adverb. *(2 points per sentence.)*

1. We climbed the sand dunes.

_____

2. Dune buggies raced up the dunes.

_____

3. Sand blew in our faces.

_____

4. Children laughed.

_____

5. The day ended.

_____

Part III: Proofreading (30 points)
Complete the following steps:

1. Add missing commas.

2. Correct any adjective or adverb errors.

3. Identify and write the part of speech of each of the words in **bold print.** Use these symbols:

    N = noun   **V** = verb   **ADJ** = adjective   **ADV** = adverb

4 pts. The **street**^{ADJ} vendors pushed **their**^{ADJ} colorful, homemade carts through the narrow,

2 pts. **crowded**^{ADJ} streets. Their carts were overflowing with trinkets, woodcarvings, handmade

1 pt. bracelets, seashells, and souvenirs of every **conceivable**^{ADJ} kind. The merchandise on

1 pt. one cart looked **identical**^{ADJ} to the merchandise on every other cart. Some of the

3 pts. **vendors**^N **often**^{ADV} stopped near the end of the **bustling**^{ADJ} street to visit with friends.

1 pt. However, they were all on the lookout for any tourists within yelling or running

3 pts. **distance.**^N Once tourists were spotted, unbelievable noise, pandemonium,

2 pts. and an incredible **surge**^N of energy burst in the direction of the **visitors**^N with money.

2 pts. The vendors **aggressively**^{ADV} hollered out their prices, waved their hands ~~frantic~~ frantically in the

3 pts. air, and **shoved**^V trinkets ~~direct~~ directly into the tourists' faces. Each of the vendors was

3 pts. determined to win a sale with the **lowest**^{ADJ} prices. Frequently, the **stunned,**^{ADJ} horrified

2 pts. tourists **retreated**^V ~~quick~~ quickly into nearby stores or restaurants to regain a sense of security.

2 pts. The tourists had **not**^{ADV} been **adequately**^{ADV} forewarned about the local street culture or the

1 pt. urgency and determination of the local vendors to make a sale to put food on **their**^{ADJ}

0 pts. tables at home.

CHAPTER 8

Compound Sentences

In Chapter 8, you will learn three methods for constructing **compound sentences,** which are sentences that consist of two or more independent clauses. With each method, you will learn the correct punctuation to use. This chapter also includes work with run-on sentences, comma splices, and subject-verb agreement.

> ### Understanding compound sentences will help you do the following:
>
> 1. Add sentence variety and sophistication to your writing
> 2. Combine independent clauses correctly to show various relationships between clauses
> 3. Avoid the common writing errors of comma splices and run-on sentences
> 4. Prepare a foundation for future sentence-combining skills that involve complex and compound-complex sentences

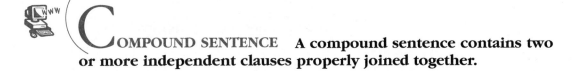

COMPOUND SENTENCE   **A compound sentence contains two or more independent clauses properly joined together.**

In Chapter 4, you learned that one independent clause standing by itself is a simple sentence. When two or more independent clauses are joined together, the result is a compound sentence.

SIMPLE SENTENCE	COMPOUND SENTENCE
ONE INDEPENDENT CLAUSE	TWO OR MORE INDEPENDENT CLAUSES JOINED TOGETHER
Twenty students enrolled in the course. Only nineteen students remained at the end of the term.	Twenty students enrolled in the course, **but** only nineteen students remained at the end of the term.
Record rain fell overnight. Roads were closed due to mudslides.	Record rain fell overnight; roads were closed due to mudslides.
Cindy is transferring to the university. She wants to take transferable courses.	Cindy is transferring to the university; **therefore,** she wants to take transferable courses.

Three Methods of Constructing Compound Sentences

In a compound sentence, independent clauses are joined in one of three ways:

1. By a comma and one of the seven coordinating conjunctions: *and, but, for, nor, or, so, yet.*

    independent clause
    The blockade was not complete, and

    independent clause
    small, fast ships routinely slipped through it.

2. By a semicolon alone.

    independent clause
    Both sides built ironclad war vessels;

    independent clause
    the *Monitor* and the *Virginia* battled in 1862.

3. By a semicolon, a conjunctive adverb (like *however, furthermore, therefore*), and a comma.

    independent clause
    The South had hoped Britain would help them; however,

    independent clause
    Britain declined to get involved.

The following diagram shows the structure of a compound sentence. S-V represents an independent clause with a subject and a verb. Each subject and verb forms a complete thought. As noted on page 216, one of three methods can be used to connect the independent clauses to result in a compound sentence.

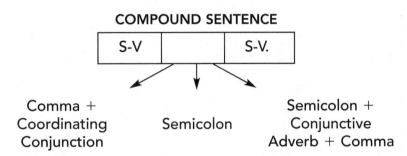

COMPOUND SENTENCE

| S-V | | S-V. |

Comma + Coordinating Conjunction

Semicolon

Semicolon + Conjunctive Adverb + Comma

Compound Sentences Using Coordinating Conjunctions

 COORDINATING CONJUNCTION   A coordinating conjunction joins two or more items. In compound sentences, it joins two independent clauses. The seven coordinating conjunctions *and, but, for, nor, or, so,* and *yet* join two independent clauses (simple sentences) that are of equal importance. A comma is used before the coordinating conjunction when it joins two independent clauses.

To learn more about each of the seven coordinating conjunctions, study the following chart carefully. Notice the meaning of each coordinating conjunction and how it is used in sentences. Cover up the coordinating conjunction in each sentence; notice how an independent clause (a group of words that stand alone as a complete sentence) appears on each side of the coordinating conjunction.

COORDINATING CONJUNCTIONS		
COORDINATING CONJUNCTION	FUNCTIONS	EXAMPLES
And	-shows clauses of equal value -adds information -means "in addition to" or "along with"	My youngest sister is a nurse, **and** my oldest sister is a veterinarian. I attended all the lectures, **and** I completed my term paper. My parents bought me a new computer, **and** I signed up for an email account.
But	-shows an opposite idea, a contrast, or a difference	I wanted to attend your wedding, **but** I could not afford the airfare.

(Continue on page 218)

COORDINATING CONJUNCTIONS

COORDINATING CONJUNCTION	FUNCTIONS	EXAMPLES
But	-means "except" or "however"	We were going to go to the concert Saturday, **but** the band had to cancel.
		My taxes are due in a few days, **but** I do not have time to complete the forms.
For	-shows how the first clause occurs because of the action of the second clause -shows a reason or cause -means "because"	Robert could not order a transcript, **for** he had forgotten his identification.
		Maurice is transferring to Chicago, **for** his fiancée accepted a job with a newspaper there.
		I did not receive the magazine, **for** my subscription had not been renewed.
Nor	-joins two negative ideas -means "not"	My study partner is not supportive, **nor** is he interested in helping me with my research paper.
		I cannot get a job, **nor** can I find a place to live.
		The students could not gather enough signatures on the petition, **nor** could they organize enough volunteers.
Or	-shows a choice between two equal options or possibilities	I could pick up the groceries, **or** you could stop on your way home.
		Professor Wilson will be in his office, **or** he will leave the information posted on his door.
		We can go to the mall, **or** we can rollerblade in the park.
So	-shows that the first clause causes the action in the second clause to occur -means "therefore"	I studied until four o'clock in the morning, **so** I am tired.
		My mother knows sign language, **so** she agreed to interpret for a deaf woman in the grocery store.
		I was sorry for my rude comments, **so** I apologized.
Yet	-shows that one action occurs in spite of the other action -means "however," "nevertheless," or "but still"	Walking and running are good cardiovascular exercises, **yet** many people fail to make time for exercise.
		The bus is an inexpensive form of transportation, **yet** few students ride the bus to school.
		Smoking causes health problems, **yet** millions of people continue to smoke.

By rearranging the first letters of each of the **seven coordinating conjunctions,** a mnemonic, or memory trick, can be created to help you remember them. The mnemonic is **FAN BOYS.** Practice naming the conjunction represented by each letter of the mnemonic:

For   **A**nd   **N**or   **B**ut   **O**r   **Y**et   **S**o

Practice 1   *Adding Coordinating Conjunctions in Compound Sentences*

Write a coordinating conjunction (one of the "FAN BOYS" conjunctions) to complete the following sentences in a logical way. Refer to the Coordinating Conjunctions chart on pages 217–218 for the meanings of conjunctions if necessary.

Example: The jeans were not on sale, _nor_ were the running shoes.

1. I did not acknowledge her, _____for_____ I could not remember her name.

2. My boyfriend might enroll in the National Guard, _____or_____ he might join the Coast Guard.

3. Last year my brother sent my mother flowers, _____but_____ this year he is sending her an airplane ticket.

4. The hard drive was not affected by the virus, _____nor_____ were the files contaminated.

5. The hikers had a guide, _____but_____ they still managed to get lost.

6. The meter had expired, _____so_____ the meter maid placed a ticket on the windshield of the car.

7. The rally started at noon, _____and_____ live television coverage started at the same time.

8. The smoke alarms went off, _____so_____ everyone had to evacuate the building.

9. The documentary was televised locally, _____and/for_____ the topic was about a boy in this community.

10. Sarina reached the credit limit on her credit card, _____yet/but_____ she continued to try to use it.

Special Notes About Coordinating Conjunctions

1. Coordinating conjunctions are used to join words, phrases, clauses, and sentences. A comma is used before a coordinating conjunction *when it joins two independent clauses*. However, do *not* use a comma when a coordinating conjunction is simply joining two words or phrases.

   Natalie <u>swam</u> four laps **and** <u>did</u> water exercises.
   [No comma is needed to join two verbs.]

The <u>tourists</u> **and** their <u>guide</u> <u>climbed</u> to the peak of the mountain.
[No comma is needed to join two subject nouns.]

<u>I</u> <u>will</u> probably <u>order</u> shrimp **or** fettuccine.
[No comma is needed to join two nouns that are direct objects.]

<u>Mark</u> <u>will leave</u> the key under the mat **or** in the flowerpot.
[No comma is needed to join two prepositional phrases.]

2. Compound sentences that use the coordinating conjunction *nor* have an inverted subject-verb pattern in the second independent clause. Two possible patterns may be used with the coordinating conjunction *nor*:

   S-V, nor V-S:

   The <u>joke</u> <u>was</u> not funny, **nor** <u>was</u> <u>it</u> appropriate.

   <u>Recording</u> the call <u>was</u> not honest, **nor** <u>was</u> <u>it</u> legal.

   S-V, nor helping verb-S-main verb:

   The telephone <u>company</u> <u>did</u> not <u>receive</u> my payment, **nor**
   <u>did</u> <u>it</u> <u>receive</u> my cancellation request.

   <u>Hannah</u> <u>could</u> not <u>reach</u> the key, **nor** <u>could</u> <u>she</u> <u>find</u> a chair to
   stand on.

Practice 2   *Simple and Compound Sentences*

Read each sentence carefully. Mark the prepositional phrases, the infinitives, the subjects, and the verbs. Look at the pattern of the subjects and the verbs to decide whether the sentence is a simple sentence or a compound sentence. On the blank, write **S** for *simple sentence* and **C** for *compound sentence*.

Examples: __S__   (After a long wait), the <u>curtain</u> finally <u>opened</u> (on the new stage).

__C__   The colored <u>lights</u> <u>flooded</u> the stage, and the <u>production</u> <u>began</u>.

__S__   1. The antique <u>coffeepot</u> <u>was</u> rusty and tarnished.

_____ S _____   2. The antique dealers worked (through the night) (to set up) their exhibits.

_____ C _____   3. Several trees will need (to be cut) down, for they obstruct the view.

_____ C _____   4. The brakes (on my van) are frayed, so I cannot drive it.

_____ S _____   5. The judge reviewed the evidence and set a trial date.

_____ S _____   6. The lease (for our new office space) will begin (in six weeks).

_____ S _____   7. Movers will haul the office equipment and work supplies (to the new site).

_____ C _____   8. The flu epidemic has started, but many elderly people have not received flu shots (for this season).

_____ C _____   9. My Financial Aid papers were incomplete, for I did not have my tax return (with me).

_____ S _____   10. I estimated my tax situation (for this year) and used that information (on the forms).

Compound Sentences with Semicolons

SEMICOLON   A semicolon is a punctuation mark that can replace a period between two independent clauses that are closely related.

A compound sentence is formed when a semicolon joins two independent clauses.

COMPOUND SENTENCE

S-V	;	S-V.

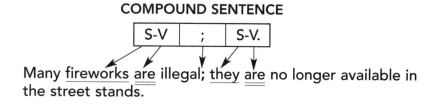

Many fireworks are illegal; they are no longer available in the street stands.

The following examples show effective use of the semicolon. Notice that the capital letter is removed from the beginning of the second sentence when a compound sentence is formed.

Heavy ice pulled down power lines. Hundreds of homes lost electricity.

Heavy ice pulled down power lines; hundreds of homes lost electricity.

Practice 3   *Punctuating Compound Sentences*

Each compound sentence lacks proper punctuation. Add a comma or a semicolon to punctuate each sentence correctly.

1. Writing tutors are available; the tutoring services are free.

2. Instructors train the writing tutors, so the tutors are familiar with your assignments.

3. Tutors are willing to suggest writing topics, but you need to come prepared with ideas.

4. Writing tutors will not write your papers; that is your responsibility.

5. Proofreading for errors is difficult for many students; tutors can help with the process.

6. I do not type, nor do I use a computer to write my papers.

7. Many spelling errors can be corrected on a computer, but computers do not correct errors with homonyms or word usage.

8. I enjoy writing book summaries, and I enjoy writing poetry.

9. An essay on an assigned topic is the most difficult for me, for I prefer to select my own topic and research ideas to use in my papers.

10. I submitted a short story for a writing contest; I won $150.

11. I had never entered a writing contest before, nor had I even won money in any kind of contest.

12. Winning one contest was a motivational experience; now I want to try to enter more contests.

13. For some contests, only a few entries are received, so the competition is not fierce.

14. The odds of winning a writing contest are actually pretty good, but your essay or short story still must be well written and convey an important message or emotion.

15. I wrote about a humbling experience; the judges must have liked my willingness to express my personal feelings and reactions.

Compound Sentences with Conjunctive Adverbs

 CONJUNCTIVE ADVERB   A conjunctive adverb works like a conjunction to join two independent clauses.

A semicolon precedes a conjunctive adverb; a comma follows the conjunctive adverb. Frequently, conjunctive adverbs help the reader understand the relationship between the two sentences that are being joined together. Following is the compound sentence pattern that is used with conjunctive adverbs.

COMPOUND SENTENCE

S - V	; conjunctive adverb	S - V.

Gasoline prices skyrocketed; **consequently,** the government intervened.

The following chart shows common conjunctive adverbs and transitional phrases, plus the relationships they suggest.

CONJUNCTIVE ADVERBS AND TRANSITIONAL PHRASES			
CONJUNCTIVE ADVERB	**MEANING OR RELATIONSHIP**	**CONJUNCTIVE ADVERB**	**MEANING OR RELATIONSHIP**
accordingly	consequently, thus	in fact	indeed
additionally	also, in addition	later	next in time
afterward	later	likewise	also, furthermore
also	in addition	moreover	furthermore, in addition
as a result	consequently	nevertheless	however, nonetheless
besides	in addition, moreover	next	following in time
consequently	as a result, therefore	nonetheless	however, nevertheless
contrarily	on the other hand	on the other hand	however
earlier	before in time	otherwise	in contrast, contrarily
finally	at last, lastly	second	in time sequence
first	beginning of a sequence	similarly	also, likewise, thus
for example	for instance	still	however, furthermore
for instance	for example	subsequently	after, consequently
fortunately	luckily	suddenly	abruptly, quickly
furthermore	in addition, moreover	then	after, next in time
hence	therefore, as a result	therefore	consequently
however	but	third	in time sequence
in addition	also	thus	therefore, consequently
in conclusion	finally	unfortunately	sadly, unluckily
indeed	in fact	yet	however, still

Special Notes About Conjunctive Adverbs

1. Notice that conjunctive adverbs are the same adverbs that can be used as introductory adverbs at the beginning of simple sentences (see Chapter 7, page 200). Many additional adverbs that end in *-ly* can also function as conjunctive adverbs that join two independent clauses.

> Mary decided to move to Reno. **Surprisingly,** her parents were supportive.

> Mary decided to move to Reno; **surprisingly,** her parents were supportive.

> The ski patrol was near the avalanche. **Remarkably,** everyone escaped injury.

> The ski patrol was near the avalanche; **remarkably,** everyone escaped injury.

2. In addition to joining two independent clauses, a conjunctive adverb can work in other ways. A conjunctive adverb can appear at the beginning, middle, or end of a sentence. A conjunctive adverb in the middle of a sentences is a **sentence interrupter.**

> *Beginning:*   These forms will not take you long to complete. **For example,** the application is only one page long.
>
> *Middle:*   You must, **however,** answer all fifty questions.
>
> *End:*   The questions are routine but important, **nonetheless.**

3. To determine whether a conjunctive adverb is working to join two independent clauses, cover up the conjunctive adverb. If you see an independent clause (a complete subject and verb) on each side of the conjunctive adverb, the sentence is a compound sentence and requires a semicolon and a comma for punctuation. If the adverb is a sentence interrupter, use a comma before and after the adverb.

> The <u>movie</u>, **however,** <u>received</u> rave reviews.
> [The adverb is a sentence interrupter and is not joining two independent clauses. This is a simple sentence, not a compound sentence.]

> <u>I</u> <u>wanted</u> to express my opinion; **therefore,** <u>I</u> <u>wrote</u> a review for the newspaper.
> [The conjunctive adverb joins two independent clauses. This is a compound sentence.]

Practice 4   *Using Conjunctive Adverbs*

Select an appropriate conjunctive adverb to complete each of the following compound sentences. Avoid using a conjunctive adverb more than one time. Add the required punctuation before and after the conjunctive adverb. *Answers may vary. Possible answers are given.*

Example: Erik lost his winning lottery ticket ; thus, he was unable to claim the money.

1. Clara is extremely self-reliant ; consequently, she never asks anyone for help.

2. The storm ripped along the coast ; as a result, the beaches were covered with debris.

3. The largest tree in America has been identified ; however, the Forest Service is keeping the location of the tree a secret.

4. My roommate must pay half of the phone bill ; otherwise, our phone will be disconnected.

5. Many languages are spoken in the United States ; nevertheless, only one language is recognized as the official language of the nation.

6. Spanish is spoken by many Americans ; unfortunately, I have not yet learned to speak Spanish.

7. Television now offers more accommodations for deaf and hard-of-hearing viewers ; for example, many programs use live captioning on the bottom of the screens.

8. I heard a loud noise ; suddenly, I felt a sharp jolt.

9. I refuse to sign this disclaimer ; furthermore, I refuse to do business with you again.

10. My elderly grandmother fell on the sidewalk ; fortunately, a kindhearted stranger came to her rescue.

Practice 5   *Identifying and Punctuating Simple and Compound Sentences*

Work with a partner, in a small group, or on your own to complete the following directions. Mark the prepositional phrases, the infinitives, the subjects, and the verbs. On the blank, write **S** if the sentence is a *simple sentence.* Write **C** if the sentence is a *compound sentence.*

Example: __S__   (In the year 2100), the American population will double.

_____C_____ 1. The <u>Census Bureau</u> <u>predicts</u> population figures (for the next century); shockingly, (in the year 2100), 571 million <u>Americans</u> <u>will live</u> (in the United States).

_____S_____ 2. <u>Will</u> the <u>United States</u> <u>be</u> overcrowded?

_____C_____ 3. <u>Overcrowdedness</u> <u>is</u> avoidable, for <u>Americans</u> <u>have</u> ample undeveloped or underdeveloped land (on which)(to sprawl).

_____C_____ 4. The U.S. population <u>density</u> <u>is</u> low; many European <u>countries</u> already <u>have</u> much higher density rates.

_____S_____ 5. (In the year 2100), the <u>prediction</u> (for American population density) <u>is</u> 161.4 people (per square mile).

_____S_____ 6. The population <u>density</u> (in Germany and the United Kingdom) currently <u>is</u> four times greater than the population density (in the United States).

_____S_____ 7. The <u>profile</u> (of the American population) <u>will change</u> (during the next century).

_____C_____ 8. The <u>population</u> <u>will be</u> older; an estimated 5.3 million <u>people</u> <u>will be</u> (over the age) (of 100).

_____C_____ 9. Today, 0.02 <u>percent</u> (of the population) <u>is</u> (over the age)(of 100); however, this <u>percentage</u> <u>will change</u> (in 2100)(to 0.9 percent).

_____S_____ 10. Better medical <u>care</u> <u>will increase</u> the longevity figures.

_____S_____ 11. <u>Advances</u> (in medical technology and research) <u>will lengthen</u> the life span.

_____C_____ 12. The largest age <u>group</u> (in 2100) <u>is</u> likely [to be] teenagers; (in fact), 6.4 <u>percent</u> (of the population) <u>will be</u> (in the 15-to-19-year-old age bracket).

_____S_____ 13. Population <u>growth</u> and the contributing <u>factors</u> (for population growth) <u>are</u> quite interesting.

_____S_____ 14. The U.S. <u>population</u> (in 1800) <u>was</u> 5.3 million people.

_____S_____ 15. The <u>population</u> <u>jumped</u> (in that century)(to a whopping 75.9 million people)(in 1900).

[Adapted from Randolph Schmid, AP, "Century from Now, U.S. May Double Population," *Register Guard*, January 13, 2000.]

COMMA SENSE

1. Use a comma before a coordinating conjunction when the conjunction joins two independent clauses to form a compound sentence. The coordinating conjunctions are *and, but, for, nor, or, so,* and *yet.*

> I have many acquaintances, **but** I have few close friends.

> I enjoy talking with my friends, **and** I enjoy going to movies with them.

> Jacob is not my boyfriend, **nor** is he my friend.

2. Use a comma after a conjunctive adverb when it is used to join two sentences to form a compound sentence. (Note that a semicolon is used before the conjunctive adverb in a compound sentence.)

> I have many acquaintances; **however,** I have few close friends.

> I enjoy talking with my friends; **in addition,** I enjoy going to movies with them.

3. Use a comma before and after an adverb inside an independent clause when the adverb interrupts the flow of the sentence. You will hear yourself pause at the point of the adverb when you read the sentence out loud. The adverb is not essential to the overall meaning of the sentence.

> Fifty employees, **unfortunately,** will be laid off in January.

> The manager wants, **therefore,** to give the news to her employees.

Practice 6   *Punctuating with Commas*

Add commas where they are needed in the following sentences.

1. Fish, snakes, owls, and chimpanzees are on exhibit at the zoo, but the zoo no longer has birds, lions, or giraffes.

2. None of the members of the board, however, want to vote to change the budget.

3. A wide variety of performers will appear onstage; consequently, this concert will sell out quickly.

4. Therefore, everyone was asked to sign the petition or to take time to campaign.

5. This project is not a high priority for me; nevertheless, I will participate.

6. Your interview skills are excellent; on the other hand, your resumé needs refining.

7. Thus, I would like to be considered for a promotion.

8. My daughter begged me to consider her request; finally, I gave her my permission.

9. The bill is first sent to Congress for approval; next, the bill is sent to the President to sign.

10. The President, however, has the power to veto any bill.

Run-On Sentence and Comma Splice Errors

Two common writing errors occur when correct punctuation is not used in compound sentences: run-on sentences (RO) and comma splices (CS). Both errors are easy to correct with proper punctuation and conjunctions.

 RUN-ON SENTENCE ERROR   A run-on sentence occurs when two or more independent clauses follow each other without any punctuation.

A common pattern of a run-on sentence looks like this:

The <u>roads</u> <u>were</u> too icy <u>we</u> <u>had</u> to stop at a motel.

Traction <u>devices</u> <u>were</u> necessary <u>we</u> <u>did</u> not <u>have</u> any.

You can correct a run-on sentence error by using one of these four methods:

1. Separate the two sentences by using a period at the end of the first sentence.

    The roads were too icy. We had to stop at a motel.

    Traction devices were necessary. We did not have any.

> **JUST SO YOU KNOW...**
>
> Run-on sentences are also referred to as *fused sentences.*

2. Use a comma with a coordinating conjunction (one of the FAN BOYS).

The roads were too icy, **so** we had to stop at a motel.

Traction devices were necessary, **but** we did not have any.

3. Use a semicolon between the two sentences.

The roads were too icy; we had to stop at a motel.

Traction devices were necessary; we did not have any.

4. Add a semicolon and a conjunctive adverb. Remember that a comma follows the conjunctive adverb.

The roads were too icy; **therefore**, we had to stop at a motel.

Traction devices were necessary; **however**, we did not have any.

 COMMA SPLICE ERROR   A comma splice error occurs when two independent clauses are joined with only a comma. A comma is too weak of a punctuation mark to use to make a compound sentence.

A common sentence pattern for a comma splice error looks like this:

You can correct a comma splice error by using one of these four methods:

1. Separate the two sentences by using a period at the end of the first sentence.

Cars slid into ditches. One truck jackknifed.

The storm came suddenly. Drivers were unprepared.

2. Add a coordinating conjunction after the comma.

Cars slid into ditches, **and** one truck jackknifed.

The storm came suddenly, **so** drivers were unprepared.

3. Replace the comma with a semicolon.

Cars slid into ditches; one truck jackknifed.

The storm came suddenly; drivers were unprepared.

4. Replace the comma with a semicolon and add a conjunctive adverb, followed by a comma.

Cars slid into ditches; **also,** one truck jackknifed.

The storm came suddenly; **consequently,** drivers were unprepared.

Practice 7   *Identifying Run-On Sentence and Comma Splice Errors*

Analyze the subject-verb patterns in the following sentences. Use the following abbreviations to indicate sentence errors or complete sentences. For RO and CS errors, draw an arrow to point to the place in the sentence where the error occurs.

RO = run-on error   **CS** = comma splice error

SENT = sentence without errors

Example: __RO__   Your car needs a tune-up it also needs new tires.

__RO__   1. Our server is down we cannot access email or the Internet.

__SENT__   2. Many businesses rely on their computer systems for their daily operations.

__CS__   3. One day, the electricity was out, the phone lines were dead.

__RO__   4. One grocery store had to stop checking out groceries the cashiers could not add up long sums in their heads.

__SENT__   5. Computers are used extensively in businesses, government, schools, and people's homes.

__CS__   6. At the turn of the century, people were paranoid, fear of Y2K (year 2000) was on many people's minds.

__RO__   7. This fear was exploited by commercial vendors people bought excessive supplies for their homes and special software programs for their computers.

_____SENT_____ 8. One man spent $20,000 to stockpile food, water, firearms, and fuel for his family.

_____RO_____ 9. He must have felt foolish on January 1 ↓ well, he won't need to shop for quite some time.

_____CS_____ 10. Most of my friends did buy extra water, ↓ some also bought flashlights, firewood, and canned foods.

Practice 8   *Matching Punctuation to Conjunctions*

Assume that each of the following conjunctions is being used to join two independent clauses to form a compound sentence. Show the punctuation that you would use before and/or after each type of conjunction in a compound sentence.

1. S-V; thus, S-V.

2. S-V; however, S-V.

3. S-V; finally, S-V.

4. S-V, for S-V.

5. S-V; indeed, S-V.

6. S-V; in fact, S-V.

7. S-V, or S-V.

8. S-V, so S-V.

9. S-V; as a result, S-V.

10. S-V, and S-V.

11. S-V, but S-V.

12. S-V, yet S-V.

13. S-V; therefore, S-V.

14. S-V, nor V-S.

15. S-V; nevertheless, S-V.

Subject-Verb Agreement in Compound Sentences

 SUBJECT-VERB AGREEMENT   **The term *subject-verb agreement* means that singular subjects must use the singular form of the verb; plural subjects must use the plural form of the verb.**

Subject-verb agreement applies specifically to present tense verbs in the third person and to the helping verbs in verb phrases.

> **JUST SO YOU KNOW...**
>
> The same rules for agreement you learned previously apply to the independent clauses in compound sentences. (Chapter 5, page 110 and Chapter 6, page 153.)

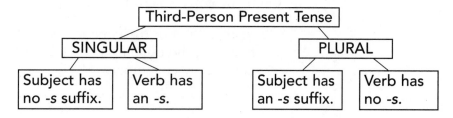

Third-Person Present Tense			
SINGULAR		**PLURAL**	
Subject has no -*s* suffix.	Verb has an -*s*.	Subject has an -*s* suffix.	Verb has no -*s*.

In compound sentences, the subjects and the verbs must agree in each of the independent clauses. The following examples show subject-verb agreement in both independent clauses:

Singular subject-verb agreement:

singular · *singular*

Robert appears at many community events, **for** he wants people to become familiar with his name and his political platform.

Plural subject-verb agreement:

plural

Both candidates want a positive race; **however,** political

plural

campaigns often become negative.

Singular and plural subject-verb agreement:

plural · *singular*

The people on the street favor Mildred, **but** the editor of the

singular

local newspaper favors Robert.

To proofread for subject-verb agreement in compound sentences, cover up the conjunction that joins the two sentences and analyze each independent clause (sentence) separately.

Subject-verb agreement:	*plural* The candidates want to debate, but *plural* the networks do not offer free airtime.
Lack of subject-verb agreement:	Neither senior citizens nor young *plural / singular* college students on this campus turns *plural* out to vote, but local leaders hope to change this pattern of noninvolvement.

Practice 9   *Using Subject-Verb Agreement in Compound Sentences*

Circle the correct verb for the following compound sentences.

1. Neither she nor the contractors (want) wants) further delays; however, the building permit for the two structures (is) are) delayed by city paperwork.

2. Each owner of the condos (has, have) the right to vote on the plan, but many owners (fail, fails) to complete the ballot.

3. All of my planner pages (is, are) filled with appointments; thus, more engagements (does, do) not fit on my schedule.

4. Several of the articles (needs, need) approval from the editor; however, the editor (lacks, lack) time to approve them in a timely manner.

5. The fabric for the curtains (match, matches) the furniture, but the owners (want, wants) more contrast in the room.

6. The highlighter pens (come, comes) in four colors, but many teachers (prefer, prefers) to use only black pens.

7. The remains of the monument (is, are) threatened by vandals, so visitors to the site (is, are) not allowed to walk past the fences.

8. One Internet site (auction, auctions) unusual artifacts; dinosaur bones from archaeological digs (sell, sells) for hundreds of thousands of dollars.

9. Dog owners from all over the United States (gather, gathers) every year to show their pedigreed dogs, and each (hope, hopes) to leave with a first-place ribbon.

10. Each contestant at national dog shows (pay, pays) an entry fee, and each dog in the competition (receive, receives) a complete physical examination.

Special Notes About Subject-Verb Agreement

1. **Collective nouns** are nouns that describe a group of people or things. Following are some common collective nouns.

COLLECTIVE NOUNS				
audience	collection	faculty	league	society
band	college	family	orchestra	squad
board	committee	firm	panel	staff
bunch	company	flock	population	team
cast	council	government	public	tribe
choir	couple	group	quartet	troop
chorus	crew	herd	school	troupe
class	crowd	jury	series	union

A collective noun requires a singular verb when the noun suggests a group is acting as one unit.

> The **family** <u>moves</u> every five years.

> The **team** <u>travels</u> throughout the season

> The **couple** <u>glides</u> smoothly across the dance floor.

However, a plural verb is required when the members of the group are acting individually.

> The **family** usually <u>arrive</u> for the reunion over the course of three or four days.

> The **team** <u>practice</u> at various times throughout the day.

> The **couple** <u>vote</u> differently in every election.

If a plural verb sounds awkward to you with a collective noun in which members act as individuals, you can usually rewrite the sentence with the word *members* or another word that makes sense:

> The family **members** usually <u>arrive</u> for the reunion over the course of three or four days.

> The **members** of the team <u>practice</u> at various times throughout the day.

> The **husband** and **wife** <u>vote</u> differently in every election.

2. Some nouns that end in *-s* are singular nouns and require singular verbs for subject-verb agreement.

aerobics	economics	mumps	summons
athletics	gymnastics	news	United Nations
checkers	headquarters	physics	United States
civics	mathematics	politics*	whereabouts
economics	measles	statistics*	

Politics and *statistics* are singular when they refer to a profession, a science, an art, or a course:
> *Politics is a stressful job. Statistics is my most challenging course.*

Politics and *statistics* may also be plural. *Politics* is plural when the word refers to different opinions or activities of individuals. *Statistics* is plural when the word refers to numbers and data:
> *Internal politics are destroying the team spirit.*
> *Crime statistics are available from the government.*

singular

Aerobics provides excellent cardiovascular exercise.

singular

Economics has been one of my favorite classes.

singular

The United States has many national monuments.

singular

Athletics keeps many young adults in good physical condition.

Practice 10   *Identifying Subject-Verb Agreement*

In each of the following compound sentences, select the correct verb to match the subject. Underline the subjects once and the complete verbs twice in each independent clause.

Example: Uncle Joe's estate is not yet mine, for the family (intends, intend) to contest the will.

1. Checkers (is, are) one of my favorite games to play, but I also (enjoy, enjoys) chess and card games.

2. The jury (is, are) going to be sequestered; consequently, the members of the jury will not have access to media coverage of the trial.

3. I do not enjoy going to the movie theater downtown, for the young audience often (ruin, ruins) the movie for other moviegoers.

4. Our graduation committee (meet, meets) every Thursday, but no specific plans for graduation (is, are) yet available.

5. The company (releases, release) its financial report in January; ample statistics (is, are) in the report.

6. The team (wait, waits) for the whistle to blow; the whistle (signals, signal) the beginning of the swim meet.

7. The president of the college (wants, want) greater focus on ethnic studies; the faculty (agree, agrees) with the president.

8. Each team (want, wants) to go to the state championship; however, only eight teams in the state (earn, earns) that privilege.

9. The soccer team (win, wins) all of its home games; unfortunately, the team consistently (loses, lose) on the road.

10. Both parents (has, have) accepted jobs in Pennsylvania; thus, the family (has, have) decided to relocate.

11. <u>Politics</u> (require, <u>requires</u>) a high level of commitment and energy, but <u>it</u> also (require, <u>requires</u>) a large amount of money and financial backing.

12. The young <u>couple</u> (<u>was</u>, were) married last week in Las Vegas; <u>they</u> (plans, <u>plan</u>) to be gone for two weeks.

13. The <u>faculty</u> at the local community college (<u>was</u>, were) praised for its commitment to quality education; faculty <u>members</u> (deserves, <u>deserve</u>) the recognition.

14. <u>Physics</u> (involve, <u>involves</u>) the study of energy systems; <u>biophysics</u> (deal, <u>deals</u>) with biological phenomena in relation to physics.

Practice 11   *Proofreading for Errors*

Proofread the following compound sentences for punctuation errors and subject-verb agreement errors. Correct the errors.

1. Everyone held ~~their~~ [his or her] breath, for the committee was ready to announce the winners of the contest.

2. That couple take separate vacations every year, yet they ~~seems~~ [seem] to be happily married.

3. The faculty ~~has~~ [have] been assigned parking spaces; however, they must pay for their spaces.

4. Electronics ~~frighten~~ [frightens] many freshman students, but I love the subject and the teacher.

5. The high school orchestra gives a spring concert; unfortunately, I am never able to attend it.

6. Their jazz band is the best in the state, so ~~they receive~~ [it receives] all the attention.

7. The city council ~~are~~ [is] hoping to see public support for Measure 52, but local support is not likely.

8. Our group always gathers at the beach during spring vacation[no semicolon]but[no comma] this year three of our members will not be present.

9. The news on most television stations ~~cover~~ [covers] current events, but events are frequently sensationalized to increase the station's ratings.

10. The board ~~approve~~ [approves] all of the college's bids for construction, but the process often involves long delays.

© Michael Zide

Work with a partner, in a small group, or on your own to complete this exercise. Proofread the following paragraphs. Add any missing punctuation or capital letters. Delete unnecessary punctuation. Correct any subject-verb agreement errors. *Answers may vary. In the key that follows, semicolons may be replaced with periods.*

SACAGAWEA

The Susan B. Anthony silver dollar was a futile attempt to change ᴬamerican currency. This silver dollar was minted from 1979 to 1981; however, the silver dollar was not popular. It was the size of a quarter, so many Americans confused it with the quarter. The Anthony dollar depicts the 19th-century suffragette Susan B. Anthony. Her profile on the coin shows a stern look. Americans saved the silver dollar in drawers or piggy banks at home; they did not circulate or spend the dollars. Approximately 857 million Susan B. Anthony dollars were minted; this stockpile of ˢsusan ᴮb. ᴬanthony silver dollars ~~were~~ ᵂᵃˢ almost depleted at the end of the millennium, but the U.S. mint decided not to produce more silver dollars. Instead, a plan for a "golden dollar" emerged.

The "golden dollar" was designed to replace the unpopular Susan B. Anthony silver dollar. The new "golden dollar" is unlike any other coin. This dollar is not made of gold; it is made of copper, manganese, nickel, and zinc. The dollar is the color of gold.

The "golden dollar" is called the Sacagawea dollar. Sacagawea was a young Shoshone Indian woman. She guided ᴸlewis and ᶜclark on their historic expedition to the ᴾpacific ᴺnorthwest. Sacagawea is featured carrying her son on her back. ˢshe has a warm, proud look on her face. The back of the coin portrays an eagle with outstretched wings.

The U.S. mint wanted to get this new "golden dollar" into the hands of consumers, so it decided to distribute the golden coins through the nation's largest retailer. On January 28, 2000, all 3,000 of the nation's Wal-Mart stores received their first shipment of golden dollars. each store eventually received 30,000 golden dollars to circulate among customers. Instantly, thousands of people flocked to the Wal-Mart stores to pocket the new coins. The gold coins disappeared rapidly from the tills; the supply could not keep up with the demand. In January, the U.S. Mint had a backlog of orders for the golden dollars, so the production for the coin was doubled to five million a day. By the end of February 2000, more than 200 million golden dollars were in circulation. The U.S. mint estimates it will produce more than one billion of these dollars for circulation.

Has the U.S. Mint finally produced a "winner"? Will the Sacagawea dollar remain popular over the years, or was the instant interest in the golden dollar merely a fad or an opportunity to add a coin to a personal coin collection? Will Americans carry the coins in their purses or pockets, or will they tuck Sacagawea safely in a drawer next to Susan? Time will tell.

[Adapted from *New York Times*, January 23, 2000; *Register Guard*, February 12, 2000; *Register Guard*, February 16, 2000.]

EXERCISE 8.2   **Writing Compound Sentences**

Name _____ Date _____

Select a general theme to use in all of your sentences. For example, you might use the name of your town, a favorite hobby, a television show or a movie, your school, an interesting career, or a place you have visited. Write compound sentences that use the following conjunctions. *Write your sentences on separate paper. Answers will vary.*

1. and	4. but	7. yet	10. nor
2. for	5. however	8. unfortunately	11. for example
3. therefore	6. consequently	9. thus	12. or

EXERCISE 8.3 Combining Sentences

Name _____ Date _____

Use any of the three methods discussed in this chapter to combine each pair of sentences into a compound sentence. Remember to use the proper punctuation. *Write your sentences on separate paper. Answers will vary. Each compound sentence should contain a comma and a coordinating conjunction; a semicolon; or a semicolon, a conjunctive adverb, and a comma. One possible answer is shown.*

1. My lawyer is often nervous in the courtroom. He does not show this nervousness to a judge or a jury. My lawyer is often nervous in the courtroom; however, he does not show this nervousness to a judge or a jury.

2. The rain has set new rainfall records. Several rivers are above their flood stages. The rain has set new rainfall records; consequently, several rivers are above their flood stages.

3. The rescue mission was dangerous. The Coast Guard was willing to attempt the rescue. The rescue mission was dangerous, but the Coast Guard was willing to attempt the mission.

4. The public relations officer was enraged. The lawsuit would damage the company's image. The public relations officer was enraged, for the lawsuit would damage the company's image.

5. Jackie's grandfather served in World War I. Veterans Day has special significance for him. Jackie's grandfather served in World War I, so Veterans Day has special significance for him.

6. I searched everywhere for my final paper. I could not locate it anywhere in my apartment. I searched everywhere for my final paper, but I could not locate it anywhere in my apartment.

7. I was born in Boston. I spent my teenage years in New Orleans. I was born in Boston, but I spent my teenage years in New Orleans.

8. The team was once called the Oilers. Now they are called the Titans. The team was once called the Oilers; now they are called the Titans.

9. Lucinda does not speak Spanish. She does not speak French. Lucinda does not speak Spanish, nor does she speak French.

10. Amateur investors lose large amounts of money with online trading. Only a few show profits. Amateur investors lose large amounts of money with online trading; in fact, only a few show profits.

EXERCISE 8.4 Sentence Variety Name _____ Date _____

Use two methods to combine each of the following sentences to make compound sentences. First, combine the two sentences by using an appropriate coordinating conjunction. Second, combine the two sentences by using an appropriate conjunctive adverb. You may rearrange the order of the independent clauses if you wish. Be sure to use proper punctuation. *Write your sentences on separate paper. Answers may vary. Possible answers are given.*

Example: Russell's clothes stank. He had been cleaning fish.
Russell's clothes stank, **for** he had been cleaning fish.
Russell had been cleaning fish**; consequently,** his clothes stank.

1. Census takers visited each home. They visited shelters for the homeless. Census takers visited each home, and they visited shelters for the homeless. Census takers visited each home; furthermore, they visited shelters for the homeless.

2. The house was dark. We left a note. The house was dark, so we left a note. The house was dark; therefore, we left a note.

3. The museum occupies the first three floors. It still lacks sufficient space. The museum occupies the first three floors, yet it still lacks sufficient space. The museum occupies the first three floors; unfortunately, it still lacks sufficient space.

4. I missed my stop. I fell asleep on the subway. I missed my stop, for I fell asleep on the subway. I fell asleep on the subway; consequently, I missed my stop.

5. I planned my time well. My research paper was thorough. I planned my time well, so my research paper was thorough. I planned my time well; as a result, my research paper was thorough.

6. The companies merged. People lost their jobs. The companies merged, so people lost their jobs. The companies merged; unfortunately, people lost their jobs.

EXERCISE 8.5   Proofreading   Name _____ Date _____

Each sentence has at least one error. Proofread carefully and correct all the errors you find in each sentence. *Answers will vary. Periods may be used instead of semicolons.*

1. The agreement was perfect for us; we both saved money.

2. You can use the restroom; however, you need to get the key from the front desk.

3. John's new puppy is frisky and hyperactive; he chews on John's slippers, furniture, and rug.

4. My neighbor's youngest daughter, however, is graduating from high school early.

5. I do not see ~~good~~ well, so I have to get some new glasses.

6. My math teacher and my art teacher ~~is~~ are new to town, but both are making friends ~~quick~~ quickly.

7. The president of the board, therefore, asked each member of the audience for ideas.

8. The unexpected high winds destroyed roofs ~~,~~ no comma and uprooted many trees in the neighborhood.

9. The New Year's Eve celebration always lasts until dawn, but I do not.

10. An email message alerted me to a new virus, so I refused to open some of my files.

EXERCISE 8.6   **Sentence Combining**   Name _____ Date _____

The following list of sentences and parts of sentences can be combined into one paragraph. Decide on the best method to combine the following information. *On separate paper,* write a complete paragraph using the twenty items in the list below. Use a variety of simple and compound sentences in your paragraph. *Answers will vary. Check answers for proper sentence structure and punctuation.*

1. Shelf after shelf of human brains are carefully preserved and stored

2. in plastic boxes

3. more brains are stored in huge freezers

4. doctors studied the brain of one Alzheimer's patient

5. it was lighter in weight

6. it had deeper grooves than a disease-free brain

7. many people donate livers, kidneys, or other organs to research

8. too few people consider donating their brains

9. researchers need more brain donations

10. to study brain diseases

11. they also need donations from people with psychiatric illnesses

12. they need normal brains to use for comparisons

13. with more brain donations

14. doctors could possibly find cures for Alzheimer's

15. Lou Gehrig's disease

16. schizophrenia, manic depression

17. and a host of other brain diseases

18. people hesitate to donate brains

19. doctors try to tell grieving families about the importance

20. of brain donations for research

[Adapted from Lauran Neergaard, AP, "Researchers Long for Brain Donors," *Register Guard*, November 6, 1999.]

Circle the correct verb to agree with each subject. Then write one additional independent clause to create a compound sentence. You may use any method to combine the two independent clauses. *Answers will vary for the second independent clause. Carefully check the second independent clause for correct pronoun usage. Examples are given below.*

1. Mathematics (require, (requires)) an analytical mind, and it requires accuracy and attention to details.

2. There ((is), are) a committee to explore the options, but it does not meet until next month.

3. The team ((order), orders) their meals in advance, for every person has a different preference or dietary need.

4. Politics ((is), are) in the news every day; therefore, people have ample opportunities to be well informed.

5. The church choir (want, (wants)) a new director, for its current director has shown little interest in his work.

6. Our local cable company (plan, (plans)) to add three new channels, so viewing options will be better.

7. The chorus (sing, (sings)) traditional hymns; however, sometimes it sings contemporary music.

8. The public (favor, (favors)) tax reductions, for it feels overtaxed.

9. The audience (laugh, (laughs)) at all of her jokes, but I do not see the humor.

10. The faculty (was, (were)) given different benefit packages and salaries; the differences were based on seniority and job descriptions.

EXERCISE 8.8 **Sentence Review** Name _____ Date _____

The following excerpt from a marketing textbook has been altered to provide practice with proofreading and identification of simple and compound sentences. The original text was error-free. Each sentence is numbered; use the following symbols to label the sentences on the numbered lines below each paragraph:

S = simple sentence   C = compound sentence

CS = comma splice error   RO = run-on sentence error

[1]Differences in the marketing environment may require special adaptations in product packaging. [2]Different climatic conditions often demand a change in the package to ensure sufficient protection or shelf life. [3]The role a package assumes in promotion also depends on the retailing structure. [4]In countries with a substantial degree of self-service merchandising, a package with strong promotional appeal is desirable; these requirements may be scaled down for over-the-counter service merchandising. [5]In addition, distribution handling requirements are not identical throughout the world. [6]In high-wage countries, products tend to be packaged to reduce further handling by retail employees all merchandisers have to do is place the products on the shelves. [7]In countries with lower wages, individual orders may be filled from larger packaged units, extra labor is required by the retailer.

1. ____S____ 2. ____S____ 3. ____S____ 4. ____C____

5. ____S____ 6. ____RO____ 7. ____CS____

[8]Packages can assume almost any shape, customs and traditions of each market often affect the shape. [9]Materials used for packaging can also differ widely. [10]For example, Americans prefer to buy mayonnaise and mustard in glass containers; consumers in Germany and Switzerland prefer to buy these products in tubes. [11]Cans are customarily used to package beer in the United States, but glass bottles are preferred in Europe. [12]International marketing is complex manufacturers need to adjust their packaging to accommodate and attract international consumers.

8. ____CS____ 9. ____S____ 10. ____C____

11. ____C____ 12. ____RO____

[Adapted from Jeannett Hennessey, *Global Marketing Strategies*, Houghton Mifflin Co., 1998, pp. 361–362.]

EXERCISE 8.9   CS and RO Errors   Name _____ Date _____

Work with a partner, in a small group, or on your own to complete this exercise. Write **CS** above any comma splice errors and **RO** above any run-on sentence errors. Use any method to correct these errors. Add any other missing commas. *Correction methods will vary. Possible methods of correction are given.*

A blind man can read large letters and navigate around big objects, a tiny camera is wired directly to his brain. The camera works like an artificial eye, but it mainly serves as a navigational device. This first brain implant was done in 1978, but scientists need to work to improve the software. The subject wears special sunglasses with a tiny pinhole camera mounted on one lens and an ultrasonic range finder on the other lens both devices communicate to a small computer carried on the subject's hip and to an adjacent computer. The camera sends signals to the brain through wires, the wires are implanted in the subject's brain. Electrodes are attached to sections of the brain. The signals stimulate certain sections of the brain, the subject sees specks of light. In the future, this artificial vision may help thousands of blind individuals to perform visual tasks.

[Adapted from The Associated Press, "Vision Aid for Blind Being Tested by Sight Researcher," *Register Guard*, January 17, 2000.]

Chapter 8 Summary

1. **Compound sentences** are made by joining two or more independent clauses by using one of three methods:

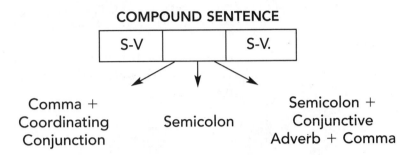

2. **Coordinating conjunctions,** also nicknamed "FAN BOYS," are the words *for, and, nor, but, or, yet,* and *so.* A comma is used before the coordinating conjunction when the conjunction joins two independent clauses: *I was nervous,* **yet** *I felt confident.*

3. A **semicolon** can be used to join two independent clauses to form a compound sentence. The semicolon replaces the period that might be used with the first independent clause: *I had practiced my speech many times; I knew the content well.*

4. A **conjunctive adverb** can also join two independent clauses. Words such as *therefore, thus, however, for example,* and *consequently* are conjunctive adverbs. A semicolon is used before the conjunctive adverb; a comma is used after the conjunctive adverb: *My speech included humor;* **therefore,** *the audience was attentive.*

5. **Run-on sentence errors** occur when two independent clauses are joined without any punctuation between the clauses. Run-on sentence errors can be corrected by inserting a period or a semicolon. Run-on errors can also be corrected by using a coordinating conjunction or a conjunctive adverb and the corresponding punctuation.

6. **Comma splice errors** occur when two independent clauses are joined with only a comma. Comma splice errors can be corrected by using the same methods as are used to correct run-on sentence errors.

7. **Subject-verb agreement** in compound sentences must occur in both independent clauses. Singular subjects require the singular form of the verb; plural subjects require the plural form of the verb.

8. **Collective nouns** such as *audience, choir, committee,* and *staff* represent a unit of people or things. Collective nouns almost always use singular verbs unless the members of the group act individually.

9. Some nouns, such as *athletics, economics, news,* and *United States,* seem to be plural because they end in *-s,* but they are singular nouns and require singular forms of verbs.

Writing Topics for Chapter 8

Select one of the writing options below. Write a paragraph or two about the selected topic. Proofread your work before you turn it in.

 1. Use the Internet or your library to learn more about Sacagawea. Where was her tribe located? How did she become the guide for Lewis and Clark? Why did they value her as a guide? Why is she being commemorated on the new "golden dollar"? Summarize the information you read about Sacagawea. With your summary, include a copy of the source of your information.

 2. Use the Internet or your library to learn more about American currency. What currencies are in circulation? What is the largest bill in print? Who appears on the different American coins and paper currencies? Where is the U.S. Mint? Where are coins minted, and where is the paper currency printed? Summarize what you learn about American currency. With your summary, include a copy of the source of your information.

3. Locate an international student in your school or your community. Discuss the product packaging differences that were discussed in Exercise 8.8. Ask the student to help you identify other product packaging differences between the United States and the student's country. How are stores the same? How are they different?

4. Modern medical technology provides many people with new alternatives and treatments that lead to healthier or more manageable lives. Discuss how medical technology has influenced the life of one person you know or have heard about through the media.

Web Site Learning Experiences

See the web site for this book to locate companion exercises and links related to the grammar topics in this chapter.

Go to: http://college.hmco.com. Click on "Students." Type *Sentence Essentials* in the "Jump to Textbook Sites" box. Click "go" and then bookmark the site. Click on Chapter 8.

CHAPTER 8 • Review   Name _____ Date _____

Total Possible: 50   Your Score: _____

Part I: Simple and Compound Sentences (30 points)

Mark the subjects and the verbs in the following sentences. On the blank, write **S** if the sentence is a *simple sentence;* write **C** if the sentence is a *compound sentence. Give one point for sentence identification, one for the correct subject(s), and one for the correct verb(s).*

_____S_____ 1. Fresh <u>flowers</u> always <u>improve</u> my mother's mood.

_____C_____ 2. The <u>concert</u> <u>has started</u>, but <u>we</u> still <u>have</u> not <u>found</u> our tickets.

_____C_____ 3. The lecture <u>hall</u> <u>was</u> nearly empty, for a flu <u>epidemic</u> <u>had hit</u> the campus.

_____S_____ 4. <u>I</u> <u>took</u> a deep breath and <u>started</u> the engine of my new car.

_____C_____ 5. The <u>plane</u> <u>landed</u> safely, and <u>everyone</u> <u>debarked</u> with a sigh of relief.

_____C_____ 6. An emergency <u>light</u> <u>flashed</u> in the cockpit, but <u>it</u> <u>was</u> a false alarm.

_____C_____ 7. <u>We</u> <u>boarded up</u> the windows, for a devastating <u>storm</u> <u>was approaching</u>.

_____S_____ 8. The <u>winds</u> <u>tore</u> the awning and the shutters off the house.

_____S_____ 9. Neither my <u>speech</u> nor my written <u>report</u> <u>was</u> ready for class on Monday.

_____C_____ 10. The <u>professor</u> <u>granted</u> me an extension, but <u>I</u> <u>was</u> still too sick to concentrate.

Part II: Sentence Writing (8 points)

Write four compound sentences that use the following conjunctions. Underline the subjects and the verbs in your sentences. *Give 0–2 points per sentence. One point can be for the correctly punctuated conjunction; the other can be for correct subject and verb identification.*

1. but _____

_____

2. nor

_____

3. therefore

_____

4. however

_____

Part III: Proofreading (12 points)

Proofread the following paragraphs for comma splice and run-on sentence errors. Use any method to correct the errors, making sure to add any necessary punctuation and capitalization. _Corrections must be made at the point of the arrows._

In Medford, Oregon, a self-described miser left a $9 million legacy to several social service agencies. His wealth surprised many people he lived in an unheated house, slept in a sleeping bag, wore secondhand clothes, and often held up his secondhand pants with a bungee cord. He ate free holiday meals at the local Salvation Army, he pedaled his bicycle around Jackson County and collected bottles and cans he could get a five-cent deposit refund for each one, this unusual man once taught a cat to ride with him on his bike he had a weakness for cats. He frequently adopted felines from the animal shelters; some of his neighbors complained about the number of cats in and around his house.

This miser was actually a bright, articulate person he started a savings plan as a child his father had given him money to invest in a savings plan later in life, he became a self-taught TV technician he was frugal, and he was wise he amassed his fortune by saving and investing wisely in the stock market one salesman at a local automobile showroom spent many hours with the miser the miser loved fine automobiles and enjoyed talking about automobile technology. The car salesman said, "You had to look beyond the clothes. I learned a valuable lesson from the miser. You can't really judge people by their physical appearance."

[Adapted from Associated Press, January 29, 2000.]

CHAPTER 9

Complex Sentences

In Chapter 9, you will learn about **complex sentences** and **dependent clauses.** You will learn to combine two or more sentences by using adverb clauses with subordinate conjunctions and adjective clauses with relative pronouns. Additional ways to avoid fragments are also presented in this chapter.

Understanding complex sentences will help you do the following:

1. Achieve greater sentence variety and more sophisticated sentences

2. Punctuate more advanced sentence structures correctly

3. Improve your proofreading and editing skills

4. Avoid writing fragments

 COMPLEX SENTENCE   **A complex sentence has one independent (main) clause and at least one dependent (subordinate) clause.**

Both clauses in a complex sentence have subjects and verbs.

If I leave now, I will arrive at the marina by noon.

The boat that I rented was old and unreliable.

 DEPENDENT CLAUSE **A dependent clause is a group of words that has a subject and a verb but cannot stand alone as a complete sentence.**

Dependent clauses, which are also called subordinate clauses, must be attached to an independent (main) clause. Dependent clauses begin with either a subordinate conjunction or a relative pronoun.

Subordinate conjunctions and relative pronouns are two kinds of words that signal the beginning of a dependent clause. They are used to form three different kinds of dependent clauses: adverb, adjective, and noun clauses. Even though we will not be labeling or classifying dependent clauses into these three categories, an overview of the three kinds of dependent clauses shows their functions and the key words that begin each type of clause. Both subordinate conjunctions and relative pronouns will be discussed in greater detail in this chapter.

1. **Adverb clause:** A dependent clause that begins with a **subordinate conjunction** shows a relationship between the dependent clause and the verb in the independent (main) clause. *After, because, before, if, since,* and *when* are common subordinate conjunctions.

   Because the forecast was for severe weather, we donned

   our life vests.

   Notice how the event in the dependent clause is related to the action *donned* in the independent clause. The meaning of the dependent clause relates to the verb in the independent clause; thus, this is an adverb clause.

2. **Adjective clause:** A dependent clause that begins with a **relative pronoun** shows a relationship between the dependent clause and a noun or a pronoun in the independent (main) clause. *Who, whom, whose, which,* and *that* are common relative pronouns.

   The Coast Guard officer who rescued us is a hero.

   Notice how the word *who* relates to the noun *officer*. The clause describes or modifies the noun *officer;* thus, this is an adjective clause.

3. **Noun clause:** Some dependent clauses function like nouns within a sentence. These dependent clauses may begin with either a subordinate conjunction or a relative pronoun. *What, whatever, who, whoever, that, what, when* and *where* are common words that begin noun clauses. To identify a noun clause, consider whether it can be replaced with the word *something* or *someone*. If it can, the dependent clause is a noun clause.

independent clause   dependent clause
We did what we had to do.

There is no noun immediately before the word *what;* therefore, *what* is not modifying a noun and does not form an adjective clause. It also does not modify the verb *did* in the independent clause; therefore, it is not an adverb clause. The only option left is a noun clause. To test whether it is a noun clause, substitute the word *something:* We did *something*.

Type 1 Dependent Clause: Adverb Clause with a Subordinate Conjunction

 SUBORDINATE CONJUNCTION   A subordinate conjunction is a word that begins a dependent clause and shows a relationship between the dependent clause and the independent (main) clause.

The relationship between a dependent and an independent clause may show time, place, manner, condition, cause, result, purpose, comparison, or contrast. The subordinate clause is grammatically less important than the main clause.

The following chart shows some common subordinate conjunctions. Note that some subordinate conjunctions consist of more than one word. (Also see the conjunction chart in Chapter 10 beginning on page 312.)

SUBORDINATE CONJUNCTIONS			
after	even if	once	until
although	even though	provided that	when
as	if	since	whenever
as if	in order that	so long as	where
as long as	in that	so that	whereas
as soon as	less than	than	wherever
as though	more than	though	whether
because	no matter how	till	while
before	now that	unless	

The subordinate conjunctions in the following dependent clauses are shown in italics. Each dependent clause has a subject and a verb; by itself, it is not a complete sentence.

After I received the news

As soon as the mail arrived

Because food was scarce

If you want to apply for a scholarship

Since you are new to town

When I receive the check

Whenever my mother comes to visit

Note that an independent clause that can stand on its own as a complete sentence occurs when you remove the subordinate conjunction.

~~*After*~~ I received the news.

~~*As soon as*~~ The mail arrived.

~~*Because*~~ Food was scarce.

~~*If*~~ You want to apply for a scholarship.

~~*Since*~~ You are new to town.

~~*When*~~ I receive the check.

~~*Whenever*~~ My mother comes to visit.

Connecting Dependent and Independent (Main) Clauses

Dependent clauses with subordinate conjunctions may be placed before or after the independent (main) clause. In the following examples, the dependent clause appears *before* the independent clause. A comma is placed at the end of the dependent clause. The sentence pattern looks like this:

dependent clause   independent clause

| *Subordinate conjunction* S-V, | S-V. |

After I received the news, I was stunned.

Because food was scarce, many people were dying from starvation.

If <u>you</u> <u>want</u> to apply for a scholarship, <u>you</u> <u>must write</u> two essays.

Once the <u>director</u> <u>receives</u> all the applications, the selection <u>process</u> <u>begins</u>.

Since <u>you</u> <u>are</u> new to town, <u>I</u> <u>would like</u> to show you around.

When <u>I</u> <u>receive</u> the check, <u>I</u> <u>will pay</u> you.

Whenever my <u>mother</u> <u>comes</u> to visit, our household routine <u>changes</u> drastically.

Whether <u>you</u> <u>win</u> or not, the <u>tournament</u> <u>is</u> a memorable experience.

Dependent clauses may also appear *after* the independent (main) clause. When the dependent clauses comes after the main clause, no comma is used. The sentence pattern looks like this:

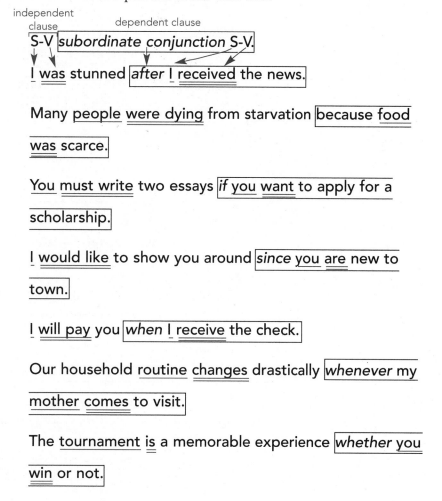

independent clause
dependent clause

S-V *subordinate conjunction S-V.*

<u>I</u> <u>was</u> stunned *after* <u>I</u> <u>received</u> the news.

Many <u>people</u> <u>were dying</u> from starvation *because* <u>food</u> <u>was scarce.*

<u>You</u> <u>must write</u> two essays *if* <u>you</u> <u>want</u> to apply for a scholarship.

<u>I</u> <u>would like</u> to show you around *since* <u>you</u> <u>are</u> new to town.

<u>I</u> <u>will pay</u> you *when* <u>I</u> <u>receive</u> the check.

Our household <u>routine</u> <u>changes</u> drastically *whenever* my <u>mother</u> <u>comes</u> to visit.

The <u>tournament</u> <u>is</u> a memorable experience *whether* <u>you</u> <u>win</u> or not.

Practice 1   *Identifying Dependent Clauses*

In each of the complex sentences below, draw a box around the dependent clause and write the subordinate conjunction. Underline the subjects once and the verbs twice in the dependent clauses.

Example: when   The band played loudly when the ambassador entered the room.

____While____   1. While you were out to lunch, you received two important phone messages.

____Because____   2. Because Beth is traveling by herself, she will borrow my cell phone.

____After____   3. After I receive my check, I will buy a new battery for my car.

____before____   4. Grandpa had no symptoms before he had his stroke.

____even if____   5. I am continuing with school even if I have to work at the same time.

____If____   6. If you arrive before 7:00 P.M., you will be able to sit near the stage.

__provided that__   7. My parents' insurance will cover me provided that I enroll in school.

____since____   8. She has lost thirty pounds since she started the vegetarian diet.

____when____   9. I moved to Washington when I was only three years old.

____Though____   10. Though the winters have been harsh, the plants in my garden have survived.

Practice 2   *Identifying and Punctuating Dependent Clauses*

In each sentence, draw a box around the dependent clause and circle the subordinate conjunction. Add a comma if one is needed between the two clauses.

Example: If you maintain your current grade point average, you will qualify for the grant.

1. Ross cannot get a promotion until he has worked in his position for three years.

2. [*Although* Nikki is old enough to vote,] she has not taken the time to register.

3. [*As soon as* I gather up my courage,] I will invite her to dinner.

4. [*Even though* the deadline has passed,] I am still going to mail in the application.

5. [*Before* I shower and dress each day,] I enjoy a fresh cup of herbal tea.

6. [*If* you fry the potatoes in butter,] you add excess calories and fat.

7. [*While* Ryan was at work,] a small fire started in his garage.

8. [*Though* the first rainstorm helped the crops,] the second storm flooded the field.

9. The employees of the company are paid well [*because* management wants to keep a stable work force.]

10. Janet's doctor was concerned [*because* Janet postponed her checkup twice.]

Practice 3 *Identifying Subjects and Verbs in Clauses*

In each sentence, draw a box around the dependent clause and circle the subordinate conjunction. Underline the subjects once and the verbs twice in both the dependent clauses and the independent clauses.

Example: [*When* the stock market falls,] bargain shoppers buy new stocks.

1. I decided to sell my car [*because* it was costing me too much money to maintain.]

2. The food was delicious [*even though* the portions were small.]

3. [*As soon as* we raise the money,] we will buy the team new uniforms.

4. [*Although* Colleen passed her bar exam last summer,] she has not found a job.

5. [*As* the line of people filed past the memorial,] admiration lit up their faces.

6. The television cameras appeared [*before* the mayor arrived.]

7. The viewing audience was small because *Monday Night Football was on the other station.*

8. When a rainbow appears in the sky, many people make wishes for prosperity.

9. No matter how difficult the hike will be, I want to reach the top of the mountain.

10. The boys played basketball on the weekends even though they did not make the team.

Special Notes About Complex Sentences with Subordinate Conjunctions

1. Some words that work as subordinate conjunctions can also work as prepositions. To determine whether a word is working as a subordinate conjunction or a preposition, examine the word in context. If the word forms a phrase that ends with a noun or a pronoun and no verb appears in the phrase, the word is a preposition. If the word forms a clause that has a subject and a verb, the word is a subordinate conjunction.

   Preposition:

   preposition   noun
   (After the dance), we took our compact disks home.

   Subordinate conjunction:

   conjunction   subject   verb
   After the dance ended, we went to my house for breakfast.

   Preposition:

   preposition   noun
   (Since that day), I have always enjoyed that swimming hole.

   Subordinate conjunction:

   conjunction   subject   verb
   Since the water is warm, I have always enjoyed that swimming hole.

2. A complex sentence may have more than one dependent clause. Notice in the following example that the complex sentence has two dependent clauses and that each clause has its own subject-verb pattern.

   dependent clause   independent clause
   After the hikers reached the peak, they ate, rested, and

   dependent clause
   told stories before they began their descent.

Practice 4   *Recognizing Simple Sentences and Complex Sentences*

Mark the prepositional phrases, infinitives, subjects, and verbs in the following sentences. Analyze the subject-verb patterns to determine whether each sentence is a simple sentence or a complex sentence. On the line, write **S** for *simple* sentence and **CX** for *complex* sentence.

Examples: S   The stakes [to mark] the location (of the posts) appeared every five feet.

    CX   Because my car needs a major tune-up, I hesitate [to drive] (over the mountains).

    S   1. (Between us) a bond (of friendship) will always exist.

    CX   2. Although she appears calm, she is a bundle (of nerves)

    CX   3. Grandpa mellows whenever he thinks (of his grandchildren)

    S   4. (Prior to the accident) the bus driver reported problems (with the brakes)

    CX   5. I can go (to the conference) unless my child is sick.

    CX   6. Though both students were late, they managed [to hear] most (of the lecture)

    S   7. (In class) several students had some difficulty (with the complex terminology)

    CX   8. When I retire, I will dedicate more time (to community volunteer work)

    S   9. (For this specific job) I am well qualified.

    CX   10. Now that you have passed the course, perhaps you could tutor me.

COMMA SENSE

1. Comma review:

   - Use a comma after introductory words:

     First, I must gather up all my notes to study for the final exam.

     However, time is of the essence.

   - Use a comma after introductory prepositional phrases:

     (In the meantime), focus on your primary goals.

     (Despite the loss), the team was optimistic about its chance to be in the playoffs.

   - Use a comma after introductory phrases that begin with an infinitive:

     [To win] the Boston marathon, the runner had to train over the course of several years.

     [To comprehend] better, read more slowly and highlight the key points.

2. Use a comma after a dependent clause that begins a complex sentence. A subordinate conjunction signals the beginning of a dependent clause.

   While you were gone, several important packages arrived.

   Because my tax refund check has not arrived, I cannot pay this bill.

Do not use a comma if the independent (main) clause appears first in a complex sentence.

   Several important packages arrived while you were gone.

   I cannot pay this bill because my tax refund check has not arrived.

Practice 5 *Identifying Sentence Types and Adding Punctuation*

Identify each sentence type as follows:

S = simple
C = compound
CX = complex

Add any missing punctuation to make the sentences complete.

Example: __C__ The space shuttle was schedule to land Saturday, but weather conditions caused a delay.

___C___ 1. The average cost of my groceries for one week is $100; however, sometimes I spend much less than that.

___C___ 2. The movie has been out for a month, but I have not seen it yet.

___CX___ 3. If everyone wants to go, we will not have room in the car.

___C___ 4. Blake just bought a motorcycle, but he does not yet have insurance.

___CX___ 5. Whenever I hear his name, my heart beats a little faster.

___S___ 6. All of our umbrellas flipped inside out in the wind yesterday.

___CX___ 7. Even though my intentions were good, I need to file for another tax extension.

___S___ 8. Young workers should set aside some money for future families and retirement.

___S___ 9. At the end of the debate, each candidate, however, wanted to make one last point.

___C___ 10. Mary has worked with the company for twelve years, yet she has not received a single promotion.

Type 2 Dependent Clause: Adjective Clause with a Relative Pronoun

 RELATIVE PRONOUN   **A relative pronoun replaces or refers to a preceding noun in the independent (main) clause.**

A relative pronoun clause tells *which one* or *what kind of.* The relative pronouns *who, whom, whose, which,* and *that* begin a dependent (subordinate) clause and function to connect or relate the dependent clause to the independent clause. Both the dependent and the independent clauses have subjects and verbs.

> independent clause
> dependent clause
> Dan researched the topic | *that* his teacher had assigned.

Notice how the sentence begins with an independent clause. The relative pronoun *that* refers to the preceding noun *topic.* The dependent clause begins with the relative pronoun.

> independent clause
> dependent clause
> Mr. Ramos, | who is my literature teacher, | provided us with several topics.

Notice how the dependent clause is inserted between the subject and the verb in the independent clause. The relative pronoun *who* refers to the preceding noun, *Mr. Ramos.*

The most common relative pronouns are shown in the box.

Relative Pronouns

who	whom	whose	which	that

- Use *who* when the clause needs a subject and the pronoun refers to a person.

- Use *whom* when the dependent clause already has a subject and the pronoun refers to a person.

- Also use *whom* inside prepositional phrases or as direct or indirect objects in sentences.

- Use *whose* when the pronoun refers to a person and shows ownership or possession.

- Use *which* when the dependent clause is not essential to the meaning of the sentence and when the pronoun refers to things instead of people. As you will see later in the chapter, a nonessential clause is set off by commas.

- Use *that* when the dependent clause is essential to the meaning of the sentence and when the pronoun refers to things instead of people. A dependent clause that begins with *that* is not set off by commas.

Who, *whom*, *whose*, *which*, and *that* are the most common relative pronouns. However, you will also encounter the following words working as relative pronouns at the beginning of dependent clauses:

| whoever | whomever | what | whatever | whichever |

Placement of Dependent Clauses with Relative Pronouns

In the following complex sentences, notice how the relative pronoun begins the dependent clause. The arrows point to the noun (the antecedent) in the independent clause that the relative pronoun refers to or replaces. In these examples, the relative pronoun is right next to the noun it refers to or replaces.

JUST SO YOU KNOW...

Relative pronoun clauses are also called *relative clauses*. When relative clauses modify nouns or pronouns and tell *which one* or *what kind of*, they are called *adjective clauses* or *adjectivals*.

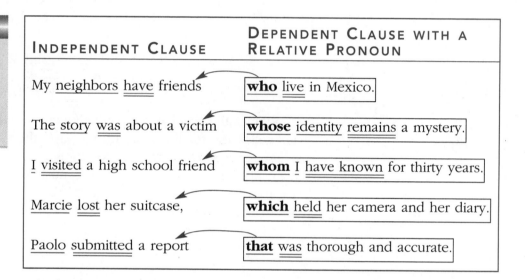

INDEPENDENT CLAUSE	DEPENDENT CLAUSE WITH A RELATIVE PRONOUN
My neighbors have friends	**who** live in Mexico.
The story was about a victim	**whose** identity remains a mystery.
I visited a high school friend	**whom** I have known for thirty years.
Marcie lost her suitcase,	**which** held her camera and her diary.
Paolo submitted a report	**that** was thorough and accurate.

The relative pronoun clause must be placed as close as possible to the noun (the antecedent) it refers to or replaces. If the relative pronoun clause is placed incorrectly, the intended meaning of the sentence is lost.

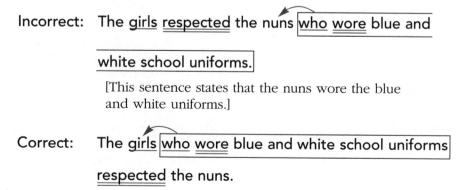

Incorrect: The girls respected the nuns who wore blue and white school uniforms.

[This sentence states that the nuns wore the blue and white uniforms.]

Correct: The girls who wore blue and white school uniforms respected the nuns.

Incorrect: The school <u>bazaar</u> <u>brings</u> people from all over the

city, | <u>which</u> <u>is</u> sponsored by the PTA. |

[This sentence states that the city is sponsored by
the PTA.]

Correct: The school <u>bazaar</u>, | <u>which</u> <u>is</u> sponsored by the PTA, |

<u>brings</u> people from all over the city.

Incorrect: The city <u>ordinance</u> <u>irritated</u> some patrons | <u>that</u>

<u>prohibits</u> skateboards and smoking on city buses. |

[The meaning of the sentence is unclear because
of the placement of the dependent clause.]

Correct: The city <u>ordinance</u> | <u>that</u> <u>prohibits</u> skateboards and

smoking on city buses | <u>irritated</u> some patrons.

Sometimes the relative pronoun clause (the dependent clause) is embedded inside the main clause. In this case, the subject and verb of the main sentence are split apart and the relative pronoun clause is inserted. Once again, the relative pronoun clause must be placed next to or as close as possible to the noun it refers to or replaces (the antecedent). To avoid confusion, always ask yourself, "What noun does this relative pronoun refer to or replace?"

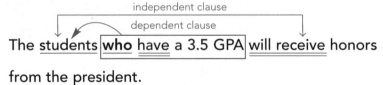

The <u>students</u> | <u>who</u> <u>have</u> a 3.5 GPA | <u>will receive</u> honors

from the president.

The dependent clause has been inserted between the subject and the verb of the independent clause. The relative pronoun *who* is placed next to the noun *students*.

In the next example, a prepositional phrase is placed between the relative pronoun and its antecedent.

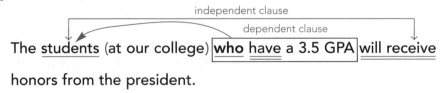

The <u>students</u> (at our college) | <u>who</u> <u>have</u> a 3.5 GPA | <u>will receive</u>

honors from the president.

In the previous example, the relative pronoun clause cannot be placed directly next to the noun it refers to or replaces because there is a prepositional phrase. The relative pronoun clause, however, is as close as possible to the noun it refers to or replaces.

Special Notes About Relative Pronoun Clauses

The following examples provide you with additional information about complex sentences created with relative pronoun clauses. The arrows point to the noun the relative pronoun refers to or replaces.

1. Use the relative pronoun *whom* when the dependent clause already has its own subject.

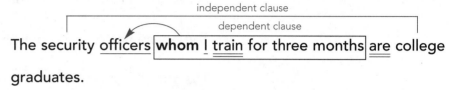

   graduates.

2. Use the relative pronoun *whose* to show possession or ownership.

   citations.

3. Use the relative pronoun *that* when the dependent clause is essential to the meaning of the sentence. In the following example, without the dependent clause, we would not know what song will be on the new CD.

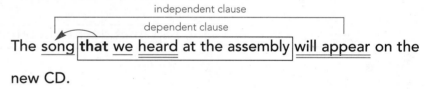

   new CD.

4. Use the relative pronoun *which* to introduce information that is not essential to the overall meaning of the sentence. In the following example, the noun *Sony* is a proper noun and a clearly understood subject. The dependent clause is set off by commas to show that it provides extra information but that information could be omitted without affecting the meaning of the sentence.

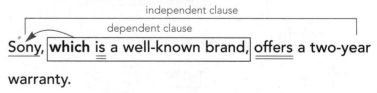

   warranty.

Subjects of Dependent Relative Pronoun Clauses

Both the dependent clause and the independent clause have at least one subject and one verb. In the following sentences, all of the relative pronouns are the subjects of the dependent clauses. Notice that a verb immediately follows the relative pronoun.

My neighbors have friends ⎡who live in Mexico.⎤

Several men ⎡who were skydivers⎤ landed in the middle of the football field.

Leroy submitted a report ⎡that was thorough and accurate.⎤

The house has one balcony ⎡that overlooks the river.⎤

The street festival, ⎡which occurs in November,⎤ brings people from all over the city.

I completed my third lab report, ⎡which covered Chapters 6 and 7.⎤

A relative pronoun always signals the beginning of a dependent clause. However, the relative pronoun is not always the subject of the dependent clause, as shown in the following examples. Arrows remind you that a relative pronoun must be placed next to or as close as possible to the noun it refers to or replaces.

The park ⎡that the neighborhood group built⎤ was inside the city limits.

The new Four Corners Rodeo Arena, ⎡which my uncles designed,⎤ will open in July.

Security officers ⎡whom I trained for three months⎤ are college graduates.

The story was about a victim ⎡whose identity remains a mystery.⎤

Practice 6   *Recognizing Relative Pronoun Clauses*

In each sentence, draw a box around the relative pronoun clause. Underline the subjects once and the verbs twice in the dependent clause.

Example: Janice, ⎡whom I met today for the first time,⎤ is in charge of Financial Aid.

1. The man who helped me with a flat tire was a retired police officer.

2. I saw a beautiful statue that I want for my backyard.

3. The garbage disposal, which does not work, needs to be replaced.

4. His sister, who is dating Bernie, still does not have her driver's license.

5. The lava that flowed freely from the volcano poured into the ocean.

6. The water slide, which is on the north side of the park, is the most popular attraction.

7. A special protective paint is used on the bottom of cars that travel on heavily salted roads.

8. Pierre laughed at my omelet, which had fallen apart and turned into scrambled eggs.

9. Samantha, who lost money in the stock market, wanted to sell her shares.

10. My track coach, who has lived in Texas all his life, has never traveled out of the state.

 ### Who and Whom

Who and *whom* are both relative pronouns that refer to people, but they are not interchangeable. Use *who* when the relative pronoun is the subject of the dependent clause. In the subject position of a dependent clause, the word *who* is followed by a verb.

> **who** live in metropolitan areas
>
> **who** enjoy traveling
>
> **who** prefer restaurant dinners several times a week

Use *whom* when the dependent clause already has a subject and verb. *Whom* is an object pronoun; it cannot be used as the subject of a dependent clause.

whom I would like to meet

whom they trust with all their hearts

whom she has supported for three years

Practice 7   *Identifying Subjects and Verbs*

Work with a partner, in a small group, or on your own to complete the following directions. In each sentence, draw a box around the relative pronoun clause. Underline the subjects once and the verbs twice in both the dependent clause and the main clause. Notice that some of the clauses are set off by commas; the use of commas before and after some relative pronoun clauses will be discussed later in this chapter.

Example: Don Carter, whom I have known for years, is an excellent

electrician.

1. Anyone who wants to attend the dance must purchase a ticket in
advance.

2. The night clerk, whom I called on the phone, gave me a room
near the swimming pool.

3. The young accountant who had just started this job was unfamiliar
with the forms.

4. No one enjoys filling out this year's tax forms, which have long,
complicated directions.

5. None of the players on the team that won the championship had
ever been to New York City.

6. Four antique rugs, which were worth fifty thousand dollars,
were available at the auction.

7. Here is the herbal tea that you ordered.

8. I <u>met</u> the person who <u>placed</u> the ad for the nanny position.

9. <u>Three</u> of the writing tutors whose <u>names</u> <u>were</u> on the board <u>read</u> and <u>critiqued</u> my paper.

10. <u>Most</u> of the reward money that <u>I</u> <u>received</u> <u>went</u> to charity.

Practice 8   *Using* **Who** *and* **Whom**

Write *who* or *whom* on the blanks in each sentence. The dependent clauses are shown in italic print.

Examples: The Williams sisters, *who* *competed against each other at Wimbledon,* are both excellent tennis players.

         Their father, *whom* *I met at the tennis match,* coaches them.

1. Randy, _____*who*_____ *is my neighbor,* plans to sell his house this year.

2. My last boss, _____*whom*_____ *I truly admire,* has been a manager for twenty years.

3. Senator Jackson, _____*who*_____ *decided not to run for office again,* wants to spend more time with his family.

4. This picture of Martin Luther King, Jr., _____*who*_____ *became the spokesperson for the Civil Rights movement,* is one of my prized possessions.

5. Coach Bengal, _____*who*_____ *told my daughter about the scholarship,* supports his students in many different ways.

6. Online investors _____*who*_____ *conduct thorough research* can profit from the stock market.

7. Jake's personal lawyer, _____*who*_____ *also represented Martin,* will take this new case.

8. Mason McDaniels, _____*whom*_____ *I hired last year,* is an outstanding employee.

9. My grandma, _____*who*_____ *loves old movies,* still enjoys *The Honeymooners.*

10. My dentist has a son _____*who*_____ *decided to travel around Europe for three months.*

Whose and Who's

Whose is a relative pronoun that shows possession. *Whose* refers to a person; however, it can also refer to objects and animals.

The race car driver whose car is sponsored by Quaker Oil

appeared on *The Tonight Show.*

My precious cat, whose paw was cut on broken glass,

curled up on my lap and purred.

The personnel director, whose name is difficult to pronounce,

will open new positions.

The tree, whose bark was carved with initials, was more

than one hundred years old.

Who's is a contraction that means *who is* or *who has.* Contractions are informal constructions and should be avoided in most types of formal writing. Anytime you use *who's,* you should be able to substitute the words *who is* or *who has* in the sentence.

who is
That is the man who's going to challenge the mayor.

who has
Sister Maria, who's been very sick, does not want

company at this time.

Practice 9   *Using* **Whose** *and* **Who's**

Write *whose* or *who's* on the blanks in the following sentences. The dependent clauses are shown in italics.

1. My English professor, _____*whose*_____ *degree is from Stanford,* has written a new novel.

2. The girls _____*whose*_____ *parents signed permission forms* are going on the field trip.

3. Robert is the man _____*who's*_____ *sponsoring the summer baseball camp.*

4. The artist_____*whose*_____ *work is on exhibit in the library* is from New Zealand.

5. The cruise ship_____*whose*_____ *engine caught on fire* offered the passengers full refunds.

6. The lady _____*whose*_____ *name appears on the building* donated $5 million.

7. The police identified the man _____*whose*_____ *fingerprints were on the cookie jar.*

8. The actor _____*who's*_____ *starring in the movie Space Cowboys* used to play the part of a detective on a television series.

9. The zookeeper, _____*who's*_____ *been gone for several weeks,* finally returned to work.

10. Malinda Jones, _____*who's*_____ *my sister-in-law,* volunteers at the local YWCA.

 ## Essential and Nonessential Relative Pronoun Clauses

You have likely noticed that some relative pronoun clauses are set off from the rest of the sentence by commas. Commas placed before and after a clause signal that the clause is not essential to the general meaning of the sentence. The clause provides extra information that can be omitted. To identify nonessential clauses, ask yourself, "Is the noun or the subject in the independent clause specific and clearly defined without the relative pronoun clause?"

In the following examples, the subject is a proper noun, which means that the subject is specific and clearly defined. Therefore, the relative pronoun clause is *nonessential.* The commas before and after the clause indicate the nonessential nature of the clause.

        specific   nonessential

George Burns, **whose marriage to Gracie Allen was kept a secret,** starred with Gracie in an early television show.

        specific   nonessential

Michael J. Fox, **who is battling a muscular disease,** inspires many people.

When the subject or the noun that the relative pronoun refers to or replaces is specific but not a proper noun, the same rule for commas applies.

        specific   nonessential

Your grandmother, **whose ninetieth birthday will soon be here,** has wisdom and insight.

[Setting the relative pronoun clause off with commas implies that a specific grandmother is being discussed. There is no confusion as to which grandmother has wisdom.]

specific   nonessential

My youngest sister, who lives in Albuquerque, is a

hospice provider.

[Only one sister is the youngest, so *youngest sister* is specific.]

Essential clauses are not set off by commas. They are necessary for the overall meaning of the sentence. Notice how the nouns the relative pronouns refer to or replace are not specific and not clearly defined without the relative pronoun clause.

not specific   essential

Men who marry tend to live longer lives.

[What men tend to live longer? The relative pronoun clause specifies which men, so the clause is essential to the meaning of the sentence.]

not specific   essential

The young girl who was crying appeared to be lost.

[The relative pronoun clause is essential in order to understand which young girl appeared to be lost.]

Special Notes About *That, Whom,* and *Which*

1. The relative pronouns *that* and *which* are often used interchangeably when they refer to things and ideas. However, these relative pronouns have subtle differences.

   That is used only for essential (restrictive) clauses. Relative pronoun clauses that begin with *that* cannot be omitted from the sentence without causing the sentence to lose some of its meaning or clarity. A dependent clause that begins with *that* provides necessary or essential information abouts the noun that the pronoun has replaced (the antecedent). Note in the following examples that the relative pronoun *that* can work as the subject of the dependent clause, or it can introduce a dependent clause that already has a subject and a verb.

   The waterfall that is at the end of the trail is spectacular.

   [Which waterfall is spectacular? The relative pronoun clause is essential in order to know which waterfall is spectacular.]

   None of the fabric that you ordered last week has

   arrived yet.

   [Without the relative pronoun clause, the sentence says that no fabric has arrived. The relative pronoun clause clarifies that only the fabric that was ordered last week has not arrived.]

2. Frequently, writers use *that* to refer to people; for many teachers and grammarians, the use of *that* is acceptable. However, the relative pronoun *who* or *whom* is associated only with people. For stronger writing, strive to use *who* or *whom* for people, and limit the use of *that* to things, ideas, and animals.

JUST SO YOU KNOW...

Essential clauses are called *restrictive clauses*. Essential clauses are not set off by commas. The clauses are needed to help define, clarify, or specify a noun in the independent clause.

JUST SO YOU KNOW...

The relative pronoun *that* can be a subject relative pronoun or an object relative pronoun. Relative pronoun clauses that begin with *that* are always essential (restrictive).

Informal: The administrators *that enforce the rules* don't understand the issues.

Formal: The administrators who enforce the rules don't understand the issues.

Informal: Taxpayers *that filed before April 15* will not be charged late fees.

Formal: Taxpayers who filed before April 15 will not be charged late fees.

3. Sometimes the relative pronouns *that* and *whom* are understood rather than explicitly stated. On occasion, when you analyze the subject-verb patterns in sentences and identify clauses, you will encounter clauses with the implied or understood *that* or *whom*.

At first glance, you might think you have discovered a run-on sentence.

At first glance, you might think that you have discovered a run-on sentence.

[The first sentence has the understood or implied relative pronoun *that*. The second sentence clearly states the relative pronoun. Both sentences are correct.]

My parents exchanged addresses (with the people) they met on the trip.

My parents exchanged addresses (with the people) whom they met on the trip.

[The first sentence has the understood or implied relative pronoun *whom*. The second sentence clearly states the relative pronoun. Both sentences are correct.]

4. *Which* is a relative pronoun used for specific things, ideas, or animals. In formal usage, *which* is used for nonessential (nonrestrictive clauses). Therefore, dependent clauses that begin with *which* should be set off by commas.

specific   nonessential

This year's ballot, which is a mail-in ballot, asks voters to vote on five measures.

specific
nonessential

My car, which is ten years old, will soon need major

repairs.

specific
nonessential

Whales, which migrate every year, can be seen in the

coastal waters.

Practice 10   *Using* Who, Whom, That, *and* Which

Select the most appropriate relative pronoun for each of the following blanks. Use these suggestions:

- Use *who* when a subject is needed and the pronoun refers to a person.

- Use *whom* when the dependent clause already has a subject and the pronoun refers to a person.

- Use *whose* when the dependent clause shows possession.

- Use *that* when the dependent clause is essential and the pronoun refers to things.

- Use *which* when the dependent clause is nonessential and the pronoun refers to things.

1. People _____who_____ want to save money can purchase airline tickets in cyberspace.

2. Internet ticket sales, _____which_____ are supported by most major airlines, are growing.

3. One Internet service _____that_____ lets travelers name their own prices for tickets has the endorsement of all the major airlines.

4. The airlines provide the company with a specific number of seats _____that_____ can be sold at the last minute at reduced rates.

5. Friends _____whom_____ I have traveled with in the past have purchased hotel rooms and car rentals online for many of their trips.

6. One Internet company allows travelers to name a price _____that_____ they are willing to pay for airfare, hotels, and car rentals.

7. Cyberspace buyers _____who_____ use this site are locked into the price _____that_____ they name.

8. The online services _____that_____ they request are billed directly to their credit cards.

9. The company _____whose_____ sales doubled last year plans to develop a new Web site.

10. My travel agent, _____whom_____ I have known for many years, does most of her work with online booking companies.

 ## Subject-Verb Agreement Within Relative Pronoun Clauses

When a relative pronoun is a subject pronoun (the subject of the dependent clause), the verb in the dependent clause must agree in number with the antecedent (the noun that the relative pronoun refers to or replaces). The antecedent is always another noun or pronoun in the independent clause; the antecedent may or may not be the subject of the independent clause.

To ensure subject-verb agreement in dependent clauses with relative pronouns in the subject position, begin by asking "What is the antecedent? What noun in the independent clause does the relative pronoun refer to or replace?" Then follow these guidelines:

1. If the antecedent is singular, the verb in the dependent clause must use a singular form.

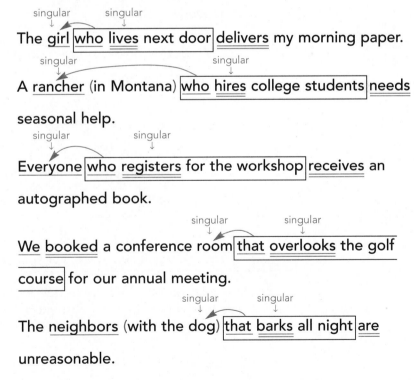

The girl who lives next door delivers my morning paper.

A rancher (in Montana) who hires college students needs seasonal help.

Everyone who registers for the workshop receives an autographed book.

We booked a conference room that overlooks the golf course for our annual meeting.

The neighbors (with the dog) that barks all night are unreasonable.

2. If the antecedent is plural, the verb must use a plural form.

The girls who live next door deliver my morning paper.

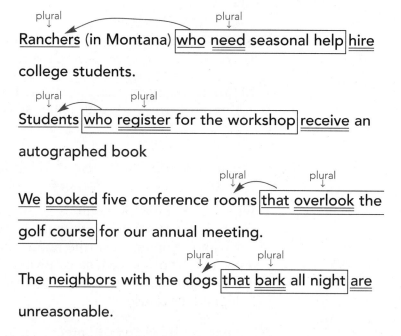

Ranchers (in Montana) [who need seasonal help] hire
plural ← *plural*

college students.

Students [who register for the workshop] receive an
plural ← *plural*

autographed book

We booked five conference rooms [that overlook the
plural ← *plural*

golf course] for our annual meeting.

The neighbors with the dogs [that bark all night] are
plural ← *plural*

unreasonable.

3. If the sentence has the phrase *one of those,* the relative pronoun refers to the noun at the end of the prepositional phrase. In the following examples, with *one of those dogs, one of those animals,* and *one of those tools,* the relative pronoun refers to the plural noun at the end of the prepositional phrase. It does not refer to the subject or the word *one.* Use a plural form for the verb in the dependent clause.

My dog is one (of those dogs) [that like to sleep at the
plural ← *plural*
foot of my bed.]

Llamas are one (of those animals) [that kick hard.]
plural ← *plural*

A Phillips screwdriver is one (of those tools) [that have
plural ← *plural*
many uses.]

Practice 11   *Working with Dependent Clauses*

Draw a box around all the dependent clauses in the following sentences. Circle the subordinate conjunction or the relative pronoun that begins each dependent clause. Add any missing commas.

Example: Special light bulbs [(that) have a shatter-resistant coating] are

used in the labs. [(If) the bulb bursts,] the glass particles

accumulate inside the bulb.

1. The young man [(who) painted my house] finished the job in less

than a week.

2. Martin, who is Mario's brother, won a $5,000 scholarship for school next year.

3. The person who called you did not leave a message.

4. Anyone who jogs three times a week shows signs of dedication.

5. That man in the tuxedo whom you met at the opera is a production manager.

6. Because flash floods hit the village, many of the villagers were unprepared.

7. The villagers, who sensed a flood was imminent, had nowhere to go.

8. My brother could not find the flashlight that I had left underneath the sink.

9. Whenever the power goes out, we light candles and just wait.

10. I feel unsafe because all of the windows in the new building are sealed shut.

Combining Sentences by Using Relative Pronouns

Complex sentences with relative pronoun clauses can be created by combining simple sentences. When a noun from the first sentence is repeated in the second sentence, the noun in the second sentence can be replaced with a relative pronoun to form a dependent clause. The dependent clause can then be inserted into the first sentence.

Two sentences:	Several <u>men</u> <u>landed</u> in the middle of the football field. The <u>men</u> <u>were</u> skydivers.
Convert to a pronoun:	Several men landed in the middle of the football field. ~~The men~~ *who* were skydivers.
Place the dependent clause in the first sentence next to the noun it replaces:	Several <u>men</u> who were skydivers <u>landed</u> in the middle of the football field.

Two sentences: My <u>resumé</u> <u>is</u> comprehensive.
                       <u>It</u> <u>shows</u> my complete work history.

Convert to a pronoun: My resumé is comprehensive.

                       ^{which}
                       ~~It~~ shows my complete work

                       history.

Place the dependent   My resumé, | **which** shows my |
clause in the first
sentence next to the   complete work history, | <u>is</u>
noun it replaces:
                       comprehensive.

COMMA SENSE

1. Use a comma before and after any relative pronoun clause that is not essential to the meaning of the sentence. In other words, the clause could be omitted and the reader would still understand the sentence. The antecedent is specific enough that it does not need the help of the relative pronoun clause to have meaning.

   Relative pronoun clauses that begin with *who, whom, whose,* or *which* may need to be set off by commas. Relative pronoun clauses that begin with *that* are never set off by commas.

   The Freedom Trail, *which is in Boston,* is a popular tourist attraction.

   Your English teacher, *whom I met last term,* is impressive.

   Peter Jennings's documentary, *which airs on Sunday,* is the result of months of investigative work.

   The sandwich *that I made* had too much mustard.

2. Use a comma before and after a relative pronoun clause that modifies or refers to a proper noun. The proper noun (the antecedent) is already specific, so the dependent clause is not essential. Proper nouns always start with capital letters.

   Joshua, *who graduates in June,* has received a job offer from Nike.

   Mrs. Alamo, *who is my economics teacher,* will retire this year.

   Curtis Selgado, *who moved to Portland,* is a great musician.

Type 3 Dependent Clause: Noun Clause

NOUN CLAUSE   **A noun clause functions as a noun in a complex sentence.**

As discussed on p. 251, a noun clause may begin with one of the same words that are used in adverb clauses (subordinate conjunctions) and adjective clauses (relative pronouns): *who, whoever, that, whose, when, what,* and *where.* Unlike adverb clauses and adjective clauses, noun clauses do not replace or refer to other words in the main clause. Instead, the entire clause functions as a noun.

Noun clauses are essential. If the noun clause is removed, the remaining sentence lacks sufficient meaning to be a complete thought.

noun clause
The chairman of the board decides who will be promoted.

noun clause
The widow believes that she can trust the insurance

company.

noun clause
I cannot find what you wanted for your birthday.

In the following examples, notice that the word *something* or *someone* can replace this kind of dependent clause (a noun clause).

noun clause = subject | verb
Whoever completes the puzzle first will win the grand prize.
[*Someone* will win the grand prize.]

noun clause = subject | verb
Whatever you write interests me.
[*Something* interests me.]

noun clause = subject | verb
That you had a second interview is a good sign.
[*Something* is a good sign.]

Avoiding Fragments

FRAGMENT   **A fragment occurs when a part of a sentence is punctuated as if it were a complete sentence.**

Fragments are pieces or fragments of a complete sentence. A complete sentence must have a subject and a complete verb, and it must form a complete thought. A sentence must be able to stand on its own. Here are three kinds of fragments and methods you can use to correct them:

1. A prepositional phrase or a series of prepositional phrases is a fragment because there is no subject, complete verb, and complete thought.

   (Throughout his long career) (as an airline pilot) (for a major international airline company).

   (After skating) (on the outdoor rink) (in Hibbing).

   (Despite your valuable contributions) (on the marketing project) (for the new athletic shoes).

   Correction method: Add a subject and a complete verb. Make sure the sentence forms a complete thought and can stand on its own.

   Throughout his long career as an airline pilot for a major international airline company, my uncle has maintained a spotless record.

   After skating on the outdoor rink in Hibbing, we decided to start our own hockey team.

   Despite your valuable contributions on the marketing project for the new athletic shoes, we cannot renew your contract with our firm.

2. A dependent clause that begins with a subordinate conjunction is a fragment if the clause is not attached to an independent clause. Though the dependent clause has a subject and a complete verb, the subordinate conjunction prevents the group of words from forming a complete thought.

   Since each of the desserts looks good.

   When the wild horses were rounded up.

   Because I have no plans.

   Correction method 1: Attach the dependent clause to an independent (main) clause.

   Since each of the desserts looks good, I will sample each one.

   When the wild horses were rounded up, they were placed in an adoption program.

   Because I have no plans, I am available to babysit for you.

Correction method 2: Remove the subordinate conjunction to form a simple sentence.

~~Since~~ Each of the desserts looks good.

~~When~~ The wild horses were rounded up.

~~Because~~ I have no plans.

3. A relative pronoun clause is a fragment if the clause is not attached to an independent clause. It cannot stand on its own as a complete declarative sentence (a statement). Sometimes it can stand on its own as a question with a question mark as the ending punctuation.

Which appeared throughout the article.

Who is well known and loved.

That was rejected by five publishers.

Who ventured into the wilderness.

Correction method 1: Attach the dependent clause to an independent (main) clause.

The foul language, which appeared throughout the article, was offensive to many readers.

Dan Marino, who is well known and loved, retired from his professional football career.

The manuscript that was rejected by five publishers was bought by a television producer.

The tourists who ventured into the wilderness were found after an extensive air search.

Correction method 2: Add a question mark if you want an interrogative statement.

Which appeared throughout the article?
Who is well known and loved?
That was rejected by five publishers?
Who ventured into the wilderness?

Practice 12   *Identifying Fragments*

Read each of the following statements. Write **F** if the statement is a *fragment*. Write **S** if the statement is a complete *sentence*.

Examples: __F__   If the public transit workers go on strike.

        __S__   Commuters will be stranded if the public transit workers go on strike.

__F__   1. Before the worst storm of the century hit our town.

__S__   2. Hurricanes often drench the southeastern coastlines of the United States.

__F__   3. Within three hours of the alert siren for the county.

__F__   4. According to the state police and the meteorologists in the area.

__S__   5. More than half a foot of rain fell in North Carolina.

__F__   6. When the strongest winds moved out to sea.

__S__   7. The National Hurricane Center is located in Miami, Florida.

__F__   8. A hurricane with winds up to 90 miles per hour.

__S__   9. Flash flooding occurred throughout the valley.

__F__   10. Torrential rains in front of the hurricane's core.

__S__   11. Community members and troops piled sandbags.

__F__   12. With gale force winds along the coastline.

__F__   13. Since evacuations occurred in five of the main urban areas.

__S__   14. People slept in temporary shelters.

__S__   15. Tropical storms occur frequently in the months of July through October.

EXERCISE 9.1   **Folk Wisdom**   Name _____   Date _____

© Michael Zide

Work with a partner, in a small group, or on your own to complete this exercise. Draw a box around all the dependent clauses. Add commas where they are needed.

FOLK WISDOM

Psychologist Robert Epstein, Ph.D., who examines how proverbs are passed down for generations, found that folk wisdom is not always true, reliable, or consistent. Most proverbs coexist with their exact opposites or with proverbs that give somewhat different advice. Does absence make the heart grow fonder? Are loved ones out of mind when they are out of sight? Is variety the spice of life? Do birds of a feather flock together? Does haste make waste? Is patience a virtue? If money is power, why are the best things in life free?

Hundreds of well-known proverbs exist in the English-speaking world, but proverbs that proclaim how we are supposed to live do not always supply useful advice. In fact, sometimes we use proverbs merely to justify what we already do or believe. Many people have an uncanny tendency to switch proverbs to suit their current values and ideas. In one situation, a person may justify his or her actions by quoting the proverb "You only live once." In a different situation, the same person may abide by the proverb "Better safe than sorry."

The behavioral sciences use a set of methods for testing the validity of statements about human behavior. How well does folk psychology stand up to scientific inquiry?

Surprisingly, some of the folk wisdom passed along through proverbs is supported by scientific studies.

"All work and no play makes Jack a dull boy." Does all work and no play make a person dull? Is too much work harmful? Research suggests that the answer is yes with one possible exception. If you love your work and have been able to make your avocation your vocation, then work may provide you with some of the benefits of play. For many people, however, work has become a necessity in order to earn a living and pay bills. Study after study confirm the dangers of overwork. Though work may not make you a dull person, it dulls your mind. One study shows that long work shifts increase reaction time and lower alertness. Overwork increases errors and impedes judgment. Conversely, leisure activities have been shown to relieve stress, improve mood, increase life satisfaction, and even boost the immune system. Numerous studies show that if you spend too much time doing things you do not want to do, your performance, health, and sense of well-being will suffer.

"Early to bed and early to rise makes a man (person) healthy, wealthy, and wise." This proverb, which is often attributed to Benjamin Franklin, actually seems to have originated in the late 1400s. Research suggests that the proverb does give sound advice to about half of the population. The body has natural rhythms or cycles, which are called circadian rhythms. These 24-hour cycles, which include cycles of temperature change, wakefulness, and eating, are highly resistant to change. Two distinctly different circadian rhythm patterns exist. The first pattern is called "the larks." Larks are people whose cycles peak early in the day. Larks awaken early and start the day strong. The second pattern, which is called "the owls," identifies people who peak late in the day. In both patterns, the peaks are associated with better performance on memory tasks, quicker reaction times, heightened alertness, and cheerful moods. Unfortunately for the owls, many important human activities are conducted during the daylight hours, which are the hours in which the larks have a distinct advantage. Owls, who often feel out of sync, are forced to adjust to the larks' sleep patterns, and to wake up when they do not want to wake up. Owls may be more restless and have lower performances early in the day. One study suggests that people who sleep well make considerably more money than people who sleep poorly. Thus, the larks have the advantage because their internal clocks are more in sync with the business world and the stock exchange.

[Adapted from Robert Epstein, Ph.D, "Folk Wisdom," *Psychology Today*, November/December 1997, pp. 46–50, 76.]

EXERCISE 9.2   **Working with Adverb Clauses**

Name _____ Date _____

Attach the following dependent clauses to independent clauses by placing them before or after an independent (main) clause. Write your sentences below. *Answers will vary.*

Example: *before his job terminates*

Mike wants to take advantage of his benefits *before his job terminates*.

1. after I called my uncle _____

    _____

2. as soon as the radio station went on the air _____

    _____

3. if you order online _____

    _____

4. as if she knew the answer _____

    _____

5. because the car is new _____

    _____

6. once the topic was selected _____

    _____

7. so that everyone has an equal opportunity _____

    _____

8. whatever you want for our anniversary _____

    _____

9. unless the roads are sanded _____

    _____

10. when the boxes arrived _____

    _____

EXERCISE 9.3   **Combining Sentences**   Name _____ Date _____

Combine the following sentences by changing one of the sentences to a dependent clause that begins with a subordinate conjunction. Write the complete sentences on separate paper. *Answers will vary. Possible answers are given.*

Example: The fish were caught. We cleaned them and cooked them on the open fire.

After the fish were caught, we cleaned and cooked them on the open fire.

1. I moved away. I have not written to him.
   Since I moved away, I have not written to him.
2. The conditions are right. We can fly our kites.
   If the conditions are right, we can fly our kites.
3. The roller coaster is so much fun. It is the most popular ride.
   Because the roller coaster is so much fun, it is the most popular ride.
4. Many people visit national monuments. They take a lot of photographs. Many people take a lot of photographs when they visit national monuments.
5. Sally usually does well. She failed the geology test.
   Even though Sally usually does well, she failed the geology test.
6. We got stuck in a huge traffic jam. We missed our flight.
   Because we got stuck in a huge traffic jam, we missed our flight.
7. My son fell on the court. He got up and continued to play.
   After my son fell on the court, he got up and continued to play.

EXERCISE 9.4   **Using Adjective Clauses**   Name _____ Date _____

Combine the following sentences into one sentence by using a relative pronoun clause. Write your sentences on separate paper. *Answers will vary. Possible answers are given.*

Example: Alicia's grandfather lives on a farm. Her grandfather is my mechanic.

Alicia's grandfather, who is my mechanic, lives on a farm.

1. The students were able to network. The students went to a conference in New York. The students who went to a conference in New York were able to network.
2. Rachel is my best friend. I trust her with all my secrets.
   I trust Rachel, who is my best friend, with all my secrets.
3. Mr. Randolph is the president of the firm. The firm is listed on the New York Stock Exchange. Mr. Randolph is the president of the firm, which is listed on the New York Stock Exchange.
4. The committee recommended Liza for the job. Liza has the most experience. The committee recommended Liza, who has the most experience, for the job.
5. The network aired the show. The show was watched by millions of people. The network aired the show, which was watched by millions of people.

Chapter 9 Summary

1. **Complex sentences** have one independent clause and at least one dependent clause.

2. **Dependent clauses** cannot stand by themselves as sentences. Each dependent clause has a subject and a verb. Dependent clauses begin with a **subordinate conjunction** or a **relative pronoun.**

3. Subordinate conjunctions are words such as *after, because, before, if, though, until,* and *when.* Subordinate conjunctions signal the beginning of a dependent clause. These dependent clauses are movable; they may be placed before or after the independent clause.

4. When a dependent clause that begins with a subordinate conjunction begins a sentence, use a comma at the end of the dependent clause. When it appears after the independent clause, do not use a comma.

5. The relative pronouns *who, whom, whose, which,* and *that* signal the beginning of a dependent clause that refers to a noun or a pronoun in the independent clause. Relative pronoun clauses are placed next to the noun they refer to or replace.

6. *Who, whom,* and *whose* relate to people, but each word has its own function, so the words are not interchangeable. *That* and *which* refer to places or things; *that* is used in essential clauses, and *which* is used in nonessential clauses.

7. **Nonessential *(nonrestrictive)* relative pronoun clauses** are set off from the rest of the sentence with commas. The information is not essential to the overall meaning of the sentence. **Essential *(restrictive)* relative pronoun clauses** are necessary for the sentence to have meaning. They are never set off by commas.

8. Subjects and verbs in dependent clauses must show agreement in number. You can tell whether a relative pronoun functions as a singular or a plural noun by locating the antecedent in the sentence. If the antecedent is singular, the relative pronoun functions as a singular word; use the singular form of the verb. If the antecedent is plural, the relative pronoun functions as a plural word; use the plural form of the verb.

9. **Fragments** are only pieces of a full sentence. A fragment occurs when a sentence is missing a subject or a complete verb, or when the words to do not form a complete thought. Use appropriate methods to correct these three kinds of fragments:

a. Fragments that consist of a series of prepositional phrases

b. Fragments that consist of a dependent clause that begins with a subordinate conjunction

c. Fragments that consist of a dependent clause that begins with a relative pronoun

Writing Topics for Chapter 9

1. Select any three proverbs from the following list. Write three to five sentences to explain what each proverb means to you. You may include examples from "real life" to explain the proverb.

Once bitten, twice shy.

Old habits die hard.

Every cloud has a silver lining.

Misery loves company.

To lengthen thy life, lessen thy meals.

Two heads are better than one.

Well done is better than well said.

When the cat's away, the mice will play.

Genius without education is like silver in the mine.

Whatever is begun in anger, ends in shame.

 2. Use library resources or the Internet to locate three interesting proverbs. Make a list of proverbs you like. Under each proverb, explain what it means to you.

 3. Use the Internet to locate information about circadian rhythms. Write a paragraph to share what you learned. Use your own words; do not copy directly from your sources. Include a copy of the web pages you used for the information.

Web Site Learning Experiences

See the web site for this book to locate companion exercises and links related to the grammar topics in this chapter.

Go to: http://college.hmco.com. Click on "Students." Type *Sentence Essentials* in the "Jump to Textbook Sites" box. Click "go" and then bookmark the site. Click on Chapter 9.

CHAPTER 9 • Review   Name _____   Date _____

Total Possible: 50   Your Score: _____

Part I: Identification of Dependent Clauses (10 points)
Draw a box around the dependent clauses in the following sentences.
Give one point for correctly identifying each dependent clause.

1. I called │because I was not able to keep the appointment.│

2. I built a storage shed │where the old shed previously stood.│

3. My insurance covers dental crowns, │which are expensive.│

4. I completed all of the papers │that were necessary for the loan application.│

5. │Since the job is listed in the classified ads,│ I know │that many people will apply.│

6. │When Joan and Bob chose a site for their reception,│ they had to make a $150 deposit.

7. │Before you make a final decision,│ you should consult with your parents.

8. │Now that the story has been printed in the papers,│ I receive a dozen calls a day.

9. The gymnasts │whose bus is delayed in traffic│ will not be here for the opening ceremony.

Part II: Simple, Compound, and Complex Sentences (15 points)

Identify the sentence patterns in the following sentences. Write **S** for *simple*, **C** for *compound*, and **CX** for *complex*. Add the missing commas. *Give one point per sentence pattern answer and one point for each comma.*

_____S_____ 1. Behind the picture frame, we found a hidden safe.

_____CX_____ 2. After the doctor called my house, I was afraid to call her back.

_____C_____ 3. Suddenly, sparks were flying; the welders started their final projects.

_____CX_____ 4. Ralph, who wanted attention, tried to scale a thirty-story building downtown.

_____CX_____ 5. I know that he is upset.

_____CX_____ 6. Conspiracy theories continued to surface after the investigation was closed.

_____C_____ 7. Winter was unseasonably warm, but the causes are not clear.

_____CX_____ 8. If gas prices continue to rise, many people will resort to public transportation.

Part III: Sentence Writing (25 points)

On separate paper, use the following words to write five complex sentences. Underline the subjects and the verbs in the dependent and the independent clauses of your sentences. *Give three points per sentence: one for writing a complex sentence, one for identifying all the subjects, and one for identifying all the verbs.*

1. that

2. if

3. who

4. which

5. after

CHAPTER 10

Sentence Builders

In Chapter 10, we will explore some additional sentence-combining techniques. You will learn to combine sentences by using **appositives, participial phrases,** and **words in a series.** Your sentence combining may result in a new simple, compound, complex, or **compound-complex sentence,** a new sentence pattern that will be discussed in this chapter. Also included in this chapter is work with **parallelism** and correcting fragments. Chapter 10 will provide you with additional options to organize and express your ideas.

Understanding sentence builders will help you do the following:

1. Assist you in writing tighter, more economical sentence structures through the use of appositives, participial phrases, combining items in a series, and compound-complex sentences

2. Develop a more sophisticated style of writing through the use of an array of sentence builders, including the use of parallelism

3. Improve your proofreading and editing skills for punctuating series of items, appositives, participial phrases as well as for correcting dangling modifiers

 **Appositives**

> **APPOSITIVE**   **An appositive is a noun, noun phrase, or noun clause that renames a previously mentioned noun and provides additional information about the noun.**

Sponges, a natural product of the ocean, last for many years.

My truck, a relic from my college years, breaks down frequently.

Appositives sometimes are referred to as *noun repeaters* because they use new words to explain or expand information about a specific, previously mentioned noun. Appositives can be used effectively in your writing in the following ways:

1. They can add descriptive details to your writing, help ideas flow together more smoothly, and eliminate unnecessary wordiness.

2. They can provide greater sentence variety, thereby increasing reader interest.

3. They can be used to substitute a familiar word for an unfamiliar term or to provide a brief definition for an unfamiliar word.

A person with apnea, a sleep disorder, temporarily stops breathing.

4. They can be used to combine two or more sentences into one sentence. Key information from one or more sentences is shortened to create an appositive.

Combining Sentences by Using Appositives

In the following examples, two sentences are combined into one sentence by using an appositive. Arrows point to the noun that the appositive renames. As the examples show, there may be more than one way to combine two sentences by using an appositive.

Two sentences:

Tourism in Rio de Janeiro increases every year.
Rio is the former capital of Brazil.

Combined with an appositive:

Tourism in Rio de Janeiro, the former capital of Brazil, increases every year.

appositive

Tourism in the former capital of Brazil, Rio de Janeiro, increases every year.

Two sentences:

Brasilia is the current capital of Brazil. The government built this modernistic city.

Combined with an appositive:

appositive

Brasilia, *a modernistic city that the government built,* is the current capital of Brazil.

appositive

Brasilia, *the current capital of Brazil,* is a modernistic city that the government built.

You can use appositives to combine information from more than two sentences into one sentence. Notice how the following sentences sound choppy when they are presented as simple sentences.

Sentence 1:	San Francisco attracts tourists.
Sentence 2:	Tourists come from all over the world.
Sentence 3:	Chinatown is in San Francisco.
Sentence 4:	Fisherman's Wharf is in San Francisco.
Sentence 5:	The Golden Gate Bridge is in San Francisco.
Sentence 6:	Tourists come to see these famous landmarks.

Combined with an appositive:

appositive

San Francisco, *the home of famous landmarks such as*

Chinatown, Fisherman's Wharf, and the Golden Gate Bridge,

attracts tourists from all over the world.

Practice 1   *Identifying Appositives*

Draw a box around the appositives in the following sentences. Remember that the appositive will be located right after the noun that it renames.

appositive

Example: Ronald, *an electrician and an all-around handyman,* has been self-employed for three years.

1. Marci's father, a local banker, created two new scholarships for finance majors.

2. My English composition project, a twenty-page research paper, has been an interesting challenge.

3. My neighbor, an absolute car fanatic, washes his car every day.

4. My latest poem, a haiku, was published in our school magazine.

5. Martin, a local artist, sells his prints at several galleries.

6. I found this Victorian table, a rare antique, in an old barn.

7. My golf clubs, a gift from my partner, will be put to good use this summer.

8. King Elementary, the newest school in the district, opened at the beginning of this year.

9. The story took place in a small town, a fishing village on the northern shore of Hawaii.

10. Asia, the largest of all the continents, is the birthplace of several major religions.

11. The bus, a rolling pep rally, was packed with zealous fans.

12. Poi, a food made from taro root, is always on a luau menu.

13. The baseball bat, an old wooden relic from the past, cracked when José hit the ball.

14. Jeannie, a freelance writer, asked her best friend for a loan.

15. Vog, a coined word in Hawaii for volcanic haze, is a form of smog that consists of water vapor, carbon dioxide, and sulfur dioxide from volcanic emissions.

Special Notes About Appositives

1. Because an appositive renames or repeats a noun, the noun and its appositive are interchangeable in the sentence. Notice in the following examples how the appositive (a noun) and the noun it renames are interchangeable.

   noun   appositive   noun
   Geckos, *small harmless lizards,* are believed to bring good luck.

   noun   appositive   noun
   Small harmless lizards, *geckos,* are believed to bring good luck.

   noun   noun   appositive
   Petroglyphs, *carvings in stone,* are found in many archaeological sites.

   noun   appositive   noun
   Carvings in stone, *petroglyphs,* are found in many archaeological sites.

2. Some appositives are essential and some are nonessential. The punctuation rules you learned for essential and nonessential relative pronoun clauses apply to appositives as well. Most appositives are not essential and are set off by commas. Appositives that rename or refer to proper nouns are always nonessential and are set off by commas.

   My youngest sister, *Mary,* lives in Albuquerque.

   Mary, *my youngest sister,* lives in Albuquerque.

   Portland, *the home of the Trailblazers,* is not the capital of Oregon.

   The home of the Trailblazers, *Portland,* is not the capital of Oregon.

   Doctor Matsuura, *my plastic surgeon,* has performed many operations on burn victims.

   My plastic surgeon, *Doctor Matsuura,* has performed many operations on burn victims.

   Notice how all of the above sentences could be understood without the appositives. The appositives simply supply more descriptive details to the sentence.

   My youngest sister lives in Albuquerque.

   Mary lives in Albuquerque.

JUST SO YOU KNOW...

Nonessential elements in a sentence are also called nonrestrictive. Since these elements are not essential for the meaning of the sentence, they can be omitted without altering the meaning of the sentence. All nonessential (nonrestrictive) elements are set off with commas.

Portland is not the capital of Oregon.

The home of the Trailblazers is not the capital of Oregon.

Doctor Matsuura has performed many operations on burn victims.

My plastic surgeon has performed many operations on burn victims.

On the other hand, if appositives are essential to make general nouns more specific, do not set them off with commas. Essential appositives are needed for the reader to understand the noun clearly. In the following three examples, the appositives are essential, so they are not set off by commas.

Demetri's brother *Dante* works as a security guard.
[Demetri has more than one brother, so the appositive is essential in order to know which brother is a security guard.]

The movie *Hurricane* received many five-star reviews.
[The name of the movie is important (essential) in order to know which movie received five-star reviews.]

Carl gave his daughter *Vicki* a dog for her birthday.
[The daughter's name is treated as an essential idea; this implies that Carl has more than one daughter.]

3. Many appositives can be thought of as relative pronoun clauses that have been shortened by eliminating the relative pronoun and the linking verb from the verb *to be (am, is, are, was, were)*. Shortening the relative pronoun clause (the dependent clause) to an appositive (a noun form) is a writer's option; both sentence structures are correct.

Complex sentence: The marketing manager, *who is my uncle*, won the annual award. [relative pronoun clause]

Remove words: The marketing manager, ~~who is~~ my uncle, won the annual award.

Appositive: The marketing manager, *my uncle*, won the annual award. [appositive]

Complex sentence: The Mill Creek Restaurant, *which is the big red building on the edge of town*, serves excellent food. [relative pronoun clause]

Remove words: The Mill Creek Restaurant, *which is the big red building on the edge of town,* serves excellent food.

Appositive: The Mill Creek Restaurant, *the big red building on the edge of town,* serves excellent food.

Practice 2   *Creating Appositives from Relative Pronoun Clauses*

Convert the relative pronoun clauses to appositives by crossing out the relative pronoun and the linking verb. Retain the existing commas.

Example: The taxi driver, ~~who is~~ a Nigerian, talked about the history of the city as he drove us from one tourist sight to another.

1. Andy sat on the log, ~~which was~~ the only dry place to sit, and waited for a ride into town.

2. My son, ~~who is~~ an energetic four-year-old, shows good coordination when he plays video games.

3. Hibiscus, ~~which is~~ the state flower of Hawaii, has large, colorful flowers.

4. My first car, ~~which was~~ a Volvo station wagon, ran well for twelve years.

5. The new quarterback, ~~who is~~ a native of the state, earned the starting position this season.

6. Sarina, ~~who is~~ my best friend, gives me a ride to work each night.

7. Bill's company, ~~which is~~ Rapid River Adventures, takes people on three-day rafting trips on the Snake River.

8. *Butterfly Lost,* ~~which is~~ my cousin's first novel, is about a Native American woman.

9. Sandy, ~~who is~~ a weight trainer, was able to move the heavy desk by herself.

10. Kona, ~~which is~~ a small town on the big island of Hawaii, is near many coffee plantations.

11. This is the first year of teaching for Maria Gonzales, ~~who is~~ my new math teacher.

12. The interviewer, ~~who was~~ a woman, entered the men's locker room to talk to the players.

Participial Phrases

You learned in Chapter 5 (pages 120–130) that verbs have present and past participle forms. The present participle, which ends in *-ing,* and the past participle, which ends in *-ed* or another form for irregular verbs, can be used with a helping verb to form a verb phrase.

PRESENT PARTICIPLE	VERB PHRASE	PAST PARTICIPLE	VERB PHRASE
walking	is walking	walked	has walked
thinking	are thinking	thought	have thought
drawing	was drawing	drawn	had drawn
writing	were writing	written	have written

PARTICIPIAL PHRASE   **A participial phrase is a group of words that begins with a present participle or a past participle.**

A participial phrase, which often refers to the subject of the sentence, must be placed close to the noun or pronoun it refers to or renames. It may be placed before or after the noun or pronoun. The participial phrase does not have a subject or a helping verb.

participial phrase

Wanting a new challenge, Randy requested a transfer to a larger store.

[The participial phrase appears first as an introductory phrase. The phrase begins with a present participle and refers to the subject, *Randy.*]

participial phrase

Ollie, *tired of the heat in Atlanta,* requested a transfer to Chicago.

[The participial phrase appears after the subject, *Ollie.* The phrase begins with a past participle and refers to the subject.]

participial phrase

Waving his arms and shouting, the man attracted the attention of pedestrians and motorists.

[The participial phrase appears first as an introductory phrase. The phrase begins with a present participle and refers to the subject, *man.*]

Though participial phrases frequently refer to the subject of the sentence, some participial phrases refer to other nouns in the sentence. Remember that the participial phrase, regardless of where it is located in a sentence, must be placed close to (before or after) the noun that it refers to or renames.

participial phrase

In the distance, I saw Sam *limping toward the car.*
[The present participle *limping* refers to *Sam. Sam* is not the subject of the sentence; *Sam* is the direct object of the verb *saw.*]

participial phrase

The poster shows the man *wanted for questioning.*
[The past participle *wanted* refers to *man*. The subject is *poster,* so the participial phrase does not refer to the subject. Instead, it refers to the direct object, *man.*]

JUST SO YOU KNOW...

Verb forms that are not working as verbs in a sentence are called *verbals*. There are three kinds of verbals:

1. Infinitives
2. Present participles
3. Past participles

Past and present participles form the base of *participial phrases*, which work as adjectives.

When the present participle (an *-ing* word) works as a noun, it is called a *gerund*.

Two methods are commonly used to create participial phrases:

Method 1: When two sentences both have the same subject, convert one of the verbs to a participial phrase. Notice that you will need to omit some words in the sentence when you create the participial phrase. Participial phrases are frequently placed at the beginning of sentences as introductory phrases; however, they may also be placed after the subject.

Consider the following two sentences:

Melissa wore excessive makeup and outrageous hairdos to work.

She wanted attention.

We can convert the second verb to a participial phrase:

Melissa wore excessive makeup and outrageous hairdos to work.

wanting
~~She wanted~~ attention.

We then have two options for placement of the participial phrase:

participial phrase

Wanting attention, Melissa wore excessive makeup and outrageous hairdos to work.

participial phrase

Melissa, *wanting attention,* wore excessive makeup and outrageous hairdos to work.

Or we can convert the first verb to a participial phrase:

wearing excessive makeup and outrageous hairdos to work
~~Melissa wore excessive makeup and outrageous hairdos to work.~~

She wanted attention.

Again, we have two options for placement of the participial phrase:

participial phrase

Wearing excessive makeup and outrageous hairdos to work, Melissa wanted attention.

participial phrase

Melissa, *wearing excessive makeup and outrageous hairdos to work,* wanted attention.

[Notice that the proper noun *Melissa* was used instead of the pronoun *she*. Minor adjustments such as this often occur when you combine sentences through the use of participial phrases.]

Thus, as shown in the above sentences, we have four options for combining the sentences through the use of participial phrases. As a writer, your task is to decide which of the sentences expresses your desired idea most clearly and effectively.

In the following examples, two sentences are combined through the use of participial phrases. Notice how some of the sentence-combining options sound awkward or distort the relationship between the sentences. Again, your role as a writer is to select the most effective option to express your ideas.

Two sentences:

Billy was accustomed to starting his day with chores.

Billy grew up in rural America.

Sentence-combining options:

1. *Growing up in rural America,* Billy was accustomed to starting his day with chores.

2. Billy, *growing up in rural America,* was accustomed to starting his day with chores.

3. *Accustomed to starting his day with chores,* Billy grew up in rural America.

4. Billy, *accustomed to starting his day with chores,* grew up in rural America.

Two sentences:

The college students found furniture bargains at garage sales.

They hoped to save money by renting an unfurnished apartment.

Sentence-combining options:

1. *Hoping to save money by renting an unfurnished apartment,* the college students found furniture bargains at garage sales.

2. The college <u>students</u>, *hoping to save money by renting an unfurnished apartment,* <u>found</u> furniture bargains at garage sales.

3. *Finding furniture bargains at garage sales,* the college <u>students</u> <u>hoped</u> to save money by renting an unfurnished apartment.

4. The college <u>students</u>, *finding furniture bargains at garage sales,* <u>hoped</u> to save money by renting an unfurnished apartment.

Method 2: When a sentence has a relative pronoun clause with a verb phrase, remove the relative pronoun and the helping verb to make a participial phrase. The participial phrase will automatically follow the noun that it refers to or renames; however, the participial phrase may be moved to the front of the sentence as an introductory phrase.

Complex sentence with a relative pronoun clause:

relative pronoun clause
<u>Paul</u>, *who was tired of studying for his real estate exam,* <u>decided</u> to exercise for an hour.

Remove the relative pronoun and the helping verb:

participial phrase
<u>Paul</u>, ~~*who was*~~ *tired of studying for his real estate exam,* <u>decided</u> to exercise for an hour.

Sentence-combining options:

1. <u>Paul</u>, *tired of studying for his real estate exam,* <u>decided</u> to exercise for an hour.

2. *Tired of studying for his real estate exam,* <u>Paul</u> <u>decided</u> to exercise for an hour.

Complex sentence with a relative pronoun clause:

relative pronoun clause
The juvenile <u>offender</u>, *who was troubled by past problems,* <u>decided</u> that it was time to change.

Remove the relative pronoun and the helping verb:

participial phrase
The juvenile <u>offender</u>, ~~*who was*~~ *troubled by past problems,* <u>decided</u> that it was time to change.

Sentence-combining options:

1. The juvenile <u>offender</u>, *troubled by past problems,* <u>decided</u> that it was time to change.

2. *Troubled by past problems,* the juvenile <u>offender</u> <u>decided</u> that it was time to change.

Practice 3   *Identifying Participial Phrases*

Draw a box around the participial phrases in the following sentences. Underline the subjects once and the verbs twice. Remember, the participles that appear without helping verbs are not the verbs of the sentence.

Example: Anticipating a favorable turnout at the forum, the planning committee ordered additional tables and chairs for the room.

1. Determined to win the dance competition, Rosa and her partner practiced every day for five months.

2. Blending classical, popular, and jazz music, George Gershwin composed musical comedies and concert pieces.

3. Matthew, tired of hearing his son beg for a car, decided to buy him an old junker.

4. Disappointed about her interview, the student decided to find ways to strengthen her interviewing skills.

5. Pretending not to care, Robby looked the other way when his old girlfriend walked by.

6. Each of the cosmetic consultants, wanting to win the sales award, tried different ways to advertise and promote his or her products.

7. Newlyweds, often wanting a highly memorable honeymoon, begin their married life with excessive honeymoon debts.

8. Living in a small town, most people know a lot of details about other people's lives.

9. The Willamette River, running high this time of year, poses some flood threats to residents who live on its beautiful banks.

10. Determined to get some attention, the young child started hollering in the middle of the mall.

Special Notes About Participial Phrases

1. A participial phrase is usually set off by commas when it is placed after the noun or the pronoun that it refers to or renames. If the participial phrase is needed to define or clarify the subject, then no commas are used.

   participial phrase

   Karla, *building houses for a living,* is in excellent physical shape.

   > [The participial phrase is nonessential because the subject, *Karla,* is specific and clearly understood without the participial phrase. A comma is placed before and after the nonessential participial phrase.]

   participial phrase

   The woman *playing the banjo* was arrested.

   > [The participial phrase is essential; the subject is not specific or clearly understood without the participial phrase. No commas are used to separate the participial phrase from the rest of the sentence.]

2. A participial phrase that functions as an introductory phrase at the beginning of a sentence is followed by a comma. This introductory phrase refers to or tells more about the subject.

   participial phrase

   Building houses for a living, Karla is in excellent physical shape.

   participial phrase

   Shown repeatedly on television, the videotape became familiar to most American viewers.

Dangling Modifiers

> **JUST SO YOU KNOW...**
>
> Misplaced modifiers were previously discussed with relative pronoun clauses. Participial phrases, like relative pronoun clauses, must be placed as close as possible to the nouns they modify. Misplaced participial phrases are also called *dangling modifiers.*

Introductory participial phrases must be placed next to or very close to the subject they modify. If the participial phrase is not related to the closest subject in the sentence, the result is a **dangling modifier.** Dangling modifiers are errors that you can avoid by carefully checking that the participial phrase refers to the subject of the sentence. Dangling modifiers are shown in italics.

Sentence with dangling modifier:

participial phrase —NO—

Barking all night long, the neighbors were ready to file a complaint about the dog.

> [The participial phrase does not refer to the subject of the sentence; the neighbors were not barking all night long. To correct the dangling modifier, you can reposition the participial phrase, change the subject, or change the participial phrase so the participial phrase and the noun it refers to match.]

Correcting the dangling modifier:

1. The neighbors were ready to file a complaint about

    participial phrase

    the dog *barking all night long.*

[The participial phrase was repositioned next to *dog,* the noun that it refers to or modifies.]

participial phrase

2. *Barking all night long,* the dog annoyed the neighbors so much that they wanted to file a complaint.

[The subject of the sentence is changed to match the participial phrase that refers to *dog.*]

participial phrase

3. *Listening to the dog barking all night,* the neighbors were ready to file a complaint.

[The participial phrase is changed to match the subject, *neighbors.*]

Sentence with dangling modifier:

participial phrase   —NO—

Sailing on the catamaran, the dolphins surfaced near us.

[The dolphins did not sail on the catamaran. An introductory participial phrase must modify or refer to the subject of the sentence. This dangling modifier can be corrected by changing the participial phrase so it refers to *dolphins,* or by changing the subject so it refers to the people on the catamaran.]

Correcting the dangling modifier:

participial phrase

1. *Sailing on the catamaran,* we saw the dolphins surface near us.

participial phrase

2. *Surfacing near us,* the dolphins amused us as we sailed on the catamaran.

The three basic methods to correct a dangling modifier are as follows:

Method 1: Move or reposition the participial phrase by placing it next to the noun or the pronoun that it refers to or renames.

Method 2: For introductory participial phrases, change the subject of the sentence. Use a subject that matches the participial phrase.

Method 3: For introductory participial phrases, change the participial phrase. Use a participial phrase that refers to the nearest subject of the sentence.

Practice 4   *Identifying Dangling Modifiers*

Write **S** on the blank if the **sentence** has no errors. Write **DM** if the sentence has a **dangling modifier.** The arrows show correct or incorrect modification. Students' work shows only the answers on the left.

_____DM_____   1. Longing for a juicy steak, four T-bone <u>steaks</u> were placed on the grill.

_____DM_____   2. Screaming for help, the <u>dog</u> heard the woman who was stuck on the ledge.

_____S_____   3. Concerned about the consequences, <u>Sarah</u> decided not to cheat on the test.

_____DM_____   4. Wanting to avoid the traffic delays, a <u>detour</u> was marked for motorists.

_____S_____   5. Recognized for excellence, the <u>college</u> attracted many qualified candidates.

_____S_____   6. Living in luxury, the <u>widow</u> had no desire to change her lifestyle.

_____DM_____   7. Destroyed by fire, the <u>woman</u> had no place to live.

_____DM_____   8. Pretending to be ill, the research <u>paper</u> was not turned in on time.

_____S_____   9. Marketing the new product, the <u>salesman</u> traveled to ten different states.

_____S_____   10. Insulted by her remarks, her <u>husband</u> sulked for two days.

_____S_____   11. Hanging from the highest limb, the <u>cat</u> was too frightened to move.

_____S_____   12. Dancing with a famous troupe, <u>Greta</u> had many new experiences.

_____S_____   13. Stunned by the announcement of our engagement, <u>Lisa</u> refused to talk to me.

_____DM_____ 14. 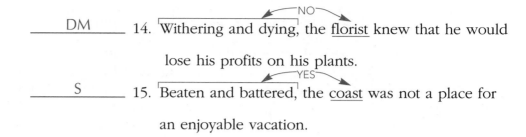 Withering and dying, the <u>florist</u> knew that he would lose his profits on his plants.

_____S_____ 15. Beaten and battered, the <u>coast</u> was not a place for an enjoyable vacation.

| **Practice 5** | *Identifying Appositives, Participial Phrases, and Dependent Clauses* |

Work with a partner, in a small group, or on your own. Draw a box around all the appositives, participial phrases, and dependent clauses in the following newspaper article about twisters that hit Fort Worth on March 28, 2000. The first paragraph is done as an example. The marginal notes, which you do not need to do, are provided to explain the highlighting.

1. dependent clause
2. participial phrase
3. participial phrase
4. dependent clause
5. appositive
6. appositive

Two tornadoes carved paths of destruction through the Fort Worth area on Tuesday, March 28, 2000. The two tornadoes were spawned amid severe thunderstorms that were accompanied by torrential rains, softball-sized hail, and strong winds. Hitting shortly after 6:30 P.M., the tornadoes shattered windows in high-rise buildings, overturned cars, and uprooted trees. Rotating in a clockwise direction, one then took a northerly route while the second moved southeast through downtown Fort Worth. Downtown Fort Worth, a city of 480,000 people, is about 30 miles west of Dallas.

About 1,200 tornadoes touch down in the United States every year, but few hit densely populated areas. "Mathematically, the United States will see an urban tornado once every year," said Jose Schaefer, director of the National Weather Service's Storm Prediction Center.

"We have a number of high-rise buildings that have sustained heavy damage," said Lt. Kent Worley, a spokesman for the Fort Worth Fire Department. "They looked like they did not have a single pane of glass left in them."

The Fort Worth tornado caused extensive damage but few deaths. At least four people were killed, one person was missing, and more than 100 were injured. Two people were crushed to death, one by a falling wall and the other by a truck trailer that flipped on him. Two others in a car were swept into the Trinity River, a river near Arlington to the east. Fearing more victims were trapped in the debris of downtown office buildings, rescue workers sealed off the city and began the search of the damaged buildings. No additional victims were found.

Extensive damage, estimated at $450 million for all of Tarrant County, occurred to many homes, businesses, and structures. Stripping brick walls off a cathedral tower and blasting out dozens of office windows, the tornado showed its force. Homes were torn apart; many residents were left with a pile of rubble. Dozens of people whose belongings were shredded or scattered were left homeless. Numerous power outages were reported. About 30,000 people were left without power at the height of the storm.

[Adapted from AP, "Fort Worth Starts Cleanup," *Register Guard*, March 29, 2000; and Stephen Hawkins, AP, "Twisters Whirl Through Fort Worth; Five Die," *Register Guard*, March 30, 2000.]

Series of Items

You can often avoid wordiness by looking for words that are repeated in a series of sentences. By combining the sentences into one simple, compound, or complex sentence, you can eliminate redundancy. Though there are many ways to combine items from several sentences into one series, the following chart summarizes ways to combine different kinds of items into a series and to place the series in a simple sentence.

SENTENCE COMBINING WITH SERIES OF ITEMS		
TYPE OF SERIES	EXAMPLE SENTENCES TO COMBINE	SIMPLE SENTENCE WITH THE COMBINED ITEMS IN A SERIES
verbs The sentences have the same subject.	In the restaurant, people heard loud, roaring noises. They dove under the tables. They covered their heads The tornado tore roofs off houses. It demolished mobile homes. It uprooted large trees and readily displaced all light objects.	In the restaurant, people heard loud, roaring noises, dove under the tables, and covered their heads. The tornado tore roofs off houses, demolished mobile homes, uprooted large trees, and readily displaced all light objects.
direct objects or objects of the preposition The sentences have the same subject.	The twister picked up patio furniture. It picked up fences. It picked up garbage cans. The town had a grocery store. The town had a small restaurant. Before the tornado, the town also had a clinic. Many farm families kept storm shelters well stocked. They had flashlights and lanterns. They had water and food. They had first-aid kits. They also had an ample supply of batteries and a radio. They had pillows and blankets.	The twister picked up patio furniture, fences, and garbage cans. Before the tornado, the town had a grocery store, a small restaurant, and a clinic. Many farm families kept storm shelters well stocked with flashlights, lanterns, water, food, first-aid kits, a radio, pillows, blankets, and an ample supply of batteries.

(Continue on page 306)

SENTENCE COMBINING WITH SERIES OF ITEMS

TYPE OF SERIES	EXAMPLE SENTENCES TO COMBINE	SIMPLE SENTENCE WITH THE COMBINED ITEMS IN A SERIES
subjects The sentences have the same verbs.	Severe <u>thunderstorms</u> <u>are</u> signs of potential tornadoes. Temperature <u>inversions</u> <u>are</u> also signs of potential tornadoes. Television <u>programs</u> <u>reported</u> the tornadoes. Radio <u>programs</u> <u>reported</u> the tornadoes. <u>Intercoms</u> in schools and businesses <u>reported</u> the tornadoes.	Severe <u>thunderstorms</u> and temperature <u>inversions</u> <u>are</u> signs of potential tornadoes. Television <u>programs</u>, radio <u>programs</u>, and <u>intercoms</u> in schools and businesses <u>reported</u> the tornadoes.
prepositional phrases The sentences have the same subjects and verbs.	The <u>trees</u> <u>were</u> (in a park). The <u>trees</u> <u>were</u> (beside the river). The <u>tornado</u> <u>moved</u> (across the field). The <u>tornado</u> <u>moved</u> (into residential areas). <u>It</u> also <u>moved</u> (through the center) (of town).	The <u>trees</u> <u>were</u> (in a park) (beside the river). The <u>tornado</u> <u>moved</u> (across the field) (into residential areas), and (through the center) (of town).
Rearranged words You can include appositives or participial phrases.	The <u>twister</u> <u>tore</u> through the town. It killed 500 people. The <u>twister</u> <u>left</u> 50,000 injured. It was unexpected. The <u>twister</u> <u>occurred</u> in Bangladesh in 1996.	The unexpected <u>twister</u> in Bangladesh in 1996 <u>tore</u> through the town, <u>killed</u> 500 people, and <u>injured</u> 50,000.

Practice 6 *Combining Sentences to Reduce Wordiness*

Work with a partner, in a small group, or on your own. Use any method to combine the following sentences into simple sentences. Write your sentences on a separate piece of paper. *Answers will vary. Possible answers are given.*

1. In my current job, I greet clients. I answer the phones. I schedule appointments. In my current job, I greet clients, answer the phones, and schedule appointments.

2. The rural town has a small library. It has a general store. The town also has a gas station and a café. The rural town has a small library, a general store, a gas station, and a café.

3. The kitchen has modern appliances. The kitchen is in my new home. The kitchen also has an island. It has recessed lighting, too. The kitchen in my new home has modern appliances, an island, and recessed lighting.

4. High school students applied for the grant. Single parents applied for the grant. Some retired citizens applied for the grant. It was a one-year educational grant. High school students, single parents, and some retired citizens applied for the one-year educational grant.

5. During the game, my friends and I ate peanuts. We yelled and screamed for our team. We enjoyed each other's company. During the game, my friends and I ate peanuts, yelled and screamed for our team, and enjoyed each other's company.

6. For my chemistry class, I need to read each chapter. I need to read carefully. I need to outline the chapter. I need to take notes. I also need to complete all the lab assignments with a partner. For my chemistry class, I need to read each chapter carefully, outline the chapter, take notes, and complete all the lab assignments with a partner.

C O M M A   S E N S E

1. Use a comma after a nonessential (nonrestrictive) appositive. The appositive is a "sentence extra" and is not needed to clearly identify the noun it represents.

> New York City, *the Big Apple,* is one of America's cultural Meccas.

2. Use a comma after an introductory participial phrase.

> *Hoping to reduce damage from storms,* the National Weather Service's Storm Prediction Center uses sophisticated equipment to warn people of potential storms.

3. Use a comma before and after a participial phrase that appears after the noun it refers to or renames. The noun is often the subject, but participial phrases may refer to other nouns in the sentence as well.

> The National Weather Service's Storm Prediction Center, *hoping to reduce damage from storms,* uses sophisticated equipment to warn people of potential storms

4. Use commas with three or more words, phrases, or clauses in a series. Commas usually are not used between prepositional phrases in a series.

> *Trees, roofs, fences, and mobile homes* were lifted into the air.

> The twister *killed four people, injured 80 people, and caused $450 million dollars in property damage.*

> The windows *(on the skyscrapers) (in the middle of the city) (of Fort Worth)* were blown out.

 **Parallelism**

JUST SO YOU KNOW...

The following coordinators are also used in parallel structures:

either . . . or
neither . . . nor
not only . . . but also
whether . . . or
not . . . but
. . . as well as . . .

PARALLELISM Parallelism occurs when words, phrases, or clauses in any series are all in the same or similar grammatical structure.

Parallel structures are usually joined by a coordinating conjunction, such as *and* or *or*. Nouns are parallel to nouns, verbs are parallel to verbs, relative pronoun clauses are parallel to relative pronoun clauses, and so on. Parallel structure makes the content of the sentence flow together smoothly; it provides coherence.

In the following examples, the parallel structures are shown in italics.

Parallelism with words:

> Sandra grows *orchids, dahlias,* and *roses.*
> [direct object nouns]

> Your accounting method is *accurate, logical,* and *detailed.*
> [adjectives]

> The basketball players *run, lift* weights, and *visualize.*
> [verbs]

> The young children responded *enthusiastically* and *honestly.*
> [adverbs]

Parallelism with phrases:

> All my life, my parents worked hard *to budget* their money and *to save* for my college fund.

> *Eating out* every night and *buying* unnecessary gadgets put a dent in a person's pocketbook.

> *Attending* classes, *doing* homework assignments, and *studying* for tests are keys to college success.

> The tornadoes were *destroying* crops, *causing* property damage, and *taking* lives.

Parallelism with clauses:

> During a drought, *the forests dry out,* and *the crops wither.*

> I realized *that I had made* some poor decisions but *that I had learned* some valuable lessons.

> My grandfather was a man *who cared* about others and *who dedicated* his life to social issues.

Special Notes About Parallelism

1. The coordinating conjunctions *and* and *or* are commonly used in parallel constructions. However, the following examples show that other types of conjunctions, or *correlatives,* which are shown in **bold print,** can be used. The words in the parallel structure are shown in italics.

> **Neither** *the computer programmers* **nor** *the software developers* had a solution.

> **Both** *the college placement test* **and** *the SAT scores* predicted her ability to succeed in the honors college program.

2. **Faulty parallelism** occurs when sentence elements are not in the same grammatical structure. The items joined may not be the same part of speech, or they may not use the same sentence structure.

Faulty parallelism:	My English teacher has a great **sense** of humor **and** very **knowledgeable.**
Correct:	My English teacher *has* a great sense of humor **and** *is* very knowledgeable. My English teacher has a great *sense* of humor **and** a *wealth* of knowledge. [In the first sentence, parallelism can be achieved by adding a verb. In the second sentence, parallelism can be achieved by adding the noun *wealth* and changing *knowledgeable* to its noun form, *knowledge.*]
Faulty parallelism:	Paul wrote about Chaucer, **and** James had written about Shakespeare.
Correct:	Paul *wrote* about Chaucer, **and** James *wrote* about Shakespeare. [Parallelism is achieved by changing *had written* to *wrote* so both sentences have the same verb tense.]
Faulty parallelism:	In addition to playing the piano **and** I sing in the choir, I square-dance on the weekends.
Correct:	In addition to *playing* the piano **and** *singing* in the choir, I square-dance on the weekends. [Parallelism is achieved by adding an *-ing* suffix to *sing* so both words are in the same form.]

Practice 7   *Identifying Faulty Parallelism*

Circle the conjunction *and, or,* or *nor* in the following sentences. Then identify the items that the conjunction is joining. On the line, write **P** for sentences that use correct *parallelism.* Write **FP** for sentences with *faulty parallelism.* Use any method to correct the sentences with faulty parallelism.

Examples: _FP_   Every student must pay tuition, get a photo identification card, (and) attend classes.

        _P_   Every student in class read the book, saw the movie, (and) participated in the discussion.

_____FP_____ 1. I enjoy skating, jogging, (and) ~~walks~~ ^{walking} along the river.

_____FP_____ 2. Rachel buys her clothes from catalogs, ~~at~~ garage sales, (or) ~~she goes to~~ Goodwill.

_____P_____ 3. Many students need to learn time management (and) techniques for studying more effectively for tests.

_____P_____ 4. Getting good grades (and) learning new skills are important goals for many students.

_____FP_____ 5. The bargain shoppers arrived early, charged into the store, (and) ~~were filling~~ ^{filled} their shopping bags.

_____FP_____ 6. The lecture series covers nutrition, ~~exercising~~, ^{exercise} (and) mental health.

_____FP_____ 7. The telemarketer was rude (and) ~~showing signs of inconsideration.~~ ^{inconsiderate}

_____FP_____ 8. My job was emptying the garbage (and) ~~to sweep~~ ^{sweeping} the cafeteria.

_____FP_____ 9. Neither rain (nor) ~~snowy days affect~~ ^{snow} ^{affects} postal delivery services.

_____FP_____ 10. The young missionaries, eager (and) ~~having lots of motivation~~, ^{motivated} met many people.

 Sentence Variety

The following chart reviews the simple, compound, and complex sentence patterns we have discussed in previous chapters.

SENTENCE PATTERNS		
SIMPLE SENTENCES	COMPOUND SENTENCES	COMPLEX SENTENCES
S-V pattern The <u>windows</u> <u>exploded</u>. **SS-V pattern** <u>Trees</u> and <u>roofs</u> <u>flew</u> through the air. **S-VV pattern** The <u>tornado</u> <u>touched</u> down and <u>approached</u> the city. **SS-VV pattern** The <u>police</u> and the <u>firemen</u> <u>blocked</u> off the area and <u>searched</u> for victims.	**S-V, coordinating conjunction S-V pattern** The <u>damage</u> <u>was</u> heavy, but few <u>lives</u> <u>were</u> lost. **S-V; S-V pattern** Four <u>people</u> <u>died</u>; eighty <u>were</u> injured. **S-V; conjunctive adverb, S-V pattern** The <u>damage</u> <u>was</u> extensive; however, <u>it</u> <u>could have been</u> worse.	**subordinate conjunction S-V, S-V pattern** Before the <u>tornado</u> <u>hit</u>, the <u>skies</u> <u>were</u> dark. **S-V subordinate conjunction S-V pattern** The <u>skies</u> <u>were</u> dark before the <u>tornado</u> <u>hit</u>. **S, relative pronoun V, V pattern** <u>Fort Worth</u>, <u>which</u> <u>is</u> near Dallas, <u>experienced</u> a tornado. **S, relative pronoun S-V, V pattern** The <u>Dallas airport</u>, which <u>I</u> <u>have visited</u>, <u>halted</u> all flights. **S-V, relative pronoun S-V pattern** The <u>airline</u> <u>evacuated</u> the terminal, which <u>they</u> <u>were</u> required to do. **S-V relative pronoun S-V pattern** <u>I</u> <u>know</u> that <u>you</u> <u>are</u> responsible.

Your writing will be more interesting, more sophisticated, and more effective when you use a variety of sentence structures. In addition to using simple, compound, and complex sentences, you can also use appositives, participial phrases, items in a series, and parallelism to enhance your sentence-writing skills.

When you combine sentences, selecting the appropriate conjunction to convey the relationship between the clauses is important. The following summary chart shows common relationships used between two clauses. The chart also shows three ways to form compound sentences and two ways to form complex sentences.

COMPOUND SENTENCES				COMPLEX SENTENCES	
Relationship	Coordinating Conjunctions	Semicolon	; conj. adverb,	Subordinate Conjunction (adverbial clauses)	Relative Pronouns (adjective clauses)
addition	and	;	accordingly again also besides furthermore in addition moreover		A relative pronoun clause with an independent clause forms a complex sentence. The relative pronouns refer to nouns in the main clause. They do not show the relationships in the left column of this chart.
comparison, similarity	and	;	also in the same way likewise similarly	as as if as though just as	
contrast or opposition	but or yet	;	however in comparison in contrast instead nevertheless on the contrary on the other hand otherwise still unfortunately	although even though though whereas whether while	
time	and and (then)	;	afterward at the same time finally first furthermore in the meantime later meanwhile next second subsequently then third	after as as long as as soon as before once since until when whenever while	that which whichever who whoever whom whomever whose

(Continue on page 313)

COMPOUND SENTENCES				COMPLEX SENTENCES
Relationship	Coordinating Conjunctions	Semicolon	; conj. adverb,	Subordinate Conjunction (adverbial clauses)	Relative Pronouns (adjective clauses)
illustration		;	for example for instance in fact		
manner				as if as though like	
concession	but yet	;	admittedly however nevertheless	although despite the fact that even though in spite of the fact that though whereas	
purpose				in order that so that	
reason, cause, effect	for so	;	as a result consequently hence then therefore thus	as as long as because inasmuch as in order that now that since so that such that	
condition	so	;		even if even though if in case only if provided that unless whether or not	

(Continue on page 314)

COMPOUND SENTENCES				COMPLEX SENTENCES	
Relationship	Coordinating Conjunctions	Semicolon	; conj. adverb,	Subordinate Conjunction (adverbial clauses)	Relative Pronouns (adjective clauses)
summation		;	finally hence in conclusion in general in short in summary overall therefore		
emphasis		;	certainly indeed in fact to be sure		

Practice 8   *Recognizing Simple, Compound, and Complex Sentences*

Each of the sentences in the following paragraphs is numbered. Study the sentence structure of each sentence. On the numbered lines below the paragraphs, indicate the type of sentence for each numbered sentence. Write **S** for *simple,* **C** for *compound,* and **CX** for *complex.*

[1]In 1999, Hurricane Floyd battered North Carolina and caused record floodwaters. [2]Shortly after Floyd hammered North Carolina, Hurricane Irene visited the same region with 85 mph winds. [3]Torrential rains in front of Irene's core swamped dozens of roads. [4]Disastrous flooding was feared, so National Guard troops were called out to sandbag against further rising floodwaters. [5]However, sandbags didn't stop Irene; the hurricane drenched southeastern North Carolina with more than a half foot of rain and unleashed even more flooding. [6]As the storm turned northeast, its strongest winds moved away from the land. [7]Tropical storm warnings, however, remained in effect for most of the coastal region. [8]The entire state was on alert.

1. _S_ 2. _CX_ 3. _S_ 4. _C_ 5. _C_ 6. _CX_ 7. _S_ 8. _S_

[9]During the hurricane, the greatest concern was the rain, not the wind. [10]A flash flood warning was issued for a 100-mile by 50-mile swath of North Carolina. [11]Gale force winds were measured at the coast, and a tornado was reported by radar over another area of the state. [12]The state, which needed to post hurricane warnings, tropical storm warnings, flood warnings, and tornado warnings, was getting slammed by Mother Nature.

9. <u>S</u>   10. <u>S</u>   11. <u>C</u>   12. <u>CX</u>

[Adapted from AP, "Irene Inundates North Carolina," *Register Guard*, October 18, 1999.]

Compound-Complex Sentences

COMPOUND-COMPLEX SENTENCE   A compound-complex sentence contains two or more independent clauses (a compound sentence) and one or more dependent clauses (a complex sentence).

Very likely you have already written compound-complex sentences in some of your writing assignments. Since compound-complex sentences frequently occur in speech, it is very likely that you use them on a regular basis in your oral communication. The following examples show simple sentences combined to form compound-complex sentences. Notice that each of these compound-complex sentences includes the elements of a compound sentence (two independent or main clauses) and an element of a complex sentence (one or more dependent clauses). The compound-complex sentence is much more interesting to read than the short, choppy original sentences.

Original sentences: The crew was exhausted.
The they had been in the air for ten hours.
The crew boarded in Chicago.

Compound-complex sentence:

The crew, which boarded in Chicago, was exhausted, for they had been in the air for ten hours.

Original sentences: The players signed autographs.
The fans partied in the streets.
The team won the championship.

Compound-complex sentence:

After the team won the championship, the players signed autographs, and the fans partied in the streets.

Compound-complex sentences may have two or more independent clauses and two or more dependent clauses. Notice the number of clauses in the following compound-complex sentences.

Original sentences:
I had planned to take a trip to Las Vegas.
Las Vegas is a place in Nevada.
I have never seen Las Vegas.
I needed to study for my algebra exam.

Compound-complex sentence:

I had planned to take a trip to Las Vegas, which is a place in Nevada that I have never seen, but I needed to study for my algebra exam.

Original sentences:
I know.
You are intelligent.
I did not know.
You are also musically gifted.

Compound-complex sentence:

I know that you are intelligent; however, I did not know that you are also musically gifted.

Practice 9   *Identifying Types of Sentences*

Study the subject-verb patterns of the following sentences. On the line, write the letter that identifies the sentence type. *If students have problems with these sentence patterns, use class time for further discussions.*

S = simple sentence   C = compound sentence

CX = complex sentence   CCX = compound-complex sentence

Example: <u>CCX</u>   The trains that leave the station before noon are northbound, but the trains that leave the station in the afternoon and the evening are southbound. [Independent clauses: *The trains are northbound. The trains are southbound.* Dependent clauses: *that leave the station before noon* and *that leave the station in the afternoon and the evening.*]

_____S_____ 1. The messenger left the package with the lady at the front desk.

_____CX_____ 2. Mark and Lisa will be married next weekend in a small chapel that is located next to a beautiful, cascading waterfall.

_____C_____ 3. The young swimmer tried to stand up on a rock, but the rock was actually a large sea turtle.

_____CX_____ 4. The women who were carrying large bundles of clothing on their heads walked gracefully through the town plaza.

_____CCX_____ 5. I think that you are wise, but you don't always think before you speak.

_____C_____ 6. Most people enjoy a good meal, but many do not enjoy paying the price.

_____CCX_____ 7. The rain, which had pelted us for days, stopped, so we decided to explore the beaches and the coves.

_____CX_____ 8. The hot air balloon that floated above the crowd almost hit a power line.

_____CCX_____ 9. I seldom buy crab because it is so expensive; I never buy lobster for the same reason.

_____CX_____ 10. The coffee that I ordered was too strong, too bitter, and too cold.

**Fragments**

FRAGMENT **A fragment occurs when a part of a sentence is punctuated as a complete sentence.**

A fragment cannot stand by itself as a sentence because it lacks one or more of the essential elements of a complete sentence: a subject, a complete verb, a complete thought, or the ability to stand on its own without any other clauses. Sentence fragments can be corrected by adding the missing sentence elements. The following chart summarizes three common types of fragment errors and methods to correct them.

FRAGMENT ERRORS		
TYPE OF FRAGMENT	EXAMPLES	CORRECTION METHODS
Fragment errors found in simple sentences: The group of words is missing a subject, a complete verb, or a complete thought. The group of words cannot stand by itself and poses as a sentence.	The cars with loud engines. Moved to the front of the line. With pink slips in her hand. My coach swimming across the river.	1. *Add a missing subject and/or a missing verb.* The <u>cars</u> with loud engines <u>roared</u> through the streets. The impatient <u>woman</u> <u>moved</u> to the front of the line. The <u>manager</u> <u>came</u> in my direction with pink slips in her hand. 2. *Complete the verb.* My <u>coach</u> <u>was swimming</u> across the river.
Fragment errors found in complex sentences: A dependent clause that begins with a subordinate conjunction stands by itself and poses as a sentence.	After the dust settled. If you want the answer. Though the breeze was cool.	1. *Attach the dependent clause to an independent clause that appears before or after the fragment.* After the dust settled, we were able to discuss the situation. Read the chapter if you want the answer. 2. *Delete the subordinate conjunction.* The breeze was cool.

(Continue on page 319)

FRAGMENT ERRORS		
TYPE OF FRAGMENT	EXAMPLES	CORRECTION METHODS
Fragment error found in complex sentences: A dependent clause that begins with a relative pronoun stands by itself and poses as a sentence.		1. *Attach the dependent clause to the noun it refers to in the independent clause.*
	That I misplaced last year.	I found the book that I misplaced last year.
	Which was inappropriate.	The request on the invitation, which was inappropriate, offended many people.
	Whom I truly adore.	My mentor is a person whom I truly adore.
		2. *Remove the relative pronoun. Add a noun or pronoun subject.*
	Who walked the entire distance.	The eight-year-old walked the entire distance.

In this chapter, you learned about appositives, participial phrases, and items in a series. Each of these can create a fragment if it stands by itself and poses as a sentence. Each fragment is a part of a sentence. The following chart shows additional kinds of fragments that you will want to avoid. Should you find fragment errors in your writing, the correction methods show you how to add the missing sentence elements to have a complete sentence.

FRAGMENT ERRORS		
TYPE OF FRAGMENT	EXAMPLES	CORRECTION METHODS
Fragment error with an appositive: An appositive stands by itself and poses as a sentence.		1. *Attach the appositive to a main clause. Place the appositive next to the noun it modifies.*
	A city near Minneapolis.	Bloomington, a city near Minneapolis, is the home of the great Mall of America.
	A difficult language to learn.	Sonja wants to learn Japanese, a difficult language to learn.
		2. *Add a subject and a verb.*
	A river in South America.	The Amazon is a river in South America.

(Continue on page 320)

FRAGMENT ERRORS		
TYPE OF FRAGMENT	EXAMPLES	CORRECTION METHODS
Fragment error with a participial phrase: A participial phrase stands by itself and poses as a sentence.		1. *Attach the participial phrase to a main clause. Place the participial phrase next to the noun/subject it refers to.*
	Used to prevent scurvy.	Used to prevent scurvy, vitamin C also aids the healing of wounds.
		2. *Add a subject and a helping verb.*
	Spinning out of control.	The <u>motorcycle</u> <u>was spinning</u> out of control.
Fragment error with items in a series: A series of items stands by itself but does not have a subject and a complete verb or form a complete thought.		1. *Add the missing subject and/or verb to form a complete sentence.*
	With the money in her hand.	The actress went to the attorney with the money in her hand.
	Completed the form, signed it, and mailed it.	My dad completed the form, signed it, and mailed it.

As you work with the sentence-combining skills in the remainder of the chapter, check carefully that you have complete sentences. Check that every sentence has a subject and a complete verb, forms a complete thought, and can stand by itself without any other clauses. Remember that both independent clauses and dependent clauses must have subjects and complete verbs. Use the preceding charts to correct any fragment errors that slip by you but are brought to your attention by your teacher, a tutor, or a peer.

EXERCISE 10.1 **Hurricanes** Name _____ Date _____

Dave Martin/© AP-Wide World Photos

Work with a partner, in a small group, or on your own to complete this exercise. Read the following paragraphs, which have numbered sentences. On the numbered lines below each paragraph, use the following abbreviations to indicate what is represented by each numbered line:

S = correct sentence; no errors   **F = fragment**

RO = run-on sentence error   **CS = comma splice error**

HURRICANES

[1]Tropical cyclones batter islands and produce massive human suffering and property damage every year. [2]Tropical cyclones are whirling masses of wind and rain that form around a low-pressure center. [3]Or a tropical depression. [4]Originate over very warm waters near the equator. [5]A tropical depression occurs when heated air is carried aloft in the atmosphere. [6]The tropical depression pulls in cold, drier air from the surrounding atmosphere. [7]The air that is pulled in begins to swirl it spins counterclockwise in the northern hemisphere and clockwise in the southern hemisphere. [8]With the mixtures of air, the moist air condenses it begins to rain. [9]The condensation releases heat, this increases the amount of humid air located above the storm system and reduces the pressure near the center or the eye of the storm even further. [10]More air gets sucked into the eye of the storm, creating more winds and increased rainstorms. [11]These violent, low-pressure tropical storms are usually confined to latitudes of 15 to 20 degrees north and south of the equator. [12]They tend to move westward and often strike coastal lands.

1. <u>SENT</u>   2. <u>SENT</u>   3. <u>FRAG</u>   4. <u>FRAG</u>   5. <u>SENT</u>   6. <u>SENT</u>

7. <u>RO</u>   8. <u>RO</u>   9. <u>CS</u>   10. <u>SENT</u>   11. <u>SENT</u>   12. <u>SENT</u>

S = correct sentence; no errors   F = fragment

RO = run-on sentence error   CS = comma splice error

[13]Tropical cyclones begin near the equator and move westward. [14]Gathering intensity and size. [15]They advance slowly, usually at about 10 to 15 miles per hour. [16]The circular winds around the center are very strong, they may reach speeds of 155 miles per hour. [17]The diameter of a cyclone can be as large as 300 miles. [18]The heavy rains and powerful winds, which are characteristic of cyclones. [19]Can cause severe land and property damage. [20]Lives are often taken. [21]A violent and destructive rush of seawater, called a storm surge, often follows a cyclone. [22]The storm surge is often more destructive than the powerful winds of the cyclone. [23]When the eye of the storm, the low-pressure center, moves onto shore, the water level rises. [24]However, when the eye moves away, the water level suddenly drops back, producing a huge wall of water that floods inland.

13. SENT   14. FRAG   15. SENT   16. CS   17. SENT   18. FRAG

19. FRAG   20. SENT   21. SENT   22. SENT   23. SENT   24. SENT

[25]Tropical cyclones are called hurricanes or typhoons. [26]Depending on the location of the tropical cyclone. [27]Hurricanes occur in the western Atlantic and the Caribbean oceans. [28]From June to November, with September often the most active month. [29]They begin as tropical storms that develop from low pressure in the trade winds. [30]When the speed of the tropical storm winds surpasses 75 miles per hour. [31]The tropical storm officially becomes a hurricane. [32]A category 5 hurricane is the most powerful and destructive hurricane hurricanes often measure 200 to 300 miles in diameter. [33]The wind speeds can range from 75 m.p.h. to more than 155 m.p.h. the storm surges range from 4 to 18 feet. [34]The eye of the hurricane, the center of the hurricane, is calm. [35]Storm clouds, called wall clouds, surround the eye; the strongest winds and the heaviest rain of a hurricane occur within its wall clouds. [36]The Caribbean islands and the coastal communities of the southeastern United States and Mexico are threatened annually by hurricanes.

25. SENT   26. FRAG   27. SENT   28. FRAG   29. SENT   30. FRAG

31. SENT   32. RO   33. RO   34. SENT   35. SENT   36. SENT

[Adapted from http://www.worldbook.com.]

EXERCISE 10.2   Using Appositives   Name _____ Date _____

Combine the following pairs of sentences into one sentence by using appositives. Write your sentences on separate paper. *Answers may vary; possible answers are given.*

Example: The *Observer* has forty thousand readers. The *Observer* is a daily newspaper.

The *Observer*, a daily newspaper, has forty thousand readers.

1. Stan looks like a movie star from the 1940s. Stan is my acting instructor.   Stan, my acting instructor, looks like a movie star from the 1940s.

2. Timothy rents two videos every weekend. He is a film major.
Timothy, a film major, rents two videos every weekend.

3. The sails on the boat flapped in the wind. The boat was a small four-person sailboat.   The sails on the boat, a small four-person sailboat, flapped in the wind.

4. Camping in the park was prohibited. The park was a remote county park on the top of a cliff.   Camping in the park, a remote county park on the top of a cliff, was prohibited.

5. The judge ordered restitution. The judge is a fair and impartial woman.   The judge, a fair and impartial woman, ordered restitution.

6. The formulas were written on the board and explained. Each formula had at least four steps.   The formulas, each with at least four steps, were written on the board and explained.

7. Lora Lynn helped me file the petition. Lora Lynn is my program adviser.   Lora Lynn, my program adviser, helped me file the petition.

8. My cousin served in the military most of his life. My cousin is a former Marine.   My cousin, a former Marine, served in the military most of his life.

9. The campaign manager predicted a landslide. He is an optimistic man.   The campaign manager, an optimistic man, predicted a landslide.

10. Several footprints were left in the mud. The footprints were not from a human.   Several footprints, not from a human, were left in the mud.

EXERCISE 10.3   **Sentence Combining**   Name _____ Date _____

Combine the following pairs of sentences into one sentence by converting one of the sentences to an appositive, a participial phrase, or a dependent clause. Write your sentences on separate paper. *Answers may vary; possible answers are given.*

Example: Funnel clouds are one type of tornado. Funnel clouds do not touch the ground.

participial phrase

Option 1:   Not touching the ground, funnel clouds are one type of tornado.

appositive

Option 2:   Funnel clouds, one type of tornado, do not touch the ground.

dependent clause

Option 3:   Funnel clouds, which do not touch the ground, are one type of tornado.

1. Tornadoes are produced inside powerful thunderstorms. Tornadoes are also called twisters. Tornadoes, or twisters, are produced inside powerful thunderstorms.

2. Tornadic thunderstorms produce tornadoes. Thunderstorms occur when warm, moist air is trapped below stable, colder air. Tornadic thunderstorms, which produce tornadoes, occur when warm, moist air is trapped below stable, colder air.

3. Supercells spawn tornadoes. Supercells are intense weather systems with large, powerful thunderstorms. Supercells, which spawn tornadoes, are intense weather systems with large, powerful thunderstorms.

4. The warm, humid air punches through the stable air. The warm air spirals upward. Spiraling upward, the warm, humid air punches through the stable air.

5. The spiraling winds gain velocity. The spiraling winds are rotating updrafts. The spiraling winds, which are rotating updrafts, gain velocity.

6. Doppler weather radar measures the velocity of winds from afar. Doppler weather radar was first used to measure wind speeds in 1971. Doppler weather radar, which measures the velocity of winds from afar, was first used to measure wind speeds in 1971.

7. Federal agencies are installing Doppler radar networks across the country. Federal agencies want to improve tornado warning capabilities. Wanting to improve tornado warning capabilities, federal agencies are installing Doppler radar networks across the country.

8. The Fujita Scale links tornado damage to wind speed. The Fujita Scale is the official classification system for tornadoes. The Fujita Scale, the official classification system for tornadoes, links tornado damage to wind speed.

9. The Fujita Scale goes from F0 to F6. The Fujita Scale is used after a tornado has struck. The Fujita Scale, which goes from F0 to F6, is used after a tornado has struck.

10. Tornadoes do varying degrees of damage. Tornadoes last from a few minutes to more than an hour. Lasting from a few minutes to more than an hour, tornadoes do varying degrees of damage.

EXERCISE 10.4   **Using Parallelism**   Name _____ Date _____

Locate the faulty parallelism in the following sentences. Correct each sentence by writing your corrections above the words, phrases, or clauses that cause the faulty parallelism or by deleting the words that cause the faulty parallelism. *Answers may vary; possible answers are given.*

Example: The endorsement was encouraging, lucrative, and ~~a benefit~~. ^{beneficial}
[Parallelism is achieved by using a series of adjectives.]

1. The architects built a new building that was modern, ~~showed~~ ^{elegant} ~~elegance~~, and beautiful.

2. I intend to arrive early, to be thorough, and ~~want~~ to be a team player.   (Note: The word *to* may be omitted in the infinitives *to be*.)

3. The chef placed cinnamon rolls, croissants, bear claws, and ~~put~~ fruit on the food cart.

4. The train moved through the town, past the orchards, and ~~headed~~ toward the coast.

5. Each of the basketball players must enroll as a full-time student, attend classes on a regular basis, and ~~be earning~~ ^{earn} a 3.0 GPA.

6. With the increase in the cost of gasoline and ~~higher~~ insurance rates, I am seriously considering riding the bus more frequently.

7. The magazine article was inaccurate, excessively long, and ~~found to be~~ extremely boring.

8. I was standing on the steps, watching the sunset, and ~~thought~~ ^{thinking} about our time together.

9. August, September, and ~~the month of~~ November are months with frequent tropical storms.

10. Our latest production netted a good profit, built community support, and ~~will provide~~ ^{provided} students with valuable experiences.

EXERCISE 10.5 **Combining Sentences** Name _____ Date _____

Use any method to combine the following pairs of sentences into one sentence. The combined sentence may be a simple, a compound, a complex, or a compound-complex sentence. Write your sentences on separate paper. *Answers may vary; possible answers are given.*

1. Tsunamis are associated with earthquakes. The earthquakes occur in oceanic and coastal regions. Tsunamis are associated with earthquakes that occur in oceanic and coastal regions.

2. Tsunamis are a series of waves. The waves have extremely long wavelengths and duration. Tsunamis are a series of waves that have extremely long wavelengths and duration.

3. In deep water, the length of the wave can be 300 miles. The wave can last for a period of one hour. In deep water, the wave can be 300 miles long and can last for a period of one hour.

4. Tsunamis are generated by impulsive disturbances. The impulsive disturbances displace large sections of water. Tsunamis are generated by impulsive disturbances, which displace large sections of water.

5. Disturbances such as earthquakes, landslides, volcanic eruptions, explosions, or meteorites can generate tsunamis. Tsunamis begin in the deep ocean waters. Disturbances such as earthquakes, landslides, volcanic eruptions, explosions, or meteorites can generate tsunamis in the deep ocean waters.

6. The powerful sea wave is called a tsunami. *Tsunami* is a Japanese word that is translated as "harbor wave." The powerful sea wave is called a *tsunami*, a Japanese word that is translated as "harbor wave."

7. The period of a tsunami wave is about one hour. The period of a wave is the time between two successive waves. The period of a tsunami wave, the time between two successive waves, is about one hour.

8. Tsunamis move faster in deep water. Tsunamis can travel 550 miles per hour in deep water. Moving faster in deep water, tsunamis can travel up to 550 miles per hour

9. Tsunamis can travel at high speeds for long periods of time. They slow down as they approach land. Tsunamis can travel at high speeds for long periods of time, but they slow down as they approach land.

10. When they reach the coast, they hit with tremendous amounts of energy. They have great erosion potential and can strip the sand off beaches. Hitting with tremendous amounts of energy when they reach the coast, they have great erosion potential and can strip the sand off beaches.

[Adapted from http://observe.ivv.nasa.gov/nasa/exhibits/tsunami.]

Chapter 10 Summary

1. **Appositives** are nouns, noun phrases, or noun clauses that rename or give more specific information about a previously mentioned noun or pronoun. They are sometimes referred to as noun repeaters. Appositives are placed before or after the nouns they modify.

2. Present participles and past participles are used to create participial phrases. Present participles use an *-ing* suffix. Past participles use an *-ed* suffix for regular verbs and a different form of the verb for irregular verbs.

3. **Participial phrases** are groups of words that begin with a participle. A participial phrase refers to the closest noun or pronoun. When it refers to the subject, it may be placed at the beginning of the sentence as an introductory phrase, or it may be placed after the subject.

4. **Dangling modifiers** are introductory participial phrases that do not refer to or modify the subject of the sentence. Dangling modifiers can usually be corrected by repositioning the participial phrase in the sentence, or by changing either the subject or the participial phrase in order to have the subject and the participial phrase match or refer to each other.

5. Series of items that are the same part of speech can be used to combine sentences. Commas are used between the items in the series.

6. **Parallelism** occurs when words, phrases, or clauses in any series are the same part of speech or have the same grammatical structure. Items on both sides of a coordinating conjunction must be parallel. Faulty parallelism occurs when the same part of speech or the same grammatical structure on each side of a coordinating conjunction is not used.

7. Sentence variety is achieved by using simple, compound, complex, and compound-complex sentences. Sentence variety also occurs through the use of appositives, participial phrases, and items in a series.

8. **Compound-complex sentences** are sentences that have at least two independent clauses and one or more dependent clauses.

9. **Fragments** are parts of sentences that cannot stand by themselves as a complete sentence. A fragment is a writing error that can be corrected by using a variety of methods to make a complete sentence with a subject, a complete verb, and a complete thought. The sentence must be able to stand on its own as a sentence to be complete.

10. Commas are used

    a. Before and after a nonessential (nonrestrictive) appositive

    b. After an introductory participial phrase

    c. Before and after a participial phrase that appears after the noun it refers to or renames (The participial phrase often refers to the subject.)

    d. With three or more words, phrases, or clauses in a series (Commas are not usually used between prepositional phrases in a series.)

Writing Topics for Chapter 10

1. Have you or anyone you know personally been in the vicinity of a natural disaster? If yes, write about the experience. What type of disaster did you experience? When did it occur? What were the outcomes?

 2. Hurricanes are named alphabetically each year. Use library resources or the Internet to locate a list of hurricanes. Select one hurricane for this assignment. Read about the hurricane and then use your own words to summarize what you learned. Provide a printed copy of the source of your information.

 3. Use the Internet to locate more information about any one of the world's natural disasters: tornadoes, hurricanes, typhoons, tsunamis, volcanoes, or earthquakes. Use your own words to summarize the information you located. Provide a copy of the source of your information.

Web Site Learning Experiences

See the web site for this book to locate companion exercises and links related to the grammar topics in this chapter.

Go to: http://college.hmco.com. Click on "Students." Type *Sentence Essentials* in the "Jump to Textbook Sites" box. Click "go" and then book-mark the site. Click on Chapter 10.

CHAPTER 10 • Review   Name _____   Date _____

Total Possible: 50   Your Score: _____

Part I: Identification of Sentences and Fragments (10 points)

Read each statement carefully. Write **F** if it is a *fragment*. Use these letter codes to indicate sentence types: *Give one point per answer.*

S = simple	**C = compound**
CX = complex	**CCX = compound-complex**

_____CCX_____ 1. I know that everyone has a special talent, but I have not yet discovered mine.

_____CX_____ 2. Sitting in the stadium, I wondered what Jeremy was doing at home.

_____C_____ 3. Because of the severe weather, the shelters opened two weeks early, and the soup kitchens started serving meals twice a day.

_____C_____ 4. The line extended for two blocks; after three hours, it disappeared.

_____FRAG_____ 5. Dangling modifiers in sentences that I wrote last night for my final paper.

_____CX_____ 6. The lava rocks, which were coarse and prickly, cut my bare feet.

_____CCX_____ 7. I thought that I had made a wise decision, but later I was proven wrong.

_____CCX_____ 8. Homestays, which are available for exchange students, provide students with room and board, but they do not always fulfill students' social needs.

_____S_____ 9. The study of languages interests Richard, a polyglot.

_____CX_____ 10. If you have some time available, I would like to give you a tour of our campus.

Part II: Correcting Fragments (20 points)

On separate paper, correct the following fragments by writing complete sentences. *Give 0–4 points per sentence. Deduct points for errors. Give 4 points for error-free sentences.*

1. The ticket stubs from the theater.

2. When you want to see a writing tutor.

3. Who I consider to be the perfect friend.

4. One of the largest bodies of water in our state.

5. Planning to continue in his major.

Part III: Sentence Writing (20 points)

Follow the sentence-combining directions for each of the following pairs of sentences. Write your sentences on separate paper. *Give 0–4 points per sentence. Deduct points for errors. Give 4 points for error-free sentences. Answers may vary. Possible answers are shown.*

1. Combine the following sentences by using a participial phrase:

   I joined a study group. I needed to pass the class.
   Needing to pass the class, I joined a study group.

2. Combine the following sentences by using an appositive:

   Olaf runs five miles every morning. He is an avid runner.
   Olaf, an avid runner, runs five miles every morning.

3. Combine the following sentences by using parallelism:

   The clouds were dark gray. The clouds looked ominous and eerie.
   The clouds were dark gray, ominous, and eerie.

4. Combine the following sentences by using items in a series:

   The salesman rang the doorbell. He waited two minutes. He finally left.
   The salesman rang the doorbell, waited two minutes, and finally left.

5. Combine the following sentences into a compound-complex sentence:

   The meteorologist warned viewers about flash flooding. Flash flooding can occur quickly. He cautioned motorists not to drive in high waters.
   The meteorologist who warned viewers about flash flooding, which can occur quickly, also cautioned motorists not to drive in high water.

APPENDIX A

Punctuation Guide

The following punctuation guide, arranged in alphabetical order, can assist you with using punctuation marks correctly in your writing. Rules and examples for the most commonly used punctuation marks are included in this section.

This punctuation guide works well as a general reference for many of your writing needs. This punctuation guide, however, does not consist of all the rules of punctuation. For more complex rules, you can check a comprehensive punctuation guide or the punctuation glossary in the back of many hardbound dictionaries, or speak with your writing instructor.

Apostrophe

1. Use an apostrophe to form contractions. The apostrophe is inserted at the place where letters are dropped when two words are combined. Contractions may be used in informal writing; however, they should be avoided in formal writing.

I am = I'm	let us = let's	they have = they've
I would = I'd	it has = it's	I had = I'd
it is = it's	what is = what's	was not = wasn't
you would = you'd	he has = he's	you had = you'd
he is = he's	who is = who's	were not = weren't
she would = she'd	she has = she's	he had = he'd
she is = she's	where is = where's	has not = hasn't
he would = he'd	I have = I've	she had = she'd
you are = you're	there is = there's	have not = haven't
we would = we'd	you have = you've	it had = it'd
we are = we're	is not = isn't	had not = hadn't
they would = they'd	we have = we've	we had = we'd
they are = they're	are not = aren't	does not = doesn't

they had = they'd	should not = shouldn't	he will = he'll
do not = don't	it will = it'll	could not = couldn't
I will = I'll	would not = wouldn't	they will = they'll
did not = didn't	she will = she'll	will not = won't
you will = you'll	cannot = can't	

2. Use the apostrophe to form singular possessive nouns and possessive indefinite pronouns. Possessive nouns indicate ownership. Place the apostrophe at the end of the word and then add -s.

car's engine	dog's dish
tree's blossoms	Mary's sister
James's surname	everyone's wish
month's sales figures	New Year's resolution

3. Use the apostrophe to form plural possessive nouns that end in -s. Place the apostrophe at the end of the word.

waitresses' tips	girls' uniforms
boys' coach	birds' nests

4. Use the apostrophe to form plural possessive nouns that do not end in -s. Place the apostrophe at the end of the word and then add -s.

children's toys	men's suits
women's goals	mothers-in-law's birthday

5. Do not use an apostrophe to form the plural of a word that is not a possessive.

The ~~river's~~ rivers merge north of the North Fork Bridge.

The young ~~cheerleader's~~ cheerleaders were excited about the national competition.

6. Do not use an apostrophe in a possessive pronoun (*yours, his, hers, ours, and theirs*).

My notes are well organized; ~~your's~~ yours could be improved by using more structure.

Our apartment overlooks the river, but ~~their's~~ theirs overlooks the alley.

Brackets

1. Use brackets to show alterations or clarifications within quoted material.

   Councilman Patello proclaimed, "She [Councilwoman Wallace] distorted the facts and misrepresented the sequence of events that led to this internal investigation."

2. Use brackets to enclose parenthetical information (information that belongs inside parentheses) that appears inside a larger group of words that are themselves inside parentheses.

   (In fact, studies [see Diagram 3] show the reverse trend is more prominent.)

Colon

1. Use a colon after the formal greeting (salutation) in a business letter.

   Dear Ms. Crawford: Dear Human Resources Director:

2. Use a colon between the hour and the minutes when you refer to time.

   10:35 A.M.   2:10 P.M.

3. Use a colon to introduce a list of items. A complete independent clause must appear before the colon.

   Correct: Several survival items should be stored in your storm shelter: food, water, flashlights, batteries, blankets, a radio, and a first-aid kit.

   Do not use a colon for a series of items that follow the linking verbs *are* or *were*.

   Incorrect: The questions on the test were: long, complicated, baffling, and unsolvable.

4. Use a colon between independent clauses when the second clause explains the meaning of the first clause. The colon in this case signals a stronger relationship between the two clauses than would be signaled by a semicolon. The second independent clause must clarify the first independent clause.

   Legislators are voicing their concerns about the initiative process to get measures on a ballot: too many special-interest groups are hiring out-of-state people to collect the required number of signatures to qualify an initiative for a ballot.

5. Use a colon to emphasize an appositive that appears at the end of a sentence. The appositive clarifies or explains the statement that appears before the colon.

> The alarming increase in mortality in Africa is attributed to one disease: AIDS.

6. Use a colon before a question.

> I want to ask you one question: Were you present at the crime scene?

7. Use a colon to introduce a quotation.

> During Dr. Martin Luther King, Jr.'s keynote address at the March on Washington, D.C., on August 28, 1963, he delivered the famous words: "So I say to you, my friends, that even though we must face the difficulties of today and tomorrow, I still have a dream. It is a dream deeply rooted in the American dream that some day this nation will rise up and live out the true meaning of its creed—we hold these truths to be self-evident, that all men are created equal."

Comma

1. Use a comma to separate nouns in a series of three or more nouns.

> The final report contained charts, quotes, and sales predictions.

> Men, women, and children were welcome at the exhibit.

Do not use a comma between two nouns:

Incorrect: We looked at an apartment, and a house in your area.

Correct: We looked at an apartment and a house in your area.

2. Use a comma between three or more verbs or verb phrases that tell the action of the subject. Include a comma before the conjunction that leads to the last verb or verb phrase. Verbs shown in the examples are underlined twice.

> The audience <u>laughed</u>, <u>cheered</u>, and <u>applauded</u> throughout the performance.

> Rafael <u>applied</u> for the job, <u>completed</u> the interview, and <u>took</u> the drug test.

> The fierce winds <u>had destroyed</u> the pier, <u>damaged</u> the coastal buildings, and <u>uprooted</u> most of the trees along Main Street.

3. Use a comma between two or more adjectives that describe the same noun whenever the word *and* can be placed between the adjectives.

                 [and]

     adjective ˄ adjective

Troy is a strong, fast wide receiver.

Do not use a comma when the word *and* cannot be inserted between the adjectives.

Incorrect:	The three, young boys played baseball in the street.
Incorrect:	The three *and* young boys played baseball in the street.
Correct:	The three young boys played baseball in the street.

4. Use a comma between three or more adverbs whenever the word *and* can be placed between them. Place a comma before the conjunction that leads to the last adverb.

                                     adverb

The student council responded to the emergency quickly,

 [and]

 ˄ adverb   adverb

responsibly, and maturely.

5. Use a comma between three or more phrases or clauses in a series.

                       phrase   phrase

The bulldozers rumbled down the street, past the intersection, and

       phrase

into the field behind our house.

             clause   clause

The players went into the dugout, the fans retreated to the covered

                       clause

areas, and the field crew pulled a huge tarp over the field.

6. Use a comma before a coordinating conjunction when the conjunction joins two independent clauses to form a compound sentence. The coordinating conjunctions are *for, and, nor, but, or, yet,* and *so.*

           independent clause   independent clause

The flight was scheduled to leave at noon, but fog delayed the

departure time.

               independent clause

I wanted to attend a university in my home state, so I applied to

                   independent clause

Portland State University and the University of Oregon.

7. Use a comma after a conjunctive adverb when it is used to join two sentences to form a compound sentence. Conjunctive adverbs are words such as *therefore, however, thus, nevertheless, consequently,* and *finally.*

<u>independent clause</u>   <u>independent clause</u>
Your grades are excellent; therefore, we would like to offer

you a scholarship.

If you use a comma instead of a semicolon between two independent clauses, you will create a comma splice error. To correct the comma splice, replace the comma with a semicolon.

comma splice error
↓
Incorrect: **The final game was rescheduled, fortunately, I was able to attend the game.**

Correct: **The final game was rescheduled; fortunately, I was able to attend the game.**

8. Use a comma after a dependent clause when the dependent clause begins a complex sentence. The dependent clause begins with a subordinate conjunction. Words such as *if, when, because, since, before, after,* and *though* are subordinate conjunctions.

<u>dependent clause</u>   <u>independent clause</u>
If you want to do well in the interview, you should practice

answering questions in front of a small group of people.

9. Use a comma before and after a relative pronoun clause (a dependent clause) that is nonessential or nonrestrictive. A relative pronoun clause that modifies or refers to a proper noun is always a nonessential dependent clause. Relative pronouns are the words *that, which, who, whom,* and *whose.*

<u>dependent clause</u>
The Vietnam Veterans Memorial, which is located in

Washington, D.C., is a powerful tribute to thousands of soldiers.

<u>dependent clause</u>
Rev. Jesse Jackson, who founded the Rainbow Coalition, will participate in a public forum next week.

Do not use a comma if the dependent clause is essential to the meaning of the sentence. In the following example, the reader would not know which men are being referred to if the relative pronoun clause were not present.

Men *who* are *married* tend to live longer than other men.

10. Use a comma after a nonessential (nonrestrictive) appositive. Nonessential information is not essential for the meaning of the sentence. An appositive refers to or renames the closest noun.

    appositive

    Sputnik I, *the world's first satellite*, was launched by the Soviet Union in 1957.

11. Use a comma before and after a participial phrase that appears after the subject of a sentence. The participial phrase in this position must refer to or rename the subject.

    subject   participial phrase

    Six college freshmen, *wanting to save some money*, decided to share a house together.

12. Use a comma after an introductory adverb.

    adverb

    Fortunately, every faculty member supported the president.

13. Use a comma after an introductory phrase at the beginning of a sentence. The phrase may be a prepositional phrase, an infinitive phrase, or a participial phrase.

    prepositional phrase

    For some viewers, the media attention became annoying.

    infinitive phrase

    To pass the driver's test, you must study the handbook.

    participial phrase

    Wanting to teach young children about the dangers of drugs, the actor became a national spokesperson for the war against drugs.

14. Use a comma before and after an adverb that appears inside an independent clause when the adverb interrupts the flow of the sentence. This is called a parenthetical word.

    adverb

    Your great uncle, *therefore*, will contribute to your college fund.

15. Use a comma to indicate a pause in the voice before a terminal word (a word at the end of a sentence).

    We supported the cause, too.

    Passing the bar exam requires knowledge, not luck.

16. Use a comma between the name of a city and the state or country. Use a comma after the state or country to separate it from the rest of the sentence.

    My family comes from Hibbing, Minnesota.

    The Eiffel Tower in Paris, France, is an architectural wonder.

17. Use a comma after the salutation of a personal letter and after the closing of a letter.

    Dear Robert,   Sincerely,   With Love,

18. Use a comma after a person's name followed by his or her title.

    James Motovin, Ph.D., published his research in this month's journal.

    Charles Wallace, Jr., has his father's physical traits.

19. Use a comma after a direct address (name of a person) in an imperative or an interrogative sentence.

    Michael, remove your muddy boots before you come into the house.

    Karla, have you received a response yet from the manufacturer?

20. Use a comma after introductory information that follows with a direct quotation.

    The college coach replied, "I am proud of the team's accomplishments on the field and in the classroom."

21. Use a comma after a direct quotation if the direct quotation is followed by identification of the speaker.

    "Your generous donation is greatly appreciated," proclaimed the program director.

    Do not use a comma before an indirect quotation that does not show the speaker's actual words.

    The mayor told the reporters that funds were approved for the new intersection.

Dash

A dash is made by placing two hyphens together without any spaces between the hyphens and the words that appear before or after them. A typeset dash looks like a long hyphen.

1. Use a dash to set off or emphasize a group of words that explains preceding information. (Note that the dashes in this case replace commas.)

    Many individuals—the district attorney, the defense lawyers, the jury, and the judge—were disturbed by the unexpected outburst.

2. Use a dash before and after words, phrases, or clauses that interrupt the main structure of the sentence. (Note that dashes replace commas.)

> Anna broke her engagement to Russell—a decision she later regretted—because she was afraid of making a long-term commitment.

3. Use a dash to emphasize an explanatory word or phrase that appears at the end of the sentence. (Note that a comma or a colon could also be used.)

> By the look on his face, I knew he wanted only one thing—revenge.

> We were not prepared for the doctor's report on my pregnancy—triplets.

Ellipsis

1. Use an ellipsis (three periods with spaces between them) to show that words, phrases, clauses, or sentences have been intentionally omitted within a quoted passage.

> Every format that you apply to text information . . . is incorporated into your document as invisible codes.

2. An ellipsis may be used on occasion to indicate a hesitation or an incomplete thought. This use of an ellipsis occurs more frequently in dialogue.

> Though the book appeared on the best-seller list for the year, I found the laws for personal growth to be nothing more than . . . hogwash.

Exclamation Point

1. Use an exclamation point after a word (called an interjection) that indicates a strong emotion or feeling.

> Aha!   Phooey!   Dang!   Yipes!   Ugh!

2. Use an exclamation point after a sentence to show strong emotion or feeling. This ending punctuation implies an urgent emphasis. Exclamation points must be used sparingly; overuse reduces the effectiveness of this ending punctuation.

> Look out!   Run!

> Drop it right now!   Call an ambulance immediately!

Hyphen

1. Use a hyphen to divide words at the end of a line of text when there is no room to handwrite or type the entire word. (Due to many word processing systems that space entire words on a line, using hyphenation for this purpose occurs only with traditional typing or handwritten work.) The hyphen must be placed at the end of the last syllable on a line.

   The donors of all of the scholarships offered through the Foundation are committed to the educational values of the institution.

   Do not divide words by syllables if only one or two letters in the word are left by themselves on a line. Consult a dictionary when you need to check how words are divided into individual syllables.

   Many employees elect to use payroll deduction to withdraw given
   amounts
   ~~amounts~~ of money from their paychecks to support specific charities

   or programs.

2. Use a hyphen for compound numbers smaller than one hundred and for fractions.

   twenty-one   fifty-five   ninety-nine   one-sixth   three-fourths

3. Use a hyphen with compound words that function as one word. (Dictionaries show hyphenated words. Consult a dictionary when you are uncertain of the need for a hyphen.)

mother-in-law	well-being of the children
self-addressed envelopes	second-guess
first-class tickets	go-between
get-together	governor-elect
long-term relationship	well-designed project

4. Some words use a hyphen between the prefix and the base word when joining the prefix to the base word would result in awkward spelling, an unusual phonetic structure, or confusion. Overall, the tendency is not to use a hyphen between prefixes and base words. Consult a dictionary when you are not sure if a hyphen is needed.

un-American	self-improvement	ex-husband
pro-life	co-op	non-native

Parentheses

1. Use parentheses to enclose definitions of unfamiliar words. Commas or dashes could also be used in these situations.

   Mangroves (tropical trees) blanketed the hillside.

   A bright pink was used on the map to show the Torrid Zone (the area between the Tropic of Cancer and the Tropic of Capricorn).

2. Use parentheses to enclose a nonessential word, phrase, clause, or sentence that is important but not grammatically essential. The information inside the parentheses may interrupt the flow of the sentence if it is not separated from the sentence by parentheses (or by commas or dashes).

   Sodium bicarbonate ($NaHCO_3$) is an antacid used in baking powder.

   The research results (see Figure 4–2) indicated a high correlation between education and income.

   I purchased IBM (International Business Machines) stock last year.

   Different plays written by William Shakespeare (1564–1616) are produced onstage every year at the Ashland Shakespearean Festival.

   By the time I had watched three plays in a row (a big mistake), I realized I could no longer pay attention to the actors or follow the plots.

3. Use parentheses to enclose citations (references) in a documented paper. The citation may be the author's name and numerical reference that corresponds to the bibliography, or the page number when the author's name is given in the text.

   "Four levels of response can be applied to answering test questions" (Wong 5).

   Wong claims that "too few students use assisted response" (396).

Period

1. Use a period at the end of a declarative sentence (a sentence that makes a direct statement) or an imperative sentence (a sentence that gives an order, gives a command, or makes a specific request). The period is one of three kinds of terminal, or ending, punctuation. (The other two kinds of terminal punctuation are the question mark and the exclamation point.)

   The moving truck arrived on time.

   Put the boxes over there by the fireplace.

2. Use a period after some abbreviations. Refer to a dictionary if you are not certain about the need for a period with a specific abbreviation.

   Mr. Tabor   Mrs. Ling   Dr. Carlton

   Sen. deFazio   Pres. Kennedy   Sr. Rodriguez

3. Use periods for abbreviations that refer to periods of time.

   1600 B.C. (before Christ)

   A.D. 1900 (anno Domini—in the year of our Lord)

   10:30 A.M. (ante meridiem—before noon)

   3:30 P.M. (post meridiem—after noon)

Question Mark

1. Use a question mark at the end of an interrogative statement. The question mark is one of three kinds of terminal punctuation that is used at the ends of sentences.

   Where do you plan to live next year?

   How do you manage so many activities every week?

2. Use a question mark inside a direct quotation if the quotation is an interrogative statement.

   The young boy asked his father, "Why are the stars so far away?"

Quotation Marks

1. Use quotation marks to enclose the exact words stated in a direct quotation. A comma or a period at the end of the quotation is placed before the closing quotation mark.

   "The tunnel will open by the end of the week," said the project engineer.

   The vegetarian said, "I don't eat anything that once had eyes."

   The cable repair person announced, "I cannot climb on a mossy roof to install another cable outlet."

   References to what a person said that do not give the exact words spoken are called indirect quotations or paraphrasing. Indirect quotations are not set off by quotation marks.

   The cable repair person said that she could not climb on a mossy roof to install another cable outlet.

2. An exclamation point or a question mark is placed before the closing quotation mark when it is a part of the quote. The exclamation mark or the question mark is placed outside of the closing quotation mark if it is a part of the entire sentence, not the quote.

   My friend bluntly asked, "How much money do you make?"

   "Put your hands up now!" shouted the security guard.

   What did you mean when you said, "I treasure you"?

3. Use quotation marks around unusual expressions or sayings to emphasize them from the other words in the sentence. Use quotation marks in this manner sparingly.

   The duchess sneered when she said that I had "common table manners."

   When my Hawaiian friend said "pau," I knew he was done eating.

4. Use quotation marks to set off titles of chapters, newspaper and magazine articles, and short stories.

   The first chapter of the book is titled "Mysteries from the Deep."

   Samantha named her short story "Tornadoes Hit Twice."

Semicolon

1. Use a semicolon to connect two independent clauses to make a compound sentence.

   > The avalanche was triggered by gunfire; the skiers skied for their lives.

   > I opened an online account; I wanted to begin day trading immediately.

2. Use a semicolon to connect two independent clauses that are connected by a conjunctive adverb to form a compound sentence. Use a comma after the conjunctive adverb.

   > The school board supports multicultural education; consequently, more funding was allocated to modify the current curriculum.

   > The textbooks were outdated; therefore, the teacher taught without books.

3. Use semicolons to separate series of phrases or clauses so as to avoid confusion. The use of semicolons in this manner is particularly important if the phrases or clauses already contain commas.

   > Awards were given to Glen Torrance, the mayor; Jennifer Lunes, the director of the Visitors Bureau; Mike Minor, the current chief of the police department; and Rachel Hernandez, the young girl who saved the lives of the elderly couple.

PUNCTUATION SUMMARY CHART		
apostrophe '	brackets [ ]	colon :
comma ,	dash —	ellipsis . . .
exclamation point !	hyphen -	parentheses ( )
period .	question mark ?	quotation marks " "
semicolon ;		

APPENDIX B
Student Answer Key

Chapter 2 Nouns

Practice 1: Identifying Nouns (page 14)

The letter **N** should be written above the following words.

1. clown, balloons, children
2. attitude, concern
3. teacher, creativity
4. parents, effects, television, children
5. engine, ship, middle, ocean
6. speeches, activists, words, hope, wisdom
7. van, traffic, freeway
8. wife, friend, basket, produce, flowers
9. report, success
10. runner, ankle

Practice 2: A/An (page 16)

The letter **N** should be written above the following words. *A* or *an* should be inserted as shown below.

1. husband's, __an__, errand's.
2. monkey's, __a__, banana's.
3. Jamie's, __an__, application's.
4. Maria's, __an__, pattern's.
5. __A__, magazine's, table's.
6. mother's, __an__, member's.
7. Sam's, __an__, ulcer's.
8. team's, __an__, team's.
9. Sue's, __a__, representative's.
10. seamstress's, __a__, hanger's.
11. book's, __an__, hero's.
12. grandfather's, __a__, hero's.

Practice 3: Identifying Nouns (page 17)

The following words that work as nouns should be circled.

bridge	traffic	drivers	speed	——	crossing
sirens	——	maps	vision	conditions	——
——	brakes	passenger	——	exit	rules
danger	——	warning	street	——	peace

Practice 4: Identifying Nouns (page 18)

An **N** should appear above all of the following words except the words that are crossed out.

Paragraph 1: psychologist, team, head, interview, ~~talked~~, athletes, ideas

Paragraph 2: ~~started~~, focus, training, ~~strengthen~~, skills, performance, ~~improves~~, stress management, self-regulation, visualization, goal-setting, concentration, focus, relaxation, motivation, ~~helps~~, future, steps, athletes, progress, week, ~~small~~, programs, goals

Paragraph 3: ~~is~~, part, visualization, ~~begins~~, minutes, training, aspect, game, equivalent, practice, golfer, ~~correct~~, muscles, ~~start~~, swing, Performance, improvement

Practice 5: Using Noun Markers to Identify Nouns (page 19)

The letter **N** should be written above the words shown. The words in *italic print* should be highlighted on your page to show they are noun markers.

1. *your,* wish, *my,* command
2. *Three,* individuals, *the,* interference
3. *His,* beliefs, *the,* introduction
4. *The,* fear, *their,* eyes, *our,* attention
5. *My family's* treasures, *this* vault
6. *The,* beauty, *the,* scenery, *the,* photographer
7. *The,* thought, *his,* departure
8. Ramon, *a,* journalist, *the,* tabloid
9. *His,* relatives, *five,* tickets, *that,* meet
10. *My,* group, *seven,* ideas, *the,* class

Practice 6: Naming Proper Nouns (page 21)

Answers will vary, but every answer that is a proper noun must begin with a capital letter.

Practice 7: Capitalizing Proper Nouns Related to People (page 23)

The following nouns must be capitalized. They are all proper nouns.

1. Mike, Jimmy, Father Danielson
2. Aunt Sue
3. Canadian, American

4. Native American, Chief Joseph
5. Norwegian

Practice 8: Capitalizing Proper Nouns Related to Places (page 24)

The following nouns must have capital letters.

1. Black Hills, South Dakota
2. Mississippi River, Gulf of Mexico
3. Sun Valley, Boise, Idaho
4. Hoover Tower, Stanford University
5. West
6. Broadway Avenue
7. Latin American, Spanish, Brazil
8. Americans, Singapore

Practice 9: Capitalizing Proper Nouns Related to Things (page 26)

The following nouns must have capital letters.

1. Jewish, Passover, Exodus, Egypt
2. Stone Age
3. Democratic, Republican, Chamber of Commerce
4. Federal Reserve Board
5. National Honor Society, Wednesday

Practice 10: Working with Common and Proper Nouns (page 28)

The following nouns should be highlighted. Nouns that must be capitalized are shown with **bold** capital letters. All other nouns should begin with a lowercase letter.

1. students, **C**onversational **E**nglish II, term
2. family, *Touched by an Angel,* week, dinner
3. **P**owell's book, *My American Journey,* list
4. **W**all **S**treet **J**ournal, **P**sychology **T**oday
5. **T**oni **M**orrison's book *Beloved,* **E**nglish, assignment
6. **P**rofessor **L**ong, instructor, **P**sychology 202, concepts, **S**teven **R**eiss's article "**S**ecrets of **H**appiness"

Practice 11: Identifying nouns (page 30)

The following words should be highlighted as nouns.

1. replacement, Cleveland, week
2. lot, commotion, station, Fifth Avenue
3. flatness, desert, tourists
4. elder, composure, middle, speech

5. teller, Norwest Bank, transaction
6. conductor, train, cars, tickets
7. Laziness, carelessness, irresponsibility, office
8. Lisa, award, Rotary Club, excellence
9. reputation, company, performance, employees
10. shortage, teachers, problem

Practice 12: Identifying Nouns and Noun Markers (page 30)

The noun markers are circled. The letter **N** is written above every noun.

1. (The) quartet, (the) stage
2. (The) blow, (my) funny bone, (my) arm
3. (The) period, history, times, (the) Middle Ages
4. (The) cosmetologist, (her) eyebrows
5. (My) (uncle's) criticism, (my) feelings
6. (The) staircase, (that) church, tourists
7. OPEC, (the) acronym, (the) Organization of Petroleum Exporting Countries
8. (The) Richter scale, (the) intensity, earthquakes
9. (Five) neighborhoods, programs
10. (The) patient, (his) doctor, (a) prognosis

Chapter 3 Prepositions

Practice 1: Making Prepositional Phrases (page 45)

Answers may vary. Possible answers are shown.

1. from
2. For; across
3. through
4. under; for
5. Before

6. inside
7. next to
8. with; despite
9. by; in
10. Throughout

Practice 2: Identifying Prepositional Phrases with Noun Objects (page 47)

The following prepositional phrases should be marked.

1. (about the lost sailors)
2. (Above the fireplace) (of four generations)

3. (According to leading authorities)
4. (for relevant facts)
5. (As children) (to our parents)
6. (in San Diego) (around noon)
7. (at the movie theater) (by seven o'clock)
8. (behind the garage)
9. (below his waist)
10. (around the brick building)

Practice 3: Using Object Pronouns in Prepositional Phrases (page 48)

1. (beside me)
2. (because of her)
3. (toward him)
4. (beneath the bridge) (with them)
5. (with whomever)
6. (To whom)
7. (through us)
8. (behind him)
9. (Between you and me) (for Matt)
10. (around them)
11. (between them)
12. (With her)
13. (to dinner) (with whom)
14. (of the youth group) (with us)
15. (Prior to her)

Practice 4: Identifying Prepositional Phrases (page 49)

The following prepositional phrases should be marked.

1. (to the phone) (with her report)
2. (with them)
3. (by the exotic fish) (in the new aquarium)
4. (on the table) (as well as the flowers) (from her son)
5. (According to my grandfather) (in all situations)
6. (on my way) (to work)
7. (for the week) (after their wedding)
8. (with her sick grandfather) (throughout his illness)
9. (of protesters) (outside the courthouse)
10. (in his pockets) (under the furniture) (throughout his car) (for the ring)

Practice 5: Identifying Prepositional Phrases (page 50)

The following prepositional phrases should be marked.

1. (with the rowdy children) (with hamburgers and milk shakes)
2. (between you and her)
3. (Between you and me) (of her hair)
4. (with salt and pepper)
5. (amid the chaos) (of the fire)
6. (but me)
7. (due to snow and ice) (on the runways)
8. (to a charity) (in lieu of flowers or gifts)
9. (between parent and child) (from one culture) (to another)
10. (among the tomatoes and green peppers)

Practice 6: Identifying Prepositional Phrases and Infinitives (page 52)

Prepositional phrases and infinitives should be marked as follows.

1. (to Memphis) (in two hours)
2. [to stay] (in the downtown area)
3. (in town) [to play]
4. [to eat] [to stretch] [to relax] (in the hotel)
5. (to the lounge) [to play]
6. [to go] (to their rooms) [to read] [to nap]
7. [to call] (from their rooms)
8. [to call] (from pay phones) (in the lobby)
9. (for the players) (for eleven o'clock)
10. (of the players) [to sleep]

Chapter 4 Subjects and Verbs in Simple Sentences

Practice 1: Finding the Subjects of Sentences (page 66)

The following words should be underlined as the subjects of sentences.

1. detective
2. friends
3. neighbors
4. Lenny
5. noise
6. deer
7. Members
8. Players
9. men
10. psychic

Practice 2: Identifying Subject Pronouns (page 68)

The prepositional phrases, infinitives, and subjects should be marked as follows.

1. Everyone (at the assembly)
2. (after midnight) all (of the emergency sirens)
3. You (in the Career Information Center)
4. None (of these books)
5. (During the early years) (of her life) she (to Japan) [to visit]
6. Several (of the wealthy aristocrats)
7. (According to the salesman) neither (of the stereo systems) (with a five-year warranty)
8. All (of my closest friends) (about outer space aliens)
9. Many (of the applicants) (for the management position) (from Stanford)
10. Some (of the sculptures) (in her garden) (by her nephew)

Practice 3: Identifying Single and Compound Subjects (page 70)

The sentences should be marked as follows.

1. (According to Peter) <u>dinner</u>
2. <u>Mr. Lane</u> <u>Mrs. Montague</u> (with meat sauce)
3. <u>Tractor</u> <u>equipment</u> (in the barn) (in the north field)
4. <u>They</u> <u>I</u> [to attend]
5. (In the morning) <u>kitten</u> <u>squirrel</u> (around the yard)
6. <u>I</u> (on the table) (in the café)
7. <u>brother</u> <u>man</u> (from next door) (into the house)
8. <u>Several</u> (of the workers) <u>two</u> (of the managers)
9. <u>newspaper</u> <u>Historical Society</u> (about the first land deal)
10. <u>memory</u> (in my computer, my modem, and my printer)
11. <u>tickets</u> <u>confirmation</u> (in the mail)
12. (In June) <u>Mom</u> <u>Dad</u> [to travel] (to Hawaii)
13. <u>hula hoop</u> <u>pogo stick</u> (in the 1960s)
14. <u>park</u> <u>docks</u> (at ten o'clock) (in the evening)
15. <u>sister</u> <u>brother</u>

Practice 4: Using Subject and Object Pronouns (page 71)

The prepositional phrases and infinitives should be marked as follows. The correct subject or object pronoun that should be circled is in **bold** print.

1. **She** [to shop] (at the new K-Mart store)
2. (After the dance) **she** [to drive] (to the coast)
3. (to **us**) (for retraining)
4. (Within minutes) (by **them**)
5. **He** [to request] (with the manager)
6. (between you and **him**)
7. **I** (for this job)
8. **They** [to disagree] (about everything)
9. (Without **him** and his dog)
10. (with **them**)

Practice 5: Combining Sentences (page 72)

Answers may vary. One possible answer with the compound subjects is given below.

1. Mesh and plastic tarps can be used to make a tent.
2. Mangoes, peaches, and plums have pits.
3. Inflammation and itching may cause some discomfort.
4. Mason and Hector had the winning lottery ticket.
5. The dog and the policeman chased the car down the alley.
6. Cory and I finished the summary last night.

Practice 6: Identifying Subjects and Action Verbs (page 74)

The subjects, verbs, prepositional phrases, and infinitives should be marked as follows.

1. children write (to their grandparents)
2. All (of the students) read
3. They dream (of adventures) (in foreign countries)
4. She pretends [to be]
5. (by six o'clock) newspaper lands (on my front porch)
6. lake fills (with water) (during the spring)
7. Alice possesses [to sing] (without accompaniment)
8. (At midnight) owner closed
9. student opened
10. We laughed (for several hours) (at her corny jokes)

Practice 7: Identifying Verbs in Simple Sentences (page 77)

The sentences should be marked as follows.

1. moon disappeared (behind a bank) (of clouds)
2. (For an aerobic workout) Nancy goes (to the gym)
3. cream does (for blemishes)
4. jury was (throughout the trial)
5. Tortillas rice beans are (in many countries)
6. (After the movie) I felt
7. father brother look (to Mom) (for advice)
8. team (of volunteers) cleans (during spring vacation)
9. machine is
10. coins (in my uncle's coin collection) are [to insure]

Practice 8: Identifying Subjects, Verbs, and Simple Sentence Patterns (page 78)

Sentences should be marked as follows.

S-VV   1. mechanic tuned rotated (on my car)

S-VV   2. I drink eat (at the restaurant) (on the corner)

SS-V   3. cat dog wanted [to get] (inside the house)

S-V   4. cost (of the leather sofa) was

SS-V   5. Fire Department Police Department merged (in January)

S-V   6. Lenders (of home mortgages) advertise (in the newspaper)

S-V   7. I grew [to enjoy] (for relaxation)

S-V   8. He <u>has</u>

S-VV   9. Anita <u>hauled</u> (from the garage) <u>washed</u>

SS-V   10. You I <u>study</u> [to pass]

Practice 9: Reviewing Elements of a Sentence (page 82)

Sentences should be marked as follows.

1. officials <u>were watching</u> (for unsportsmanlike conduct)

2. I <u>will understand</u>

3. visitors <u>had eaten</u> (of the cheesecake)

4. Rodents <u>gnawed</u> (on the wood) <u>damaged</u>

5. <u>noise</u> (from the construction site) <u>is hindering</u> [to concentrate]

6. (Aside from that one incident) <u>they</u> <u>have behaved</u>

7. report <u>was read</u> <u>approved</u> (by the board)

8. You <u>may apply</u> (for the scholarship)

9. You <u>should go</u> (to the rally) (at noon)

10. offender <u>had asked</u> (for a lawyer)

Practice 10: Identifying Fragments and Complete Sentences (page 84)

The sentence elements should be marked as follows.

_S_   1. <u>Delays</u> (in Financial Aid) <u>were</u> (due to the national holiday)

_S_   2. I <u>had noticed</u> (in the neighborhood)

_F_   3. <u>burst</u> (of energy) (from the power bar)

_F_   4. Andrew <u>became</u> (at the state university)

_F_   5. <u>Flown</u> (through the smoke) (from the fires) (in the northern part) (of the state)

_F_   6. <u>Wanted</u> (for tampering) (with the fire alarms) (in the school)

_S_   7. <u>team</u> (of consultants) <u>might consider</u> [to merge]

_S_   8. Mario <u>does attend</u>

_S_   9. buggies vehicles <u>destroyed</u>

_F_   10. <u>Both</u> (of the candidates) (for the Senate seat) (in our state)

Practice 11: Rewriting Inverted Sentences (page 88)

The sentences should be rewritten as follows.

1. Many options are available.
2. A brave woman stands here.
3. Children are in the park every day.
4. Four candidates can be on the ballot.

5. My letter of resignation is here.

6. The packages from today's delivery are here.

Practice 12: Finding Subjects and Verbs in Questions (page 89)

The following words should be marked as follows.

1. did you honk (at me)

2. did expedition originate

3. were you prepared (for the test)

4. Can you lend

5. Shall we schedule (with the president)

6. Are all (of the verbs)

7. is tax calculated

8. Do all (of the students) need [to register] (for the workshop)

9. will they file

10. Should we plan (for Friday)

Practice 13: Subjects and Verbs in Imperative and Declarative Sentences (page 91)

Subjects and verbs should be marked as follows.

1. [You] bake

2. are prizes

3. [You] Close

4. [You] Attach

5. are ways

6. [You] deliver

7. [You] Call

8. [You] count

9. [You] Donate

10. [You] File

11. [You] Drop

12. [You] Contact

13. [You] Do call

14. is reason

15. [You] Create

Chapter 5 Verb Forms

Practice 1: Simple Verb Tenses (page 109)

The labels for past, present, and future should be in the blanks. Sentences should be marked as follows.

P	1. fog settled (into the valley)
PR	2. I search (for inexpensive train tickets) [to see]
F	3. waitress will bring (to your table)
PR	4. You get (in the movie theater)
PR	5. Ali arrives (by 7:00 A.M.)

_____PR_____ 6. Latisha <u>pretends</u> [to be]

_____P_____ 7. Daydreaming <u>caused</u> (in school)

_____P_____ 8. assistant <u>copied</u> (of notes) (for me)

_____F_____ 9. driver <u>will get</u> (to the meeting) (on time)

_____PR_____ 10. resumé <u>looks</u>

Practice 2: Identifying Person (page 110)

Sentences should be marked as follows.

_____3_____ 1. <u>Wildflowers</u> <u>cover</u>

_____3_____ 2. <u>people</u> <u>choose</u>

_____1_____ 3. <u>I</u> <u>plan</u> [to attend] (in three years)

_____2_____ 4. <u>You</u> <u>spend</u> (on the phone)

_____3_____ 5. <u>niece</u> <u>will compete</u> (in a gymnastics tournament)

_____1_____ 6. <u>We</u> <u>decided</u> [to present] (for our class project)

_____3_____ 7. <u>electricians</u> <u>belong</u> (to a union)

_____3_____ 8. <u>papers</u> <u>outline</u>

_____3_____ 9. <u>They</u> <u>care</u> (about their possessions)

_____3_____ 10. <u>exhibit</u> <u>is</u>

Practice 3: Using Simple Present Tense (page 112)

Sentences should be marked as follows.

1. <u>desserts</u> (on the menu) <u>tempt</u> [to try]

2. <u>I</u> <u>enjoy</u>

3. <u>She</u> <u>wants</u> [to go] (to the movies)

4. <u>report</u> (about the floods) <u>needs</u>

5. <u>friend</u> (with the two German shepherds) <u>enters</u>

6. <u>They</u> <u>buy</u>

7. <u>We</u> <u>consult</u> (with our grandfather) (for advice)

8. <u>You</u> <u>need</u>

9. <u>storms</u> (in the Caribbean) <u>develop</u> (into hurricanes)

10. <u>planes</u> (in Houston) <u>depart</u> (on time)

Practice 4: Proofreading for Subject-Verb Agreement (page 112)

Many species of bats <s>is</s> ^{are} considered endangered. The bat population worldwide <s>are</s> ^{is} declining. Bats in Colorado <s>is</s> ^{are} roosting in caves, in hollow trees, beneath bridges, and in attics, cellars, and mine tunnels. In the past, inactive ~~mine~~ *mines* were closed to prevent danger to people. Mines were blasted to backfill the tunnels and to seal the openings with concrete. Thousands of bats were entombed alive. They were shut off from their food source and eventually starved to death. Now the Colorado Division of Wildlife ~~operate~~ *operates* a program to provide bat habitats in the inactive mines. "Bat gates" are installed to allow bats to fly in and out. The man-made habitats in Colorado ~~is~~ *are* important for the conservation and preservation of the bat species.

Practice 5: Using Regular Action Verbs in Past Tense (page 113)

Answers will vary. Check that you used a one-word verb and that it ends in *-ed*. Check the spelling of the simple past tense verb you wrote on each line. Possible answers are shown.

1. yelled	3. ordered	5. created	7. attended	9. subsided
2. stained	4. turned	6. signed	8. cried	10. halted

Practice 6: Using Irregular Action Verbs in Past Tense (page 115)

The following irregular past tense verbs should be written on the lines.

1. froze, burst	6. made, paid	11. crept, hid
2. broke	7. struck, awoke	12. laid, went
3. dealt, bid	8. fled	13. quit, left
4. led	9. swam, dove or dived	14. spun, wove
5. shrank or shrunk	10. chose, fell	15. swung, hit

Practice 7: Knowing Past Tense (page 116)

Check the spelling of the following past tenses.

1. thought	8. studied	15. caught
2. planned	9. stole	16. heard
3. counted	10. bottled	17. cut
4. woke	11. stuck	18. dealt
5. sped	12. proved	19. fed
6. sprang or sprung	13. strapped	20. cried
7. chose	14. bought	21. sprayed

Practice 8: Using the Correct Verbs in Present Tense (page 117)

Sentences should be marked as follows.

1. <u>prizes</u> (in the contest) <u>are</u>

2. <u>are</u> <u>boots</u>

3. <u>Are</u> <u>statues</u> (on the shelf)

4. <u>waitresses</u> (at the diner) <u>have</u>

5. <u>are</u> <u>checks</u> (in the mail) (for you)

6. <u>is</u> <u>balloon</u>

   7. hogs (on the farm) have

   8. industry has [to make] (to the public)

   9. Are concerts (in the park)

 10. boxes (in the storage room) have

 11. child (in those commercials) has

 12. are results (of the latest poll)

 13. students (in the media arts program) have

 14. workers (at the scene) (of the earthquake) are

 15. Are photos (of your child)

Practice 9: Using Future Tense (page 119)

The prepositional phrases, infinitives, subjects, and verbs should be marked as follows.

   1. Alfredo will take (on Tuesday)

   2. Will you submit

   3. union will ask [to vote]

   4. rally will create (for security)

   5. photographs will appear (in the Sunday paper)

   6. Investments (on the Internet) will guarantee

   7. program will include

   8. will we plan (for this summer)

   9. agent will book make (for you)

 10. neighbors will watch water

Practice 10: Forming Progressive Verb Phrases (page 122)

   1. is considering or was considering
   2. is borrowing or was borrowing
   3. is taking or was taking
   4. are exploring or were exploring
   5. are inspecting or were inspecting
   6. was fishing
   7. are talking or were talking
   8. is hoping or was hoping
   9. am applying
 10. are cooking or were cooking

Practice 11: Identifying Subjects and Verbs (page 124)

Sentences should be marked as follows.

   1. babies were crying (in the movie theater) (on Sunday)

   2. Two (of the crying babies) were

3. <u>man</u> <u>was snoring whistling</u> (through his teeth)

4. <u>boys</u> <u>were imitating</u>

5. <u>girls</u> (in the row) (behind me) <u>were watching</u>

6. <u>children</u> <u>were running</u> (in the aisles)

7. <u>Parents</u> <u>were yelling</u> (at the children) <u>telling</u> [to sit]

8. <u>Ignoring</u> <u>was</u>

9. <u>Following</u> (of the movie) <u>was</u>

10. <u>I</u> <u>will</u> be going (to Saturday matinees) (at this theater)

Practice 12: Identifying Complete Sentences and Fragments (page 124)

1. S	3. F	5. F	7. S	9. S
2. F	4. S	6. F	8. F	10. S

Practice 13: Reciting the Verb Forms (page 128)

No written work is required for this practice work.

Practice 14: Identifying Subjects and Perfect Tense Verbs (page 130)

Prepositional phrases, infinitives, subjects, and verbs should be marked as follows.

1. <u>drivers</u> <u>will have raced</u> (for five hours)

2. <u>grandmother</u> <u>had reached</u>

3. <u>eclipse</u> <u>has appeared</u> (for the first time)

4. <u>transparencies</u> <u>pens</u> <u>have improved</u>

5. <u>Marcus</u> <u>has mastered</u> (of cribbage) (at an early age)

6. <u>widow</u> <u>had wanted</u> [to sell]

7. <u>roses</u> <u>daisies</u> (in the vase) <u>had wilted</u> (after one week)

8. <u>waters</u> <u>have overflowed</u> <u>flooded</u>

9. <u>driver</u> <u>passenger</u> <u>had exchanged</u>

10. <u>Rosie</u> <u>Patrick</u> <u>will</u> have dated (for four years)

Practice 15: Using Past Participles Correctly (page 131)

1. broken	6. shrunk	11. slept
2. shot	7. come	12. chosen
3. stolen	8. become	13. spoken
4. fled	9. taken	14. hurt
5. gone	10. eaten, drunk	15. seen

Practice 16: Using Simple Past Tense and Past Participles (page 132)

1. became, become
2. froze, frozen
3. grew, grown
4. held, held
5. fed, fed
6. cast, cast
7. forgot, forgotten
8. ate, eaten

Practice 17: Identifying Verb Phrases (page 134)

Sentences should be marked as follows.

1. I <u>do</u> <u>intend</u> [to enroll] (in school) (during the summer)
2. <u>Do</u> <u>you</u> <u>plan</u> [to attend]
3. <u>We</u> <u>had</u> <u>seen</u>
4. <u>attorney</u> <u>had</u> <u>proven</u> (in front of a jury)
5. <u>professor</u> <u>does</u> <u>give</u>
6. <u>All</u> (of the speakers) <u>will</u> <u>have</u> <u>spoken</u> (to the council members) (at the public forum)
7. <u>I</u> <u>have</u> <u>swept</u>
8. <u>neighbors</u> <u>will</u> <u>be</u> <u>having</u> (on Saturday)
9. <u>parents</u> <u>had</u> <u>known</u>
10. <u>Someone</u> (in the cafeteria) <u>had</u> <u>stolen</u>
11. <u>ducks</u> <u>geese</u> <u>had</u> <u>swum</u> (near the docks)
12. <u>mourners</u> <u>had</u> <u>wept</u> (for a long time) (at the grave)
13. <u>Three</u> (of the freshmen) <u>did</u> <u>elect</u> [to live] (off campus)
14. <u>Have</u> <u>nuns</u> <u>organized</u> (in the past)
15. <u>dean</u> <u>had</u> <u>posted</u> <u>made</u>

Practice 18: Forming Verb Phrases (page 137)

1. had chosen
2. could have
3. has edited
4. must have set
5. had chosen
6. should have seen
7. had gone
8. had dealt
9. must have cost
10. must have given
11. had stolen
12. have drunk
13. had dived
14. had swum
15. had broken

Chapter 6 Pronouns and Pronoun Agreement

Practice 1: Using Subject Pronouns (page 155)

1. He
2. It
3. she, he, they; They
4. They
5. Any two: He, she, we, they, I, you
6. They

7. They

8. It

9. It

10. She, He, *or* They

Practice 2: Using Object Pronouns (page 158)

Subjects and verbs should be marked as follows. The word in **bold** print is the correct pronoun that should be circled.

1. Karen watched **me**

2. announcer called **him**

3. attendant gives **them**

4. **him me** we are

5. professor told **us**

6. **him** I am

7. inspectors told **her**

8. magazines show **them**

9. **us** refund will pay

10. sailors waved **us**

Practice 3: Working with Possessive Pronouns (page 160)

The following possessive pronouns should be circled.

1. Your, their

2. yours

3. its

4. his, yours

5. my, yours

6. ours

7. Ours

8. your

9. Their

10. mine

Practice 4: Working with *its* and *it's* (page 160)

1. It's

2. its

3. its

4. its

5. it's

6. It's

7. Its

8. It's

9. it's

10. Its

Practice 5: Working with Pronoun Agreement (page 161)

The antecedent, which should be circled on your page, is shown in *italic* print. The pronoun follows the antecedent.

1. *reviews,* them

2. *notes,* them

3. *papers,* They

4. *winds,* They

5. *power,* it

6. *petition,* it

7. *door,* it

8. *Sirens,* They

9. *rocks,* They

10. *dig,* it

11. *controls,* Their

12. *Norma, Raeleen,* Their

13. *children,* They

14. *deer,* They

15. *green,* It

Practice 6: Using Reflexive and Intensive Pronouns (page 163)

1. themselves

2. itself

3. herself

4. himself

5. myself

6. himself or herself

7. themselves

8. ourselves

9. himself or herself

10. herself

Practice 7: Working with Subject-Verb Agreement (page 167)

Sentences should be marked as follows.

1. Everybody makes (of my colorful hair)
2. Both (of the movies) are (about historical events)
3. Most (of the garbage) stinks
4. Neither appeals (to me)
5. Several (of my uncles) work (for Sony Disk Manufacturing)
6. None (of the current options) match
7. Some (of the factories) close (for the holidays)
8. writers make
9. Nobody (on the bus) wants (for the duration) (of the trip)
10. Someone was (at the door) (in the middle) (of the night)
11. Something was (inside the mysterious box)
12. All (of the recycling) saves (of dollars)
13. petitions have
14. All (of the loose change) goes (into a jar) (for a vacation)
15. Nothing works (on my new computer)

Practice 8: Working with Subject-Verb Agreement with Indefinite Pronouns (page 169)

Sentences should be marked as follows.

1. Each has
2. children deserve
3. Some believe
4. patience runs
5. Anything needs
6. Someone needs
7. Both cry
8. Most have
9. She one are
10. employees complete
11. No one waits
12. Many arrive
13. Many are
14. None tells
15. All taste

Practice 9: Working with Pronoun and Verb Agreement (page 169)

Sentences should be marked as follows.

1. loves, his
2. is, his or her
3. have, their
4. forget, their
5. has, its
6. give, their
7. loses, his or her
8. enters, his or her
9. wants, his or her
10. leaves, her
11. agrees, his or her
12. takes, his or her
13. pay, their
14. leaves, his or her
15. wear, their

Practice 10: Working with *either . . . or* and *neither . . . nor* (page 173)

Sentences should be marked as follows.

1. Purdue Notre Dame was
2. psychology sociology is
3. check card is
4. salad platter is
5. Paul cousins want
6. Francis Samuel plays
7. instructor students expect
8. paper presentation is

9. salesmen manager works
10. photographs painting was
11. dogs cat is
12. chicken scallops were
13. you she is
14. you accountants are
15. aunts uncles are

Chapter 7 Modifiers

Practice 1: Using Adjectives to Describe Nouns (page 189)

Answers will vary. A noun (person, place, thing, or idea) should follow each adjective on lines 1–10. An adjective should appear before the noun on lines 11–20.

Practice 2: Identifying Adjectives in Sentences (page 190)

Sentences should be marked as follows.

1. Our firm landed sizable [to market] innovative electronic

2. managerial meeting lasted four

3. vice president distributed detailed (to every department manager)

4. Six departments (within the main branch) agreed [to make] this new

5. urgent memo (to each employee) stated several

6. Many crucial questions needed immediate

7. detailed list (of mandatory meetings) appeared (in the company newsletter)

8. Fifty-two employees signed up (for additional training and orientation)

9. Employees received huge bonuses overtime

10. Everyone (in this marketing firm) wanted [to be] (of this unique and creative project)

Practice 3: Using Commas Between Adjectives (page 192)

Sentences should be marked as follows. Pay close attention to the placement of the commas.

1. (His) father <u>operates</u> (heavy) (at the (old)(steel) plant) (on Mill Street)

2. (In the (quarterly) reports), <u>you</u> <u>will find</u> (unemployment)

3. (Heather's)(older) brother <u>works</u> (long) (at the (family's)(equestrian) center)

4. (His)(inappropriate,)(abusive) language <u>created</u> (many)

5. (Marty's)(pleasant) personality <u>landed</u> (many)(lucrative)

6. (attractive,)(detailed) resumé <u>strengthens</u> (your)(application)

7. Clarissa <u>used</u> (appropriate) format (for (her)(cover) letter) (to the (potential) employer)

8. (confident,)(ambitious)(college) graduate <u>looked</u> (to (her)(first) interview)

9. (Pedro's)(closest) friends <u>envied</u> (his)(strong,)(articulate)(interviewing)

10. (Today's)(classified) ads <u>lists</u> (eight) (in the (popular) field) (of data entry)

Practice 4: Identifying Adjectives (page 193)

The following adjectives should be circled. Pay close attention to the commas that have been inserted between some of the adjectives.

1. My aging purebred my
2. Gradual weight America's leading
3. Many concerned library's
4. Upscale furnished two thousand
5. brief peaceful old
6. diligent many stolen
7. perfect math special
8. inactive nuclear power toxic
9. airline's reservation stressful
10. One prominent local scholarship
11. mysterious shiny dark autumn
12. Every department incredible holiday
13. Their dishonest business
14. Betty's outstanding administrative
15. side active medicine

Practice 5: Identifying Subjects, Verbs, and Adjectives (page 195)

The subjects and verbs should be underlined as shown. The adjectives should be circled as follows.

1. <u>Each</u> <u>is</u> (knowledgeable) (resourceful)

2. <u>Many</u> (my) (closest) <u>are</u> (honest) (ambitious)

3. (Many) <u>drivers</u> <u>are</u> (careless) (dangerous) (inconsiderate)

4. (Warm) (homemade) <u>bread</u> <u>tastes</u> (delicious)

5. (new) <u>product</u> <u>looks</u> (exciting) (challenging) (unique)

6. <u>voice</u> (my) (answering) <u>sounded</u> (distraught) (confused)

7. <u>Sharon</u> <u>feels</u> (bad)

8. <u>All</u> (porcelain) <u>are</u> (valuable)

9. <u>Mark</u> <u>seemed</u> (bothered) (your)

10. (Several) <u>ballots</u> <u>were</u> (invalid)

Practice 6: Identifying Adjectives (page 197)

The adjectives in **bold** print should be circled on your paper. The arrows indicate the noun that the adjective modifies.

1. The **bronco** rider had the **wildest** ride of **his** life **last** night.

2. The party was **noisier** after midnight.

3. **This** bread is **fresher** than **that** one.

4. **Jazz** dancing is **livelier** than the **traditional** waltz.

5. The **heaviest** box in the van is the **last** one.

6. *Dallas* was a **successful television** series for **many** years.

7. J. R. Ewing was a **loathsome, egocentric, cunning** man.

8. The **famous** restaurant on the pier serves the **freshest** fish in town.

9. Grapefruit is **sweeter** during the **summer** months.

10. The **current weather** predictions for the **coastal** areas are **awful.**

Practice 7: Identifying Adjectives and Adverbs (page 201)

1. ADJ	6. ADV	11. ADJ
2. ADV	7. ADJ	12. ADV
3. ADV	8. ADJ	13. ADV
4. ADV	9. ADV	14. ADV
5. ADV	10. ADV	15. ADJ

Practice 8: Identifying Adverbs (page 202)

The following adverbs should be boxed on your paper.

1. Tomorrow, too, soon
2. surprisingly, quite
3. seldom, promptly
4. almost
5. never
6. really
7. poorly
8. too, here, yesterday
9. extremely
10. so
11. seldom
12. late
13. much, too
14. definitely
15. not, early, enough

Practice 9: Using Adjectives and Adverbs (page 203)

1. happily	6. loudly	11. quickly
2. beautifully	7. content	12. softly
3. nervous	8. wonderful	13. different
4. quickly	9. slowly	14. tightly
5. gracefully	10. quietly	15. firm

Practice 10: Using *Good* and *Well* (page 205)

1. good	6. good	11. well
2. well	7. well	12. well
3. good	8. good	13. good
4. well	9. well	14. well
5. well	10. well	15. well

Practice 11: Using Adjectives and Adverbs (page 205)

Answers will vary. Discuss your answers with your partner.

Chapter 8 Compound Sentences

Practice 1: Adding Coordinating Conjunctions in Compound Sentences (page 219)

1. for	3. but	5. but	7. and	9. and/for
2. or	4. nor	6. so	8. so	10. yet/but

Practice 2: Simple and Compound Sentences (page 220)

Sentences should be marked as follows.

___S___ 1. The antique coffeepot was rusty and tarnished.

___S___ 2. The antique dealers worked (through the night) [to set up] their exhibits.

___C___ 3. Several trees will need [to be cut] down, **for** they obstruct the view.

___C___ 4. The brakes (on my van) are frayed, **so** I cannot drive it.

___S___ 5. The judge reviewed the evidence and set a trial date.

___S___ 6. The lease (for our new office space) will begin (in six weeks).

___S___ 7. Movers will haul the office equipment and work supplies (to the new site).

___C___ 8. The flu epidemic has started, **but** many elderly people have not received flu shots (for this season).

___C___ 9. My Financial Aid papers were incomplete, **for** I did not have my tax return (with me).

___S___ 10. I estimated my tax situation (for this year) and used that information (on the forms).

Practice 3: Punctuating Compound Sentences (page 222)

The missing punctuation is shown in **bold** print.

1. available; the
2. tutors, so
3. topics, but
4. papers; that
5. students; tutors
6. type, nor
7. computer, but
8. summaries, and
9. me, for
10. contest; I
11. before, nor
12. experience; now
13. received, so
14. good, but
15. experience; the

Practice 4: Using Conjunctive Adverbs (page 225)

Answers may vary. Possible answers are shown below. Check that a semicolon is used before the conjunctive adverb and that a comma is used after the conjunctive adverb.

1. ; consequently,
2. ; as a result,
3. ; however,
4. ; otherwise,
5. ; nevertheless,
6. ; unfortunately,
7. ; for example,
8. ; suddenly,
9. ; furthermore,
10. ; fortunately,

Practice 5: Identifying and Punctuating Simple and Compound Sentences (page 225)

Sentences should be marked as follows. **S** or **C** should be indicated on the line.

___C___ 1. The Census Bureau predicts population figures (for the next century); shockingly, (in the year 2100), 571 million Americans will live (in the United States).

___S___   2. <u>Will</u> the <u>United States</u> <u>be</u> overcrowded?

___C___   3. <u>Overcrowdedness</u> <u>is</u> avoidable, for <u>Americans</u> <u>have</u> ample undeveloped or underdeveloped land (on which) [to sprawl].

___C___   4. The U.S. population <u>density</u> <u>is</u> low; many European <u>countries</u> already <u>have</u> much higher density rates.

___S___   5. (In the year 2100), <u>prediction</u> (for American population density) <u>is</u> 161.4 people (per square mile).

___S___   6. The population <u>density</u> (in Germany and the United Kingdom) currently <u>is</u> four times greater than the population density (for the United States).

___S___   7. The <u>profile</u> (of the American population) <u>will change</u> (during the next century).

___C___   8. The <u>population</u> <u>will be</u> older; an estimated 5.3 million <u>people</u> <u>will be</u> (over the age) (of 100).

___C___   9. Today, 0.02 <u>percent</u> (of the population) is (over the age) (of 100); however, this <u>percentage</u> <u>will change</u> (in 2100) (to 0.9 percent).

___S___   10. Better medical <u>care</u> <u>will increase</u> the longevity figures.

___S___   11. <u>Advances</u> (in medical technology and research) <u>will lengthen</u> the life span.

___C___   12. The largest age <u>group</u> (in 2100) <u>is</u> likely [to be] teenagers; (in fact), 6.4 <u>percent</u> (of the population) <u>will be</u> (in the 15-to-19-year-old age bracket).

___S___   13. Population <u>growth</u> and the contributing <u>factors</u> (for population growth) <u>are</u> quite interesting.

___S___   14. The U.S. <u>population</u> (in 1800) <u>was</u> 5.3 million people.

___S___   15. The <u>population</u> <u>jumped</u> (in that century) (to a whopping 75.9 million people) (in 1900).

Practice 6: Punctuating with Commas (page 227)

Check the location of the commas inserted in the following sentences.

1. Fish, snakes, owls, and chimpanzees are on exhibit at the zoo, but the zoo no longer has birds, lions, or giraffes.
2. None of the members of the board, however, wants to vote to change the budget.
3. A wide variety of performers will appear onstage; consequently, this concert will sell out quickly.
4. Therefore, everyone was asked to sign the petition or to take time to campaign.

5. This project is not a high priority for me; nevertheless, I will participate.
6. Your interview skills are excellent; on the other hand, your resumé needs refining.
7. Thus, I would like to be considered for a promotion.
8. My daughter begged me to consider her request; finally, I gave her my permission.
9. The bill is first sent to Congress for approval; next, the bill is sent to the President to sign.
10. The President, however, has the power to veto any bill.

Practice 7: Identifying Run-On Sentences and Comma Splice Errors (page 230)

An arrow should be drawn between the two words shown below. **RO, CS,** or **SENT** should be written on the line.

RO	1. down ↓ we
SENT	2.
CS	3. out ↓ the phone lines
RO	4. groceries ↓ the cashiers
SENT	5.
CS	6. paranoid ↓ fear
RO	7. vendors ↓ people
SENT	8.
RO	9. January 1 ↓ well
CS	10. water ↓ some also bought

Practice 8: Matching Punctuation to Conjunctions (page 231)

Pay close attention to the punctuation shown in the following patterns.

1. S-V; thus, S-V.
2. S-V; however, S-V.
3. S-V; finally, S-V.
4. S-V, for S-V.
5. S-V; indeed, S-V.
6. S-V; in fact, S-V.
7. S-V, or S-V.
8. S-V, so S-V.
9. S-V; as a result, S-V
10. S-V, and S-V.
11. S-V, but S-V.
12. S-V, yet S-V.
13. S-V; therefore, S-V.
14. S-V, nor V-S.
15. S-V; nevertheless, S-V.

Practice 9: Using Subject-Verb Agreement in Compound Sentences (page 232)

1. want, is
2. has, fail
3. are, do
4. need, lacks
5. matches, want
6. come, prefer
7. are, are
8. auctions, sell
9. gather, hopes
10. pays, receives

Practice 10: Identifying Subject-Verb Agreement (page 235)

Subjects and verbs should be marked as follows.

1. Checkers is, I enjoy
2. jury is going, members will have
3. I do enjoy, audience ruins
4. committee meets, plans are
5. company releases, statistics are
6. team waits, whistle signals
7. president wants, faculty agrees
8. team wants, teams earn
9. team wins, team loses
10. parents have accepted, family has decided
11. Politics requires, it requires
12. couple was, they plan
13. faculty was, members deserve
14. Physics involves, biophysics deals

Practice 11: Proofreading for Errors (page 236)

Sentences should be marked as follows.

1. Everyone held ~~their~~ [his or her] breath, for the committee was ready to announce the winners of the contest.

2. That couple take separate vacations every year, yet they ~~seems~~ [seem] to be happily married.

3. The faculty ~~has~~ [have] been assigned parking spaces; however, they must pay for their spaces.

4. Electronics ~~frighten~~ [frightens] many freshman students, but I love the subject and the teacher.

5. The high school orchestra gives a spring concert; unfortunately, I am never able to attend it.

6. Their jazz band is the best in the state, so ~~they receive~~ [it receives] all the attention.

7. The city council ~~are~~ [is] hoping to see public support for Measure 52, but local support is not likely.

8. Our group always gathers at the beach during spring vacation~~;~~ [,] but~~,~~ this year three of our members will not be present. [no comma]

covers
9. The news on most television stations ~~cover~~ current events, but events are frequently sensationalized to increase the stations' ratings.

approves
10. The board ~~approve~~ all of the college's bids for construction, but the process often involves long delays.

Chapter 9 Complex Sentences

Practice 1: Identifying Dependent Clauses (page 254)

Dependent clauses should be marked as follows. Subordinate conjunctions should be written on the lines.

While	1.	While you were out to lunch,
Because	2.	Because Beth is traveling by herself,
After	3.	After I receive my check,
before	4.	before he had his stroke,
even if	5.	even if I have to work at the same time.
If	6.	If you arrive before 7:00 P.M.,
provided that	7.	provided that I enroll in school.
since	8.	since she started the vegetarian diet.
when	9.	when I was only three years old.
Though	10.	Though the winters have been harsh,

Practice 2: Identifying and Punctuating Dependent Clauses (page 254)

A box should enclose the following dependent clauses. The subordinate conjunction should be circled.

1. (until) he has worked in his position for three years.
2. (Although) Nikki is old enough to vote,
3. (As soon as) I gather up my courage,
4. (Even though) the deadline has passed,
5. (Before) I shower and dress each day,
6. (If) you fry the potatoes in butter,
7. (While) Ryan was at work,

8. *Though* the first rainstorm helped the crops,

9. *because* management wants to keep a stable work force.

10. *because* Janet postponed her checkup twice.

Practice 3: Identifying Subjects and Verbs in Clauses (page 255)

Sentences should be marked as follows.

1. I decided to sell my car *because* it was costing me too much money to maintain.

2. The food was delicious *even though* the portions were small.

3. *As soon as* we raise the money, we will buy the team new uniforms.

4. *Although* Colleen passed her bar exam last summer, she has not found a job.

5. *As* the line of people filed past the memorial, admiration lit up their faces.

6. The television cameras appeared *before* the mayor arrived.

7. The viewing audience was small *because* *Monday Night Football* was on the other station.

8. *When* a rainbow appears in the sky, many people make wishes for prosperity.

9. *No matter how* difficult the hike will be, I want to reach the top of the mountain.

10. The boys played basketball on the weekends *even though* they did not make the team.

Practice 4: Recognizing Simple Sentences and Complex Sentences (page 257)

Sentences should be marked as follows.

  S 1. (Between us), a bond (of friendship) will always exist.

  CX 2. Although she appears calm, she is a bundle (of nerves).

  CX 3. Grandpa mellows whenever he thinks (of his grandchildren).

<u>S</u>   4. (Prior to the accident), the bus <u>driver</u> <u>reported</u> problems (with the brakes).

<u>CX</u>   5. <u>I</u> <u>can go</u> (to the conference) unless my <u>child</u> <u>is</u> sick.

<u>CX</u>   6. Though both <u>students</u> <u>were</u> late, <u>they</u> <u>managed</u> [to hear] most (of the lecture).

<u>S</u>   7. (In class), several <u>students</u> <u>had</u> some difficulty (with the complex terminology).

<u>CX</u>   8. When <u>I</u> <u>retire</u>, <u>I</u> <u>will dedicate</u> more time (to community volunteer work).

<u>S</u>   9. (For this specific job), <u>I</u> <u>am</u> well qualified.

<u>CX</u>   10. Now that <u>you</u> <u>have passed</u> the course, perhaps <u>you</u> <u>could tutor</u> me.

Practice 5: Identifying Sentence Types and Adding Punctuation (page 259)

Check each sentence for correct punctuation. Sentence types should be marked as follows.

<u>C</u>   1. The average cost of my groceries for one week is $100; however, sometimes I spend much less than that.

<u>C</u>   2. The movie has been out for a month, but I have not seen it yet.

<u>CX</u>   3. If everyone wants to go, we will not have room in the car.

<u>C</u>   4. Blake just bought a motorcycle, but he does not yet have insurance.

<u>CX</u>   5. Whenever I hear his name, my heart beats a little faster.

<u>S</u>   6. All of our umbrellas flipped inside out in the wind yesterday.

<u>CX</u>   7. Even though my intentions were good, I need to file for another tax extension.

<u>S</u>   8. Young workers should set aside some money for future families and retirement.

<u>S</u>   9. At the end of the debate, each candidate, however, wanted to make one last point.

<u>C</u>   10. Mary has worked with the company for twelve years, yet she has not received a single promotion.

Practice 6: Recognizing Relative Pronoun Clauses (page 264)

The relative pronoun clauses (dependent clauses) should be marked as follows.

1. | who <u>helped</u> me with a flat tire |

2. [that I want for my backyard.]

3. [which does not work,]

4. [who is dating Bernie,]

5. [that flowed freely from the volcano]

6. [which is on the north side of the park,]

7. [that travel on heavily salted roads.]

8. [which had fallen apart and turned into scrambled eggs.]

9. [who lost money in the stock market,]

10. [who has lived in Texas all his life,]

Practice 7: Identifying Subjects and Verbs (page 266)

Sentences should be marked as follows.

1. Anyone [who wants to attend the dance] must purchase a ticket in advance.

2. The night clerk, [whom I called on the phone,] gave me a room near the swimming pool.

3. The young accountant [who had just started this job] was unfamiliar with the forms.

4. No one enjoys filling out this year's tax forms, [which have long, complicated directions.]

5. None of the players on the team [that won the championship] had ever been to New York City.

6. Four antique rugs, [which were worth fifty thousand dollars,] were available at the auction.

7. Here is the herbal tea [that you ordered.]

8. I met the person [who placed the ad for the nanny position.]

9. Three of the writing tutors [whose names were on the board] read and critiqued my paper.

10. <u>Most</u> of the reward money │that <u>I</u> <u>received</u>│ <u>went</u> back to charity.

Practice 8: Using *Who* and *Whom* (page 267)

1. who	3. who	5. who	7. who	9. who
2. whom	4. who	6. who	8. whom	10. who

Practice 9: Using *Whose* and *Who's* (page 268)

1. whose	3. who's	5. whose	7. whose	9. who's
2. whose	4. whose	6. whose	8. who's	10. who's

Practice 10: Using *Who, Whom, That,* and *Which* (page 272)

1. who	3. that	5. whom	7. who, that	9. whose
2. which	4. that	6. that	8. that	10. whom

Practice 11: Working with Dependent Clauses (page 274)

The following clauses should be boxed and the subordinate conjunctions and relative pronouns circled. Pay close attention to the commas that have been added.

1. (who) painted my house

2. , (who) is Mario's brother,

3. (who) called you

4. (who) jogs three times a week

5. , (whom) you met at the opera,

6. (Because) flash floods hit the village,

7. , (who) sensed a flood was imminent,

8. (that) I had left underneath the sink.

9. (Whenever) the power goes out,

10. (because) all of the windows in the new building are sealed shut.

Practice 12: Identifying Fragments (page 280)

1. F	4. F	7. S	10. F	13. F
2. S	5. S	8. F	11. S	14. S
3. F	6. F	9. S	12. F	15. S

Chapter 10 Sentence Builders

Practice 1: Identifying Appositives (page 291)

The following appositives should be boxed.

1. a local banker
2. a twenty-page research paper
3. an absolute car fanatic
4. a haiku
5. a local artist
6. a rare antique
7. a gift from my partner
8. the newest school in the district
9. a fishing village on the northern shore of Hawaii
10. the largest of all the continents
11. a rolling pep rally
12. a food made from taro root
13. an old wooden relic from the past
14. a freelance writer
15. a coined word in Hawaii for volcanic haze

Practice 2: Creating Appositives from Relative Pronoun Clauses (page 295)

The following relative pronouns and verbs should be crossed out.

1. Andy sat on the log, ~~which was~~ the only dry place to sit, and waited for a ride into town.
2. My son, ~~who is~~ an energetic four-year-old, shows good coordination when he plays video games.
3. Hibiscus, ~~which is~~ the state flower of Hawaii, has large, colorful flowers.
4. My first car, ~~which was~~ a Volvo station wagon, ran well for twelve years.
5. The new quarterback, ~~who is~~ a native of the state, earned the starting position this season.
6. Sarina, ~~who is~~ my best friend, gives me a ride to work each night.
7. Bill's company, ~~which is~~ Rapid River Adventures, takes people on three-day rafting trips on the Snake River.
8. *Butterfly Lost,* ~~which is~~ my cousin's first novel, is about a Native American woman.
9. Sandy, ~~who is~~ a weight trainer, was able to move the heavy desk by herself.
10. Kona, ~~which is~~ a small town on the big island of Hawaii, is near many coffee plantations.
11. This is the first year of teaching for Maria Gonzales, ~~who is~~ my new math teacher.
12. The interviewer, ~~who was~~ a woman, entered the men's locker room to talk to the players.

Practice 3: Identifying Participial Phrases (page 300)

The participial phrases should be marked as follows. The subjects and verbs should be underlined as shown.

1. [Determined to win the dance competition,] <u>Rosa</u> and her <u>partner</u> <u>practiced</u> every day for five months.

2. [Blending classical, popular, and jazz music,] <u>George Gershwin</u> <u>composed</u> musical comedies and concert pieces.

3. <u>Matthew</u>, [tired of hearing his son beg for a car,] <u>decided</u> to buy him an old junker.

4. [Disappointed about her interview,] the <u>student</u> <u>decided</u> to find ways to strengthen her interviewing skills.

5. [Pretending not to care,] <u>Robby</u> <u>looked</u> the other way when his old <u>girlfriend</u> <u>walked</u> by.

6. <u>Each</u> of the cosmetics consultants, [wanting to win the sales award,] <u>tried</u> different ways to advertise and promote his or her products.

7. <u>Newlyweds</u>, [often wanting a highly memorable honeymoon,] <u>begin</u> their married life with excessive honeymoon debts.

8. [Living in a small town,] most <u>people</u> <u>know</u> a lot of details about other people's lives.

9. The <u>Willamette River</u>, [running high this time of year,] <u>poses</u> some flood threats to residents <u>who</u> <u>live</u> on its beautiful banks.

10. [Determined to get some attention,] the young <u>child</u> <u>started</u> hollering in the middle of the mall.

Practice 4: Identifying Dangling Modifiers (page 303)

1. DM	4. DM	7. DM	10. S	13. S
2. DM	5. S	8. DM	11. S	14. DM
3. S	6. S	9. S	12. S	15. S

Practice 5: Identifying Appositives, Participial Phrases, and Dependent Clauses (page 304)

The following groups of words should be boxed on your paper.

Paragraph 1: that were accompanied by torrential rains, softball-sized hail, and strong winds; Hitting shortly after 6:30 P.M.; Rotating in a clockwise direction; while the second moved southeast through downtown Fort Worth; a city of 480,000 people; director of the National Weather Service's Storm Prediction Center

Paragraph 2: that have sustained heavy damage; a spokesman for the Fort Worth Fire Department; like they did not have a single pane of glass left in them

Paragraph 3: one by a falling wall and the other by a truck trailer; that flipped on him; a river near Arlington to the east; Fearing more victims were trapped in the debris of downtown office buildings

Paragraph 4: estimated at $450 million for all of Tarrant County; Stripping brick walls off a cathedral tower and blasting out dozens of office windows; whose belongings were shredded or scattered

Practice 6: Combining Sentences to Reduce Wordiness (page 306)

Answers will vary. All answers must be simple sentences. Possible answers follow.

1. In my current job, I greet clients, answer the phones, and schedule appointments.
2. The rural town has a small library, a general store, a gas station, and a café.
3. The kitchen in my new home has modern appliances, an island, and recessed lighting.
4. High school students, single parents, and some retired citizens applied for the one-year educational grant.
5. During the game, my friends and I ate peanuts, yelled and screamed for our team, and enjoyed each other's company.
6. For my chemistry class, I need to read each chapter carefully, outline the chapter, take notes, and complete all the lab assignments with a partner.

Practice 7: Identifying Faulty Parallelism (page 310)

The conjunction that should be circled is shown in **bold** print. Corrections show parallelism.

_____ FP _____   1. I enjoy skating, jogging, **and** ~~walks~~ _walking_ along the river.

_____ FP _____   2. Rachel buys her clothes from catalogs, ~~at~~ garage sales, **or** ~~she goes to~~ Goodwill.

_____ P _____   3. Many students need to learn time management **and** techniques for studying more effectively for tests.

_____P_____   4. Getting good grades **and** learning new skills are important goals for many students.

_____FP_____   5. The bargain shoppers arrived early, charged into the store, **and** ~~were filling~~ ^filled^ their shopping bags.

_____FP_____   6. The lecture series covers nutrition, ~~exercising~~ ^exercise^, **and** mental health.

_____FP_____   7. The telemarketer was rude **and** ~~showing signs of inconsideration~~ ^inconsiderate^.

_____FP_____   8. My job was emptying the garbage **and** ~~to sweep~~ ^sweeping^ the cafeteria.

_____FP_____   9. Neither rain **nor** ~~snowy days~~ ^snow^ affects postal delivery services.

_____FP_____   10. The young missionaries, eager **and** ~~having lots of motivation~~ ^motivated^, met many people.

Practice 8: Recognizing Simple, Compound, and Complex Sentences (page 314)

1. S	4. C	7. S	10. S
2. CX	5. C	8. S	11. C
3. S	6. CX	9. S	12. CX

Practice 9: Expanding a Basic Sentence (page 317)

1. S	3. C	5. CCX	7. CCX	9. CCX
2. CX	4. CX	6. C	8. CX	10. CX

INDEX